Stephen McLaughlin retired in 2017 after working for 35 years as a l[...] Public Library. In addition to contributing regularly to *Warship*, he is th[...] *Soviet Battleships* (US Naval Institute Press, 2003, reissued 2021) and is co-editor of an annotated version of the controversial *Naval Staff Appreciation of Jutland* (Seaforth Publishing, 2016).

Kathrin Milanovich has been researching the history of the Imperial Japanese Navy for many years and is a regular contributor of feature articles to *Warship*.

Jean Moulin has written widely on the French Navy, and is the author of several monographs on warships of the interwar period. Jean is the co-author, with John Jordan, of *French Cruisers 1922–1956* (2013) and *French Destroyers 1922–1956* (2015). Books on the 'stealth' frigates of the *La Fayette* class and the Tripartite MCM vessels were published by Lela Presse in 2018 and 1921 respectively.

Dirk Nottelmann is a marine engineer by profession, and is currently working for the German shipping administration. He has contributed to *Warship*, *Warship International* and various German magazines, as well as being author of *Die Brandenburg-Klasse* (Mittler, 2002) and co-author of *Halbmond und Kaiseradler* (Mittler, 1999). His book *The Kaiser's Cruisers* (with Aidan Dodson) was published by Seaforth Publishing in late 2021.

John Roberts is a former editor of *Warship*. He is the author of many books and articles on the Royal Navy, including the seminal *British Battleships of World War Two* (Arms & Armour, 1976) and *British Cruisers of World War Two* (Arms & Armour,1980), both with Alan Raven. He also initiated the Anatomy of the Ship series with *The Battlecruiser Hood* (Conway, 1982), followed, in the same series, by *The Aircraft Carrier Intrepid* (1982) and *The Battleship Dreadnought* (1992). Recent publications include *The Battlecruiser Repulse* (2019) and *The Destroyer Cossack* (2020) in Seaforth's 'original builders' plans' series.

Ian Sturton is a regular contributor of articles and illustrations to naval publications, including *Warship*, *Warship International* and *Jane's Fighting Ships*. He edited *Conway's Battleships: The Definitive Visual Reference to the World's All-Big-Gun Ships*.

Sergei Evenevich Vinogradov trained as a civil engineer, graduating from the Moscow Engineering and Construction Institute in 1982. He has published many works on the capital ships of the Imperial Russian Navy, including books on the predreadnought battleship *Slava*, the dreadnought *Imperatritsa Mariia*, and never-built designs for Russian battleships with 16in guns. He currently works at the Central Museum of the Armed Forces in Moscow.

Conrad Waters is the author of numerous articles on modern naval matters and editor of *World Naval Review* (Seaforth Publishing). He also edited Seaforth's *Navies in the 21st Century*, shortlisted for the 2017 Mountbatten Award. His history of the Royal Navy's Second World War 'Town' class cruisers was published in 2019 and he is currently writing a sequel on the *Fiji* class and their successors.

WARSHIP 2023

WARSHIP 2023

Editor: **John Jordan**

Assistant Editor: **Stephen Dent**

OSPREY
PUBLISHING

Title pages: The Milhaud finger piers at Toulon between
November 1960 and January 1961, with the recently-arrived
Clemenceau in the foreground, *Arromanches* in the centre, and
La Fayette on the left of the picture. Note the comparatively large
size of *Clemenceau* and the fully-angled deck. *Clemenceau* and
her sister *Foch* are the subject of an article by John Jordan and
Jean Moulin in this year's annual. (Jean Moulin collection)

OSPREY PUBLISHING
Bloomsbury Publishing Plc
Kemp House, Chawley Park, Cumnor Hill, Oxford OX2 9PH, UK
29 Earlsfort Terrace, Dublin 2, Ireland
1385 Broadway, 5th Floor, New York, NY 10018, USA
E-mail: info@ospreypublishing.com
www.ospreypublishing.com

OSPREY is a trademark of Osprey Publishing Ltd

First published in Great Britain in 2023

A catalogue record for this book is available from the British Library.

ISBN: HB 9781472857132; eBook 9781472857125; ePDF 9781472857101; XML 9781472857118

23 24 25 26 27   10 9 8 7 6 5 4 3 2 1

Cover design by Stewart Larking
Page layout by Stephen Dent
Printed and bound in India through Replika Press Private Ltd.

Osprey Publishing supports the Woodland Trust, the UK's leading woodland conservation charity.

To find out more about our authors and books visit www.ospreypublishing.com. Here you will find extracts,
author interviews, details of forthcoming events and the option to sign up for our newsletter.

CONTENTS

EDITORIAL

Warship 2023 sees the welcome return of John Roberts. John is a former editor of *Warship* and the author/coauthor of many books on Britain's Royal Navy, including the seminal *British Battleships of World War Two* and *British Cruisers of World War Two* (Arms & Armour Press). He has chosen as the subject of his article the loss of HMS *Audacious* to a mine north of Ireland in the autumn of 1914. *Audacious* was one of Britain's latest 'super-dreadnought' battleships, and her loss was a wake-up call, highlighting the threat posed to even major surface units by the mine and the torpedo. John's detailed account of the ship's loss demonstrates that although the set procedures for coping with a large ingress of water were broadly followed (aided by the presence of Albert P Cole of the Naval Constructor Corps), the ship was lost to progressive flooding via apertures that could not be sealed off – including the soil pipe for the captain's WC. Pumping arrangements were found to be inadequate, and because the generators were powered exclusively by steam all electrical power was lost. There were many lessons taken from this disaster, which sparked a fundamental review both of underwater protection and pumping arrangements, and which led to the development of systems that could better contain the explosive force of a mine or torpedo warhead and could deal with (or compensate for) the flooding of large compartments below the waterline.

Battleship design is something of a theme this year. Stephen McLaughlin concludes his series on Soviet battleship designs of the 1930s with an article on Italian influences, with a particular focus on Ansaldo's UP.41 proposal for a 43,000-tonne fast battleship that would have been armed with nine 406mm (16in) guns and no fewer than twelve 180mm (7.1in) guns. The main and the secondary guns would have been mounted in triple turrets in an arrangement similar to that of the Italian *Littorio*. This surprising collaboration between Fascist Italy and the Communist USSR was driven on the one hand by Italy's need to secure export orders in order to develop and sustain its relatively small naval arms industry, and on the other by the loss of Russia's most experienced ship designers following the October Revolution, which led to the crude and derivative Project 21, inspired by the British *Nelson* class. The UP.41 design was never built, but exercised a major influence on subsequent Soviet battleship design, which culminated in the ambitious *Sovetskii Soiuz* (see *Warship 2021*).

Ironically, at a time when Stalin was contemplating the construction of ever-larger and more powerful battleships capable of dominating the seas around the Soviet Union, the Italian *Regia Marina* was embarking on studies for battleships of moderate size comparable to the French *Dunkerque* and *Strasbourg*. A series of studies by General Luigi Barberis of the Italian Naval Engineering Corps during the early 1930s was followed by studies by the distinguished naval architect Umberto Pugliese for a battleship of 'moderate displacement'. Both sets of studies were prompted by British proposals for limitations on the displacement and gun calibre of future battleships, first at the London Conference of 1930 and then in anticipation of the Second London Conference of December 1935. Neither came to fruition, and in the end the *Regia Marina* opted to extend the *Littorio* construction programme by ordering a further two units.

Philippe Caresse continues his series on the older French battleships of the *Flotte d'échantillons* with an article on the fourth of the five ships of the 1890 programme, *Masséna*. Designed by the eminent (but ageing) naval architect Louis de Bussy, *Masséna* incorporated a number of innovations, which included a vaulted stern and the prominent 'plough bow' that had been a feature of de Bussy's *Dupuy-de-Lôme*. Neither feature proved successful, and *Masséna* never fired a shot in anger, ending an undistinguished career with employment as a breakwater at Gallipoli in 1915.

Finally, Sergei Vinogradov follows up his Warship Note published in *Warship 2021* on the unusual career of the Russian battleship *General Alekseev* with a full feature article in which he chronicles the even more surprising odyssey of her 305mm (12in) guns after the ship was scrapped. Subsequent employment included the mounting of the guns in coast defence batteries on the Finnish islands and Guernsey (Channel Islands), and on Soviet TM-3-12 railway mountings. Some guns currently survive as museum exhibits.

The remaining feature articles this year cover a variety of periods, navies and types of warship. Kathrin Milanovich has submitted an article on the powerful protected cruisers *Takasago*, *Kasagi* and *Chitose* built for the Imperial Japanese Navy. Designed by Sir Philip Watts of Armstrongs, they mounted 8in (20cm) guns fore and aft at the insistence of the Japanese, who were keen to counter the modern European-built armoured vessels in service with the Chinese Navy. The first, *Takasago*, was built on the Tyne by Armstrongs, the other two in the United States with a view to repairing Japanese-US relations and mollifying opposition to Japanese immigration to the West Coast. The 8in guns proved to be too heavy for these relatively lightly-built warships, and the hull of the two US-built ships had to be enlarged to accommodate them successfully.

Aidan Dodson and Dirk Nottelmann have embarked on a two-part article on another set of lesser-known vessels: the German Flak ships of the Second World War. Intended to defend the approaches of German harbours against hostile air attack, the Flak ships were conversions of obsolescent cruiser-sized vessels of German or ex-enemy origin and were equipped with state-of-the-art

The IJN battleship *Nagato* during her power trials in Sukumo Bay on 27 October 1920. Not only was she the first capital ship to mount 16in guns, but she was fast and well protected. In the lead article of *Warship* 2024 Hans Lengerer will look at the principles behind her conception, and will also explore the controversy surrounding authorship of the design. (Lars Ahlberg collection)

anti-aircraft guns and control systems. Part I covers the former German cruisers *Arcona* and *Medusa* and the two former Norwegian coast defence vessels *Tordenskjold* and *Harald Haarfagre*.

Part II of Hans Lengerer's article on the development of the Yokosuka Navy Yard during the latter half of the 19th century traces the steady decline of French influence, the move in naval construction from wood to iron and steel, the eventual replacement of foreign expertise by home-grown talent, and the 'tug-of-war' between French and British naval design principles (and between metric and imperial measurements).

When *Warship* was first published in 1977, the Second World War was a relatively recent period of history. It is now 78 years since the war ended, and much of the postwar era is now the distant past. Much archival material that previously would have been classified is now freely available, so articles covering the more technical aspects of the ships, weapons and electronics of the period 1945 to 1990 are not only feasible, but are essential if we are to put naval developments into a broader context. The Editor's article on the French carriers *Clemenceau* and *Foch* falls into this category, as does Peter Marland's detailed technical study of postwar developments in electronic warfare (EW) in Britain's Royal Navy. Conrad Waters then brings us up to the present with a perceptive account of the US Navy's new strategy termed 'Distributed Maritime Operations' (or DMO), devised to meet the challenges posed by Chinese naval expansion.

The annual concludes with the customary Warship Notes, Naval Books of the Year and Gallery. This year's Gallery is from Dirk Nottelmann, who has submitted some stunning images of ships of the Imperial German Navy in port during the period 1890–1918, together with his own detailed explanatory captions.

The list of feature articles for *Warship* 2024 is already fixed. The new edition will lead with a ground-breaking account by regular contributor Hans Lengerer of the design of the IJN battleships *Nagato* and *Mutsu*. Other scheduled features will include an acount of the brief naval engagement off the Bosphorus on 10 May 1915 between SMS *Goeben* and the Russian Black Sea Fleet by naval historian Toby Ewin, and studies of the Italian-built Soviet flotilla leader *Tashkent* (Przemysław Budzbon), the French missile frigates *Suffren* and *Duquesne* (John Jordan), and the IJN escort destroyers of the *Matsu* and *Tachibana* classes (Kathrin Milanovich). Dirk Nottelmann will be embarking on a two-part article on the famous German WWI commerce raider *Seeadler* using information that has only recently come to light, and Dirk and Aidan Dodson will be concluding their two-part article on the German WW2 Flak ships. Philippe Caresse's series on the French battleships of the *Flotte d'échantillons* will conclude with a study of *Bouvet*, arguably the most successful ship of the type despite her catastrophic loss at the Dardanelles. Enrico Cernuschi will return with a major article on Italian midget submarines which will include a surprising amount of new information, Jon Wise will trace the evolution of the Royak Navy's fishery protection vessels since the war, and Stephen McLaughlin will present a short feature on the reconstruction of the former Russian battleship *Orel* as the Japanese *Iwami*.

John Jordan
March 2023

A SERIES OF UNFORTUNATE EVENTS: THE LOSS OF HMS *AUDACIOUS*

The loss of HMS *Audacious* to a mine off the coast of Ireland in October 1914 reduced the numerical advantage of the Grand Fleet over the High Seas Fleet to small margins. The British were so concerned that they attempted to conceal the loss of the ship from the Germans and from the general public. *Audacious* was one of the Royal Navy's latest 'super-dreadnoughts', and her loss to progressive flooding suggested a concerning vulnerability to underwater damage. **John Roberts** provides a comprehensive account of the ship's sinking and an analysis of the reasons for her loss.

At 5pm on 13 October 1914 the 2nd Battle Squadron (BS), comprising *Ajax, Audacious, Centurion, King George V, Conqueror, Orion* and *Thunderer*,[1] sailed from Scapa Flow to patrol an area to the northeast of Muckle Flugga (at the northern extremity of the Shetlands). This was part of a fleet operation the purpose of which was to intercept '… enemy ships and trade attempting to pass out of or into the North Sea, [while] keeping the battlefleet and cruisers well to the northward in order to minimise the submarine menace'.[2]

The 'submarine menace' referred to the steadily increasing activity of German U-boats in the northern North Sea and the vulnerability of the Grand Fleet's northern bases to submarine incursion. Following multiple real and false reports of submarine sightings and the sinking of *Hawke* of the 10th Cruiser Squadron (CS) by *U.9* on 15 October it was decided to initiate a relocation of the Grand Fleet to temporary bases while the anti-submarine defences of Scapa Flow were strengthened. The main base chosen for this purpose was Lough Swilly, on the northern coast of Ireland. Since this could not accommodate the entire fleet, Loch na Keal (Isle of Mull) and Broadford Bay (Isle of Skye) were designated as additional anchorages. The 1st BS and 4th BS with the cruiser *Blonde* left Scapa at 6am on 16 October for gunnery practice prior to patrolling to the westward of Orkney and Shetland during the following two days. At 4.18pm in the afternoon of the same day a (false) report of the sighting of a U-boat between Switha and Cantick Head on the west side of the southern entrance to the Flow prompted a general retirement of most of the ships that remained in harbour. Sailing during the late evening of the 16th were the two ships of the 2nd Battle Cruiser Squadron (BCS), *Liverpool*[3] of the 1st Light Cruiser Squadron (LCS), *King Edward VII* and *Dominion* of the 3rd BS, and the minelaying cruisers *Naiad* and *Thetis*. The fleet flagship, *Iron Duke,* did not leave until 3.20am on the 17th as she was in the process of re-tubing her condensers and had to temporarily stop this work before leaving.[4] She re-joined the fleet later the same day but was detached to East Loch Roag, Isle of Lewis, on the 19th to complete the condenser repairs before again re-joining the fleet at sea early on the 20th. Following sweeps to the westward of the Hebrides *Iron Duke,* 1st and 4th BS proceeded to Lough Swilly where they arrived on the morning of the 22nd.

In the meantime, the ships of the Grand Fleet involved in supporting the Northern Patrol were also ordered to withdraw on 16 October. The 2nd BS was ordered to Broadford Bay, but later the same day this destination was changed to Loch na Keal. This westward withdrawal also included the 3rd BS, the 1st BCS, the 2nd CS, and the 1st LCS, which left only the 3rd CS and 10th CS on blockade duty with their patrol area moved further north to the NNW of the Shetlands (for the organisation of the Grand Fleet during this period see page 197). This effectively removed British patrols between northern Scotland and Norway at just the right time to give the German raider *Berlin* a clear run to the north as she entered the southern end of this abandoned area in the late afternoon of the 17th. The *Berlin* (Captain Hans Pfundheller) was a 17-knot, 16,786grt Norddeutscher liner that had been converted to an auxiliary cruiser/minelayer during August– September and was heading to the Atlantic with orders to lay her 200 mines in the approaches to the Clyde and then raid the fishing fleets and trade routes to the north of Norway during her return.[5]

During the 17–18th *Berlin* headed northward, approximately along the longitude of 2°E, turned NW on reaching the area of 61°N, thus skirting the British cruiser patrols to the NNW of Shetland, before altering course to pass, during the 19th, through the centre of the Iceland/Faeroes passage, which at this time had no cruiser patrol. She continued far out into the Atlantic, turned southward at 20°W and, on reaching 56°N, altered course eastward to pass to the north of Ireland. As she approached the Irish Coast late on the 22nd she

The almost completed *Audacious* in the river Mersey shortly after being undocked from No 7 graving Dock, Tranmere Yard, Birkenhead on 16 July 1913. She is not yet fitted with a director, searchlights, net defence or the after compass. The latter was fitted, on the platform above her after superstructure, before she sailed on the 22nd. (Author's collection)

Audacious sailed from the Mersey on 22 July 1913 and arrived at Spithead, via Plymouth, on the 29th having carried out her steam trials en route. Here she is seen entering Portsmouth harbour on the 30th to prepare for her gun and torpedo trials, which took place on 5–6 August. (Author's collection)

Audacious in No 7 Dock, Birkenhead, which she occupied for the second time during 18 September – 14 October 1913; she had returned to the Mersey on 7 August. Her builder, Cammell Laird, was the first private contractor to fully complete and inspect a British dreadnought before she entered service – previously the final stages of fitting-out and subsequent inspection were carried out in one the Royal Dockyards. Note that she now has her director tower, twin 24in searchlights and torpedo net booms. (Author's collection)

began to pick up heavy wireless traffic, in particular from the 2nd CS, patrolling to the west of the Flannan Islands, and the battleships *Albemarle* and *Exmouth* patrolling across Stanton Banks. In addition, to the southward of her were the cruiser *Iris* (11th CS) and the battleships *Russell* and *Duncan*. Since the Germans had no intelligence regarding the movement of the Grand Fleet to the west, this level of British naval activity came as a surprise to Pfundheller. After coming close to running ashore on the Isle of Aran, he turned northward to find that most of the local navigation lights were off. This decided him that the Clyde operation was unlikely to succeed, and that a minefield across the main trade route from the British west coast ports to North America would be an acceptable alternative. Another factor which may have influenced this decision was that if he continued, he would have arrived off the Clyde after sunrise. However, if *Berlin* had proceeded to the Clyde, she might well have avoided interception since the only warship she was likely to have encountered was the armed boarding vessel (ABV) *Tara* patrolling in the narrow North Channel between Fairhead and the Mull of Kintyre. Considering that the ABV was a smaller vessel, armed only with three 6pdr (57mm) guns against *Berlin*'s two 105mm and six 37mm guns, any engagement was likely to have favoured the German ship, although it is probable that *Tara* would at the least have raised the alarm. As it turned out, the nearest that *Berlin* came to any British ship was at 1am on 23rd when she was about 10nm south of *Exmouth*,

just as that ship turned from a southerly to a northerly course during her patrol of Stanton Banks.

Between 11.35pm on the 22nd and 12.10am on the 23rd, *Berlin* laid her mines in an area about 20nm north of Tory Island. Three days later, at 2.15pm on 26 October, the minefield claimed its first victim, the 5,363-ton SS *Manchester Commerce* outward bound from Manchester to Montreal. Fourteen of the crew, including her captain, were lost with the ship. Twenty-four hours later 30 survivors were picked up from a lifeboat to the west of Malin Head by the trawler *City of London* and taken to Fleetwood, Lancashire. On the way the loss *and its cause* were reported to the police at Carnlough on the northeast coast of Ireland. This information was passed to the war signal station at Torr Head and then telegraphed to Kingstown, Dublin. From Kingstown the news was forwarded to Buncrana naval station at Lough Swilly and from there signalled to the flagship *Iron Duke*. The message was received by Admiral Jellicoe at 1.08pm on the 27th.[6] Had the *City of London* elected to go to Lough Swilly instead of Fleetwood, although she would not have been aware of any reason to do so, Jellicoe would have known much sooner – possibly soon enough to stop the unfortunate event that was about to take place.

The Mining of *Audacious*

The 2nd Battle Squadron arrived at Loch na Keal at midday on 18 October and settled down for a rest period

A view from the quarterdeck of *Audacious* taken at Portsmouth in December 1913. The wedding garland, hung from the rigging of the fore-topmast, is in celebration of the marriage of the ship's commanding officer, Captain CF Dampier, which took place in Chelsea on the 11th. The item on top of the capstan is one of the ship's night lifebuoys which would normally have been stowed in one of two frames attached to the guardrails at the after end of the upper deck. Forward of the capstan is the skylight which on 27 October 1914 served for passing orders down to the hand steering compartment – note that the port side of the skylight is hidden by the capstan. (IWM Q38197)

at 6 hours notice for sea.[7] Six days later, at 5pm on the 26th, the squadron sailed with orders to carry out gunnery practice to the north of Tory Island. At the same time, the tugs *Plover* and *Flying Condor*, each towing a battle practice target, left Lough Swilly escorted by *Liverpool* to rendezvous with the 2nd BS on the following morning at 55°45'N, 08°30'W. According to the Grand Fleet Narrative it was intended that the practice should take place 'in this vicinity'. The 2nd BS passed through this position, heading SW, at about 3am but continued in the same direction for 2 hours before turning back, and met *Liverpool* and the two tugs at 6.50am. At 7.28am course was altered from ENE to SSE for a position about 15nm from the original rendezvous. While this may well have been considered to be in the same vicinity, it was an unfortunate choice both in

distance and direction since it ended very close to where *Manchester Commerce* had been mined. The initial practice, due to begin at 9am, was to be made by the *King George V* class, while the *Orion*s were in the target line, presumably to serve as marking ships. At this time *Audacious* had a displacement of about 26,500 tons, allowing for the coal being '300 tons short of war stowage' and the war outfit of 13.5in ammunition. Her mean draught was about 31ft, she was fully stored and had 112rpg (rounds per gun) for her 13.5in guns and the standard outfit of 150rpg for her 4in guns.

At 8.40am *Audacious* was about 20nm north of Tory Island steering SSE. The wind was WSW Force 5–6 and there was a long Atlantic swell. In line ahead of her were *Centurion* and *Ajax* while *King George V* followed astern. Two minutes later *Audacious* sounded general

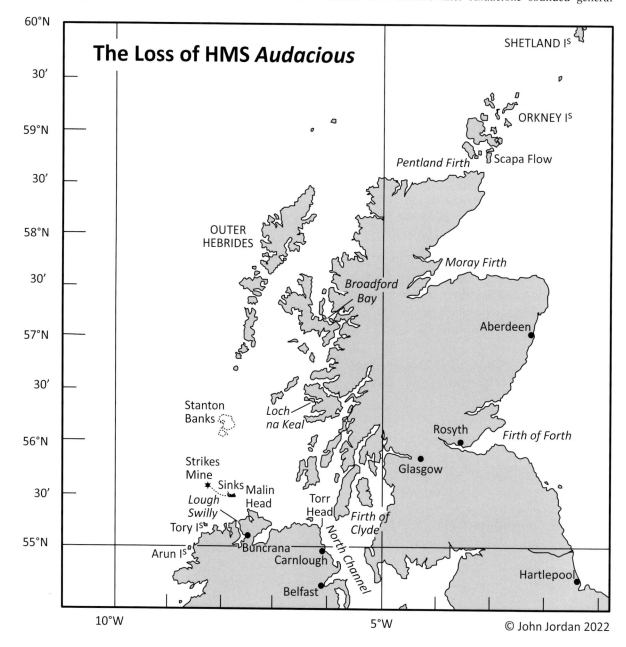

The Loss of HMS *Audacious*

© John Jordan 2022

Audacious at anchor in 1914, probably at Spithead. (Author's collection)

quarters to initiate preparations for gunnery practice which included opening doors and hatches for access to magazines and shell rooms. In sequence the ships turned to the intended firing course of SW, *Audacious* turning slightly inside her next ahead (*Ajax*). At about 8.45am, as her stern swung round, she struck a mine on the port side just forward of the after engine-room bulkhead. Her approximate position at this point was 55°34'N, 8°13.5'W. From the bridge, the explosion generated a slight shock and relatively little noise but it became clear that something serious had occurred when the ship failed to right herself as the helm was returned to amidships after the turn.[8] The commanding officer of *Audacious*, Captain CF Dampier, ordered all watertight doors to be closed, the counter-flooding of double bottom compartments and after boiler room bunkers on the starboard side, and 'hauled out of line to starboard into the wind and sea to try to keep the ship steady'. With two minor exceptions (see later) all watertight doors and hatches had been closed by 9am, at which point the ship was rolling between 10 and 15 degrees to port. About 45 minutes later the counter-flooding had reduced this to 0–9 degrees.

Although it was uncertain whether *Audacious* had been mined or torpedoed, the initial assessment favoured the latter.[9] Consequently the other ships of the 2nd BS were ordered to move out of the danger area and, after continuing their SW course for about 30 minutes, steamed away rapidly to the NW. The light cruiser *Liverpool* stood by *Audacious*, circling her charge at speed to reduce the threat to herself from torpedo attack.

From Lough Swilly Jellicoe ordered the fleet collier *Thornhill* (which was equipped with towing hawsers) to the scene, escorted by the ABV *Cambria* and the hospital ship *Soudan*. In addition, all the available destroyers and small craft at Lough Swilly and Loch na Keal were sent out to provide cover against the assumed submarine.

Down by the stern and listing to port, *Audacious* set course at about 9.20am for Lough Swilly, running the starboard engines at maximum power which, according to the Forbes Log, gave her a speed of 9 knots. The sea swell on her starboard quarter caused her to steer badly. The centre engine room had begun to flood slowly, and at about 9.45am Captain Dampier went to inspect this compartment personally. He found it '... very dark, being only lit with hand oil lamps, and there was about 5 to 6 feet of water in the Engine Room Bilge, and the [starting] platform was covered with oil, and [there was] much oil about, but I found Engineer-Lieutenant-Commander Macey and his men working away with the greatest coolness and energy endeavouring to cope with the water. He told me he hoped to be able to steam for two hours.'[10]

At about 11am, after travelling about 13nm, flooding made it necessary to stop the starboard engine, and shortly after this the engine rooms were evacuated and closed down. Now, after turning her head to sea, work began on hoisting out several of the ship's boats to take off non-essential personnel. However, it was soon found necessary to close down the boilers and evacuate the boiler room personnel since the movement of the ship, primarily a tendency to hang at the end of her port roll, indicated that

Members of the crew of *Audacious* posing on the upper deck to port of 'Q' turret. On the deck in front of them is the ship's badge – the wreathed head of a bull with the motto 'Viribus Audax', 'Bold with Strength' – other translations are possible. The same badge appeared on the tompions for the ship's 13.5in guns. (Author's collection)

HMS *Audacious* leaving Grand Harbour, Malta, on 28 February 1914. She arrived here during a three-week Mediterranean cruise with the other ships of the 1st Division of the 2nd BS, Home Fleet, *Ajax*, *Conqueror* and *King George V* and the squadron's attached cruiser *Boadicea*. They also visited Gibraltar, on both the outward and homeward voyages, Corfu and Palermo. The boat in the foreground is a 45-foot Admirals barge. (Richard Ellis)

Audacious under way in June or July 1914, probably entering or leaving Portsmouth. (Author's collection)

her stability was dangerously low.[11] This meant losing power for the hydraulically-operated main boom and the electric deck winches. With or without power the 42-foot launch, 36-foot pinnace and three 32-foot cutters were got out with some difficulty, although it seems unlikely that this was possible without power in the case of the launch and pinnace, which weighed 7.85 tons and 5 tons respectively. During this period boats were also sent from the cruiser *Liverpool* and some of the destroyers, and from the liner *Olympic* which had arrived about noon in answer to *Audacious*' calls for assistance. About 550 seamen, marines and boys were removed from the ship, leaving an estimated 250 seamen on board together with the ship's officers.[12] By about 2pm heavy seas were sweeping across the quarter deck, while the waist was 'practically impassable' at times due to the heavy rolling.

Between 2pm and 5pm three attempts were made to take the battleship in tow. The first to try was the *Olympic*, the cable being taken over to the liner by the destroyer *Fury* – which provided the same service for the two subsequent attempts. The *Olympic* successfully pulled *Audacious* round from her heading of west to SSE, the direction for Lough Swilly, but without her steam steering gear the battleship proved unmanageable, and as the tow began she yawed away into wind and parted the cable. The second attempt was made by *Liverpool*, but the line was fouled by one of the cruiser's port propellers and cut. In the final attempt, by *Thornhill*, the cable parted as soon as the line took the load. Prior to receiving the news of the mining of the *Manchester Commerce* Jellicoe had been reluctant to send out a battleship to tow *Audacious* because of the assumed submarine threat. He

then held back under the impression that she was already under tow by the *Olympic*. It was not until 5pm that the pre-dreadnought *Exmouth*, which had been on standby for some hours, sailed from Lough Swilly. She arrived too late to be of assistance.

By 5pm the quarterdeck of *Audacious* was awash and a considerable amount of water was flooding into the stern through vent trunks whose mushroom tops had been damaged and, in some cases, completely removed by loose items on the quarterdeck which had come adrift and had been washed across the deck by the sea. Principal among these was one of the ship's accommodation ladders which had gradually broken up. A gig and a whaler, stowed to port and starboard of the quarter deck respectively, also broke adrift, the gig being washed over the side while the whaler ended up against the starboard side of the after superstructure. There was further uncontrolled flooding of the stern from other causes, and it was clear that the ship would soon be in danger of capsizing due to loss of stability. With night approaching, Captain Dampier decided to have the majority of those that remained on board taken off, but asked for fifty volunteers to stay with the ship. Fifty-six seamen and a number of officers actually stayed on board but, with the ship rolling sluggishly and more heavily, Dampier soon decided that the ship should be abandoned for the night in the hope that it would be possible to return to her at daylight. This process was complete by about 7pm, the last men to leave the ship being Captain Dampier and Vice Admiral Sir Lewis Bayly (commander of the 1st BS, who had arrived in the ABV *Cambria* and boarded *Audacious* at about 2.15pm).

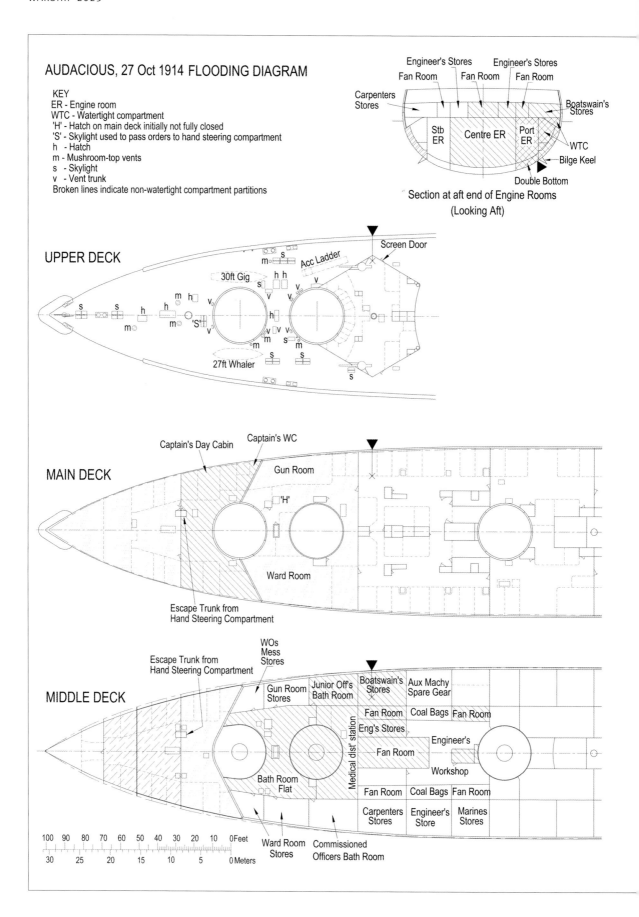

AUDACIOUS, 27 Oct 1914 FLOODING DIAGRAM

KEY
ER - Engine room
WTC - Watertight compartment
'H' - Hatch on main deck initially not fully closed
'S' - Skylight used to pass orders to hand steering compartment
h - Hatch
m - Mushroom-top vents
s - Skylight
v - Vent trunk
Broken lines indicate non-watertight compartment partitions

Engineer's Stores
Engineer's Stores
Fan Room
Fan Room
Fan Room
Carpenters Stores
Boatswain's Stores
Stb ER
Centre ER
Port ER
WTC
Bilge Keel
Double Bottom

Section at aft end of Engine Rooms
(Looking Aft)

UPPER DECK

Screen Door
Acc Ladder
30ft Gig
'S'
27ft Whaler

MAIN DECK

Captain's Day Cabin
Captain's WC
Gun Room
'H'
Ward Room

Escape Trunk from
Hand Steering Compartment

MIDDLE DECK

Escape Trunk from
Hand Steering Compartment
WOs Mess Stores
Gun Room Stores
Junior Off's Bath Room
Boatswain's Stores
Aux Machy Spare Gear
Fan Room
Coal Bags
Fan Room
Eng's Stores
Medical dist' station
Engineer's
Fan Room
Workshop
Bath Room Flat
Fan Room
Coal Bags
Fan Room
Carpenters Stores
Engineer's Store
Marines Stores

100 90 80 70 60 50 40 30 20 10 0 Feet
30 25 20 15 10 5 0 Meters

Ward Room Stores
Commissioned Officers Bath Room

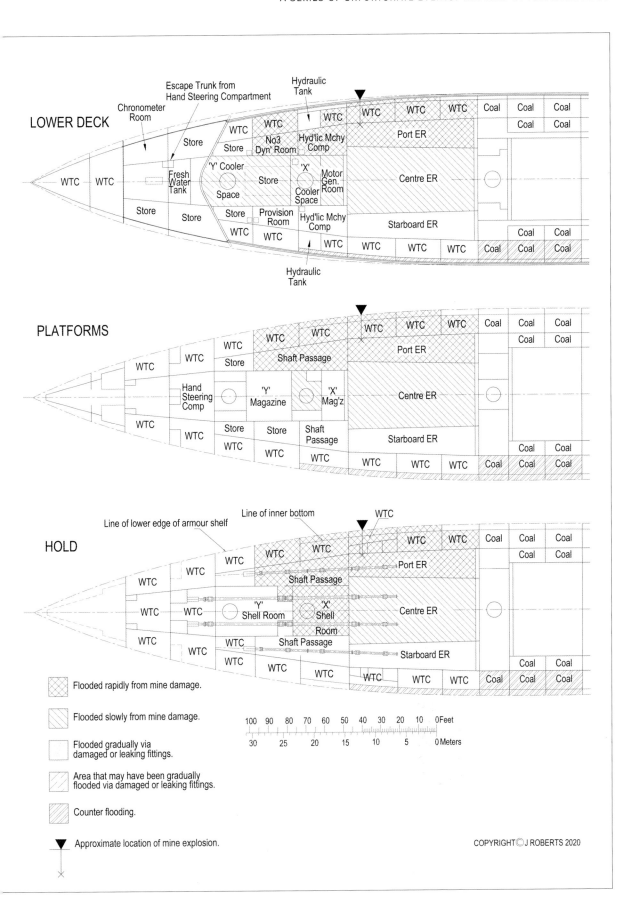

AUDACIOUS: LAYOUT OF ENGINE ROOMS

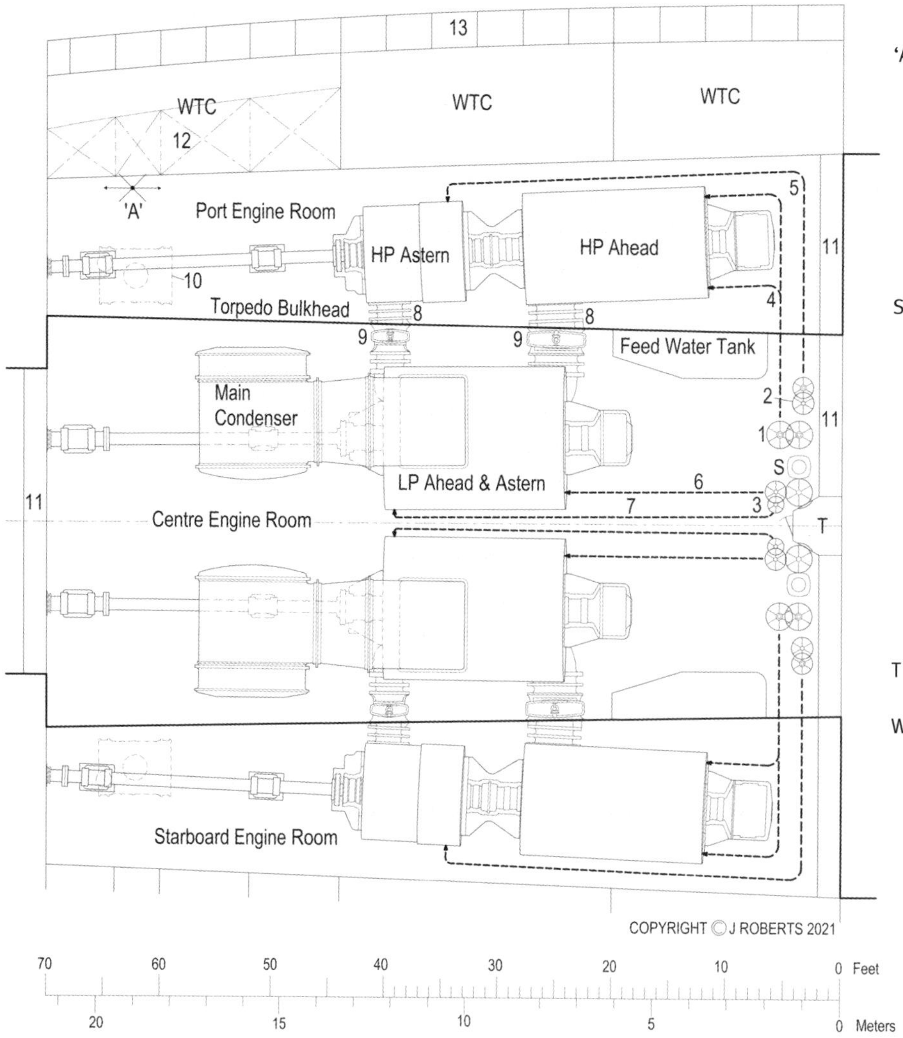

'A' Approximated location of mine explosion, centred on mean point of contemporary estimated position; the arrows indicate the fore-and-aft range of this estimate (5ft).

S Main steam pipe running vertically linking a horizontal pipe at top of forward centre engine room bulkhead (supplied directly from the boilers) and horizontal pipes running below the starting platform supplying the control valves.

T Telephone cabinet.

WTC Watertight compartment.

COPYRIGHT © J ROBERTS 2021

Key:

1 Control wheel for manoeuvring valve of port engine.
2 Control wheel for manoeuvring valve of port astern engine.
3 Control wheels for regulating valves of LP turbine when operated independently from HP turbine.
4 Main steam line to ahead turbines.
5 Main steam line to astern turbines.
6 Main steam line to LP ahead turbine (for independent operation).
7 Main steam line to LP astern turbine (for independent operation).
8 Steam connections from HP to LP turbines via torpedo bulkhead.
9 Slide shut-valves to steam supply from HP to LP turbines.
10 Outline of auxiliary condenser (over).
11 Air space.
12 Lubrication oil tanks in lower section of WTC. From forward to aft: Valvoline, mineral, olive and rapeseed.
13 Double bottom.

Notes:

– Arrangement of port and starboard engines and the wing compartments was identical apart from being mirror images of each other.
– The port and starboard turbine groups were each considered as a single engine (ie 'port engine' / 'starboard engine').
– The run of the main steam pipes to the engines is diagrammatic.
– The valves for the supply to the HP turbines were combined manoeuvring/intermediate valves, while those giving direct supply to the LP turbine comprised a single intermediate valve and separate ahead/astern regulating valves. Note that the control wheels for the intermediate and regulating valves do not have key numbers as their association with those valves that do have numbers is obvious. Intermediate/regulating valves provided basic control of engine speed, while the manoeuvring valves added more precision and faster reaction to that control.

At about 8.50pm *Audacious* heeled to port, hung there for a few seconds and then rolled over and began to sink by the stern. At 9pm, when her keel line reached an angle estimated at 30 degrees by one witness and 45 degrees by another, the forward magazines exploded, sending a sheet of flame into the air variously estimated at between 200 and 400 feet high. At least one explosion was seen in the air at the top of the column of flame and, as this produced black smoke, it was put down to the detonation of 4in lyddite shell(s) blown into the air. The flash of the explosion was seen, and its sound heard, at Lough Swilly 13nm away. The generally favoured conclusion as to the cause of the magazine explosion was that one or more 13.5in nose fused HE shell had detonated as the contents of the shell bins fell onto the deck head and/or each other as the ship rolled over, which in turn set off the cordite in the magazines. The explosion threw a considerable quantity of debris into the air, including one large section of plate from the hull. The only casualty of the loss of *Audacious* was a petty officer of *Liverpool* who was struck and killed by falling debris; all 852 men of the battleship's crew survived.[13] The wreck lies upside down at a depth of 36 fathoms in position 55°28'N, 7°45'W, about 18nm ESE from the position in which she was mined (see map).

Damage

The mine could not have struck in a worse place. Not only was it close to the after engine room bulkhead and the outer wing bulkhead but deep, close under the hull in the vicinity of the bilge keel and approximately 23 feet below the ship's level waterline at the time. This figure must remain a rough estimate as to the actual depth below water, given that the ship would have been heeling to port during her turn to starboard and that the swell then running may also have influenced the relative depth. This depth also implies that the mine was on a short cable, although this may have been affected by the mine swinging away from the *Audacious* due to the ship's wash and/or any deflection of the mine induced by the sea swell. The location explains the limited sound and surface splash – estimated by one witness as 16 feet above the upper deck – generated by the explosion, which would have expended most of its energy directly upward into the ship. There is also the speculative possibility that the mine detonated on hitting the edge of the bilge keel, which extended about 4 feet from the outer bottom at this point – in effect a close, non-contact explosion that could have generated more structural damage than one directly in contact with the hull. Even had this not occurred it was considered probable that the bilge keel had been either badly distorted or torn off, creating greater damage to the outer bottom and extending it further fore and aft. At the time of the explosion, men at the forward end of the port engine room '... saw the deck [*sic*] and machinery abaft the [auxiliary] condenser suddenly rise'.[14] Given that the port engine room flooded to the waterline very rapidly, probably in

less than 5 minutes, there can be little doubt that the ship had a very large hole in both her outer and inner bottom. Apart from the port engine room, the port wing shaft passage, port after hydraulic engine room, No 3 dynamo room, 'X' shell room and several wing compartments also flooded quickly. However, all the men on duty in these compartments escaped before the compartments were closed up.

Loss of Power

Shortly after the explosion, the port engine, that is both the HP and LP turbines, stopped. Steam and other connections between the port and centre engine rooms were quickly closed except for the large sluice valves in the pipes which exhausted steam from the HP into the LP turbines. These were not completely sealed until about 9.45pm due to the pressure of water in the port engine room distorting the torpedo bulkhead and making them very difficult to close – possibly the result of the bowing of the bulkhead causing distortion of the spindles between the sluice valves and the hand wheels that operated them. Water passed through these valves into the LP turbine and began to flood the centre engine room.[15] The closing of the valves reduced but did not stop the flooding, and it was soon realised that water was also entering through structural damage caused directly by the mine, either via a crack in the double bottom in the centre engine room, damage to the lower edge of the torpedo bulkhead or a combination of the two.[16]

By the time the sluice valves were closed there was about 5 feet of water in the bilge and the rising water had brought an end to an attempt to make a bilge suction connection to the powerful centrifugal circulating pumps of the condensers. Less than an hour later the centre engine room was half full (at about the level of the starting platform from which the engines were controlled) and it soon became necessary to stop the starboard engine.[17] At about 1pm the centre engine room was half full and by 4.30pm nearly full.

Audacious also lost her main electricity supply. She had three steam-driven dynamos, one aft on the port side of the lower deck powered by a reciprocating steam engine, and two forward, on the platform deck abreast 'B' shell room, driven by turbines. On the morning of the 27th, No 1 (starboard, forward) and No 3 (port, aft) were running at about half load. The mine put No 3 out of action, leaving only No 1 to supply power, so a request was sent by messenger to Captain Dampier asking permission to open No 2 dynamo room. Unfortunately the messenger was 'nervous' and 'indistinct' and Dampier thought he said No 3 dynamo room. Being unaware that this compartment was already out of action, he refused the request on the basis that it was too close to the point of damage. This made it necessary to reduce the load, so all the primary electric circuits were broken except those for the engine and boiler room lights, the engine room ventilation fans (those for the boiler rooms were steam powered) and the winches on the upper deck. The

This and the following two photographs were taken from *Olympic* and show *Audacious* immobile and broadside on to the Atlantic swell at midday on 27 October 1913. Non-essential personnel, about 65 per cent of the ship's crew at this time, are in the process of being transferred to the ships in company. Note the extent of her roll to port in comparison with that in the next photograph, which was taken shortly after this one. (Author's collection)

connections to the electrically-powered 50-ton fire and bilge pumps outside the main machinery compartments were also retained but added no load since none of these machines were in operation, the four forward having nothing to pump while the two aft, which would have been of some use, were inaccessible. No 1 dynamo continued to run, with occasional breakdowns, until the steam power failed. The low power system, which served the telephones and other electrical instruments, failed even sooner. The power for the low power switch boards was switched from the dynamo, the supply from which was unreliable, to batteries in the hope of maintaining the ship's communications, but this failed quickly as a result of electrical instruments in the engine room being flooded and shorted out. Thus, as midday approached *Audacious* was lying broadside on to the Atlantic swell, rolling heavily, with no ability to move or steer, no operating auxiliary machinery and very limited communication.

Albert P Cole, RCNC

On board *Audacious* at the time of her loss was Assistant Constructor 2nd Class AP Cole. He had joined the Admiralty Department of the DNC (Director of Naval Construction) late in 1913 and been assigned to *Audacious* for 12 months sea service in April 1914. Captain Dampier later commented that Cole '...was invaluable to me throughout this trying day by giving me most useful reports of the state of the ship. He visited

every W. T. door which he could possibly get at and saw them all really watertight, many of them at much personal danger.'[18]

After reporting to Dampier on conditions in the engine room Cole was involved in an inspection of some of the closed compartments abaft the engine rooms. This started with the opening of a hatch on the main deck to give access to the medical distributing station on the middle deck, abaft 'X' barbette. Here about 6 inches of water and oil were washing about which originated from leaks via sealing glands to valve control rods and a hole in a fan casing. These leaks were sealed before moving down to the lower deck and into the compartment containing the after motor-generator room and 'X' cooler space. This contained 2 feet of water apparently coming from leaks behind junction boxes fixed to the port longitudinal bulkhead. On the other side of this bulkhead were the port hydraulic engine room and No 3 dynamo room, both of which were probably completely flooded. Nothing could be done since the area behind the boxes was inaccessible. It also seemed to Cole that the amount of water indicated that this was not the only cause of flooding, so the hatch to 'X' magazine was checked but found to be tight. As no other cause could be found, the compartments were evacuated and closed-up.

Moving further aft on the main deck the access hatch to the bath room flat was discovered to be not tight due to a stanchion jammed in the ladder having stopped the hatch cover from fully closing. The hatch was opened and the flat below found to be 2 feet deep in water. The cause was found in the port forward corner of the flat where the watertight door to the junior officers' bathroom was leaking due to being only 'hand tight'. This bathroom was obviously flooded so the clips were tightened with a maul (heavy hammer) and all other doors similarly treated before closing-down the compartment. Some time was then spent ensuring that ventilators and hatch covers on the quarterdeck were as secure and tight as possible – an effort largely negated by the subsequent damage to both by wreckage washing about on the deck.

Given that the ship was difficult to manage without power in the prevailing weather and that some control would be useful in the forthcoming attempt to tow her to Lough Swilly, Cole was ordered to open up the hand steering compartment. Together with an officer (Lt Craven) and twelve volunteers, he began to make his way down to the platform deck.[19] The main deck abaft 'Y' barbette was partially flooded with about 15 inches of water and oil which had entered via the soil pipe of the Captain's WC. It was considered that this was probably due to the flap valve in the pipe being jammed open by the shock of the mine explosion. The flap was inaccessible, so nothing could be done to stop the steady flooding of the compartment.

Access to the hand steering compartment was via a watertight escape trunk against the after bulkhead of the compartment. For reasons that are unclear, Cole states that he had to open a watertight door in this bulkhead in order to enter the Admiral's lobby (which was 'practically dry') so that he could open the watertight sliding shutter at the bottom of the escape trunk.[20] In the hand steering compartment it was found that the rudder was hard to starboard at 35 degrees and this was initially returned to amidships. Owing to the loss of telephone communication, a chain of men was employed to pass orders, along the upper deck, between the bridge and the hand steering compartment via a skylight above the midshipmen's study (an area on the main deck abaft 'Y' turret with a surrounding curtain). From here the officer in charge of the communication party, Lieutenant Pridham-Wippell, (later Admiral Sir HD Pridham-Wippell, KGB, CVO) passed down orders through the port forward cover of the skylight. As the ship sank lower and the swell got worse it became necessary to repeatedly close the cover to stop water washing across the deck from making its way below. Shortly after 2pm, with the hand steering proving of limited value, increasing risk to the men on the quarter deck and the danger of flooding making its way down to the hand steering compartment from both the upper and

The ships in this view, besides *Audacious*, include two destroyers of the 2nd Flotilla ('H' class) and, on the extreme right, the stern of the cruiser *Liverpool*. Following the loss of power to the hoist machinery for the main boat boom it had been left extending to starboard. Although secured by guys fore and aft it began to creep as the ship rolled, broke the after guy and took charge. It was eventually lashed to the starboard strut of the tripod foremast, as shown here, although not before it had done some minor damage. Note that the positions of the coaling derricks abreast the after funnel, and the derrick on the port side of the after superstructure, indicate that they had also been in use in getting out the boats. All the boats that were got out came from the boat deck abreast the funnels except for one – a 32-foot cutter stowed on the upper deck under the guns of 'Q' turret which capsized while being lowered over the side. (Author's collection)

main decks, Captain Dampier ordered the compartment to be evacuated and the escape trunk and quarterdeck skylight closed up.

The following observations on the behaviour of *Audacious* were included in a report by Cole and inserted in the Ship's Covers of the *King George V* class. This report is an expansion of that he originally made shortly after the ship's loss and which now resides in the National Archives at Kew:

[The] rolling of the ship and subsequent capsizing is most interesting from a theoretical point of view. Though it is doubtful that what actually occurred could have been calculated 'a proiri' owing to the several variables in operation. At the time she struck the period was approximately 15 [seconds] and the vanishing angle about 70°. A regular swell was coming from the Atlantic which under normal circumstances would probably have caused the ship to roll about 5 degrees on either side. Unfortunately, no data was taken but [there were] three remarkable phases of rolling at intervals of about 5 hours each. That this interval should have been so long can only be explained by the fact that there must have been three or more strong periodic forces acting on the ship – namely, the swell, the stability force and the free water inside the ship and that they approached synchronism at intervals of about 5 hours. The first phase took place at about 11.0am when the water in the middle engine room was just rising over the turbines. The port side of the upper deck was just rolling under the water and the swell was on the port beam. This rolling took the nature of going to the extreme angle and stopping there, then very slowly coming back. The second phase occurred about 4.0pm. The water in the middle engine room had reached to within 3ft or 4ft of the middle deck but it was very probable that the other compartments were being filled. The mean water line was about 1ft below the upper deck aft and about 4ft below the upper deck forward. The swell was on the starboard beam, the ship having turned at about 12.0pm. This rolling took the nature of going to the extreme angle, stopping,

going a little further and then slowly coming back. The ship was very sluggish. The third phase occurred between 8.30 and 9.0pm. The upper deck was then practically right under water and probably the ship was entirely water logged aft. There then would be practically no free surface but on the other hand there was also no water line so that the vanishing angle must have been very small. At about 8.45pm the ship turned to an angle of about 12deg and appeared to hang up as before, she then went slowly on, failed to recover and thus turned turtle. Almost immediately after this she blew up apparently from B magazine.

Pumping and Flooding

There is a generally held view that the loss of *Audacious* was primarily due to poor damage control combined with inadequate watertightness and pumping arrangements. While not without basis this is simplistic, and those holding this view could be accused of being wise after the event. In the case of damage control there was one serious error in that the counter-flooding aft increased her trim by the stern. Counter-flooding on the starboard side forward would have served her much better – a point made as early as February 1915 by the 3rd Sea Lord, Rear Admiral Tudor. In other respects it is difficult to criticise damage control given that what was actually possible in the way of stopping leaks *was* done. The most serious problems with the spread of flooding came from the damage at the bottom of the port wing bulkhead of the centre engine room and the decapitating of the vents on the quarterdeck, both of which it was impossible to do anything about. The same applies to the flooding through the soil pipe of the Captain's WC and leakage through sealing glands for electrical cables which in all cases were inaccessible. There were probably other leaks of a similar nature that could not be reached. Such leaks do indicate an inadequate procedure for testing the watertightness of compartments but, while these small leaks may not have helped the situation, they can hardly be viewed as a major

Audacious viewed from astern with the Atlantic swell on her port side coming up to the edge of her upper deck amidships. Just visible, at the after end of the net shelf on the port side of the quarterdeck, is the 30ft gig originally stowed abreast 'Y' turret. Shortly after this it was swept over the side.
(Author's collection)

contributor to the ship's loss, especially when account is taken of the view at the time that, had the weather not caused such heavy rolling, it was just possible that the ship might not have capsized. The weather also seriously compromised the attempts to tow *Audacious*.

For pumping purposes pre-dreadnought battleships were fitted with main drains, with sluice valves at each main transverse bulkhead running along the inner bottom down the middle line and discharged into the bilges of the engine rooms. For normal purposes fire and bilge pumps in the engine rooms were used to pump out any bilge water drained down to the engine room. In order to deal with more extensive flooding, as might occur from collision or action damage, the powerful pumps that circulated sea water through the ship's condensers were fitted with bilge suctions so that large quantities of water could be dealt with in an emergency. Other than this the only pumps available were Downton hand-pumps. In *Dreadnought* it was decided to adopt bulkheads unpierced by doors or any unnecessary pipes and connections including the main drain. In its place each primary watertight compartment between the main transverse bulkheads was provided with a dedicated pumping arrangement. The main machinery compartments had steam-driven fire and bilge pumps – two 75-ton in each engine room and one 50-ton in each boiler room – while an electrically driven 50-ton fire and bilge pump was provided in each of the compartments fore and aft.[21] In general, this was regarded as sufficient for dealing with normal pumping requirements, and the flooding of a major compartment was considered acceptable in more serious circumstances since the 'intact' bulkheads would limit the extent of flooding. Although proposals were made to omit the circulating-pump bilge suctions they were retained, albeit with reduced capacity, in *Dreadnought*, the *Bellerophon* class and the *Invincible* class. In 1907 the subject was raised again and, on the basis that the bilge suctions would be useless in dealing with flooding from serious damage, it was approved to discontinue their use in all future ships.

In January 1915 Vice Admiral HJ Oram, Engineer-in-Chief of the Fleet, commented that 'As regards accidents in peace, there have been two cases of flooding of engine rooms of battleships in comparatively recent years and in neither case were the bilge suctions of use owing to rapid flooding or other circumstances.' However, he did describe *Audacious* as a special case, a tacit agreement with those, including Tudor and Cole, who considered that the ship would have survived if her main circulating pumps had been fitted with bilge suctions. The opening that flooded the centre engine room could not have had an area much greater than about 4 square inches, equivalent to a flood rate of *c*260 tons per hour – a level well within the capacity of the circulation pumps. Not only would this have kept the flooding of the centre engine room under control but it would also have allowed the continued use of her starboard engine. Oram was correct in that the existing system relied on isolating badly damaged compartments, while the pumping arrange-

ments were only intended to deal with small leaks or to pump out compartments once any larger leak had been repaired. It was, however, clear that some serious improvement in pumping capacity was required.

This resulted in the restoration of circulating-pump bilge suctions and the introduction of other high-capacity pumping devices specifically intended for emergency use. In December 1914 it was approved to fit bilge suctions to the circulation pumps in the engine rooms of all battleships and battle cruisers of the *St Vincent* and *Indefatigable* and later classes.[22] It was also decided to provide 200-ton bilge ejectors for the boiler rooms and gland compartments of all dreadnought battleships and battle cruisers.[23] Shortly after this, ejectors were also approved for the forward submerged torpedo rooms and, by August 1915, for the after submerged torpedo rooms. In the latter case the steam ejectors for the gland spaces were omitted. In addition to this work, additional shut-valves were fitted to ventilation trunks passing through decks and watertight bulkheads to limit any future repetition of the flooding from the mushroom top vents that occurred in the after compartments of *Audacious*.

While it is certain that new construction was provided with bilge suctions, there is little evidence to clarify how much of this programme was completed in earlier ships, it being subject to the limitations of available resources and dockyard time – which was kept to a minimum for operational reasons. In addition, the existing engine room arrangements often limited the size of bilge suction that could be fitted. The subsequent introduction of electrically powered turbo-pumps and portable salvage pumps may also have reduced any urgency applied to the work.

Electric Power

One of the more serious problems suffered by *Audacious* resulted from her almost total reliance on steam power. Once this was lost, the ship was left motionless and without a means of running her auxiliary machinery, including the machinery providing steering, hydraulics and the primary electricity supply. In the early dreadnoughts one or two diesel-driven dynamos had been fitted to provide power when steam was not available. These were to some extent under trial and were not regarded as sufficiently reliable so, from *Neptune* onward, reliance was placed entirely on steam-powered dynamos. This remained the case until the *Iron Duke* class and later battleships, when oil-driven dynamos were reintroduced. During the war several of those ships that had only steam-driven dynamos were provided with an additional diesel-driven dynamo. However, it would seem that the addition was not viewed at this period as critical in relation to action damage, given that none of the sister ships of *Audacious* was so fitted.

Fates

In Britain, news of the loss of *Audacious* was suppressed for both military and political reasons which, while justified for a limited period, eventually served only to damage the reputations of both the British Government and the Admiralty. Given the fact that the fate of *Audacious* had been witnessed by foreign nationals, primarily citizens of the USA, from the deck of the *Olympic*, it was obvious that the news would soon be known to the world. The *Olympic* was held at Lough Swilly for three days, with her passengers retained on board, and the crew of *Audacious* was distributed among the ships of the Grand Fleet, while the ship's name was retained in the Navy List until February 1915. In Germany news of the loss was received 23 days after the event while the British public remained, for the most part, in ignorance until the details were officially released at the end of the war.

The luck that had attended *Berlin* on her outward journey deserted the ship during her attempt to return home. After laying her mines, she headed westward into the Atlantic until she reached about 15°W and then turned toward Greenland. Her journey was seriously hampered by bad weather and boiler problems, resulting from long periods of high-speed steaming, which substantially reduced her speed. On 30 October she turned NE to pass through the Iceland-Greenland passage. Pfundheller's original orders required him to raid the Icelandic fishing fleets but, having concluded that the weather would have driven the majority of fishing vessels to take shelter in harbour, he continued eastward to fulfil his next task – to raid the Archangel-UK trade route. On 5 November he arrived in a position to the north of Murmansk, closed the coast and followed it during the 7–8th as far as North Cape. Here *Berlin* encountered a potential target but the appearance of a second ship, identified incorrectly as a possible warship, resulted in her withdrawal to seaward. She then retraced her route westward until north of the Lofoton Islands where she altered course to follow the coast of Norway. With her coal supply running low, a problem exacerbated by high coal consumption resulting from her boiler problems, and worsening weather conditions plus the ever-present fear of interception, Pfundheller concluded that he would not be able to return to Germany and decided to seek internment in a neutral port. This option was provided for in his operational orders and early on 17 November, in a heavy snow-storm, *Berlin* arrived at Trondheim. Following the requisite period of 24 hours the ship was interned at Hommelvik. In 1919 she was surrendered to Britain, and after a brief period of trooping duties was sold to the White Star Line and renamed *Arabic*. She was sold for breaking up in 1931.

Clearing the minefield laid by *Berlin* proved to be something of a problem initially due to the limited availability of minesweepers on the west coast. The mines were also scattered to some extent by the bad weather. Initial steps involved sweeping a safe channel for shipping, but no mines seem to have been cleared until 20–22 December. These were located in an area close to where *Audacious* and *Manchester Commerce* had been mined. More were discovered on 10–11 February, in a line

extending roughly 5 miles northward from a point about 8 miles NE by E from where *Audacious* was mined. A mine in this area had already claimed a merchantman on 19 December and was to claim another on 23 April. The area was not completely cleared until August 1915.

Captain Cecil Frederick Dampier (1868–1950) was given command of *Audacious* on 30 May 1913. After her loss he was accommodated in *Marlborough* (1st BS) until Jellicoe provided him with temporary command of *Superb* (1st BS) during 3–9 November.[24] On 1 January 1915 he was appointed as Admiral of the Training Service, with the temporary rank of Commodore 1st Class until 18 February when he was promoted to Rear Admiral. On 13 March 1916 he was appointed Second-in-Command of the 3rd BS, based at Sheerness, with his flag in *Hibernia*. During 1–5 December 1916, while the squadron was between vice admirals, he was given temporary command of the squadron with his flag in *Dreadnought*. He left the 3rd BS, his last sea command, on 14 March 1917 to serve at Dover, initially as Admiral Superintendent of the dockyard (18 June 1917 – 1 June 1918), then as Rear Admiral in command of controlled minefields (2 June 1918 – 20 March 1919), and finally as temporary commander of the Dover Patrol (20 March – 15 October 1919). His active service in the Navy seems to have ended at this point and, although he attended the Senior Officers course at Greenwich Naval College during March – December 1920, he was placed on the retired list at his own request on 1 July 1922.

Albert Percy Cole joined the department of the DNC at the Admiralty in November 1913 as an Assistant Constructor 2nd Class (temporary) and spent most of his career in this office, initially in London and later at Bath, but there were a few exceptions. He does appear to have completed his twelve months of sea service since he was appointed to the battleship *Benbow* for a few months during the latter part of 1915. In late 1917 he was promoted to Assistant Constructor 1st Class and during December 1918 – April 1919 was on loan to the Director of Airship Production and Repair (together with two other Assistant Constructors). At the end of 1920 he was on loan again, to the Naval Inter-Allied Commissions Control (Berlin), presumably to provide technical advice, and in 1926 was Admiralty overseer at Fairfield's shipyard at Govan during construction of the cruiser *Berwick*. In 1929 he was promoted to Constructor and in 1934 placed in charge of the Destroyer section, subsequently being responsible for the 'Tribal' and 'J' to 'L'-class destroyers, which period saw the introduction of a new bridge design and longitudinal framing (with the 'J' class). During this time, he also gave Captain Louis Mountbatten advice on damage control which Mountbatten later said proved invaluable in saving his ship (*Kelly*) when she was torpedoed by an E-boat in May 1940. In the same month Cole was promoted to Chief Constructor, in November 1941 to ADNC (Assistant Director of Naval Construction) and in March 1945 to DDNC (Deputy Director of Naval Construction).

Acknowledgement:

My thanks are due to William Jurens for his assistance in confirming the precise location of the wreck of *Audacious*.

Primary Sources:

The Loss of *Audacious* (ADM137/1012 and ADM137/1919, TNA).

Naval Staff Monograph, Vol XI, Home Waters Sep-Oct 1914 (ADM186/620, TNA).

Naval Staff Monograph, Vol VII, The 10th Cruiser Squadron (ADM186/614).

Grand Fleet Narrative of Events, October 1914 (ADM137/416).

Ship's Covers, *King George V* Class (No260/260A, NMM).

Naval Operations Vol 1, Sir Julian S Corbett (Longmans, 1920).

Endnotes:

1   *Monarch* was absent from the squadron, docking and refitting at Portsmouth 12–16 October.

2   Grand Fleet Operational Order Number 16 of 6 October 1914 (ADM 137/2018).

3   *Liverpool* joined the 1st BS as a temporary attached cruiser in place of *Bellona*; she did not re-join the 1st LCS until 6 November.

4   After *Iron Duke* departed, the only ships remaining at Scapa were the flagship's attached cruiser *Sappho* (which sailed at 8am to join the 2nd BCS), the repair ships *Assistance* (ordered to Broadford Bay on the 17th) and *Cyclops*, a few minesweepers, and some destroyers of the 2nd and 4th Flotillas.

5   The detailed movements of the *Berlin* which follow are entirely based on Vol XI of the Naval Staff Monographs, Home Waters Sep–Oct 1914 (ADM137/416) which were in turn based on the German Navy's Official History. The British Official History (Naval Operations Vol I) was published before that of the German Navy and relied for the movements of *Berlin* on a source acknowledged as dubious. Not only has this left a false record of events but has also added speculation regarding the *Berlin*'s apparent luck in avoiding (non-existent) British patrols and the impression that she did not turn back in her progress towards the Clyde until she reached the North Channel.

6   The time 1.08pm is recorded in the Grand Fleet Narrative of October 1914 (ADM137/416). Jellicoe himself, in a report of the incident dated 30 October 1914, gives the time as 1.30pm, while the relevant Naval Staff Monograph gives the time as 2pm. In a footnote, the latter also refers to the 1.08pm given in the 'Grand Fleet Narrative' without comment on the discrepancy. It is possible that 1.08pm is a reception time, either at Buncrana or aboard *Iron Duke*, and that Jellicoe did not get to read it until later.

7   Before arrival at Loch na Keal *Conqueror* was detached to dock at Devonport. On the 19th *Monarch* re-joined from Portsmouth while the squadron's attached cruiser, *Boadicea*, sailed for Chatham to refit. The 1st BCS was also present at Loch na Keal but sailed on the 21st.

8   Captain Dampier's initial reaction was that one of the ship's after guns, or possibly one in *King George V*, had fired accidently.

9   This view was later re-enforced by *Monarch* reporting at 11.09pm that she had sighted a submarine.

10 Captain's Report on the loss of *Audacious* (ADM137/1012). Other official documents state that the depth of water in the centre engine room at this time was 5 feet.

11 Most of the original sources state that the main machinery compartments were abandoned at 'about' 11am. They also imply that the boats were hoisted out after this time. Given that the main derrick was powered by hydraulic machinery, supplied from steam-driven hydraulic pumps, it would seem that either the main derrick was only in use prior to the machinery being shut down, or that some boiler power remained available for some time after 11am. It was possible to operate the main derrick manually but this process required a large number of men and was unlikely to have been employed in a ship rolling heavily.

12 There were also about fifty officers on board and, as these are not mentioned in this initial evacuation, it is assumed that all remained in the ship.

13 One stoker was initially assumed to have been lost but was later found.

14 *King George V* Class, Ship's Covers (NMM). There were no 'decks' within the engine room so presumably this refers to the platforms, roughly 10 feet above the inner bottom at the after end of the wing engine room. In this general area were the auxiliaries for the condenser and distillation plant, and the port outer propeller shaft, but only a few of these could be accurately described as 'abaft the condenser'.

15 Had these valves been closed quickly it might have been possible to run the port LP turbine independently for a short period. There was also water entering via the port feed tank but the cause of this is unclear.

16 The suspect area could not be examined due to the flooding. The rest of the bulkhead was checked and no problem, apart from the bowing, was found.

17 According to the Engineer Commander (W Bartwell), after the LP turbine was shut down an 'attempt' was made to run the starboard HP turbine independently of the LP turbine, exhausting the steam to atmosphere. This would have required the closing of the sluice valves between the two starboard turbines and providing some other route for the exhaust steam. Presumably the attempt failed when the control valves in the centre engine room could no longer be operated due to the rising water level.

18 Captain's Report on the loss of *Audacious* (ADM137/1012).

19 Cole himself states that this was initiated by an *order* but Captain Dampier in his report suggests that Cole was one of the twelve volunteers.

20 Logic would suggest the main deck control wheel for remote opening of the shutter would have been in the same watertight section as the trunk, and not in the next compartment.

21 Note that the early dreadnoughts had two engine rooms with two 75-ton fire and bilge pumps in each. Those with three engine rooms (*Colossus* class and later) had two 75-ton in the centre engine room and one each in the wing engine rooms.

22 By February 1915 it had also been approved to increase the number of bilge suctions in the *Bellerophon* and *Invincible* classes.

23 The gland compartments were the after sections of the shaft passages adjacent to the stuffing boxes (seals) of the propeller shafts.

24 In company with the Grand Fleet, *Superb* was at sea during 3–7 November, after which the fleet returned to Scapa Flow. The previous captain of *Superb*, Price Vaughan Lewes, had been taken seriously ill and Dampier was a convenient substitute since her new captain, RW Bentinck, was not appointed until 6 November and did not arrive at Scapa to take over command until the 9th. Captain Lewes died on the same day.

CLEMENCEAU AND *FOCH*: FRANCE'S FIRST MODERN AIRCRAFT CARRIERS

France's engagement with the aircraft carrier as a type prior to the Second World War had been patchy and less than committed. Faced with a postwar world in which the battleship had effectively been displaced by naval aviation, the *Marine Nationale* drew up ambitious plans for a fleet of aircraft carriers. After some initial false steps, France finally laid down two carriers of modern design incorporating the latest technology. **Jean Moulin**, author of a number of books on French carrier design, and **John Jordan** present a detailed study of *Clemenceau* and her sister *Foch*.

The French *Marine Nationale* entered the Second World War with only a single aircraft carrier, *Béarn*, converted during the 1920s from a battleship hull (see John Jordan's article in *Warship 2020*). Too slow to operate with the battle fleet, the ship was relegated to transport duties from the outset, carrying French gold to Canada and bringing back aircraft purchased from the United States on the return journey. Two faster ships of more modern design were authorised during the late 1930s (see John Jordan's article in *Warship 2010*). Work on *Joffre* was begun in 1938 but the hull remained on the stocks at the outbreak of war; her sister *Painlevé* was never laid down.

The aircraft carrier proved its value during the Second World War, and a French study dated 20 June 1945 proposed a fleet of six, all conversions or completions of existing hulls. These plans were impractical and unrealistic. There were also numerous studies for new-build carriers, none very impressive. As an interim measure France moved to borrow or purchase aircraft carriers from her allies, Britain and the USA. The escort carrier HMS *Biter*, which had been returned to the United States in April 1945, was refitted and loaned to the French Navy, becoming *Dixmude*. The British-built light carrier *Colossus* was loaned as *Arromanches* in 1946 and purchased outright in 1951. And two of the American wartime light carrier conversions, *Langley* (CVL-27) and *Belleau Wood* (CVL-24), were loaned to the French under the Mutual Defense Assistance Program (MDAP) as *La Fayette* (1951) and *Bois Belleau* (1953) respec-

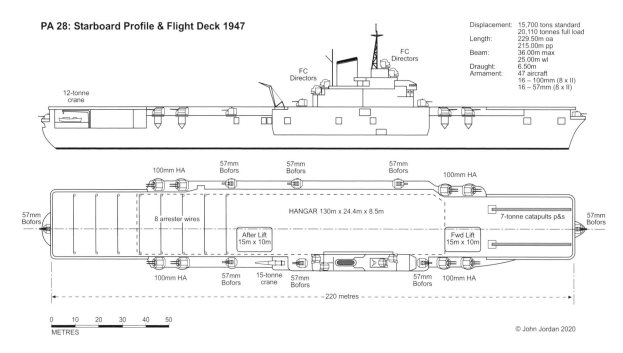

PA 28: Starboard Profile & Flight Deck 1947

12-tonne crane

FC Directors

FC Directors

FC Directors

Displacement:	15,700 tons standard
	20,110 tonnes full load
Length:	229.50m oa
	215.00m pp
Beam:	36.00m max
	25.00m wl
Draught:	6.50m
Armament:	47 aircraft
	16 – 100mm (8 x II)
	16 – 57mm (8 x II)

100mm HA
57mm Bofors
57mm Bofors
57mm Bofors
100mm HA

57mm Bofors

8 arrester wires

HANGAR 130m x 24.4m x 8.5m

7-tonne catapults p&s

57mm Bofors

After Lift 15m x 10m

Fwd Lift 15m x 10m

100mm HA
57mm Bofors
15-tonne crane
57mm Bofors
57mm Bofors
100mm HA

— 220 metres —

0 10 20 30 40 50
METRES

© John Jordan 2020

tively. The British and US carriers were not first-line ships and were due to be discarded by their own navies. However, they provided valuable experience of operating aircraft from flight decks and enabled France to build a core of naval aviators who would fly the high-performance jet aircraft that would enter service during the 1950s.

PA 28

The first serious postwar carrier proposal was PA 28 (PA = *porte-avions*), which was to be funded under the 1948 Estimates and built in one of the two large docks at Laninon, Brest, with a projected completion date of 1954. Closely modelled on the British light fleet carriers, PA 28 nevertheless incorporated a number of features more closely associated with US carrier design, such as the suspension of a large number of aircraft from the hangar roof. There were also features borrowed from the prewar *Joffre* design: the hangar was offset to port with the centre lift against its starboard edge to permit the movement of aircraft fore and aft.

The air group was to have comprised 20 SE 582 fighters suspended from the hangar roof, and five fighters and 22 NC 1070 twin-engine bombers stowed on the hangar floor, for a total of 47 aircraft. There were to be eight arrester wires with four oleopneumatic brakes, three crash barriers and two 7-tonne catapults. Aircraft could be lifted from quayside onto the flight deck by a 15-tonne crane abaft the island, and there was a 12-tonne crane to port to handle the boats. A total of 400 tonnes of avgas could be carried, and magazines for air ordnance fore and aft were served by lifts 2.8m x 0.7m. The armament was to comprise sixteen 100mm guns in twin mountings – probably the same model fitted in the battleship *Jean Bart* – with four stabilised directors for fire control atop the island. These were complemented by eight of the new 57mm twin Bofors mountings: three per side plus two at the open ends of the ship (see Profile and Plan).

After considering various types of propulsion unit already in service it was finally decided that the ship would have all-new machinery comprising four Indret Sural asymmetric boilers supplying steam for two sets of Parsons single-reduction turbines (HP, IP, LP) on two shafts for 95,000shp, rising to 105,000shp with forced draught to ensure 32 knots at deep load. Two auxiliary boilers would supply 'hotel' services, while for electrical power there were to be two turbo-alternators in the engine rooms for 2,010kW, complemented by four diesel generators in two independent spaces. Endurance was to be 7,700nm at 18 knots. PA 28 was designed as a flagship and would have had a complement of 1,806 officers and men.

The programme was authorised 14 August 1947 and Brest notified 1st September; the ship was to be named *Clemenceau*. Work continued on the plans and some items of equipment were ordered, but the keel laying was put on hold 9 October 1947 for budgetary reasons. Work

on the project ceased 7 March 1949 and the ship was cancelled on 31 May. The PA 28 project was a victim of opposition to carriers by traditionalists, financial constraints and infrastructure limitations; she was also the victim of the failed trials of the aircraft she was to embark, none of which passed the prototype stage.

From PA 28 to PA 54

On 26 Oct 1951 Admiral Henri Nomy, a former naval aviator, became Naval Chief of Staff. Nomy's accession saw a new plan published in July 1952 that aimed to take account of France's commitments to NATO and proposed the construction of three new carriers. On 28 July 1952 Navy Minister Jacques Gavini duly requested studies for an aircraft carrier of 12,500 tons to perform both the Atlantic ASW support and the overseas power projection missions. Studies began in late 1952, but 12,500 tons proved too small a displacement for operations in the Atlantic, particularly in the light of the increasing weight of modern jet and turboprop aircraft.

After further studies it was decided to pursue a more ambitious project initially designated PAX, and on 25 Mar 1953 the STCAN presented a preliminary sketch for a carrier of 19,000 tons standard, with a waterline length of 228 metres and a flight deck 245 metres long incorporating a 7-degree, 164-metre angled deck. There were to be two 50-metre British steam catapults, aircraft lifts with dimensions 16.3m x 14m and 15.3m x 9m, and tanks for 750 tonnes of furnace fuel oil (FFO) and 550 tonnes of avgas. The steam turbine machinery would deliver 120,000shp on two shafts, and protection was limited to tight subdivision. The island was modelled on that of the modernised units of the US *Essex* class, and the anti-aircraft armament was to comprise 24 x 57mm in four groupings each of three twin mountings.

An armoured variant, designated PAX-P (P for *protégé*), was presented at the same time. On a displacement of 23,000 tons standard, it would have had a flight deck 50mm thick and an internal armoured citadel with 60mm sides and a 30mm crown. Propulsion machinery would have been identical, but the increase in weight would limit maximum speed to 31 knots. An even more heavily armoured variant, designated PAX-P2 (the earlier armoured variant was redesignated PAX-P1) and presented for consideration on 20 June, would have combined a 30mm flight deck with a 80–100mm citadel; displacement increased by 720 tonnes, but 800 tonnes could be saved by suppressing the flight deck armour. It was estimated that 32 knots would require 4-shaft machinery, at a cost in both weight and volume plus a 10-metre increase in length. PAX-P2 was the variant preferred by the STCAN; Nomy likewise preferred the protected version but wanted 32 knots on two shafts. The version approved by the Minister on 8 August 1953 would be a modified PAX-P1.

There were numerous changes to the design specifications before the new ship, now designated PA 54, was laid down. In July 1953 it was proposed to replace each

The hull of *Clemenceau* is floated out of her building dock at Laninon, Brest, in a formal 'launch' ceremony on 21 December 1957, and towed to the fitting-out quay. (Jean Moulin collection)

of the twelve 57mm twin mountings by the new 100mm single mounting currently under development, which fired proximity-fuzed shells. On 19 October there was a request from Nomy to embark aircraft with a take-off weight of 20 tonnes and a landing weight of 15 tonnes. The air group was to comprise 24 British Sea Venom jet fighters (built under licence by SNCASE as the Aquilon), 24 attack and 12 anti-submarine aircraft (as yet undefined). New radars and electronic support measures (ESM) equipment of French design and manufacture would be fitted.

There was now a focus on the layout of flight deck. A study dating from late 1953 showed two catapults side by side and two aircraft lifts: one forward of the island, offset to starboard to clear the angled deck, the other as a side lift directly abaft the island. In January 1954 Paul Gisserot, head of the section *Grands Bâtiments Porte-Avions* of the STCAN, visited the US-loaned carrier *La Fayette* and criticised the flight deck layout and the low capacity of the fuel tanks and magazines. Following his visit the angled deck of PA 54 was moved to port and the angle increased, the island was moved one metre to starboard – both measures were intended to increase the area available for deck parking – and the capacity of the avgas tanks was increased from 1,000m³ to 1,200m³.

The embarked aircraft were now posing problems. Studies of the Aquilon were completed; however, the dimensions and weight of future aircraft was unclear, so the aviation installations needed to be 'future-proofed'. The forward lift was lengthened by one metre (from 16.4m x 14m to 17.4m x 13m), and the capacity of the aviation fuel tanks further increased to 1,350m³, with the bulk allocated to JP-5 jet fuel. In late 1954 the positions of the catapults were reviewed in the light of current US Navy and RN practice: one of the catapults was relocated to the angled deck to free up the forward part of the flight deck for parking to starboard.

On 14 June 1957, only six months prior to 'launch', the number of 100mm guns was reduced from twelve to eight. Finally, on 30 July 1957 Vice Admiral Aboyneau presented to the Conseil Supérieur de la Marine (CSM) a proposal for atomic bombs to be delivered by aircraft from *Clemenceau* and her sister *Foch*. This would have an impact on the arrangements for air ordnance stowage and handling.

Construction

PA 54 was authorised under the 1954 Estimates: she was to be laid down in October 1955 and ready for trials on 31 January 1959 and would be named *Clemenceau*. The turbines and gearing were contracted from the private

shipbuilder Chantiers de l'Atlantique, the boilers from the state establishment at Indret, and the propulsion and auxiliary machinery, together with the anchors and their handling gear, was to be installed by AC Bretagne. The order for the hull was duly placed with Brest Naval Dockyard on 28 May; work began in April 1955, and the keel was laid in Laninon No 9 Dock on 15 December 1955. At almost 258 metres *Clemenceau* was the longest ship yet built at Brest.

Construction of the ship was a major enterprise: there were 200 draughtsmen and technicians charged with plans, and 2,500 men worked on the ship; 3,500 orders were sub-contracted to private industry. Each of the prefabricated elements weighed a maximum of 45 tonnes, and 500 tonnes were installed each month. The ends of the flight deck were fitted as two 50-tonne modules in November 1957, by which time the weight of the hull was 12,000 tonnes. The boilers were embarked from 12 August to 6 December 1957. Water was admitted to the dock on 20 December and the hull was formally floated out the following day (see photos); the 'launch' was attended by the Navy Minister and Admiral Nomy. The hull was then towed to the fitting-out quay at Laninon.

Capitaine de vaisseau Jean Lorrain was appointed in September 1958 to command the ship and supervise completion. The turbines and gearing were embarked between 12 June and 17 October. Fitting of the after catapult began in September 1958, and the forward catapult in March 1959; the arrester gear was fitted from April 1959.

The ship was manned for trials on 26 September of the same year. As the first of class and the first of a new type of warship, *Clemenceau* underwent extensive trials of her machinery and other systems. The forward end of flight deck had to be reinforced following damage in heavy seas. Dummy aircraft were launched from her catapults in November, and the first Alouette helicopters landed on later in the same month. From 25 March 1960 there were deck landings of the new Breguet Alizé antisubmarine turboprop aircraft, followed by Aquilon jet fighters and Zéphir trainers. By 22 April there had been 77 catapult launches of the Alizé, 162 of the Aquilon and 64 of the Zéphir. There were concerns about roll and pitch of the aviation platform, and during a maintenance and modification period at Brest that lasted from 1 May to 7 July, 1,295 tonnes of lead ballast was set in concrete in the double bottom; there was also some lightening of the upperworks, particularly the framework of the hangar roof. At the same time the 100mm guns were embarked.

The next 14 months were taken up with further familiarisation with *Clemenceau*'s assigned air groups,

Table 1: **Building Data**

Name	Builder	Laid down	Floated out	Trials	Commissioned	In service
Clemenceau	Arsenal de Brest	15 Dec 1955	21 Dec 1957	26 Sep 1959	18 Mar 1960	22 Nov 1961
Foch	Chantiers de l'Atlantique/ Arsenal de Brest	15 Feb 1957	23 July 1960	28 Apr 1962	1 Jan 1963	15 Jul 1963

Clemenceau leaves Brest for the first time on 23 November 1959. Her armament and most of her electronics outfit have yet to be fitted, and there are as yet no markings on the flight deck. (Jean Moulin collection)

Clemenceau during her inclining test at Toulon. She now has her full outfit of guns and electronics. (Jean Moulin collection)

4F (Alizé) and 16F (Aquilon). The first landing of prototype 02 of the Etendard IVM strike fighter took place on 18 September, and further trials of this aircraft (destined for naval air squadron 11F) continued into December. The gun installation and the electronics outfit were completed. A missile workshop was created in the hangar and a NBC washdown system fitted. The ship left Brest on 22 October 1961 and arrived at Toulon on the 29th. She was assigned to the *Groupe des porte-avions*, and on 28 November Rear Admiral Lainé transferred his flag from *La Fayette*.

PA 55 *Foch*

Funding for a sister *Foch* (PA 55) was authorised in August 1955. The hull was to be built by Chantiers de l'Atlantique of Saint-Nazaire and the armament installed by DCAN Brest. The contract envisaged official trials taking place in January 1960, six months after *Clemenceau*. However, delays due to a shortage of labour and steel plating would lead to *Foch* entering service some 20 months after her sister.

Like *Clemenceau*, *Foch* was built in a dock, not on a slipway. The dock in question was that of the Forme Jean Bart (formerly Caquot), in which the battleship of the same name had been built. The completed hull was floated across from the 'dry' construction area to the 'wet' dock on 13 July 1959, and following stability trials was floated out of the facility and towed to Brest for fitting out. Budgetary problems then resulted in further delays, and trials began only in April 1962.

Hull & Navigation

Longitudinal construction was employed, the flight deck forming part of the hull girder as in British practice. The shell plating was 16mm, reinforced to 18–24mm at the bow. There were 1,200 Type 6Z galvanic anodes to prevent corrosion. The island was constructed of 10mm plates to port, 8mm to starboard.

Decks were as follows: Hold (Nº 3 Deck), Lower Platform (Nº 2), Upper Platform (Nº 1), Main Deck (Nº 0), First Deck (Nº 01), Hangar Deck (Nº 02), 1st Gallery (Nº 03), 2nd Gallery (Nº 04), and Flight Deck (Nº 05). The First Deck was the main circulation deck; beneath it the hull was divided into 20 watertight compartments (A forward to T aft) by 19 transverse bulkheads. The island had six levels, numbered 06–011.

The ship was controlled from an enclosed bridge on level 3 of the island; the latter housed the engine room telegraphs, the steering column, a console for the DRBN 31 navigation radar display and an IPE 6 panoramic scope. The Admiral's bridge was on level 2 of the island; it had good views around the ship, but was fitted only with an IPE 6 panoramic scope.

During the early trials the metacentric height (GM) of 1.01m at light displacement was found to be insufficient, leading to excessive heel when turning or with a beam sea, and excessive roll and pitch when operating aircraft.

Clemenceau during her trials. She has now received flight deck markings, with the angled deck prominent. She would retain these markings, albeit with some later additions, throughout her service life. (Jean Moulin collection)

Clemenceau being fitted with bulges to improve stability; the photo was taken at Toulon on 27 March 1966. (Jean Moulin collection)

The 3-degree heel experienced on trials was reduced to 2 degrees following the embarkation of lead ballast. At a displacement of 30,358 tonnes and with a GM of 2.03m, movement was much reduced. It was nevertheless decided to fit bulges (1966 in *Clemenceau*, on completion in *Foch*); these gave a GM in excess of 2 metres even at light displacement. The bulges increased waterline beam from 29.3 metres to 31.7 metres.

Protection

The flight deck had 45mm armour plating between frames 24 and 159. The machinery spaces, magazines and tanks for the aviation fuel were contained within an internal armoured box formed with a 30mm roof at the level of the Main Deck and 50mm sides, joined top and bottom by curved corners with a 1.5-metre radius (see section drawings). The armoured box was closed at its ends (F186 and F36) by 40mm transverse bulkheads, and there was a third 40mm bulkhead at frame 68 where the shafts exited the hull. The steering gear compartment was protected by a separate 40mm box, and the compartments to the sides and at the after end were filled with 360 cubic metres of a waterproof compound. The gunhouses, aviation facilities and command spaces had light bullet-proof plating.

Propulsion and Auxiliary Machinery

The high-pressure steam propulsion plant ($45kg/cm^2$, 450°C) was disposed in two boiler and two engine rooms in a 'unit' arrangement. The forward unit comprised three boilers (numbered 10–12) arranged side-by-side in a single space, followed by an engine room with the forward set of turbines driving the starboard shaft, and one of the three turbo-alternators (TA1 – see Hold drawing). The after unit was similar, with three boilers (20–22) in a single space followed by the turbines driving the port shaft, and the third of the turbo-alternators (TA3). The two propulsion 'units', each comprising a boiler room and an engine room, were separated by an auxiliary machinery room.

An Aquilon jet fighter is about to engage one of the four arrester wires on *Clemenceau* in 1962. The splash visible in the centre of the ship's wake is a target towed astern on a wire connected to a winch on the quarterdeck. It consisted of a wooden sledge with scoops at the rear to throw up a water splash, and was used to provide a moving target for carrier aircraft to attack with guns, rockets and bombs. An observer on the carrier's island could spot whether weapons went over or under the splash; sometimes a carefully positioned helicopter was used to spot left or right. The splash target was normally deployed some 1,000 metres astern of the carrier, but in the photo it may be being winched in for short stay to allow the ship to turn or is possibly being recovered – the authors extend their thanks to David Hobbs for this insight. (Jean Moulin collection)

Designated *tranche de mouillage*, it housed two Indret auxiliary boilers (rated at 27kg/cm², supplying 14t/h of steam) for use when the ship was in port and a third turbo-alternator (TA2); it was located amidships and had stabilisation tanks to the sides.

Each turbine grouping comprised high pressure (HP), intermediate pressure (MP1/MP2) and low pressure (BP) turbines and drove the shaft via single reduction gearing, which reduced the turbine shaft rotation of 2,000–3,000rpm to 200rpm for the propeller shafts.. There were two reversing turbines, HP and LP, the latter being incorporated into the main casing of the LP ahead turbine.

Each of the two engine rooms was divided vertically into two floors (see GA Plans): the upper for the control consoles and electrical switchboards; the lower for the turbines, the feed and lubrication pumps, and the turbo-alternator. *Clemenceau* as completed had a machinery control centre (*PC machines*) in the forward engine room to port and a secondary control post in the after engine room; these control spaces were enlarged and differently arranged in her sister *Foch*.

Steam for the turbines was supplied by six Indret asymmetrical Sural small-tube boilers with natural circulation and direct firing. The boilers had a single large water collector at the base and a steam collector offset at the top, and were equipped with economisers, superheaters and air reheaters. Each boiler was in its own air-tight box, and the six exhaust uptakes were combined in single funnel.

High temperatures in the machinery spaces were found to be a major problem during trials. In February 1961, *Clemenceau* ran a 2-hour trial with an external temperature of 28.6–30°; the temperature recorded at the control panel in the forward boiler room was 34–38°C, and in the after engine room 40–52°C!

The shafts were of nickel-chrome steel. The 4-bladed propellers fitted in *Clemenceau* were 5.52m in diameter and weighed 21,700 tonnes; *Foch* had a slightly different model. Pitting of 25–30mm was registered after 8,000 hours of operation, and some modifications were required during the late 1960s.

The maximum speed attained by *Clemenceau* on trials was 33.39 knots with forced draught on 11 December 1959; the maximum speed for *Foch* was recorded (following correction) as 33.27 knots on 24 August 1962. An increase in displacement of 1,000 tonnes was found to cost 0.5 knots, and there was a loss of a further 0.5 knots with a dirty hull. Peak vibration was around 28 knots (176rpm).

Electrical Supply

The electrical supply for general service was 440V. There were three Rateau-Jeumont turbo-alternators each rated at 2,000kW, located in the forward engine room, the *tranche de mouillage* and the after engine room respectively. Each generator was powered using the steam from the main turbines and had its own switchboard (*Tableau Principal* – designated TP2/3/4

Table 2: **Characteristics: *Clemenceau* as Completed**

Displacement:	22,000 tons standard
	27,520 tonnes normal
	32,570 tonnes deep load
Dimensions:	
length	238m pp; 257.5m oa
width at flight deck	46.3m
beam	29.3m wl
mean draught	8.34m deep load
	(9.25m incl propellers)
Machinery:	
boilers	6 Indret asymmetrical Sural boilers
	45kg/cm², 450°C
engines	2-shaft Parsons geared turbines
	(HP, 2 x IP, LP)
horsepower	126,000CV
speed	32 knots max (33.4kts on trials)
endurance	6,750nm at 18 knots
electricity	3 Rateau-Jeumont turbo-alternators
	each 2,000kW
	6 SACM Jeumont diesel alternators
	each 480kW
Protection:	
flight Deck	45mm (F24–F159)
citadel	50mm sides, 30mm roof
transverse b/heads	40mm
Armament:	
main guns	8 – 100/55 ACAS Mle 1953 (8 x I)
aircraft	40
Electronics:	
air search	DRBV 20C
target designation	DRBV 23
surface search	DRBV 50
fire control	DRBC 31C
navigation	DRBN 31
CCA	NRBA 50
sonar	SQS-503
Complement:	2,239 officers and men

The stern of *Foch* is seen here in dock, The large single rudder and the two four-bladed propellers are prominent. (Jean Moulin collection)

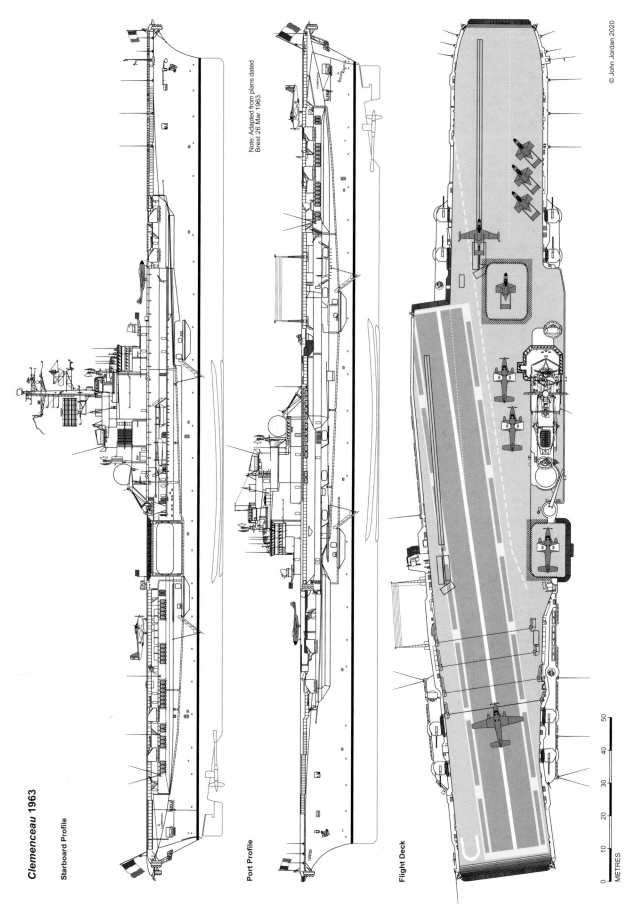

© John Jordan 2020

Note: Adapted from plans dated
Brest 26 Mar 1963.

Clemenceau 1963

Starboard Profile

Port Profile

Flight Deck

METRES
0 10 20 30 40 50

Clemenceau: GA Plans

Inboard Profile

Upper Platform Deck [Citadel]

Lower Platform Deck

Hold

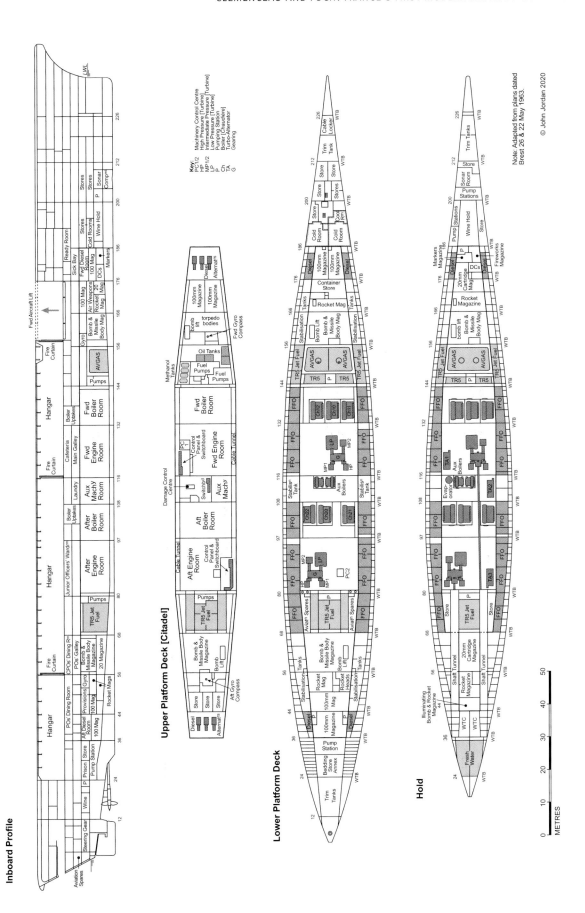

Key:
MCC / PC1/2 Machinery Control Centre
HP High Pressure [Turbine]
MP1/2 Intermediate Pressure [Turbine]
LP Low Pressure [Turbine]
P Pumping Station
Ch Boiler [Chaudière]
TA Turbo-Alternator
G Gearing

Note: Adapted from plans dated
Brest 26 & 22 May 1963.

© John Jordan 2020

from aft); the turbo-alternators could be coupled together.

For back-up and when alongside there were six SACM-Jeumont diesel alternators each rated at 480kW: three located side-by-side in the after diesel room, which was on the Upper Platform Deck at the after end of the armoured citadel, and three in the forward room, which was on the same level at the forward end (see GA Plans). The switchboards were designated TP1 (aft) and TP5 (forward), and as with the turbo-alternators the two groups could be coupled together. Normal electricity consumption at sea was 2,400kW in peacetime.

Clemenceau: Sections

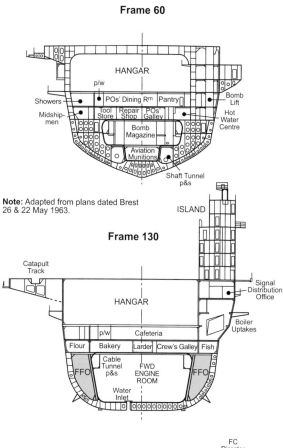

Frame 60

Note: Adapted from plans dated Brest 26 & 22 May 1963.

Frame 130

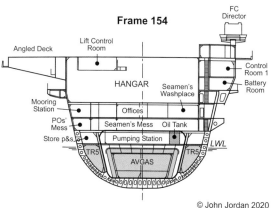

Frame 154

© John Jordan 2020

Fresh Water Supply

When completed *Clemenceau* was equipped with three evaporators each with a capacity of 160 tonnes per day, distributed between the three machinery spaces. Consumption was found to be greater than anticipated: 3 tonnes per hour for the boilers, 200/300kg per catapult launch, plus 185 tonnes of fresh water per day for the crew. In practice only 300–350 tonnes of water per day were produced to top up the initial 540 tonnes carried in the tanks. In theory endurance was unlimited with three evaporators on line provided there was no air activity, but with air operations it was only 20 days. Additional evaporators were embarked 1978–81, and a more modern osmosis unit was installed in *Clemenceau* in 1992.

Armament

Guns

Eight of the new 100mm/55 ACAS (*Automatique Contre-Avions Simple*) Mle 1953 guns were fitted on completion. The gun was housed in a pseudo-turret with a fixed ammunition hoist supplied from a working chamber directly beneath the mounting. A rotating 12-round drum (*barillet*) in the working chamber revolved around a fixed vertical hoist (3 rounds), and the feed in the gunhouse comprised two quarter-cheese trays with 18 rounds. The first 30 rounds could be fired without human intervention. Once the ready-use (RU) supply was exhausted, the drum needed to be replenished by two/three loading numbers.

The theoretical maximum rate of fire was 60rpm, but once the RU supply was exhausted this was reduced to 35rpm. The gun could be elevated to +80° and depressed to -15° and could be locked between +5° and +20° when not in use; there was water cooling for the barrel between the ejection of the cartridge and the loading of the next round.

The gun mounting could be controlled remotely using Ward Leonard RPC, or locally by the turret commander (*chef de tourelle*) using an electrical director; it was equipped with binocular sights with a wide field of vision. The mounting was manned by the turret commander, a 'supervisor' (*surveillant*), who checked that the breech opened for the first round, a gunlayer and an *aide-surveillant*, charged with supplying gun-range and deflection data in local fire. The working chamber was manned by the chamber commander (*chef de relais*) and two loading numbers. The gun could open fire without any of the gun crew present.

Ammunition

The fixed OEA Mle 1954 round was fitted with a mechanical (DM/DE) or proximity fuze. The Mle 1956 detonator activated on contact or after a predetermined interval. The OEA Mle 1954 would be superseded by the F1 with prefragmentation, then the F4 with 1,530 1-gramme balls, both intended for use against thin-skinned missiles.

The ammunition for the 100mm guns was stowed in six magazines within the armoured citadel; electric hoists raised ammunition at a rate of 20 boxed cartridges per minute to handing rooms on the 1st Gallery Deck beneath the mountings. Capacity was 9,400 OEA combat rounds plus 300 OEALp semi-ballasted exercise rounds. The fixed ammunition was stowed in individual cylindrical cases of light alloy.

Each of the eight working chambers had a RU supply of 190 rounds; fuzing was carried out in an adjacent space. The magazines were equipped with a spray system, and there was forced ventilation for the magazines and the handing rooms.

Fire Control

There was a director for each of the four groups of guns. All were fitted with radar and – unusually for the period – two were equipped with an optical stereoscopic rangefinder. The DRBC 31C radar was optimised for the automatic tracking of aerial targets, but could also be used to direct anti-surface fire (*but flottant* or BF). The 100mm guns could also be employed against an invisible target on land (*tir contre la terre* or CT) provided the ship was stationary or moored 17,000m away; this was done in local control using the auxiliary sights.

The two directors fitted with optical rangefinders, which had a base-length of 4.2-metres, were designated TT (*tourelle de télépointage optique et radar*). Each weighed 8 tonnes, was 4.5m wide, and was stabilised in four rotational axes. The director was able to train through 350 degrees, could elevate from -8° to 90°, and was stabilised for 10 degrees of pitch and 22 degrees of roll. It was normally manned by a gunlayer, a rangetaker and a control officer, but was able to operate with one man or unmanned.

The two light directors, which were designated TR (or TRA – *télépointeur radar artillerie*) were uniquely for radar-controlled fire against aircraft. The platform was again stabilised in four axes. The director carried only the antenna for the DRBC 31 radar and a black-and-white TV camera that facilitated remote optical pointing from the *Poste Central*.

Fire control groupings were as follows:

– Group 1 (starboard forward): director TT1 plus mountings 1 & 3.
– Group 2 (port forward): director TR2 plus mountings 2 & 4.
– Group 3 (starboard aft): director TR3 plus mountings 5 & 7.
– Group 4 (port aft): director TT4 plus mountings 6 & 8.

Group 2, which was forward of the angled deck, was located 1.5m lower than the others. Each of the four directors was able to control (i) its own group, (ii) the group on the same side of the ship, or (iii) both groups. Director TT1, which was on a raised deckhouse at the forward end of the island, was also able to control

Group 2. Each group had two calculating positions with three cabinets. Performance was limited to aircraft with a speed of 25m/s out to a range of 8,000 metres. The groups were under the overall command of the *chef de défense* (Platform 6 of the island) or the target designation officer (*officier de désignation d'objectif*, or ODO).

Electronics

Radars

Clemenceau was fitted on completion with a complete suite of the latest models of radar of French design and manufacture.

The DRBV 20C (with NRBI 20 IFF) was a long-range air search radar with a large rectangular mattress antenna, and was also fitted in the contemporary anti-aircraft cruiser *Colbert*. In theory it could detect a jet fighter out to 150nm, but this varied with the altitude and radar cross-section of the aircraft.

DRBV 23 (likewise with NRBI 20 IFF) was not available until mid-1961; the smaller and less capable DRBV 22C, which was widely fitted in ships of destroyer/frigate size, replaced it as a temporary measure. DRBV 23 was a long-range target designation radar capable of detecting

A close-up of the island of *Clemenceau* in 1960, with two Aquilon jet fighters parked beneath. She now has her full complement of radar antennae, which include the large mattress antenna for the DRBV 20C air search radar, the DRBV 23 target designation radar (just visible to the left of it), and two DRBI 10 heightfinders (fore and after ends of island). Note the large carrier-controlled approach radar housed within a dome at the after end.
(Jean Moulin collection)

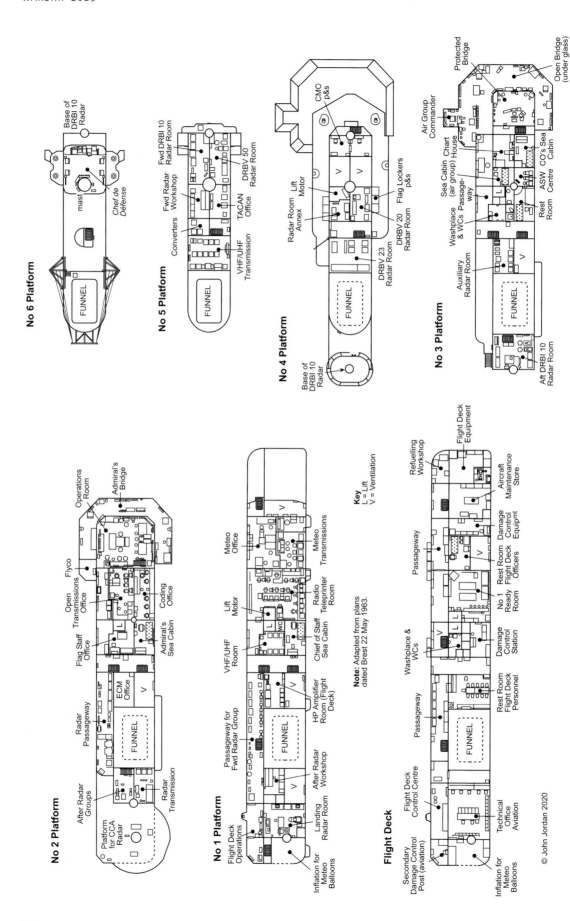

No 6 Platform

Base of DRBI 10 Radar

mast

Chef de Défense

FUNNEL

No 5 Platform

Fwd DRBI 10 Radar Room

Fwd Radar Workshop

DRBV 50 Radar Room

Converters

TACAN Office

VHF/UHF Transmission

FUNNEL

No 4 Platform

CMO p&s

Radar Room Lift Annex Motor

Flag Lockers p&s

DRBV 20 Radar Room

DRBV 23 Radar Room

Base of DRBI 10 Radar

FUNNEL

No 3 Platform

Protected Bridge

Open Bridge (under glass)

Air Group Commander

Sea Cabin Chart (air group) House

ASW CO's Sea Centre Cabin

Washplace & WCs Passage-way

Rest Room

Auxiliary Radar Room

FUNNEL

Aft DRBI 10 Radar Room

No 2 Platform

Operations Room

Admiral's Bridge

Open Flyco Transmissions Office

Coding Office

Flag Staff Office

Admiral's Sea Cabin

Radar Passageway

ECM Office

V

FUNNEL

After Radar Groups

Radar Transmission

Platform for CCA Radar

No 1 Platform

V

Meteo Office

Meteo Transmissions

VHF/UHF Room

Lift Motor

WC

L

Radio Teleprinter Room

Chief of Staff Sea Cabin

Key
L = Lift
V = Ventilation

Note: Adapted from plans dated Brest 22 May 1963.

Passageway for Fwd Radar Group

HP Amplifier Room (Flight Deck)

After Radar Workshop

V

FUNNEL

Flight Deck Operations

Landing Radar Room

Inflation for Meteo Balloons

Flight Deck

Flight Deck Equipment

Refuelling Workshop

Aircraft Maintenance Store

Damage Control Equipt

Rest Room Flight Deck Officers

Passageway

V

No 1 Ready Room

Damage Control Station

L L

V

Passageway

Washplace & WCs

Rest Room Flight Deck Personnel

FUNNEL

Secondary Damage Control Post (aviation)

Flight Deck Control Centre

Technical Office Aviation

Inflation for Meteo Balloons

© John Jordan 2020

a fighter out to 110nm; it used a parabolic antenna and was normally synchronised with DRBV 20C.

The aerial detection and tracking suite was completed by two DRBI 10 heightfinding radars, the antennae being fitted at either end of the island; they could be synchronised at an angle of 180 degrees, and detection range was 80nm on an aircraft flying at 21,000 metres.

A DRBV 50 radar for surface surveillance was fitted above DRBV 23 on a platform angled to starboard, which gave it a blind arc between 200 and 230 degrees; it could detect a large surface unit at 30nm and a destroyer at 20nm. It was complemented by the smaller DRBN 31 for navigation, which was capable of detecting a destroyer at 12nm; the antenna was fitted atop the navigation bridge and had a blind arc between 130 and 230 degrees. DRBN 31 would be replaced by the more capable DRBN 32 in 1969–70 (1971 in *Foch*).

The carrier controlled approach (CCA) radar was the NRBA 50, the aerial for which was housed within a large radome at the after end of the island (there was a 100-degree 'dead zone' forward). It could detect an Alizé ASW aircraft at 25nm and the smaller Etendard strike fighter at 15nm. A TACAN beacon, carried at the masthead, enabled a high-flying aircraft to home in on the carrier from a maximum range of 200nm. The original

A later view, taken on 19 July 2000, of the island of *Foch*. The antenna for the DRBV 23 radar has been relocated to the platform abaft the mast, and replaced by DRBV 15. (Jean Moulin)

NRBP 20A model was replaced by the more advanced SRN-6 in August 1961.

There were numerous issues with these emitters due to their close proximity, and some could not be used simultaneously at full power.

Sonar

The sonar, which was housed in a retractable dome, was SQS-503, a 10kHz medium-frequency model widely fitted in the US Navy. It was usable in good weather up to 28 knots, although performance deteriorated above 22 knots. Speed had to be reduced to 20 knots in order for the dome to be raised or lowered; at higher speeds it had to be lowered and locked. SQS-23 would be replaced by the US SQS-505 panoramic sonar around 1971.

ECM/ESM

Electronic support measures (ESM) to detect, monitor and analyse hostile emissions comprised the French ARBC 10C (detection + analysis) and the US Navy's AN/SLR-2 (analysis); these models would be upgraded during the late 1980s. There was provision for the fitting of electronic countermeasures (ECM), and ARBB 31 jammers were installed during the early 1970s. However, chaff dispensers, which were key to decoying anti-ship missiles, would not be embarked until the late 1980s.

Tactical Data and Command Systems

The French Navy was not as advanced as the British Royal Navy or the US Navy of the 1960s with regard to data processing and coordination. When *Clemenceau* and *Foch* were first completed there was only a *Central Information* (CI) housing the consoles for the DRBV 20, 23, 50 and DRBI 10 radars, located on the 2nd Gallery Deck to starboard, beneath the forward end of the island.

A *Poste Central Opérations* (PC Ops), located on Platform 2 of the island directly behind the admiral's bridge, was tasked with coordinating surface and air operations. The latter space proved too small, particularly when an admiral and his staff were embarked. The *Chef de défense*, stationed in a glazed 'gazebo' on Platform 6, provided situational input via 'indicators' (*indicateurs*).

A proposed installation of the French-developed SENIT data system was delayed by funding issues. A SENIT 2 system from the fleet escort *Jauréguiberry* (T 53 – see *Warship 2021*) was finally installed in *Clemenceau* 1977–78, and *Foch* received the SENIT 2 from her sister *Tartu* in 1980–81. The original CI was enlarged and redesignated the Operations Centre (*Central Opérations*, or CO). SENIT would subsequently be upgraded with NATO Links 11 and 14 and a doubling of computer capacity.

Complement

The theoretical complement when *Clemenceau* entered service was 179 officers, 560 petty officers and 1,500 men (total 2,239). All personnel had bunks, and there was cafeteria messing. There were separate galleys for the admiral, officers, petty officers and seamen. The change in balance between specialist petty officers and ordinary seamen during the ships' service lives led to constant modifications to the accommodation.

There was a large, well-equipped sick bay with 24 beds on the First Deck forward of the first aircraft lift. This would later be refitted as a 17-bed hospital.

Aviation Facilities

Flight Deck

The flight deck was 257.5 metres long and between 28 and 46 metres wide. At deep load it was 15.89 metres above the waterline. To starboard of the island was a narrow passageway for deck tractors and other handling gear. The angled deck measured 168m x 20m and was inclined at 8°40 to the ship's axis; its length was calculated to allow aircraft to clear the deck at the stern by at least 3 metres when landing on to allow for pilot error and pitching of the deck.

The strength of the flight deck was calculated to bear the weight of a 20-tonne stationary/catapulting aircraft and a 15-tonne aircraft on landing (once fuel had been expended and ordnance disposed of). There were 800 attachment points on the flight deck, and when the angled deck was in use there was sufficient space for 23 parked aircraft: fifteen forward, four abreast the island, two on the forward lift and one on the after lift. From 1970 there was an additional spot for aircraft to be rapidly fuelled and catapulted.

The flight and hangar decks were initially given a coat of Tankastral paint, and from 1964 Ferrox non-slip, anti-oxidising paint was applied to the flight deck. The *Poste de contrôle pont d'envol* (PCPE) organised the stowage of aircraft on deck and in the hangar using models; it controlled movement in collaboration with the *Bureau technique aviation* (BTA). Both were at flight deck level at the rear of the island: the PCPE to port and the BTA to starboard. Directly above the PCPE was the *Passerelle pont d'envol* (lit 'flight deck bridge'), which had large glazed bays that gave it good views over the flight deck.

Hangar

The hangar was offset to port, as in P 28 and the prewar *Joffre*. It was divided into three zones (*sous-hangars*) numbered 1 (F158–116), 2 (F116–56) and 3 (F56–24) by four sets of metal fire doors with electrical controls (F176, 158, 116, 56), and there were fire curtains at frames 24 and 12 to isolate the engine maintenance

Clemenceau on 14 August 1994 during a naval review to mark the 50th anniversary of the landings in Provence. Four Alizé ASW aircraft are parked on the angled deck, with two Crusader interceptors and Super-Etendard strike fighter aircraft forward. Note the launcher for Crotale surface-to-air missiles on the port after sponson which replaced the after pair of 100mm mountings after a major refit during 1986–87. (Getty Images)

spaces (see below). The layout of the hangar was a compromise between British and US practice: the starboard side of hangar was completely enclosed, with operational spaces outboard and access by air lock; the port side was partially open, with bays closed by sliding doors. The flight deck was supported from the main deck on transverse beams 1.5m high, reducing the usable height of the hangar from 8.5m to 6.9m.

The zone forward of the first lift was originally an extension of the hangar measuring 16m x 15m x 5.1m. Between March and November 1961 it was converted into a workshop for airborne missiles; *Foch* was completed with this arrangement. At the after end of the hangar, between frames 24 and 12, there was a space for dismantling and reassembly of Atar and J-57 aero-engines to starboard with associated workshops to port.

The total length of the hangar following modification was 164 metres, of which 134m was usable (taking account of the forward lift). Maximum width was 26 metres (of which an average 21m was usable). There was a control platform for the hangar at frame 122 to starboard, and damage control cabins in the centre of each of the three fire zones to port.

The spray system comprised nine networks on the hangar roof, ten water screens along the doors, four transverse water screens, plus diffusers in the lift well and water spray ramps for the control cabins and air locks. Ten foam stations on the First Deck (five per side) fed nine main

and four secondary canons, and the fire suppression outfit was completed by mobile CO_2 and water dispensers.

Heavy items could be moved by block and tackle, with five engagement points each capable of lifting 10 tonnes and one of 3 tonnes, plus two 0.5-tonne davits in the port-side bays.

Lifts

The two aircraft lifts were built by Applevage. Each was powered by two 150hp electric motors from Sautter-Harlé; a single emergency motor delivered 30hp. The lifts could raise 15 tonnes from the hangar to the flight deck. Four speeds were available: two 'normal' (one or two main motors), two 'slow' (single main motor/emergency motor); it took 9 seconds to travel the 8.5m with two motors, 1 minute with the emergency motor.

The forward lift was 17.4m long and 13m wide, and was offset 3 metres to starboard. The after, US-style side lift measured 16.4m x 11m. The access bay for this lift was 5.5m high, and was closed by double-leaved doors operating at 30m/s.

Catapults

The two British BS 5 catapults were built by Brown Bros, with the bow catapult offset to port and the second at the forward end of the angled deck, inclined at 5°21 to the axis of ship. This arrangement was adopted to maximise parking forward.

The hangar of *Foch* looking aft, also on 19 July 2000. Note the open bay for the side lift on the left, and the sliding fire doors that divided the hangar in the event of a fire. (Jean Moulin)

An Etendard IVM strike fighter on the side lift to starboard in 1970. Note the SAGEM optical landing aid directly abaft it; this would later be removed. (Jean Moulin collection)

The BS 5 could launch a 20-tonne aircraft at 90 knots with 2.8g acceleration. In theory the interval between launches was 35 seconds; in practice it was 45 seconds. There were two driving cylinders side-by-side beneath the flight deck; twin rams ran inside the cylinders under steam pressure; the rams were linked by a cradle, and a bridle was attached to the aircraft. The steam accumulators were located on the 1st Gallery Deck, the operating spaces, elevation motors for the blast deflectors, catapult workshop and stores on the 2nd Gallery Deck. The catapult had to undergo on-board maintenance after 400 launches, and a major maintenance period of six weeks in a dockyard was required after 1,600–2,000 launches.

Hinged blast deflectors abaft the catapults protected the crew and the aircraft on deck; the original MacTaggart model was replaced during the Crusader refit 1967–68. The new Breguet model had identical dimensions but had water cooling. The blast deflectors were hydraulically operated from a retractable 'howdah', and took 15 seconds to elevate or lower. When in the raised position they had a vertical angle of 60 degrees and an angle of deflection 120 degrees to port.

Initially the catapult bridles were ditched, but the bridles for the Crusader were 5–10 times more expensive, and two bridle catchers (Mk 2 Mod 2 forward, Mod 0 angled deck) were fitted in Jan 1966–Jan 1967

(*Foch* Aug 1965–Jan 1966). In 1964 *Clemenceau* carried 720 (disposable) bridles for the Etendard, and 420 for the Alizé. Following two incidents catchers were no longer used for the Etendard, but they continued in use for the Crusader.

Arrester Wires

Clemenceau was equipped with four arrester wires that ran perpendicular to the angled deck axis at frames 40, 48, 56 and 63. The cables were 114mm thick and 29 metres across at rest, extending to 65–70m when engaged by an aircraft on landing. They could cope with an 18-tonne aircraft with a maximum landing speed of 112 knots. Each cable was linked to a British MacTaggart Mk 13 hydraulic brake, comprising a cylinder filled with a glycerine-based fluid that was displaced by a piston via a small opening. A cabin located on the starboard gallery monitored the arrester wires.

In the event of a the failure of the tail hook to engage the arrester wires, a barrier could be installed between collapsible posts at frames 72–77. The force was absorbed by a system of nylon bags. The barrier was used only once, for an Aquilon on 20 February 1961.

Mirror Landing Aids

Aircraft adopted a speed of approach of 130 knots for a maximum 112 knots when engaging the arrester wires;

the angle of approach was 3°30 and the vertical speed of impact 3 metres per second. *Clemenceau* was initially fitted with a British Mk IA mirror landing aid manufactured by John Curran with SAGEM stabilisation; it was located on a platform between frames 84 and 88, with the lighting source at F37. There was also an emergency SAGEM model, which was purely optical and used Fresnel lenses, to starboard at frame 78, immediately abaft the side lift (see Profile and Plan). In 1967 *Clemenceau* had the mirror sight replaced by second optical landing aid – *Foch* had two optical models on completion; the starboard installation was landed in 1970.

Cranes

A fixed crane capable of lifting a 15-tonne aircraft was located at the after end of island forward of the side lift: it had a 300-degree radius to enable it to serve the flight deck, side lift and quay. Built by Caillard, it had a height of 22–26 metres in the raised position, a reach of 12.2–8.7 metres, and could lift or lower at 0.3 metres per second.

There was also a 27-tonne mobile crane mounted on a Berliet 90hp diesel tractor that could lift 10 tonnes at 6 metres, 15 tonnes at 3.5 metres. Some of the deck tractors initially embarked proved too lightweight for the task; they were replaced in 1967 by ten diesel tractors with a pull rating of 2.3 tonnes.

Aviation Fuel

When *Clemenceau* entered service the transition was being made from conventional propeller-driven aircraft to jets; the former used *essence aviation* (avgas), the latter TR5 jet fuel (the French equivalent of JP-5), which was less volatile and had a higher flash point. *Clemenceau* initially embarked 400m³ of the former and 1,200m³ of TR5. *Foch*, which was completed less than two years later, embarked 1,800m³ of TR5 and only a small quantity (9m³) of avgas.

The avgas tanks were of the 'saddle tank' design, and were always filled with liquid to prevent the accumulation of combustible vapours; petrol that was consumed was replaced by sea water, which because of its higher density sat on the bottom of the tank.

Clemenceau as completed had two groups of tanks forward (see GA Plans), each comprising an external reservoir, an internal reservoir and a pumping reservoir located one inside the other and surrounded with nitrogen. Distribution was via two collectors: the port side collector supplied the hangar, that on the starboard side the hangar and flight deck. There were three distribution stations (40m³/h at 7kg/cm²) for the flight deck and two for the hangar.

The TR5 jet fuel was stowed in two groups of tanks with a total volume of 1,180m³ (1,360m³ at deep load). Each group comprised two stowage tanks, two feed tanks plus two decontamination tanks. There were two electrically-driven pumps per group rated at 90m³/h at 7.5kg/cm² for distribution, two 40m³/h pumps for transfer and two water separators. Distribution was via collectors to port and starboard linked by transverse lines. *Clemenceau* had ten 40m³/h distribution stations to starboard and four to port.

The avgas capacity of *Foch* had to be increased from 9m³ to 109m³ in 1965–66 prior to the embarkation of Sikorsky HSS helicopters. However, following the retirement of the helicopters in June 1979 there was no further need for avgas, and the TR5 jet fuel capacity was increased to approximately 2,000m³ in both carriers.

Air Ordnance

A total of 1,300 tonnes of air ordnance could be embarked: on completion *Clemenceau* had no fewer that twenty magazines in two groups fore and aft of the machinery spaces, served by twelve lifts. Each of the two groupings had upper and lower bomb lifts, with transfer at the level of the First Deck, and separate lifts for rockets and cartridge ammunition.

On *Clemenceau* the upper bomb lifts emerged to port of the forward aircraft lift and directly abaft the after lift (see flight deck plan). The lifts were manufactured by Sautter-Harlé; they measured 3.8m x 1.1m and could raise ordnance 2.5m at 0.6m/sec. The length of the lifts was limited by the 4-metre distance between the frames, but had to be increased to 5.5m between 1978 and 1981 to enable them to handle the new generation of air-launched missiles.

Nuclear weapons were embarked from 1978. The AN 52 900kg gravitational bomb needed special handling arrangements and limited the number of conventional bombs carried. It would later be replaced by the ASMP air-launched missile.

When the Super Etendard was embarked in the late 1970s, stowage for the associated AM 39 Exocet missile was considered insufficient, and it was decided that additional missiles would be stowed externally in airtight canisters on the gun sponsons.

Air Group

Clemenceau and *Foch* were originally designed to operate 60 aircraft, but aircraft became larger and heavier during build, and the air group comprised 34–36 plus two rescue helicopters when they commissioned. Capacity was also reduced by the reassignment of the forward part of the hangar to stow large items. This led to some discussion about reducing the number of different types of aircraft to be embarked.

The capability of the new carriers would be limited by the performance of their embarked aircraft, which was in turn limited by the comparatively low displacement and light construction of the ships, and also by the limited funding available for specially-adapted carrier aircraft. Only the US Navy can be said to have anticipated the increase in size and weight of modern jet aircraft during the postwar period, building 'super-carriers' that could comfortably operate jets (and large turboprop aircraft such as the E-2 Hawkeye) with all-up weights in excess

An Aquilon jet fighter in the early navy blue livery of the *aéronavale*. (Jean Moulin collection)

An Alizé turboprop aircraft on board *Clemenceau*, probably in 1960. (Jean Moulin collection)

of 25 tonnes and high landing speeds. The *Aéronautique navale*, on the other hand, had to purchase (or build under licence) foreign aircraft with moderate weights and dimensions, or alternatively adapt small combat aircraft in service with the French Air Force.

The first jet strike fighter embarked was the Aquilon, a French adaptation of the British Sea Venom (see table for data). The Aquilon entered service with the

Aéronautique navale at about the same time that the Sea Venom was being superseded in the Royal Navy by the larger, heavier and more capable Sea Vixen. It was complemented by the Breguet Alizé, a large turboprop antisubmarine aircraft similar in conception to the Royal Navy's Fairey Gannet, equipped with radar, ESM detectors, sonobuoys, depth charges and A/S torpedoes. The Alizé was a successful machine, and remained in service (following a number of upgrades to its weaponry and avionics) until the year 2000.

An Etendard IVP photo reconnaissance aircraft is launched from the angled deck using the catapult. (Jean Moulin collection)

An F-8E Crusader interceptor on *Clemenceau* during the late 1960s. (Jean Moulin collection)

Foch during Operation 'Trident' off Kosovo towards the end of her career; the photo was taken on 16 October 1998. In a 1997 refit the last of the 100mm mountings were landed and replaced by the point-defence Sadral missile system. Crusader interceptors and Super-Etendard strike fighters are parked forward (Getty Images)

Table 3: **Embarked Aircraft (1961–1975)**

Aquilon

French variant of British Sea Venom built under licence.

Five prototypes (01–05) followed by 96 production models:
- 25 Mk 20 2-seat trainer (1–25) – not fitted for carrier landing
- 25 Aquilon 202 with R/F (26–50)
- 40 Aquilon 203 all-weather fighter with APQ-65 + FC computer (51–90)
- 6 Aquilon 204 2-seat trainer night fighter (91–96)

Characteristics:

Type:	Single-seat fighter
Weight:	6,820kg fully loaded
Dimensions:	11.14m(L) x 13.07m(S) x 2.31/3.00m(H)
Performance:	powered by Ghost 103 turbojet;
	960km/h at 15,000m; 420nm radius
Armament:	4 x 20mm Hispano HS 404 cannon, later 8 x 5in rockets,
	then Nord 513 AAMs *or* AS 20 ASM + 2 x Matra R 511 AAM

Flotille 11F	1955–62
Flotille 16F	1955–64

Breguet Br 1050 Alizé

Evolved from the postwar Br 965, a specialised ASW aircraft that worked in pairs: one for detection, the other for attack. The Alizé was designed for both roles. The prototype flew 5 Oct 1956. Followed by 87 production aircraft of which 75 for *Aéronavale* + 12 for Indian Navy. First flight Mar 1959.

Characteristics:

Type:	3/4-seater ASW aircraft (pilot, navigator, radar op + spare seat); later used for AEW
Weight:	8,200kg fully loaded
Dimensions:	13.86m(L) x 15.60m(S) x 5.00m(H)
Performance:	turboprop, powered by RR Dart 21;
	435km/h upwards at ground level; cruise speed 250–380km/h;
	4h 45 in flight for total range 685nm
Electronics:	DRAA 2A radar + various receivers/interrogators/detectors;
	14 sonobuoys
Armament:	5 x DC (3 in weapons bay, two underwing); also bombs & rockets;
	Mk 43>44>46 A/S torpedo *or* 2 x AS 12 ASM

Flotille 6F	1959–2000
Flotille 4F	1960–97
Flotille 9F	1960–72

The requirement for a light tactical strike fighter proved more difficult to meet. A Dassault model intermediate in size between the Mystère and Mirage land-based aircraft was developed as the Etendard IVM, and was delivered between December 1961 and May 1965. An Etendard IVP variant had its cannon replaced by a CER 10 chassis with three cameras, and was employed for photo reconnaissance. This lightweight, single-engine aircraft was not equipped for all-weather combat and had a limited night capability. Deployment was delayed following a series of four accidents, three of which were fatal, during 1963–64. It was planned to replace the Etendard with a navalised variant of the Jaguar, but this was abandoned after two years of trials. It would eventually be superseded by the Super Etendard, which was essentially an upgraded Etendard with a more powerful engine and superior avionics.

The Aquilon was already obsolescent after only two years in service, and various foreign aircraft were considered as replacements. The US McDonnell Douglas F-4 Phantom was too large and heavy to operate from *Clemenceau* and *Foch*, and following trials with two F-8 Crusader interceptors on *Clemenceau*, a contract was signed with Vought on 31 July 1963 for 40 F-8E aircraft built to French requirements plus six two-seat trainers. When development of the latter was abandoned the order was increased to 42 single-seat aircraft, to be designated F-8E (FN). The French variant incorporated a variable-incidence wing to permit supersonic speed in flight with a lowered speed on landing. Speed on take-off was reduced to 180km/h by varying the incidence of the wing and by providing Boundary Layer Control (BLC) – air blown onto the upper surfaces. The Crusader was longer and heavier than the Etendard IV, and its operation required the fitting of bridle catchers and modification to the deflection plates. This work was

Dassault Etendard IVM

Designed to meet requirement for light strike fighter to replace US Corsair F4U-7. Pre-series of 5 (02–06) ordered 31 May 1957. Followed by 69 production aircraft delivered Dec 1961 – May 1965.

Characteristics:

Type:	single-seat strike fighter
Weight:	10,800kg max catapult launch
Dimensions:	14.35m(L) x 9.60m(S) x 3.85m(H)
Performance:	powered by SNECMA Atar 8C turbojet without afterburner
	1100km/h (Mach 1.3); range 980nm
Electronics:	DRAA 2A radar + various receivers/interrogators/detectors
Armament:	2 x DEFA 30mm cannon, 2 x Sidewinder AIM-9B (later Matra Magic);
	13,560kg bombs on hardpoints, 2 x Matra rocket pods, 2 x Nord AS 20 ASM (later AS 30)

Flotille 15F	Jan 1962 – Jan 1969
Flotille 11F	Apr 1963 – Sep 1978
Flotille 17F	Jun 1964 – Jun 1980

Not equipped for all-weather combat and limited capability at night; could be refuelled in air; single engine had no back-up. Replaced from 1978 by Super Etendard.

Dassault Etendard IVP

Reconnaissance variant of above: cannon replaced by CER 10 chassis with 3 cameras; could also embark container with 3 more cameras externally. Total of 21 delivered Oct 1962 – May 1965.

Flotille 16F May 1964 – Jul 2000

To compensate for attrition of IVP, four IVM converted 1977–79. Last five aircraft retired Jul 2000; replaced by modified Super Etendard.

Vought F-8E Crusader

Replacement for Aquilon. Trials two US aircraft from *Clemenceau* Mar 1962; contract signed 31 Jul 1963 for 40 x 8E variant + 6 x 2-seat trainers built to French requirements: F-8E (FN). 2-seat version abandoned by US Navy so order modified to 42 single-seat. Order arrived from USA in two batches: 13 on *Arromanches* Oct 1964, 28 on *Foch* Feb 1965. Final machine – first completed and used for trials USA – arrived on USS *Forrestal* Sep 1965.

Characteristics:

Type:	all-weather interceptor
Weight:	13,000kg max catapult launch
Dimensions:	16.61m(L) x 10.72m(S) x 4.80m(H)
Performance:	powered by Pratt & Whitney J57-P-20A with afterburner
	2,220km/h (Mach 1.8); range 1,500nm (2.5hrs)
Electronics:	AWG-4 FC comprising Magnavox AN/APQ-104 + AN/AAS 15 infrared
	detector + gyroscopic sight and computers
Armament:	4 x 20mm Colt-Browning cannon, 2 x Sidewinder 1A (>1986) *or* Matra
	R530 (1965–91) radar/infrared *or* R550 Magic (1979>) infrared AAMs

Flotille 12F	Oct 1964 – 1999
Flotille 14F	Mar 1965 – Apr 1979
Flotille 17F	Jun 1964 – Jun 1980

Variable-incidence wing to permit supersonic speed in flight with lowered speed on landing. Speed on take-off reduced by 9% in FN model (180km/h) by varying incidence of wing (5>7°) and providing Boundary Layer Control (BLC) – air blown onto upper surfaces. Refuelled in air. 17 Crusaders underwent life extension refurbishment 1991–96 (F-8P – *Prolongé*); some updates to avionics.

carried out on *Foch* at Brest in 1965 and on *Clemenceau* during a major refit in 1966.

The Crusader was successful in service, but finding a replacement was to prove problematic. The French considered buying the F/A-18 Hornet from 1978, but this proposal was abandoned in 1989 in favour of the French-built Dassault Rafale, which was then delayed. Seventeen Crusaders therefore underwent a limited life extension refurbishment during 1991–96 (F-8P – *Prolongé*), in which the avionics were updated.

THE ITALIAN CONNECTION: ANSALDO'S UP.41 DESIGN

It has long been known that Ansaldo sold a battleship design to the Soviet Union in 1936, but recent Russian archival and published sources provide much more detail on both the design and the background to the transaction. **Stephen McLaughlin** tells the story of this odd collaboration between Fascist Italy and the Communist USSR, and assesses the importance of the connection to future Soviet battleship designs.

By the mid-1930s, when Soviet party leader Iosef Stalin decided to build a great fleet based on powerful battleships, the USSR lacked the expertise to design and construct such ships. Although tsarist Russia had trained a cadre of talented naval architects, many had died or fled the country during the years of revolution and civil war. Some experienced men remained, but they were often not trusted by the Communist regime and were relegated to teaching positions. The up-and-coming younger generation of Soviet-trained naval architects, while generally competent, lacked practical knowledge of their profession.

Recognising this reality, Stalin had declared in 1931 that 'It is necessary to start the construction of a great navy with small ships. It cannot be ruled out that in five years we will build battleships', and indeed this gradualist approach was the path the Soviets pursued.[1] The first warships designed in the USSR were the 450-ton 'guard ships' (*storozhivye korabli*) of the *Uragan* class, a type of small destroyer substitute. Eight units were built

Table 1: Soviet Battleship Designs, May–June 1936

| | —— Requirements, 15 May 1936 —— | | | |
	Pacific Battleship	Baltic Battleship	KB-4	TsKBS-1
Displacement:				
standard	55,000 tons	36,000 tons	35,000 tons	35,000 tons
full load	N/S[1]	N/S	N/S	41,000 tons
Length, overall	N/S	N/S	*circa* 235m[2]	249m
Beam, waterline	N/S	N/S	31.6m	31.8m
Draught	N/S	N/S	8.7m	8.9m
Armament:				
main guns	9 x 460mm (3 x III)	9 x 406mm (3 x III)	9 x 406mm (3 x III)	9 x 406mm (3 x III)
secondary	12 x 152mm (6 x II)	12 x 130mm (6 x II)	12 x 152mm (4 x III)	12 x 152mm (6 x II)
AA guns	16/24 x 37mm (4/6 x IV)	16 x 37mm (4 x IV)	12 x 100mm (6 x II)	14 x 100mm (7 x II)
	16 x 12.7mm MGs	24 x 12.7mm MGs	36 x 37mm (9 x IV)	26 x 37mm (13 x II)
Catapults/Aircraft	? / 4	? / 4	2 / 6	2 / 4
Protection:				
upper belt	N/S	N/S	150mm @ 0°	100mm @ 7°
main belt	420mm	360mm	380mm @ 0°	350mm @ 7°
tranvs b/hds	N/S	N/S	380mm	350mm
decks	200–250mm	150mm	60+140mm	40+25+130mm
U/w protection	N/S	N/S	Pugliese, 7.5m	'American', 7.5m
Machinery	N/S	N/S	3 x 75,000shp	3 x 57,000shp
Speed	30 knots	32 knots	30 knots	30 knots
Endurance	10,000nm at economical speed	8,000nm at economical speed	N/S	6,000nm at 20kts
Complement	N/S	N/S	N/S	1,280

Notes:

[1] N/S = Not specified

[2] Estimated from the drawing.

Source: Vasil'ev, *Lineinye korabli tipa 'Sovetskii Soiuz'*, 9, 14.

in 1928–1933, and while overweight and plagued with defects, they represented a useful start. The technical bureau at the Severnyi (Northern) Works (the former Putilov Works) in Leningrad did most of the design work, and in 1930 it was pulled out of the shipyard and renamed the Bureau of Special Design Work for Vessels (*Biuro Spetsialnogo Proektirovaniia Sudov*, or BSPS); in 1931 it was again renamed, becoming the Central Construction Bureau for Special Shipbuilding (*Tsentralnoe Konstruktorskoe Biuro Spetsiatnogo Sudostroeniia*), or TsKBS-1. In both cases 'special' vessels meant warships, and the bureau was assigned the lead role for the next major warship, the 2,100-ton flotilla leaders of the *Leningrad* class (Project 1 – for details, see the article on these ships by P Budzbon and J Radziemski in *Warship 2022*). These were far more impressive ships than the *Uragans*, and their machinery plant, based on materials submitted to an international competition, proved powerful enough to drive them at speeds in excess of 40 knots. There remained problems in both their design and construction: three ships were laid down in 1932, but the lead ship was completed only in 1936, and her two sisters were delayed until 1938.[2]

However, the problems with the *Leningrads* had not become apparent by late 1935 when the first serious Soviet battleship studies began. These called for two different types of ship: 'large' battleships for the Pacific and 'small' ships for the Baltic. The studies for large battleships included vessels displacing as much as 75,000 tons standard, armed with twelve 450mm (17.7in) guns in quadruple turrets. Some of these were drawn up by TsKBS-1, others by the Navy's own warship research group, the Scientific-Experimental Institute for Warship Construction (*Nauchno-issledovatelskii Institute Voennogo Korablestroeniia*, or NIVK). Such ships would have been far beyond the capabilities of both the Soviet designers and the shipyards, but this was the era of the Five-Year Plans, when reports of skyrocketing growth in industrial production were the order of the day, and nothing seemed beyond the potential of the Soviet state.

The Navy's requirements for a small battleship of 35,000 tons were almost as unrealistic as those for the large designs: it wanted nine 406mm (16in) guns, a 350mm belt, and a speed not less than 36 knots, a combination that more experienced constructors would have dismissed out of hand. Reality set in gradually, and on 15 May 1936 the Navy issued a revised set of requirements that were more modest but still overly ambitious, specifying a 30-knot speed for the 55,000-ton large battleship and 32 knots for the smaller one (see Table 1). However the large battleship studies were soon abandoned, as that same month negotiations began with Great Britain for a bilateral naval agreement that would bring the USSR into compliance with the 35,000-ton displacement limit of the Second London Naval Treaty. This left the 'small' battleship, now dubbed Project 21, as the only active battleship programme; at the same time, studies were undertaken of 'cruiser killers' intended to hunt down heavy cruisers and pocket battleships.

Two teams were assigned to develop competing battleship designs, TsKBS-1 and KB-4 (the construction bureau at the Baltic Works), and in June 1936 they submitted their responses to the requirements (see Table 1). Neither was able to meet the specified speed, with both estimating 30 knots as the maximum; in hindsight even this seems implausible.

To date only drawings of KB-4's design have been published. It was based on the British battleships of the *Nelson* class, a detailed description of which had been published in 1929.[3] This was probably the most up-to-date information available to the Soviet designers, and the derivation of the design is obvious from its appearance, with three main battery turrets located forward and superstructures almost identical to those of the British ship. The machinery layout was also similar, but the Soviet designers somehow expected to squeeze a three-shaft plant delivering five times *Nelson*'s horsepower in machinery spaces only about 8 metres longer, which was highly improbable – to put it mildly. Combined with a longer, slimmer hull (Length:Beam ratio about 7.4 compared to *Nelson*'s 6.62) this was supposed to boost the speed from *Nelson*'s 23 knots to 30 knots.

There were several other departures from *Nelson*'s design. Instead of twelve 152mm guns in six twin turrets, KB-4 disposed the same number of guns in four triple turrets, freeing up deck space for a stronger antiaircraft battery – twelve 100mm guns in six twin turrets instead of six 120mm (4.7in) guns in single mounts. The main armour belt was external and vertical instead of *Nelson*'s inclined internal belt, which had not been publicly described and was probably still secret at the time. The same applied to the underwater protection; instead of *Nelson*'s multi-bulkhead air/liquid sandwich system, there was an early version of the Pugliese type, based on that installed in the Italian naval oilers *Brennero* and *Tarvisio*, which had recently been discussed in a French periodical.[4] Finally, the Soviet design featured extensive aviation facilities on a broad quarterdeck, whereas *Nelson*'s design had included no aircraft.

As for the design proposed by TsKBS-1, it had been developed in two versions, one featuring a *Nelson* arrangement of the main battery, the other having two turrets forward and one aft; the latter layout was preferred by the Navy, and no more designs with an all-forward arrangement would be studied.[5] The torpedo protection was a multi-bulkhead type, which the Soviets called the 'American' system.

The KB-4 design may charitably be described as wildly optimistic; more bluntly, it was simply crude – the space allocated to the machinery plant was clearly inadequate, the armament was little more than a sketch, and the proposed armour protection could almost certainly not have been carried by a ship of such limited displacement. It appears likely that the TsKBS-1 submission was no more refined. However, it should be borne in mind that the Soviet designers were trying to make bricks without straw; they lacked detailed information about recent foreign designs that could be used as models, as well as

Project 21: Profile & Plan 1936

Displacement:	35,000 tonnes
Length:	235m oa (est)
	230m wl (est)
Beam:	31.6m wl
Horsepower:	225,000shp = 30kts
Armament:	9 x 406mm (3 x III)
	12 x 152mm (4 x III)
	12 x 100mm (6 x II)
	36 x 37mm (9 x IV)
Aircraft:	6 KOR-1 floatplanes

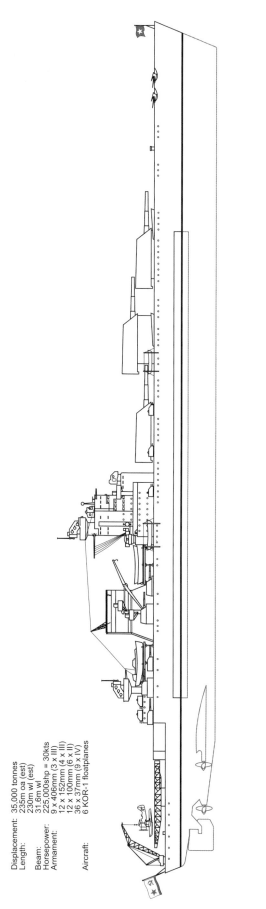

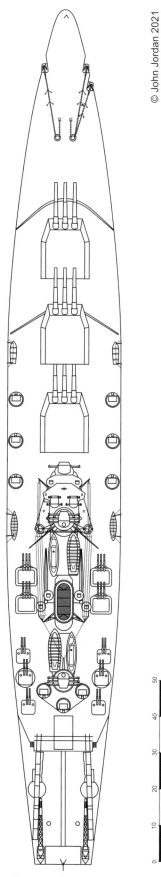

© John Jordan 2021

METRES

The Project 21 battleship design drawn up by the construction bureau at the Baltic Works, June 1936. It was obviously based on HMS *Nelson*, at that time the most modern foreign battleship for which detailed information was available. Note the over-sized main battery turrets and the under-sized secondary turrets. In addition to the two catapults with their cranes, the extensive aviation facilities on the quarterdeck would apparently have included a Hein landing mat for recovering seaplanes. This device featured a ribbed canvas mat unrolled from the stern transom, onto which a seaplane would taxi while the ship was underway. The aircraft could then be hauled aboard by the cranes and moved via the rail system back into the hangar.

© John Jordan 2021

Project 21: GA Plans

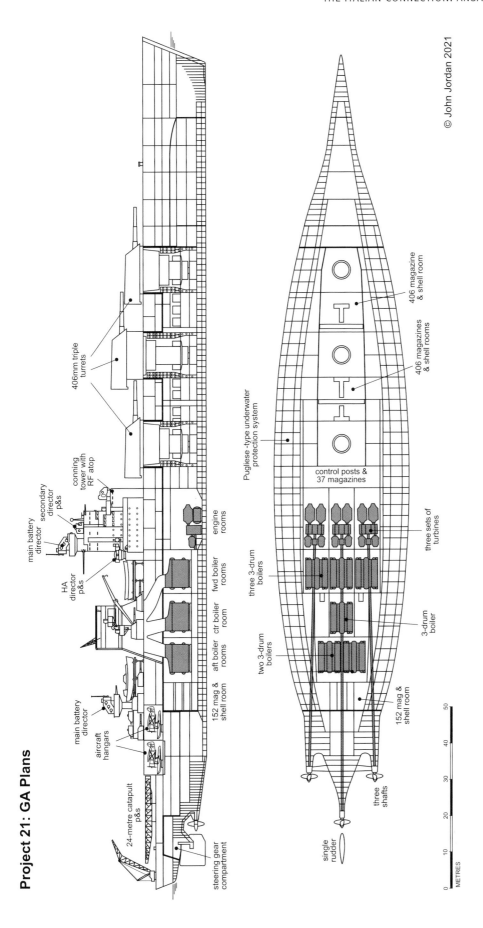

main battery director
secondary director p&s

conning tower with RF atop

main battery director p&s

HA director p&s

engine rooms

fwd boiler rooms

ctr boiler room

aft boiler rooms

152 mag & shell room

406mm triple turrets

main battery director

aircraft hangars

24-metre catapult p&s

steering gear compartment

Pugliese-type underwater protection system

406 magazine & shell room

406 magazines & shell rooms

control posts & 37 magazines

three sets of turbines

three 3-drum boilers

3-drum boiler

two 3-drum boilers

152 mag & shell room

single rudder

three shafts

METRES
0   10   20   30   40   50

Inboard profile and deck plan of KB-4's Project 21 design. The machinery layout is similar to that of HMS *Nelson*, but instead of the latter's two-shaft, 45,000shp plant Project 21 was supposed to develop 225,000shp on three shafts, foreshadowing the propulsion system of the later Project 23 (*Sovetskii Soiuz*) design. However, the machinery plant would have been extremely cramped – as indeed was the entire design.

Project 21: Protection Scheme

Profile

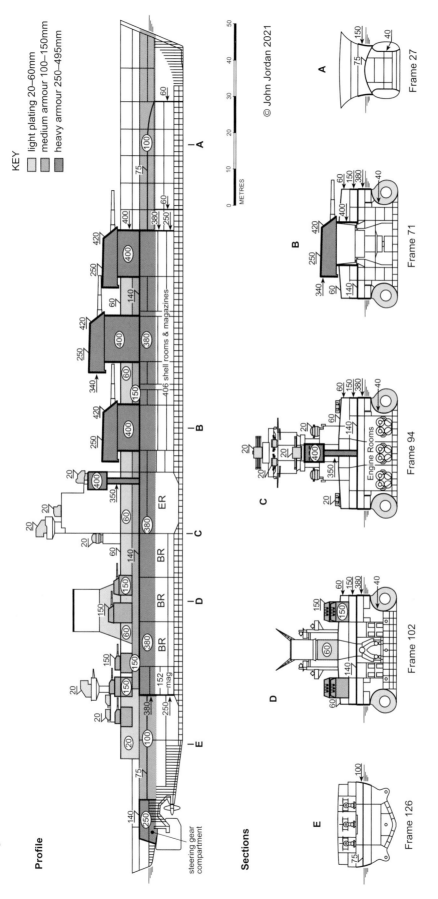

Sections

© John Jordan 2021

Project 21's protection scheme. Note in particular the early type of Pugliese underwater protection, based on the prototype systems installed in the naval oilers *Brennero* and *Tarvisio* (built in the 1920s). This system had recently been described in a French nautical magazine.

basic knowledge about how to go about designing a vessel as complex as a battleship.

The learning curve had proven to be much steeper than Stalin imagined in 1931 when he predicted that battleship construction could start in five years. The Soviet designers realised they needed foreign expertise if they were to produce realistic designs for major warships, and even before these designs had been submitted negotiations were underway with the Italian firm of Ansaldo for a battleship design.

Italian Contacts

At first sight, the relationship between Fascist Italy and the Communist Soviet Union seems paradoxical; in theory, their political regimes were diametrically opposed to one another. Despite these doctrinal differences, the two nations also had good reasons to cooperate: the Italians needed oil, coal and grain, while the USSR needed technical assistance in its aviation, automobile and shipbuilding industries.[6] Moreover, at the time both nations had an interest in countering Nazi Germany's expansionist policies; their strong stand against Hitler's attempt to absorb Austria in the summer of 1934 was only the most noteworthy example of this confluence of foreign policy.[7] The relationship found official expression in a series of agreements: for commerce in 1931, followed by a broader economic agreement in May 1933, and finally the 'Pact of Friendship, Neutrality, and Nonaggression' of September 1933.

However, contacts between the two nations and their navies predated these agreements. Italy had extended diplomatic recognition to the USSR in 1924, and the following year warships of the *Regia Marina* visited Leningrad and Odessa. Port visits by the two navies would henceforth become a regular occurrence, as did trips to Italy by Soviet military and naval representatives. The naval men were impressed by what they saw, especially by the high speeds of Italian cruisers – at this time the Soviet naval leadership considered speed to be 'the main shipbuilding element', bestowing enormous tactical advantages.[8]

The Soviets also began purchasing a considerable amount of Italian naval equipment. Otero-Terni-Orlando manufactured twelve 100mm twin AA mounts for light cruisers; Officine Galileo of Florence made fire control gear for the *Leningrad*-class flotilla leaders as well as 8-metre and 6-metre rangefinders and submarine periscopes; the Società San Giorgio produced no fewer than forty-six 4-metre rangefinders, Ditta Isotta Fraschini manufactured motors for torpedo boats, while Silurificio Italiano of Naples and Silurificio Whitehead of Fiume between them delivered 140 533mm and 450mm torpedoes.[9] Two guard ships for the NKVD's maritime border patrol, *Kirov* and *Dzerzhinskii*, were ordered from Ansaldo; they were laid down at Sestri Ponente on 8 February 1933 and delivered to Vladivostok in 1935. Finally, after a protracted series of negotiations, on 14 May 1934 a contract was signed with Ansaldo for tech-

nical assistance in the design and construction of light cruisers. The ships became the Project 26 design – the *Kirov* class (not to be confused with the earlier NKVD patrol vessel). They were built in the USSR, but were based on the *Raimondo Montecuccoli*, and the first unit had machinery manufactured in Italy. A party of Italian engineers came to Leningrad to work alongside the staff at TsKBS-1 in designing the ships and to assist in organising the construction process.

Thus by 1935 the Soviets had established a working relationship with numerous Italian firms, especially Ansaldo, which at the time was also building the battleship *Littorio*, laid down on 28 October 1934. It was therefore entirely logical that they would turn to this company for help in designing their own battleships. The exact sequence of the negotiations is, however, somewhat vague; according to one source, the Soviets approached Ansaldo in the autumn of 1935, while another says that it was Ansaldo who offered assistance in March 1936.[10] Whoever initiated the process, in the spring of 1936 a group of constructors and engineers, led by the head of TsKBS-1, V L Bzhezinskii, was sent to Italy to work out the details, and an agreement was reached for the development of several warship designs.[11]

However, Bzhezinskii's initial reports were apparently less than satisfactory, for on 10 June 1936 his boss, R A Muklevich, the head of the Shipbuilding Administration, sent him a telegram worded as follows:

> Try to get the *Littorio* design. What is needed is a battleship of 35,000 tons. This is the main task. The next design should be this: displacement 26,000 tons, 9 x 305mm, 16 x 130mm, main deck not less than 125mm, speed 33–35 knots. A cruiser would be of interest ... displacement 21,000 tons, speed 35 knots, main deck 100–125mm, side not less than 200mm. Your first submissions do not inspire confidence, beware of low-quality materials. The most reliable [method] is to obtain the design of a ship being built.[12]

From this it is clear that the Soviets were still hoping to obtain a 35,000-ton design, and were unaware that the standard displacement of the *Littorios* had already increased to more than 38,000 tons, and would soon go higher still.[13] The interest in a 26,000-ton fast battleship may have been inspired by Soviet interest in battlecruiser-type ships for the 'cruiser-killer' role – that was certainly the case with the big cruiser design Muklevich asked Bzhezinskii to obtain. It is also possible that the request was linked to the negotiations with Great Britain, which had been advocating for a reduction in battleship size since the late 1920s.[14]

Although Ansaldo refused to hand over the *Littorio* plans, on 14 July 1936 the firm did deliver no fewer than five designs to Bzhezinskii: two battleships, two battlecruisers, and an 'armoured scout' (see Table 2). Since Muklevich's telegram specifying the characteristics was sent on 10 June, this was remarkably fast work, even for preliminary designs; how had Ansaldo managed it?

The answer is simple: they already had a range of

Table 2: Ansaldo Designs for the USSR, July 1936

Type	Battleship (UP.41)	Battleship	Battlecruiser	Battlecruiser	Armoured Scout
Displacement:					
standard	42,000 tons	28,000 tons	22,000 tons	19,000 tons	3,700 tons
trials	46,200 tons	30,500 tons	23,400 tons	20,530 tons	4,050 tons
Length:					
waterline	245.0m	218.0m	235.0m	210.0m	146.0m
overall	253.0m	223.7m	241.5m	217.5m	152.5m
Beam, waterline	35.0m	30.6m	26.5m	26.0m	14.0m
Draught, trials	9.40m	8.30m	6.64m	6.64m	4.06m
Armament:					
main guns	9 x 406mm	9 x 343mm	9 x 250mm	9 x 250mm	8 x 130mm
secondary	12 x 180mm	12 x 152mm	8 x 130mm	16 x 100mm	20 x 45mm[1]
AA guns	24 x 100mm	8 x 100mm	12 x 100mm	10 x 45mm[1]	8 x 13.2mm[1]
	48 x 45mm[1]	24 x 45mm[1, 2]	32 x 45mm[1]	32 x 13.2mm[1]	–
	24 x 13.2mm[1]	24 x 13.2mm[1, 2]	24 x 13.2mm[1]	–	–
TT	–	6 x 533mm TT	6 x 533mm TT	12 x 533mm TT	9 x 533mm TT
Catapults / Aircraft	1 / 4	2 / 4	2 / 4	2 / 4	–
Protection:					
belt	370mm	300mm	220mm	200mm	65mm
decks (total)	165mm	175mm	140mm	125mm	30mm
Machinery:					
shafts	4	4	4	3	2
boilers	8	8	12	6	4
SHP	180,000	135,000	240,000	210,000	135,000shp
Speed	32.0 knots	30.5 knots	37.0 knots	35.0 knots	43.5 knots
Endurance:					
fuel oil	5,000 tons	4,000 tons	4,000 tons	4,000 tons	945 tons
range	6,300nm at 20kts	6,700nm at 20kts	7,750nm at 20kts	8,700nm at 20kts	2,750nm at 20kts

Notes:

[1] The original table gives the numbers of AA mountings, not the numbers of guns; based on the numbers for UP.41, it has been assumed that all 45mm were quads and all 13.2mm mountings were twins.

[2] Vasil'ev, p 15, gives 2 x 45mm, 20 x 13.2mm.

Sources: RGA VMF, F r-441, o 5, d 301; Vasil'ev, *Lineinye korabli tipa 'Sovetskii Soiuz'*.

designs available to offer. After the first two *Littorio*-class battleships had been laid down in the autumn of 1934, the Italian Navy undertook studies for future building programmes, including proposals for ships that would not be constrained by treaty limits. Sketch designs were developed by the Naval Corps of Engineers, headed by General Umberto Pugliese; these included a sketch design for a ship armed with 406mm guns and displacing 41,000 tons – soon increased to 42,000 tons due to the introduction of various modifications (as was happening to the *Littorio* class at the same time). This design was designated 'UP.41' for *Ufficio Piani, Umberto Pugliese* 41,000 tons.[15]

As for the other designs, the Italians had also been studying smaller capital ship possibilities since the late 1920s, both on their own initiative and in response to British proposals for reducing the Washington Treaty displacement limit.[16] Thus they had a considerable body of raw material to draw upon in preparing the smaller battleship and battlecruiser designs for the Soviets, and it seems likely that they again adapted an existing design to suit the Soviet request. Note that while Muklevich had specified 305mm guns the design delivered had 343mm

guns – a similar calibre to that adopted for the French battleships *Dunkerque* and *Strasbourg*, possible opponents of the Italian Navy.[17] A similar case probably obtained with the two battlecruiser designs. As for the 'armoured scout', its characteristics were very close to those of the later small cruisers of the 'Capitani Romani' class, and may have been a forerunner of that type.

Most, if not all of these designs had been prepared not by Ansaldo, but by the *Regia Marina*'s own construction office, for at this time Ansaldo was virtually a branch of the Italian Navy.[18] They were sold to the Soviets with the shipyard acting as a 'middleman'. Ansaldo probably introduced the minor modifications intended to bring UP.41 more into line with the Soviet requirements – or at least what the Italians assumed were Soviet requirements; these changes will be described below.

General Features

Bzhezinskii's report on the Italian battleship design, which survives in the Russian naval archives, never refers to the design as 'UP.41', instead simply calling it a

Table 3: UP. 41 Characteristics, 14 July 1936

Displacement:	
standard	43,000 tonnes (42,321 tons)
trials	46,200 tonnes (45,470 tons)
full load	48,860 tonnes (48,088 tons)
Dimensions:	236m pp, 245m wl, 252m oa x 35.5m x 9.4m trials, 9.8m full load
	774ft 3in pp, 803ft 10in wl, 826ft 9in oa x 116ft 6in x 30ft 10in trials, 32ft 2in full load
Armament:	
main guns	nine 406mm (16in)/50 (3 x III)
secondary	twelve 180mm (7.1in)/60 (4 x III)
AA guns	twenty-four 100mm (3.9in)/60 (12 x II)
	forty-eight 45mm (12 x IV)
	twenty-four 13.2mm (12 x II)
Catapults / Aircraft	1 / 4
Protection:	
main belt	370mm (14.57in) @ 6°[1]
upper belt	150mm (5.9in) @ 6°
406mm turrets	400mm (15.8in) faces, 150mm (5.9in) sides, 200mm (7.9in) roofs
barbettes	350mm (13.7in) max[2]
180mm turrets	180mm (7.1in) faces, 60mm (2.4in) sides, 90mm (3.5in) roofs
100mm turrets	100mm (3.9in) faces, 40mm (1.6in) sides, 50mm (2in) roofs
conning tower	370mm (14.6in) sides, 200mm (7.9in) roof
decks	55mm (2.2in) forecastle, 10mm (0.4in) upper, 25mm (1in) main, 65+35mm (2.6+1.4in) middle
Machinery:	eight boilers, four turbine sets,
	140,000mhp (138,085shp) normal, 180,000mhp (177,537shp) max
Speed	30 knots normal, 32 knots max
Endurance:	3,000 tonnes OF (normal), ?nm at ?kts
	5,000 tonnes OF (full load), 6,300nm at 20kts, 8,800nm at 16kts
Complement	1,600

Notes:

[1] Bzhezinskii's report gives 380mm in one place, 370mm in other places; Vasil'ev, 21 gives 370mm, as do Garzke and Dulin, 310; Cernuschi and O'Hara, 92, state that it varied from 320mm to 425mm.

[2] Bzhezinskii's report gives 370mm, but his tables give 350mm, as do Garzke and Dulin, 310.

Sources: RGA VMF, F r-441, o 5, d 301; Garzke and Dulin, *Battleships: Allied Battleships*, 310.

'Battleship of 42,000 tons standard displacement', which mirrors the Italian designation *Nave de Battaglia da 42 000 T st* (Battleship of 42,000 tons standard).[19] His report provides much detail, and serves as the basis for most of the information in the following paragraphs. However, he seems to have drafted it in something of a hurry, as there is a good deal of repetition, and in some cases there are discrepancies between the report and the accompanying data tables.

In its general features UP.41 closely resembled the contemporary *Littorio* class, with the same long forecastle, identical arrangements of the main and secondary armaments, and similar upperworks. As in the *Littorios*, the aviation facilities were on the low quarterdeck. There were also similarities in the hull structure, with both designs featuring the same one-metre frame spacing and a triple bottom throughout the citadel.[20] Both also probably had a modest bulbous bow. Although the Length:Beam ratio of UP.41 was slightly inferior to that of the *Littorio* (7.0 vs 7.17), its hull form was somewhat finer, with a block coefficient of 0.533 as opposed to 0.566.[21]

The hull was divided into twenty main watertight compartments by nineteen transverse bulkheads (compared with eighteen bulkheads in *Littorio*).[22] The damage control system was to include 'automatic balancing channels' – cross-flooding ducts that would connect the void compartments on one side of the ship to the corresponding ones on the opposite side; in the event of a breach in the hull, water would flow automatically from the damaged side to the undamaged side, reducing any list. Similar ducts had been incorporated in the *Littorio* class, and were also familiar to the Soviet designers, since they had been employed in large Russian warships since the *Borodino* class at the turn of the century. The metacentric height in the normal or trials condition (46,200 tonnes/45,470 tons) was 2.3m, considerably greater than that of the *Littorios* (1.66m at full load: 45,752 tons).[23]

The rudder arrangements differed from those of the *Littorio* class: instead of having a large centreline rudder with two smaller ones in the wakes of the outboard screws, UP.41 had only two rudders, both on the centreline, the larger one located farther aft.

Design UP.41 July 1936

Displacement: 43,000 tonnes
Length: 253m oa
              245m wl
Beam: 35.5m max
Horsepower: 180,000shp = 32kts
Armament: 9 x 406mm (3 x III)
              12 x 180mm (4 x III)
              24 x 100mm (12 x II)
              48 x 45mm (12 x IV)
              24 x13.2mm (12 x II)

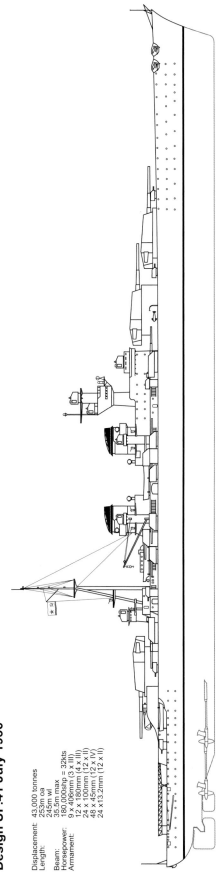

© John Jordan 2021

0   10   20   30   40   50
METRES

The UP.41 design delivered to the Soviets on 14 July 1936 by Ansaldo. This had originally been drawn up by the Italian Navy's design office under General Umberto Pugliese and generally resembled the *Littorio* class, but had a more powerful main battery and a different protection scheme. In particular, the Pugliese underwater protection system was abandoned in favour of a more conventional multi-bulkhead scheme. UP.41 was never more than a preliminary design, but even so the plans provided the Soviet constructors with many insights into the intricacies of battleship design.

Design UP.41 July 1936: GA Plans

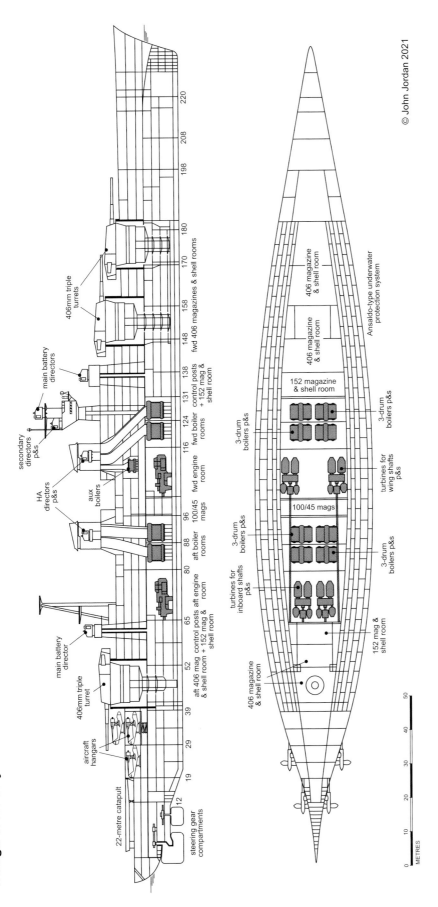

© John Jordan 2021

General arrangement drawings of UP.41. The machinery layout differed from that of the *Littorio* class: instead of a solid block of boiler rooms with engines rooms fore and aft, UP.41 had alternating boiler and engine rooms. The aviation facilities were also more extensive, with an enclosed hangar, a feature the *Littorios* lacked.

Design UP.41 July 1936

Profile: Starboard Side

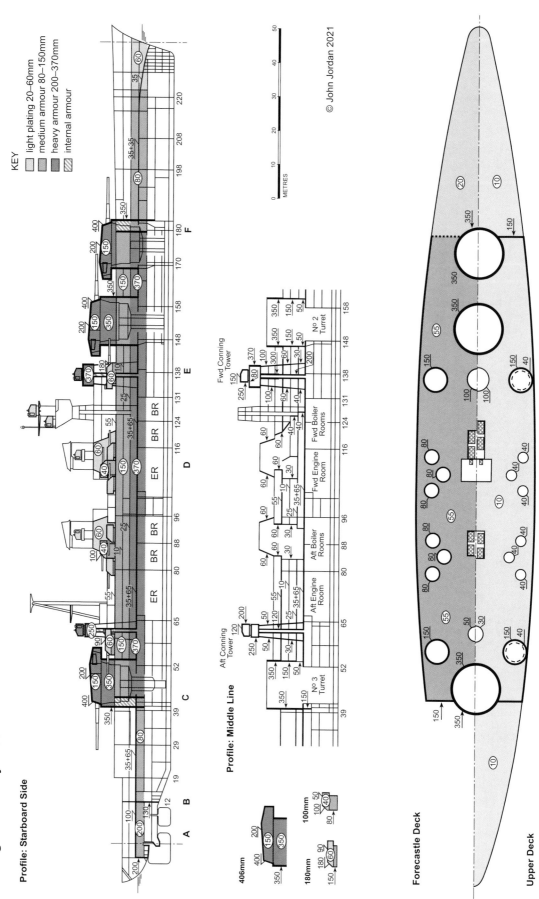

KEY
light plating 20–60mm
medium armour 80–150mm
heavy armour 200–370mm
internal armour

© John Jordan 2021

Profile: Middle Line

Fwd Conning Tower
Aft Conning Tower
Nº 3 Turret
Aft Engine Room
Aft Boiler Rooms
Fwd Engine Room
Fwd Boiler Rooms
Nº 2 Turret

406mm
180mm
100mm

Forecastle Deck

Upper Deck

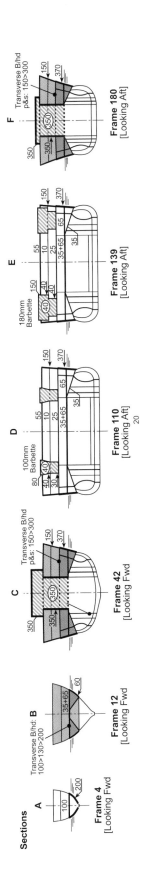

Sections

A
Transverse B/hd: 100>130>200
Frame 4
[Looking Fwd]
100 200

B
Frame 12
[Looking Fwd]
35>65 60

C
Transverse B/hd p&s: 150>300
150 370
350 350 350
Frame 42
[Looking Fwd]

D
100mm Barbette
80 40 40 30
55 10 25 35>65 35
150 370
Frame 110
[Looking Aft]
20

E
180mm Barbette
40 40
55 10 25 35>65 35
150 370
Frame 139
[Looking Aft]

F
Transverse B/hd p&s: 150>300
150 370
350 350 350
Frame 180
[Looking Aft]

UP.41's armour protection, with thicknesses in millimetres. This diagram, in combination with the midship half-section (see page 61), gives a good idea of the Italian style of protection. Instead of concentrating the heaviest possible armour over the most vital areas as in the 'all or nothing' system, there was a narrow waterline belt with extensive areas of the hull protected by lighter armour and the horizontal protection distributed over no fewer than four relatively thin decks. This system required a great deal of splinter protection scattered throughout the hull's interior.

Table 5: UP.41 Weights

Group	Description	Weight (tonnes)
A	Steel, bare hull	9,900
B	Additional hull weights	900
C	Auxiliary machinery & equipment	1,200
D	Armour[1]	17,600
E	Machinery with water	2,590
F	Armament[2]	7,100
G	Underwater fittings	50
H	Aviation equipment	50
I	Chemical protection	100
L	Electrical gear	500
M	Seagoing equipment	450
N	Margin	500
O	Water in propeller shaft recesses[3]	20
P	Various liquids in piping	40
	Total, Light ship	41,000

Consumables, etc ...	Trials	Full Load
Crew, provisions, fresh water	450	580
Ammunition	1,355	1,780
Aircraft	10	10
Consumables	80	150
Boiler reserve feed water	150	250
Fuel	3,000	5,000
Lubricants	105	155
Aviation petrol	20	20
Total	5,200	7,860
Displacements	46,200	48,860

Notes:

1 Includes weight of underwater protection.
2 Incudes weight of turret armour.
3 The meaning of this phrase is unclear.

Source: RGA VMF, F r-441, o 5, d 301.

Table 4: Hull Characteristics at Normal Displacement

Displacement	46,200 tonnes
Length (waterline)	245m
Beam (waterline)	35m
Draught (mean)	9.4m
Length:beam ratio	6.90[1]
Beam:draught ratio	3.78[2]
Block coefficient	0.553
Waterplane coefficient	0.650
Midship coefficient	0.99
Depth of hull amidships[3]	14.3m
Freeboard:	
bow	6.2m
amidships	4.9m
stern	5.4m

Notes:

[1] This is the figure given in Bzhezinskii's report, but a simple calculation gives an L:B ratio of 7.0.

[2] Again, this is the figure given by Bzhezinskii, but calculation gives 3.72.

[3] Measured at the side (not at the middle line).

Source: RGA VMF, F r-441, o 5, d 301.

Armament

The main battery comprised nine 406mm/50 guns in three triple turrets, two forward and one aft. As in the *Littorio*s, the after main battery turret was set on a tall barbette, almost as high as that of the superimposed turret forward (the height of turret 3 above the waterline at normal load was 12.80m, that of turret 2 was 13.70m); this has often been attributed to a desire to minimise the effects of blast on the aviation facilities on the quarterdeck, but in fact it was intended to give the after turret the greatest possible arc of fire on forward bearings.[24] By raising the turret over the lower levels of the superstructure and keeping the upperworks as narrow as possible, turret 3's 'dead zone' was minimised, being only 30 degrees on either side of the bow. Firing a 950kg projectile at an initial velocity of 900m/s – the propellant charge of 342kg was in six bags – the guns were expected to have a maximum range of 41,000 metres, while the rate of fire was projected to be two rounds per minute. The ammunition allowance was 60rpg at normal load and 80rpg at full load, considerably less than the 100 or more rounds per gun adopted by most of the other major navies at the time.

The secondary and anti-aircraft batteries were to be Soviet weapons, although the guns and mountings had yet to enter service. In the original UP.41 design the secondary battery had comprised twelve 152mm/55 guns in four triple turrets, as in the *Littorio* class, but as delivered to the Soviets it featured twelve 180mm guns, a considerably more powerful – and heavier – weapon. Bzhezinskii provided the data for these turrets, which were under development and had yet to reach their final

form. This explains why the turrets depicted look nothing like the ones that finally appeared in the *Kirov* class cruisers, and why the guns themselves are described as 180mm/60, whereas the guns that eventually entered service were 57-calibre weapons.[25]

The triple 180mm turret as built was a very compact mounting with all three guns in a single cradle; nevertheless, when it finally entered service in 1938 its rotating weight was 220–230 tonnes, considerably heavier than the Italian 152mm turrets it was supposed to replace, which weighed 155.6 tonnes; moreover the 180mm cruiser turret had considerably thinner armour than was projected for the battleship. The result would have been several hundred tonnes of excess weight compared to what was allowed for in the original design. Each 180mm turret had an arc of fire of 160 degrees, and the ammunition allowance was 150rpg at normal load, 200rpg at full load. Shell weight was assumed to be 100kg, compared to 97.5kg in the actual gun, while the 40kg propellant charge allowed for was exactly correct.

Bzhezinskii's report notes that an arrangement with eighteen 180mm guns was also studied, with three triple turrets on either beam, but this led to a reduction in the heavy anti-aircraft battery to eight guns, which was regarded as inadequate.

The AA battery of UP.41 was exceptionally heavy for the era, with no fewer than twenty-four 100mm/60 guns in twelve twin mounts. There was in fact no such gun or mounting in Soviet service, although a 100mm/56 gun was under development. By 1936 Italian battleship designs featured the stabilised 90mm/50 single mounting, which would eventually enter service in the *Littorio* class.[26] However, the 1935 design sold to the Soviets still featured conventional unstabilised turrets, presumably because the Italians wanted to keep their latest technology secret. The turrets are shown in two groups of three on either beam, with the centre turret raised above the other two. The ammunition outfit was 300rpg in both the normal and full-load conditions, and each round was assumed to weigh 26kg.

The close-range AA armament of the original UP.41 design may have featured the quad 37mm mount for the Breda 54-calibre guns under development at this time, which was eventually abandoned.[27] The version sold to the Soviets instead showed forty-eight 45mm guns in twelve quadruple mounts. This was probably another substitution to meet perceived Soviet requirements, as a 45mm gun, designated 21-K, had recently entered service in the Red Navy. The Soviet 21-K was a 46.1-calibre semi-automatic gun, but its rate of fire of 25 rounds per minute was inadequate, and in future fully-automatic 37mm guns would be preferred for this role. Four quad mountings are shown abreast the forward main battery turrets, while aft there are two under the barrels of the 180mm guns and two on the quarterdeck. Four further mountings are located on the superstructures. The twelve twin 12.7mm (.50in) machine guns mounts were also located on the superstructures.

The main battery was to be controlled by three

command-rangefinder posts (*komandno-dalnomernye posty*, or KDPs, equivalent to the director control tower in the Royal Navy) for the main battery: one atop the tower mast (~34m above the design waterline), one atop the forward conning tower (~20m above the waterline) and one on the after conning tower (~18m above the waterline). Each was equipped with a single 8-metre rangefinder. There were two KDPs for the 180mm guns, one on either side of the tower mast below the main battery KDP; they were about 29 metres above the waterline and featured 6-metre rangefinders. The heavy AA battery was controlled by four KDPs, two on either side on platforms projecting from the funnels; they were approximately 19.5 metres above the waterline and were equipped with 3-metre rangefinders. There were to be six 90cm searchlights mounted on or near the funnels, and four 40cm signal projectors.

The aviation facilities were similar to those of the *Littorio* class, but were more extensive. The design shows a single trainable catapult on the quarterdeck. Stowage for four seaplanes was provided under the barrels of the after main battery turret, in an enclosed two-level hangar with a lift to bring them to the upper deck.

Protection

All of the heavy vertical armour was to be Krupp cemented (KC) plate. The thicknesses specified for the main belt and decks were based on resisting shells fired from the same 406mm guns carried by the ship (950kg shells fired at 900m/s). According to calculations, the ship's vitals should have been immune to shells arriving from an angle of 25 degrees forward of the broadside at ranges between 13,500 and 30,000 metres.[28]

The main belt extended from frame 42 to 180, for a total length of 138m, or about 56 per cent of the ship's waterline length. It was 4.4m high (exactly as in *Littorio*), with 2.2m to be immersed at the design draught. However, unlike the 'composite' belt of the *Littorio*s, which featured a 70mm chrome-nickel steel plate to decap shells with a 280mm KC belt 25cm behind it, UP.41 would have had a uniform 370mm KC belt. This may have reflected doubts about the effectiveness of the 'composite' belt.[29] UP.41's belt was sloped at 6 degrees, a considerable reduction from the 15-degree incline in the *Littorio*s; approximately 1.8–2m inboard of the belt was a 30mm splinter bulkhead. Above the main belt there was a 150mm upper belt extending to the forecastle deck. It should have been able to resist 180mm shells (100kg, initial velocity 950m/s) at ranges above 8,000 metres. Both the main and upper belts were mounted on a 60mm teak backing.

The citadel was closed off fore and aft by transverse bulkheads running between the barbettes of the end turrets and the sides of the hull; below the main deck these bulkheads were 300mm, their lower edges angling upward to the middle deck to match the 35mm deck slopes. Above the main deck they were 150mm and extended up to the forecastle deck.

The horizontal protection over the citadel was distributed over four protected decks. The forecastle deck was 55mm (reduced to 20mm forward of the citadel), the upper deck 10mm, the main deck (at the top of the main armour belt) 25mm, and below that was the heaviest deck, 65mm laid on 35mm plating; the total of all four decks was 190mm. The 65mm plating extended across the full width of the deck, but over the torpedo protection system the 35mm layer formed slopes to the bottom of the main belt.

Forward of the citadel there was an 80mm waterline belt, reducing to 60mm near the bow; aft the waterline protection was 80mm. In addition there were 100mm turtleback decks both fore and aft.

The forward conning tower had 370mm sides, a 200mm roof, and a 200mm communications tube. The after conning tower had 250mm sides, an 80mm roof, and a 120mm communications tube. The command-rangefinder posts for the main battery showed unusually heavy protection – the forward one had 250mm sides and a 150mm roof, while the after post had 200mm sides and a 120mm roof.

The main battery turrets had 400mm faces, 200mm roofs and 150mm sides, with 350mm barbettes, reduced

Design UP.41 July 1936: Midship Half-section

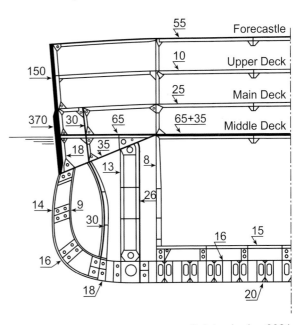

© John Jordan 2021

Midship half-section of UP.41's hull showing armour thicknesses and the underwater protection. The Pugliese cylinder of the *Littorio*s was replaced by a multi-bulkhead system, with a distinctive concave main bulkhead. The thickness of that bulkhead is not indicated in the available materials, and it has been assumed that it was a continuation of the 30mm longitudinal bulkhead behind the main belt. Note also the triple bottom, which extended throughout the citadel.

to 150mm below the 55mm forecastle deck and then to 50mm below the 25mm second deck. The secondary turrets had 180mm faces, 90mm roofs, and 60mm sides. The 100mm turrets had 100mm faces, 50mm roofs and 40mm sides.

The funnel uptakes had 60mm protection to a height of 7.3m above the forecastle deck, and were reduced to 30mm below it, where they were covered by the 150mm upper belt.

The underwater protection scheme differed from that of the *Littorio* class, the Pugliese system being replaced with a liquid-loaded multi-bulkhead type of unique design. This change was not an attempt to keep the details of the Pugliese system secret, as has sometimes been stated; in fact at the same time the Soviets obtained

Generale del Genio Navale Umberto Pugliese (1880–1961), whose department designed the *Littorio* class battleships and was responsible for the follow-up studies that produced the UP.41 design. He was appointed head of the *Direzione Generale delle Construzioni Navali e Meccaniche* in 1931, responsible for supervising the design of Italian warships. Despite a long and distinguished career that had earned him a number of awards he was dismissed after the promulgation of the Racial Laws of 1938, which barred Jews from state service. Nevertheless he was recalled to duty to assist in the salvage of the battleships sunk by the British air raid on Taranto in November 1940. Arrested and imprisoned by the Germans after the Italian surrender, he was subsequently released. After the war he served as President of the *Istituto nazionale per gli Studi e le esperienze di architettura navale* until shortly before his death. (USMM, courtesy of Michele Cosentino)

UP.41 they were able to reach an agreement with the Italian government to use the Pugliese system and so received 'practically comprehensive' information it.[30] The choice of a more conventional multi-bulkhead system was due to Italian concerns about shells falling short and penetrating the hull below the belt. In the Pugliese system the thin-walled empty cylinder would provide little protection against such hits, leaving only the 40mm main bulkhead as a significant obstacle.[31] UP.41, on the other hand, featured several bulkheads, two of which were relatively thick; this system would have offered considerably greater resistance to underwater shell hits. The most striking feature of the system was a concave longitudinal bulkhead inboard of the double bottom, which continued around the turn of the bilge to the deck slope. Inboard of the curved bulkhead were two flat bulkheads and a holding bulkhead. The total depth of the system amidships was 8m, reducing to 6m fore and aft.[32] This system was dubbed the 'Ansaldo' system by the Soviets and was used in several subsequent battleship designs. Bzhezinskii does not state what size warhead the system was designed to resist; it is known that the Pugliese system of *Littorio* was designed to withstand a 320kg torpedo warhead.[33]

The UP.41 design featured a triple bottom under the citadel, as had the *Littorio* class. The possibility of more comprehensive under-bottom protection was also studied, 'based on the principle of arches supported by longitudinal reinforced beams', but unfortunately details of the proposed system are lacking. However, it may have inspired a configuration studied by Soviet designers during the Second World War.[34] The proposed scheme would have increased displacement by more than 1,500 tonnes and its effectiveness was doubtful, so the idea was abandoned.

The hull of the Italian battleship *Littorio* under construction at Ansaldo Genoa-Sestri Ponente in 1936, showing among other features the cylinder of the Pugliese underwater protection scheme. An alternative to the heavier multi-bulkhead form of torpedo protection, it was nevertheless abandoned in UP.41 because of concerns that it was less effective in resisting underwater hits by plunging shells. However the system was later incorporated into the Project 23 (*Sovetskii Soiuz*) class battleships. (Ansaldo)

Vittorio Veneto of the *Littorio* class on 4 October 1939. With her incomplete forward tower-mast she gives some idea of how UP.41 might have looked had it been built. (F Petronio collection)

Machinery

As in the *Littorio* class there were eight boilers and four sets of turbines, but the layout of the plant differed. While the *Littorios* had a solid block of four boiler rooms amidships with a pair of turbines located forward of them and another pair aft, in UP.41 an alternating arrangement was adopted: working fore to aft, there were two boiler rooms, then a compartment for the wing shaft turbines, then two more boiler rooms, and finally a compartment for the two turbine sets for the inboard shafts.

The eight boilers would probably have been of the Yarrow 3-drum type, as in the *Littorios*. In his report Bzhezinskii noted that the steam conditions were moderate, as it was not considered 'advisable' to employ higher temperatures and pressures; although this would have allowed greater power, machinery reliability was regarded as more important than high performance in the battleship. The boiler pressure was therefore limited to 30kg/cm^2, temperature to 360°C. These were somewhat higher steam conditions than in the *Littorio* class (25kg/cm^2 and 325°C).[35] The total heating surface was 9,920m^2, as opposed to 9,440m^2 in the *Littorios*.

There were four sets of geared turbines, each comprising one high-pressure, one intermediate-pressure and two low-pressure turbines working through reduction gearing. There were no cruise turbines, but there were cruising wheels in the IP and LP turbines.

At normal output the machinery plant was to generate 140,000shp, giving a speed of 30 knots with shaft revolutions of 240rpm. The maximum output was 180,000shp, providing for a speed of 32 knots with 263rpm. The cruising speed of 20 knots would have required 44,000shp with 160rpm. (Elsewhere in the report Bzhezinskii gives a figure of 36,000shp for 20 knots.)

Electricity was to be provided by six 500kW diesel generators on the lower armoured deck in two separate compartments, four 250kW turbo-generators, and two 150kW diesel generators on the upper deck, the latter intended for harbour service, for a total of 4,300kW.

Fuel would have been stowed in the double bottom and in the side protection system. The maximum bunkerage was 5,000 tonnes, giving a steaming range when cruising at 20 knots of 6,300nm; at 16 knots range was to be 8,800nm.

In addition, 20 tonnes of aviation fuel would have been stowed in a tank forward.

Impact

In assessing the importance of UP.41 to the Soviet battleship programme, it must be borne in mind that it was never more than a preliminary design, and would have required further development and elaboration before it could have been used as the basis for actual construction. Nor was there ever any intention of building a ship to this design, the Navy's Shipbuilding Department considering that it did not 'reflect the latest achievements of Italian shipbuilding'.[36] This was an accurate assessment: UP.41 was not the latest version of the design; it dated from 1935, yet by 1936 Italian designs for ships with 406mm guns had reached 45,000 tons standard, with a waterline length of 249m.[37]

Nevertheless, UP.41 played a key role in the development of the USSR's capital ship programme. It was studied intensely by the Soviet naval administration and constructors and brought a new sense of reality to the design process. The requirements for future battleships would no longer be the result of wishful thinking; if the highly-respected Italian naval architects could not combine 406mm guns, heavy armour protection and a 30-knot speed in a 35,000-ton hull, it must have been obvious that the inexperienced Soviet constructors could not be asked to do so. The next set of staff requirements called for a ship of 41,500 tons and a speed of not less than 30 knots – suspiciously close to UP.41's characteristics. (See the author's article 'Stalin's Super Battleships' in *Warship 2021* for details of the subsequent Soviet design process.)

The hull lines and general arrangements of the next round of Soviet capital ship designs owed a good deal to UP.41, although they differed greatly from the Italian design in appearance. The design offered by TsKBS-1 featured the so-called 'Ansaldo' side protection system, while the competitive design by KB-4 at the Baltic Works adopted the Pugliese system. Alternating boiler and engine rooms would also be a feature of all future capital ship designs.

In some ways Italian design practices tallied well with trends already present in Soviet thinking, especially in the area of armour protection. Both navies rejected the American-style 'all-or-nothing' scheme, instead combining heavy but narrow side belts with extensive vertical protection against smaller-calibre projectiles and splinters. Horizontal protection was likewise distributed in several layers, with the heaviest deck at the lowest level.

After UP.41 the Soviet design teams would strike out on their own, but the Italian design provided a vital starting point for their future work and formed an essential point of departure for the process that eventually produced the mammoth Project 23 battleships of the *Sovetskii Soiuz* class.

Acknowledgements:

The author again expresses his gratitude to Sergei Vinogradov, who supplied a transcript of Bzhezinskii's report as well as other materials relevant to the design. John Jordan's excellent drawings have once again added depth, while Enrico Cernushchi provided additional materials and insights. And as always, my wife Jan Torbet applied her editorial skills to the article, greatly improving it.

Sources:

RGA VMF (Russian State Archives of the Navy), *fond* r-441, *opis'* 5, *delo* 301: 'Lineinyi korabl' standardnym vodoizmeshcheniem 42000 t. Poiasitel'naia zapiska'.

Enrico Cernuschi and Vincent P O'Hara, 'The Breakout Fleet: The Oceanic Programmes of the Regia Marina, 1934–1940', *Warship 2006*, 86–101.

Garzke, William H Jr and Dulin, Robert O Jr. *Battleships: Allied Battleships of World War II*, Naval Institute Press (Annapolis, 1980), 308–10.

Molodtsov, S V, 'Stalinskie linkory', pt. 1. *Briz*, 1996, no 9, 9–22.

Vasil'ev, A M, *Lineinye korabli tipa 'Sovetskii Soiuz'*, Galeia Print (St Petersburg, 2006).

Endnotes:

1 Molodtsov, 'Stalinskie linkory', 9.
2 I P Spasskii (editor), *Istoriia otechestvennogo sudostroeniia*, 5 vols; *Sudostroenie* (St Petersburg, 1994–1996), 4:174–7, 189–92; J N Westwood, *Russian Naval Construction 1905–1945*, Macmillan Press (London, 1994), 148–150.
3 William Berry, 'HM Battleships *Nelson* and *Rodney*', *Transactions of the Institution of Naval Architects*, vol LXXI (spring session, 1929), 1–21.
4 *Journal de la Marine Marchande*, 17 and 24 January 1935.
5 René Greger, in his article 'Sowjetischer Schlachtschiffbau' (*Marine-Rundschau*, August 1974, 461–479) published two photos of models, one of KB-4's all-forward turret design, the other apparently of a very similar model with two turrets forward and one aft; the superstructures appear identical, as do the aviation facilities. These were likely demonstration models, but it is not known what design the second model represented since KB-4 is not credited with such a design.
6 J Calvitt Clarke Jr, 'Italo-Soviet Military Cooperation in the 1930s', in: Donald J Stoker Jr and Jonathan A Grant, *Girding for Battle: The Arms Trade in a Global Perspective, 1815–1940*, Prager Publishers (Westport, 2003), 178–199, at 180.
7 For the background to this relationship, see J Calvitt Clarke Jr, *Russia and Italy Against Hitler: The Bolshevik-Fascist Rapprochement of the 1930s*, Greenwood Press (Westport, 1991).
8 Aleksandr Chernyshev and Konstantin Kulagin, *Sovetskie kreisera Velikoi Otechestvennoi: Ot 'Kirova' do 'Kaganavicha'*, Iauza, EKSMO (Moscow, 2007), 6.
9 Clarke, 'Italo-Soviet Military Cooperation', 186.
10 Jürgen Rohwer, 'The Development of Strategic Concepts and Shipbuilding Programs for the Soviet Navy, 1922–1953: Stalin's Battleships and Battlecruisers', *The Northern Mariner/Le Marin du Nord*, vol VII, no 3 (July 1997), 51–61, at 53; Vasil'ev, 15.
11 Molodtsov, 'Stalinskie linkory', 15; Vasil'ev, 15.
12 Vasil'ev, 15.
13 Erminio Bagnasco and Augusto de Toro, *The Littorio Class: Italy's Last and Largest Battleships 1937–1948*, Seaforth Publishing (Barnsley, 2011), 21, 36.
14 Bagnasco and de Toro, 25. Note that while some published accounts say that the Soviets had requested a 42,000-ton design, Muklevich's telegram makes it clear that they were looking for a 35,000-ton ship.
15 Cernuschi and O'Hara, 90–2.
16 William H Garzke Jr and Robert O Dulin Jr, *Battleships: Axis Battleships in World War II*, Naval Institute Press (Annapolis, 1990), 373–9; Bagnasco and de Toro, 25.
17 Odero-Terni-Orlando developed a design with twelve 343mm guns, so this calibre had apparently been considered by the Italians; see Robert C Stern, *The Battleship Holiday: The Naval Treaties and Capital Ship Design* (Barnsley; Seaforth, 2017), 143.
18 Cernuschi and O'Hara, 92.
19 Garzke and Dulin, 308.
20 Bagnasco and de Toro, 50–51.
21 Bagnasco and de Toro, 52.
22 Bagnasco and de Toro, 51.
23 Bagnasco and de Toro, 52.
24 Bagnasco and de Toro, 31.
25 However, the earlier model of 180mm gun, fitted in the old light cruiser *Krasnyi Kavkaz*, was a 60-calibre gun.
26 Cernuschi and O'Hara, 91. The new guns were included in a drawing of the *Littorio*s dated 30 April 1936; Bagnasco and de Toro, 42.
27 Bagnasco and de Toro, 43.
28 Note that in Bzhezinskii's report there are discrepancies between some of the armour thicknesses given in the text and those given in the tables; I have assumed that the tabular data is correct.
29 Bagnasco and de Toro, 35. According to Cernuschi and O'Hara, 92, UP.41's belt had a 'variable thickness ranging from 320mm to 425mm', but this is not mentioned in Bzhezinskii's report.
30 Vasil'ev, 15, 69.
31 Cernuschi and O'Hara, 92.
32 Vasil'ev says depth amidships was 9.8m, but this is not confirmed by the drawing of the hull cross-section in his book; see 14, 21.
33 Bagnasco and de Toro, 56.
34 Vasil'ev, 138.
35 Garzke and Dulin, 425, 434.
36 Molodtsov, 'Stalinskie linkory', 15.
37 Cernuschi and O'Hara, 92.

TAKASAGO, KASAGI AND CHITOSE:

THE IJN'S FIRST 8in-GUN PROTECTED CRUISERS

The three large protected cruisers of the *Takasago* class were ordered following the Sino-Japanese War to a design by Sir Philip Watts. The first unit was built by Armstrong in the UK, her two slightly modified sisters in the United States. **Kathrin Milanovich** looks at the design, construction and service history of these unusually powerful vessels.

When Sir Philip Watts was the chief designer of Armstrong, Mitchell & Co, one of his projects was the design of the protected cruiser *Yoshino* for the Imperial Japanese Navy (IJN). The ship attained a speed of 23.03 knots with 15,819ihp on trials – a world record for the time. Her four-cylinder triple expansion engines,

built by Humphrys, Tennant & Co, were the first of the type to be fitted in a Japanese warship when the ship was completed on 30 September 1893. *Yoshino* was armed with four 6in 40-calibre guns in a lozenge arrangement, the two side mountings being on sponsons abeam the bridge, and eight 4.7in 40-cal Armstrong QF guns (four

The second class cruiser *Takasago* anchoring off Portsmouth in May 1898, shortly before she made the passage to Japan. Like her US-built half-sister *Chitose* she had the Imperial chrysanthemum at the bow, but the carved and gilded decorations were seldom seen in other IJN warships. The large size of the 8in main gun on the forecastle compared with the side-mounted 4.7in QF guns is evident. The style of the bridge, military masts and funnels was repeated in the larger *Kasagi* class. (Hans Lengerer collection)

on either side of the ship). Much was expected from both her speed and armament, and *Yoshino* played an active part in the Sino-Japanese War (SJW) of 1894–95. However, she met her demise early in the Russo-Japanese War (RJW) when, at 0140 on 15 May 1904, she changed course in dense fog and collided with the armoured cruiser *Kasuga*, whose ram struck her abreast the port-side engine room. She heeled over quickly, and the poor weather conditions meant that only 96 men of her complement of 419 survived.

After her victory in the Sino-Japanese War Japan planned an unprecedented expansion of the Navy to cope with the changed situation in the Far East, and the construction of three protected cruisers (designated *Bogōjunyōkan* = 2nd Class Cruiser) was approved by the Diet as part of the First Period Naval Expansion Programme of 1896. The first unit, *Takasago*, was again ordered from Armstrong; she was to be built as a sister to *Yoshino* with the same principal dimensions, propulsion machinery and endurance (4,000nm at 10 knots with 1,000 tons of coal). The projected radius of action conformed to the strategic concept of operating close to Japan; operations on the high seas in far, remote places were not considered. This principle governed fuel stowage, consumables, habitability and seaworthiness. However, for tactical purposes high speed and firepower were required. Missions comprised scouting and

screening, and support of both smaller friendly units and the main force.

In order to meet this requirement the four 6in (15.2cm) guns of *Yoshino* were to be replaced by two 8in (20.3cm) 45-calibre Armstrong QF guns, mounted fore and aft on the middle line, and the number of secondary 4.7in (12cm) guns was increased from eight to twelve. However, the embarkation of this heavy gun impaired both seaworthiness and stability, and in order to avoid these defects the dimensions and displacement of *Takasago*'s American-built sisters, *Kasagi* and *Chitose* – the first warships ordered from US shipyards since 1862 – were significantly increased.

In working out the specifications for the last two ships the Japanese design team was assisted by Sir Philip Watts, who had been invited to Japan, and they emerged as a modified *Takasago* type, with the same principal characteristics but incorporating a number of significant modifications that included improvements to the ammunition supply for the main guns. As they were to have an identical gun armament to *Takasago*, both ships were completed without their weapons; *Kasagi* sailed for England following completion to be armed at Armstrongs, while the armament of *Chitose* was embarked at the Yokosuka Navy Yard.

These three vessels were the last protected cruisers ordered from abroad, and when completed they were,

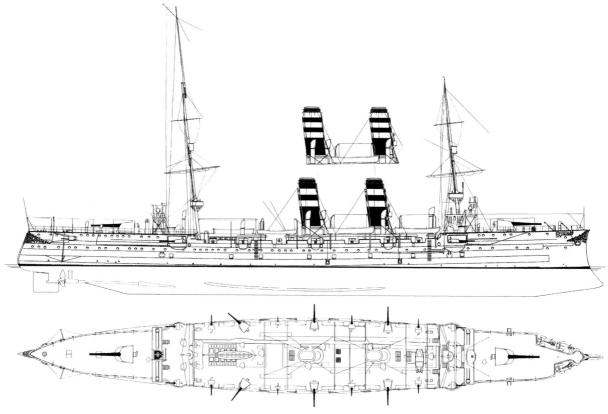

Profile and plan of *Takasago* in 1902. The funnels are painted black with two broad white rings as shown in the photo taken at Plymouth, although for clarity the drawing shows the hull unpainted. The inset shows the funnel markings (black with three white rings) dating from 1898–99. (Waldemar Trojca)

Takasago photographed on the occasion of the coronation of King Edward VII. The photo was probably taken in June 1902 off Plymouth, where she anchored from the 10th to 23rd. Note the black painted hull, funnels and masts, which contrasted with the white of the fighting tops, bridge structures, boats and ventilation cowls. As the second ship in the squadron – she accompanied the armoured cruiser *Asama*, flagship of Rear Admiral Ijuin Gōrō, from Japan – *Takasago* has two broad white rings bands on her funnels. (Hans Lengerer collection)

together with the much larger armoured cruisers, the most powerful warships of the IJN.

The Ten-Year Naval Expansion Programme 1896–1905

In July 1895, immediately after the Sino-Japanese War and the so-called Triple Intervention, Navy Minister Saigō Tsugumichi proposed an expansion programme to the cabinet. It was based upon the 1892 plans, the execution of which had been hampered by the current political situation in the Far East. However, following Japan's victory the situation had fundamentally changed, and the huge Chinese war indemnity provided the finance that had previously been lacking. Of the 111 warships proposed, 92 were approved by the cabinet, with funding to be divided into two phases.

The first *tranche* of the naval expansion programme, totalling 54 vessels, was approved at the 9th Diet session in December 1895 and the second, comprising 40 vessels – including an increase of two armoured cruisers in May 1896 – approved one year later. The budget for this ten-year program amounted to 213,100,964 yen, 84 sen, 1 rin – adjusted to 211,650,116 yen, 31 sen, 8 rin due to a

change in the exchange rate for foreign currency. In the event the total cost was 219,097,962 yen, 76 sen, 6 rin, of which 196,997,549 yen, 51 sen comprised the budget for shipbuilding and weapon production.

Three 2nd class cruisers of the *Yoshino* type were included in the first *tranche*, and the Navy Minister outlined to the cabinet the rationale for their inclusion as follows:

> … in order to decide on tactics the composition, course and speed of the enemy fleet must be known. In order to obtain this information a large number of high-speed cruisers with good manoeuvrability is essential; their purpose is to report the enemy's situation to the main force. However, the enemy will also deploy his cruisers for the same purpose, so we need to have cruisers with superior firepower to chase them out of sight and range …. [The] 2nd class cruisers [in the programme] are more powerful than those already in service with the Navy; they are fast and are armed with many QF guns … [They] are an improved *Yoshino* type ….

During the execution of this programme there were several changes, and in the event no fewer than 106

Table 1: **Building Data**

Building Data

	Builder	Laid down	Launched	Completed	Fate
Takasago	Armstrong	29 May 1896	17 May 1897	17 May 1898	Struck mine 12 Dec 1904 off Port Arthur; sank 13th; stricken 15 Jun 1906.
Kasagi	Cramp	13 Feb 1897	20 Jan 1898	24 Oct 1898	Grounded in Tsugaru Strait 20 Jul 1916; stricken 5 November.
Chitose	Union	1 May 1897	22 Jan 1898	1 Mar 1899	Sunk as target ship for naval guns and aerial bombs Saeki Bay 19 Jul 1931.

warships were built, of which 42 of the smaller ships – the largest were three 3rd class cruisers – were built in Japan, while 37 were ordered from Britain, eighteen from Germany, seven from France, and two from the USA. Of the three 2nd class cruisers, one was ordered from Britain and the other two from the USA. The orders placed in the United States were the first since the problems experienced by the Tokugawa Bakufu and the Meiji government with the first generation of warships ordered from the USA. The policy change was essentially a 'thankyou' for America's neutrality in the SJW; however, an additional factor was to undermine American opposition to Japanese immigration. At first, it was intended to order both ships from William Cramp & Sons at Philadelphia, but following discussions of rival tenders the order was split between William Cramp and the Union Iron Works of San Francisco. It would be the first time that a Japanese warship was built in a shipyard located on America's West Coast.

Sir Phillip Watts

The lead ship, *Takasago*, was designed by the chief designer of Armstrong, Elswick (UK), Sir Philip Watts, and was based on the earlier *Yoshino*. However, the preliminary design and the specifications for the two

A fine view of *Chitose* fitting out at the Union Iron Works, San Francisco. She and her sister *Kasagi* were the first ships ordered from American shipyards since the Meiji Restoration in 1867–68. The photo probably dates from early 1898 and shows the ram bow, the housing for the bow torpedo tube, and the scaffolding for erecting the sponsons. (NHHC, NH75196)

Table 2: **Characteristics and Weights**

Characteristics

	Takasago	Kasagi	Chitose
Length oa	118.16m (387ft 8in)	122.48m (401ft 10in)	120.40m (395ft)
Length pp	109.73m (350ft)	114.15m (374ft 6in)	114.93m (377ft)
Beam, max	14.78m (48ft 6in)	14.91m (48ft 11in)	14.99m (49ft 2in)
Beam, moulded	14.17m (46ft 6in)	14.85m (48ft 7in)	14.93m (49ft)
Mean draught:			
normal	5.56m (18ft 3in)	5.79m (19ft)	5.49m (18ft)
full load	6.24m (20ft 6in)	6.34m (20ft 10in)	6.04m (19ft 10in)
Displacement:			
normal	4,535 tons	5,416 tons	4,948 tons
full load	5,260 tons	6,066 tons	5,598 tons
L/B ratio	7.74	7.68	7.70
d/B ratio	0.392	0.390	0.368
D/d ratio	?	1.71	1.68
Block coefficient (CB)	0.518	0.545	0.518
Metacentric height	?	2.2m	1.9m
Propulsion machinery:			
engines	2 four-cylinder vertical triple expansion (VTE)	2 four-cylinder vertical triple expansion (VTE)	2 four-cylinder vertical triple expansion (VTE)
boilers	4 single, 4 double-ended cylindrical	12 single-ended cylindrical	12 single-ended cylindrical
speed (trials)	22.9kts with 12,990ihp	22.75kts with 13,492ihp	22.7kts with 12,500ihp
radius	4,000nm at 10 knots	4,000nm at 10 knots	4,000nm at 10 knots

Armament:	
main guns	2 – 20.3cm (8in) 45-cal Armstrong QF guns (2 x I)
secondary guns	10 – 12cm (4.7in) 40-cal Armstrong QF (10 x I)
ATB guns	12 – 7.6cm (12pdr) 40-cal Armstrong QF guns (12 x I)
	6 – 42mm (2½pdr) QF guns
torpedo tubes	5 a/w (1 bow, 4 side)
torpedoes	25 – 36cm (14in) Whitehead
Protection:	
deck	44mm (1¾in) crown, 114mm (4½in) / 89mm (3½in) / 44mm (1¾in) slopes
conning tower	114mm (4½in) walls
gunshields	114 (4½in) / 63mm (2½in)

Complement	380	405	405

Distribution of Weights

	Takasago	Kasagi	Chitose
Hull and fittings[1]	1,889t (41.6%)	2,523t (46.6%)	2,037t (41.2%)
Protection (including CT)[2]	526t (11.6%)	568t (10.5%)	602t (12.1%)
Machinery (incl feed/boiler water)	1,120t (24.7%)	1,330t (24.5%)	1,270t (25.7%)
Armament and ammunition[3]	393t (8.7%)	351t (6.5%)	380t (7.7%)
Coal (normal capacity)	300t (7.7%)	350t (6.5%)	350t (7.1%)
Equipment	257t (5.7%)	294t (5.4%)	309t (6.2%)
Normal displacement	4,535t (100%)	5,416t (100%)	4,948t (100%)

Source: Chief Naval Constructor of the contemporary IJN, Rear Admiral Sasō Sachū.

Notes:

[1] The difference of 490 tons in the weight of the hull and fittings of *Kasagi* and *Chitose* is difficult to explain. The British-built *Takasago* had the same theoretical fighting power on 881 tons less normal displacement than *Kasagi*, and 413 tons less than *Chitose*. The figures indicate that the hull scantlings were significantly strengthened in the two US-built ships, particularly in *Kasagi*.
[2] The different weights of the protective decks suggest considerable individual structural differences even though thicknesses, dimensions and arrangement are reported to have been the same.
[3] The weight of armament and ammunition is on the low side, and cannot have included the entire complement of ammunition for even peacetime service.

Editor's Note: The data supplied by the author is from Japanese-language sources and uses metric measurements. Dimensions, armour thicknesses and weapon designations would originally have been in imperial as the first ship was built at Armstrongs (UK) and the other two in US shipyards, and these have been used in the text. Metric measurements have been retained in the table, with the imperial equivalent in parentheses for dimensions, armament and protection.

ships that were to be built in the United States, *Kasagi* and *Chitose*, were drawn up by a Japanese design team in the Bureau of Military Affairs (*Gunmukyoku* – in existence from 20 March 1893 to 19 March 1900 and the immediate predecessor of the Navy Technical Department, *Kaigun kansei honbu*).

Sir Philip was invited to Japan to assist with the new programme of construction. During his stay, from the autumn of 1895 to the spring of 1896, he instructed the Japanese naval architects and conducted a study of the current state of shipbuilding in Japan. Naturally, he was also heavily involved in the specifications for *Kasagi* and *Chitose*. Although they were to be built in American shipyards, the structure and fittings were of the British type, and for the sake of uniformity both ships were armed, like *Takasago*, with Armstrong QF guns, which for *Kasagi* would be fitted at the Newcastle yard of Armstrong, Whitworth & Co, and for *Chitose* at the Yokosuka Navy Yard.

However, there were a number of differences compared to British practice:

– The top of the conning tower was secured to the sides instead of being removable, with horizontal slits provided for observation.

– No wood was used in the construction or fittings. With the exception of the planking of the upper deck and the men's mess tables everything, including the ceilings and partitions of the cabins, the walls of the officers' mess, the spokes and rims of the steering wheel, the treads of companion ladders and seating, was made of sheets of steel or other metal; even in the officers' bathrooms the enamelled baths and washstands were exclusively of metal.

– The torpedo bodies were stowed in cases made of steel wire netting.

– The arrangement of the bower anchors was reversed (as in *Takasago*), with two to port and a single anchor to starboard.

– Electric motors were employed for training and elevating the main guns, and also for the ammunition hoists.

– There was a marked absence of spare parts and stores.

– The artificers' workshop was exceptionally well equipped, with steam-operated lathes, and drilling and grinding machines.

Table 3: **Machinery**

	Takasago	**Kasagi**	**Chitose**
Boilers			
number & type	4 single-ended cylindrical 4 double-ended cylindrical	12 single-ended return type cylindrical	[as *Kasagi*]
heating surface	1,697.5m^2	1,794.5m^2	1,627,5m^2
grate surface	61.18m^2	66.44m^2	55.68m^2
Engines			
number & type	two four-cylinder, vertical triple expansion	[as *Takasago*]	[as *Takasago*]
cylinder diameter	1,016/1,524/1,676mm	1,079/1,568/1,727mm	[as *Takasago*]
length of stroke	838mm	838mm	914mm
shaft revolutions	165rpm	165rpm (161 actual)	165rpm (160.8 actual)
piston speed	276.6m/sec	276.6m/sec	281.63m/sec
pressure at engine	10.54 bar	10.54 bar	11.00 bar
pressure at boiler	10.99 bar	10.99 bar	11.00 bar
mean pressure LP cylinder	2.94 bar	2.99 bar	2.84 bar
diameter/pitch of propellers	4.20/5.03m	4.27/4.88m	3.96/5.33m
type of rudder	balanced	[as *Takasago*]	[as *Takasago*]
rudder area	14.42m^2	10.82m^2	11.64m^2
area abaft/in front of axis	10.37/4.05m^2	8.12/2.70m^2	8.41/3.24m^2
official trial results	22.9kts with 12,990ihp at 4,463 tons	22.75kts with 13,492ihp at 5,416 tons	22.7kts with 12,500ihp at 4,890 tons
coal, normal (full load)	300 tons (1,075t)	350 tons (1,000t)	350 tons (1,000t)
radius (knots- nautical miles)	4,000nm at 10 knots	[as *Takasago*]	[as *Takasago*]
Weights			
Weight of boilers	514 tons	524 tons	521.5 tons
Weight of boiler feedwater	152 tons (+9t in condenser)	197 tons (+9t in condenser)	214.5 tons (+9t in condenser)
Weight of engines	404 tons	597 tons	534 tons
Total weight of machinery	1,070 tons	1,318 tons	1,270 tons

Note: *Kasagi* had two vertical Worthington type, *Chitose* two vertical Dow type air pumps. Both ships had horseshoe-type shaft bearings rated at 18.7 bar (designed 14.74 bar) and 24.41 bar (designed 16.14 bar) respectively.

By Royal Navy standards, the large projecting sponsons for the open casemates, the proximity of the main 8in gun mountings to the stem and the stern, and the tight arrangement of the broadside guns were considered disadvantageous. Particular criticism was focused on the forecastle gun, which weighed more than 30 tons, and which combined with the three anchors and their cables to cause the ships to bury their bows in a head sea and to roll considerably. These characteristics were more marked in *Takasago* than in the larger American-built ships, and in the former vessel the fighting tops of both military masts had to be mounted unusually low to reduce topweight and improve stability. Following the RJW the fighting tops were removed, the main topmast was lengthened and a gaff mounted to improve W/T performance.

Machinery

The high-speed cruiser *Yoshino* was the first ship in the IJN to be fitted with four-cylinder vertical triple expansion (VTE) engines. These and all subsequent Japanese warships (with the exception of the battleships ordered from Britain in the 1890s) had two cylinders in the final low-pressure stage. The arrangement of the engines in all three ships was the same: (from aft) high pressure (HP), intermediate pressure (IP), then the two low-pressure (LP) cylinders.

The division of the large-diameter LP cylinder of the conventional three-cylinder engine into two smaller cylinders became necessary as horsepower increased. A four-cylinder engine avoided an excessive increase in the diameter of the LP cylinder; it also provided a good balance because of the superior linkage of the piston rods to the cranks via the connecting rods. The machinery for *Takasago* was supplied by Humphrys, Tennant & Co, who had also built the engines of *Yoshino*; that of the other ships by the shipbuilder (for engine data see Table 3). There were significant differences between designed and actual power developed by the engines – *Kaigun Kikan Shi* Vol 2, 776 claims only 11,000ihp for *Chitose* – but the contract speed was achieved even by the US-built ships, despite their greater displacement; the ihp developed per ton of machinery weight is recorded as 11.65, 10.97 and 9.43 for *Takasago*, *Kasagi* and *Chitose* respectively.

The increase in the steam pressure in the cylindrical

The two four-cylinder vertical triple expansion steam engines of *Chitose* in a shed at the Union Iron Works of San Francisco. (NHHC, NH75197)

boilers to 150psi (just over 10 bar) resulted in frequent problems that included major deformations of the furnaces and leakages from the tube ends in the back tube plates. The adoption of corrugated furnaces – *Takasago* had the Morison type to reinforce strength – was an improvement, as was the mounting of British-type ferrules. However, these modifications did not resolve the problems completely, and the cylindrical boilers were later replaced by modern water-tube types. In 1910 *Kasagi's* boilers were changed to the Miyabara large

watertube type – at that time the IJN's only locally-built model. Her sister *Chitose* followed only in 1924, but she received the Kampon (abbreviation of *Kansei honbu*) small watertube boiler which had replaced the Miyabara some years previously. The main engines remained unchanged from first to last.

Armament

The most striking feature of these ships was their heavy

A port broadside view of *Kasagi* shortly after completion by William Cramp & Sons, Philadelphia. The absence of an ensign indicates that the photo was taken prior to the ship's handover to the IJN. She is still lacking her guns, which would be fitted in the UK. (NHHC, NH75367)

Kasagi at Newcastle-upon-Tyne in March 1899 following the embarkation of her guns. The original photo was taken by Dr Oscar Parkes and presented to Fukui Shizuo in exchange for photos of Japanese warships. (NHHC, NH48200)

armament. The 8in 45-calibre Armstrong QF gun, which had a barrel length in excess of 30ft (9.14m), was unusually powerful for a ship of this size and was the first 8in gun to enter service with the IJN. The shell weighed more than twice as much as that of the 6in model which armed *Yoshino*, and the destructive power was correspondingly greater. In addition, the longer barrel (45 vs 40 calibres) made for greater penetration and an improved hitting probability due to the flatter trajectory. On the basis of the lessons of the SJW, the IJN rated the effect of the larger gun very highly and pushed strongly for a powerful armament for the new ships in relation to their displacement.

The Armstrong gun was on a centre pivot mounting. Both mountings were on the centreline: one on the forecastle, the other on the raised poop deck. Each of the guns was protected by a large, thick shield with plenty of working space for the gun crew. The front of the shield

was semicircular in plan and dimensions were: length 12ft 2in (5ft 3in before and 6ft 11in behind the trunnion axis) and 6ft 3in high. It was protected by Harveyised (*ie* cemented) steel plates 4½in (114mm) thick on the face, tapering to 2½in (63mm) at the sides.

The mounting was trained by an electric motor. In the event of failure of the electrical circuit there was manual back-up using a hand wheel, which was found to be easy and smooth to operate. The operation of the breech was manual, and was effected by a hand wheel between the breech and the trunnion axis. The arc of fire was 270 degrees, and it took less than 60 seconds to train the gun fully.

The weight of the gun itself was 17.62 tons and the mounting 11.3 tons, so the total weight of the revolving part, including the motors and gearing, was just over 30 tons. The maximum angle of depression was -5°, the maximum angle of elevation +15°, and muzzle velocity

Trans. Inst. Naval Architects, Vol. XLI., 1899.   *To Illustrate Sir Andrew Noble's Paper on the Rise and Progress of rifled naval Artillery.*   *Plate XXXIII.*

"H. I. J. M. S. TAKASAGO"

8 INCH 203 ᵐ/ₘ Q.F. GUN ON AUTOMATIC CENTRE PIVOT MOUNTING.

45 Calibre.

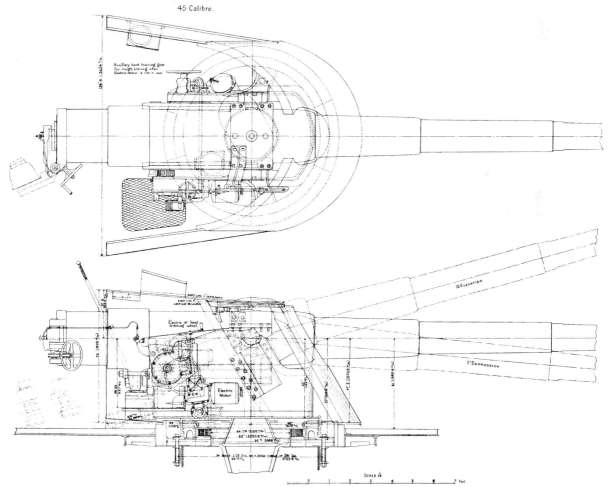

Side and plan view of the 8in 45-calibre QF gun mounting embarked in *Takasago*. The mounting was trained using an electric motor with manual back-up. Elevation was manual in *Takasago*, whereas the guns fitted in her two US-built half-sisters had a separate electric motor for elevation. Note that all measurements on the plan are imperial with the metric equivalent in parentheses, indicating that this Armstrong-designed/built gun was intended for export. (*Transactions of the Institute of Naval Architects*, Vol XLI, 1899)

was 2,740ft/sec (835m/sec) with a full charge. Maximum range was approximately 13,200 yards (12,100m).

The main gun of *Takasago* and the ammunition hoist were detailed and illustrated in Sir Andrew Noble's paper *The Rise and Progress of Rifled Naval Artillery* (*Transations of the Institute of Naval Architects*, 1899, 242 – see the accompanying drawing). Noble stated:

> … the elevating gear is worked entirely by hand, the trunnions being mounted on Mr Brankston's anti-friction arrangement, with knife edges supported on springs to relieve the shock when the gun is fired. So easily does this gear work that one man can elevate or depress the gun at the rate of 2° per second.

Noble also pointed out that the man at the sights could look over the top of the shield to have a good field of view, while his head was protected by a hood projecting from the roof of the shield.

In the US-built ships a smaller motor was employed for elevation, but auxiliary hand gear was retained in the event of the primary system being disabled.

The armour piercing (AP) shell weighed 250lbs (113.25kg) and the common shell 220lbs (99.66kg). Four aimed rounds could be fired in 64 seconds with a trained crew. This level of performance was attained only after improvements made in the American-built cruisers, which had an armoured ammunition hoist and a gun-metal 'tramway' arranged in the rear of each gun position. The circular mouth of the hoist, which led down to the magazines, projected slightly above the deck and was covered by a hemispherical solid steel cap. The projectiles and the powder charges, which were in metal cases for safety reasons, were raised from the magazine via endless chains over a roller at the top of the hoist and run out onto a waiting tray. From here the shells were conveyed to the breech by trolleys running on the small, semicircular tramway which enabled the gun to be loaded throughout its forward training arc (see drawing of *Chitose*). Tracks were provided on each side of the hoist so that the full and empty trolleys could pass one another. The use of the tramway and trolleys was necessary because of the weight of the shells, which were too heavy to be lifted by hand.

In *Takasago* 'the powder charge was brought up the centre and delivered at the side under cover of the shield'. The axial hoist for the powder supply is shown in the drawing published by *TINA* and was, in the words of Sir A Noble, 'so arranged that, when one charge is going up, the empty case is going down, thus effecting a great saving of time and labour, as the weight of the cases balance each other, and there is thus only the actual weight of the charge to lift'. In peacetime 100 rounds were carried for each gun, but this figure was doubled when the ship was on war service.

The ten 4.7in 40-cal Armstrong QF guns – the same model mounted in *Yoshino* – were evenly distributed on either side of the upper deck, and were protected by heavy shields 2½in (63mm) thick. The fore and after mountings were in open casemates that could be closed off by shutters, and could engage targets close to the ship's axis; training arcs were 130 degrees. The remaining guns were sited in the intervals between the low bulwark that ran along the sides of the ship between the forecastle and the poop deck, and could train through 100 degrees.

Each gun had an armoured ammunition hoist that worked on the same principle as those of the main guns: an endless chain powered by an electric motor. The hoists were directly behind the guns, and the top of the hoist was protected by a circular armoured cap. In peacetime 200 rounds per gun were stowed in the magazines – a figure that was likewise doubled when on war service.

Twelve 12pdr (7.6cm) 40-calibre Armstrong QF guns were arranged between the 4.7in guns amidships, with the fore and after pairs being sited atop the open case-

Bow view of *Kasagi* showing the sponsons projecting from the hull, the bow torpedo tube, the bridge – the wings of which extended across the whole beam – and the small wheel house above it. The pole masts each featured a crow's nest and a fighting top. The ship's hull is as yet unpainted and she is lacking her armament. The photo was probably taken during her machinery trials, which took place in July 1898 off Portsmouth, USA. (Hans Lengerer collection)

mates (*Takasago*) or in sponsons fore and aft (*Kasagi, Chitose*). For the supply of ammunition an electrically-operated hoist within an armoured tube was again employed. The hoist opened through a hatch into a small armour-protected compartment beneath the poop deck, and from here the fixed ammunition was supplied to the guns. Intended for defence against torpedo boats, these guns also had shields but of a much lighter type than those of the secondary guns. Three hundred rounds per gun were stowed in the magazines (600rpg when on war service), making for a total of 3,600 (7,200) rounds.

In addition, six light 2.5pdr (42mm) ATB guns of Japanese manufacture – they were built under licence from Hotchkiss – were mounted as follows: two in each of the fighting tops and two in the waist abaft the second funnel (see drawing of *Takasago*). These guns had shields of a similar configuration to those of the broadside 12pdr guns but smaller and lighter. Four hundred rounds per gun (800rpg in wartime) were provided.

In addition to the combat rounds, several types of exercise and saluting round were embarked. The total weight of ammunition (including the metal cases for the propellant charges) was 120 tons in peacetime, rising to 240 tons in wartime – an extraordinary figure for a ship of modest displacement.

The five torpedo tubes were manufactured by Armstrong and were all mounted above the waterline: one in the bow, the others on the broadside behind hinged doors fore and aft. Twenty-five 14in (36cm) Whitehead torpedoes (five per tube) were stowed in racks close to the tubes. In the American-built ships these racks were made of steel wire netting so that the rudders and propellers of the torpedo bodies were protected against accidental damage. The torpedo warheads were located separately in a magazine.

Four 24in (61cm) searchlights were mounted on rails and were distributed between the bridge and the steering position aft (see drawing of *Takasago*). The manufacturer is unknown, but is thought to have been Siemens.

Protection

The protective deck covered the ship's vitals. It was flat over the centre part of the hull and inclined at the sides, which were reinforced by thicker steel plates. The deck was sloped down towards the bow and the stern to form a carapace; the forward end of the deck supported the ram.

The flat central section was only just above the waterline at normal displacement: ½in (0.12m) in *Takasago*, ¼in (0.06m) in *Kasagi,* and ⅝in (0.16m) in *Chitose*. The slopes, which were inclined at 30 degrees to the horizontal, joined the hull some 5ft below the waterline. Precise figures recorded were: 5ft 3in (1.6m) in *Takasago*, 5ft 2in (1.58m) in *Kasagi* and 4ft 11in (1.49m) in *Chitose*.

The protective deck comprised two plates each of 7/8in (22mm) steel. It was reinforced on the upper part of the slopes, from the the forward end of the machinery spaces

Kasagi: Protection

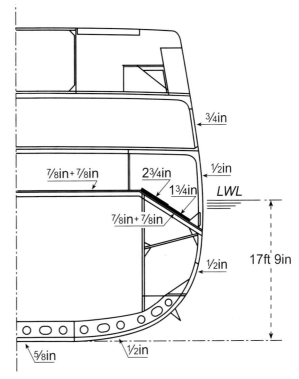

© John Jordan 2021

Midship half-section of the US-built *Kasagi* and *Chitose*. The flat of the protective deck was only just above the waterline at normal displacement. The deck comprised two layers of ⅞in steel reinforced by thicker armour plates on the slopes. (Drawn by John Jordan using material supplied by the author)

to about one-third of the after magazine, by plates 2¾in thick, giving a total thickness of 4½in (114mm), and on the centre part, from the middle of the forward magazine to the after end of the aft magazine, by plates 1¾in thick, for a total thickness of 3½in (89mm).

Above the protective deck only the gunshields, ammunition hoists (see above) and the conning tower were armoured. The latter had walls of 4½in (114mm) Harveyised steel.

Identification

Characteristics which distinguished *Takasago* from her American-built sisters were as follows:

– The spacing of the funnels was wider in *Kasagi* and *Chitose*, and the funnels were broader and flatter.
– *Takasago* had only a single large sponson on either side of the bridge structure plus a smaller one aft, whereas *Kasagi* and *Chitose* had two sponsons forward and two smaller ones aft, all below the forecastle and poop deck respectively.
– The fighting tops on the pole masts were positioned lower in *Takasago*.

– The ventilation cowls grouped around the funnels were more prominent in *Takasago* and were also differently arranged.

– The bridge structure and the after steering position had a different configuration.

Service History

Takasago

Takasago was designated No 3 Protected Cruiser in the Ten-Year Naval Expansion Programme and funded under the FY 1896 budget. Designed by Sir Philip Watts and built at Armstrong's Low Walker shipyard as the last protected cruiser ordered in Britain, she was the lone sister of the cruiser *Yoshino* but incorporated a number of modifications based on the lessons of the SJW. On the same principal dimensions, the armament was significantly increased by mounting two 8in (20.3cm) Armstrong 45-calibre QF guns in place of the four 6in (15.2cm) 40-calibre Armstrong QF guns of *Yoshino*. The number of 4.7in (12cm) Armstrong QF guns was increased from eight to ten, with twelve 12pdr (7.6cm) 40-calibre QF guns for ATB defence added. The protective deck was reinforced. The number of cylindrical boilers was reduced from twelve to eight, but the main engines were identical and developed almost the same

horsepower, so speed remained the same. The displacement was too small to mount such a heavy armament, and this resulted in excessive pitching and rolling in heavy seas. In addition, there were some defects in ammunition supply. *Takasago* was commissioned in 1898 but sank in December 1904 after striking a mine off Port Arthur, so her service in the IJN was brief – six years. Her half-sister *Yoshino* sank seven months before her on 15 May, following a collision. The battleships *Yashima* and *Hatsuse*, both designed by Watts, were also lost to mines on 15 May, and *Takasago* served for seven months as the only survivor of these four Armstrong-built ships.

1898: Delivered on 17 May, left the UK on the 25th and entered Yokosuka naval port on 14 August.

1900–01: Participated in the North China Incident ('Boxer Rebellion') and was deployed to Shanghai.

1902: Despatched to Britain to participate in the coronation fleet review of King Edward VII. She left Yokosuka on 7 April 1902 in company with the armoured cruiser *Asama*, flying the flag of Rear Admiral Ijuin Gōrō, and the destroyer *Asashio*, returning on 26 November. *Asama* had a single broad white band on the funnels, *Takasago* two. The review was to have taken place on 28 June at Spithead, but

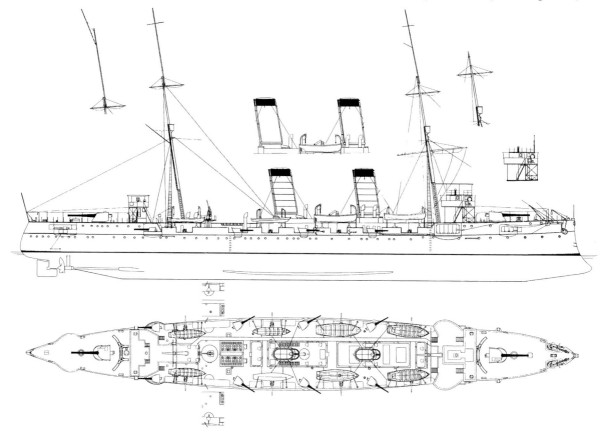

Profile and plan of *Chitose*, showing the ship as she was in 1919 after the fitting of a single 3in/8cm (actual calibre 7.6cm) HA gun on the centreline aft, and the removal of the fighting tops and the original six 2½pdr (42mm) QF guns. The insets show the masts and funnels at the time of her completion in 1898. (Waldemar Trojca)

A clear broadside view of *Kasagi* showing the raised forecastle and poop and the inclined masts and funnels typical of the class. *Kasagi* was handed over to the IJN on 24 October 1898, took part in the Fleet Review celebrating the USA's victory over Spain the following day, and left Philadelphia on 2 November, when this photo was taken. She then headed via New York and Plymouth for the Armstrong shipyard at Newcastle-upon-Tyne, where her armament was fitted. While at Newcastle she collided with a bridge on 30 November 1898, with some damage to both the bridge and the ship. (Hans Lengerer collection)

had to be postponed to 16 August due to the King's appendicitis. The Japanese ships arrived in Plymouth on 10 June after passing through the Suez Canal, and then proceeded to Spithead (Portsmouth) where, from 16 to 18 June, *Takasago* was open to visitors from the assembled warships. When the review was postponed the ships embarked on a visit to Belgium, returning to Spithead on 1 August. Following the review there were port visits to other countries in Europe (Portugal and Italy) and in Asia (Thailand). When they arrived back in Japan the ships had covered 24,718 nautical miles.

1904: During the Russo-Japanese War (RJW) *Takasago* was assigned to the 3rd Division of the 1st Fleet (*Chitose, Takasago, Kasagi, Yoshino*) under the command of Rear Admiral Dewa Shigetō. She captured the Russian steamer *Manchuria* (enrolled in the IJN as the *Kantō*) off Port Arthur on 9 February. She participated in the blockade of Port Arthur, escorted the blockade forces and took part in the Battle of the Yellow Sea on 10 August. Afterwards she was again engaged in the blockade, but at midnight on 12 December she struck a mine. The detonation took place under her port bow, and after 20 minutes *Takasago* was listing 25 degrees. By 0045 the list had increased to 30 degrees and at 0110 she capsized, disappearing within two/three minutes with the loss of 273 men. Boats from *Takasago* and the cruiser *Otowa*, which was operating close by, rescued 161 men, including the captain; the rescue operation was hindered by snowfall.

1905: Stricken from the register of Imperial warships on 15 June.

Kasagi

Kasagi was designated No 1 Protected Cruiser in the Ten-Year Naval Expansion Programme that followed the SJW and funded under FY 1896. She was designed as an improved *Takasago*, whose designer Sir Philip Watts came to Japan to assist the Japanese design team in drawing up the specifications. The dimensions of the hull were slightly larger and displacement increased in order to eliminate the defects of *Takasago*. The thickness of the protective deck and the type of engine and speed remained unchanged, but twelve cylindrical boilers were fitted. The armament was also as in *Takasago*, but the ship was completed without her guns, which were embarked in the UK. *Kasagi* was built by William Cramp & Sons of Philadelphia. She and her sister were the first warships ordered from the USA since 1862 and the first ordered by the Meiji government – only the tanker *Kamoi* was later ordered from the USA in order to trial the novel turbo-electric propulsion system.

1898–99: Delivered on 24 October 1898 and participated in the triumphant naval review that followed the Spanish-American War the following day. She left Philadelphia on 2 November for Newcastle-upon-Tyne via New York and Plymouth, where her armament was fitted at the Armstrong shipyard. After that she visited a number of French ports, arriving in Yokosuka on 16 May 1899.

1900: Assigned to the Standing (Permanent) Fleet in May and participated in the North China Incident until September, operating off the coasts of China and

Korea. She then saw action off the coast of Russia's Maritime Provinces.

1904–05: Just before the outbreak of the RJW, *Kasagi* was assigned to the 3rd Division of the First Fleet (see *Takasago* above). When war was declared she operated in the Port Arthur area in company with the 1st and 2nd Divisions (six battleships and six armoured cruisers respectively), and participated in the first attack on the Russian warships in the harbour, then several blockade operations and other actions. Following the loss of *Yoshino* on 15 May (collision with the armoured cruiser *Kasuga*), she operated with the armoured cruisers *Yakumo* (flag) and *Asama*, and the protected cruisers *Chitose* and *Takasago* at the Battle of the Yellow Sea on 10 August 1904. When *Takasago* was also lost on 13 December to a mine, the 3rd Division was reformed with *Kasagi* (flag), *Chitose*, *Otowa* and *Niitaka*. At the Battle of Tsushima in May 1905, *Kasagi* was holed at the waterline at 1510 on the 27th by an enemy shell. On fire and with one engine room flooded, her condition became critical. Admiral Dewa shifted his flag to *Chitose* and accompanied *Kasagi* to Aburatani Bay (near Tsunoshima), where she underwent emergency repairs. Casualties were ten men dead and wounded.

1910–11: The original cylindrical boilers were replaced by the Miyabara large watertube type. *Kasagi* was then assigned to the Training Fleet from 1 June 1910 to 1 April 1911, and embarked on a training cruise for the cadets of the 38th class from 16 October to 6 March in company with the armoured cruiser *Asama*, flying the flag of Rear Admiral Yashiro Rokurō. The cruise took in Hawaii and North and Central America.

1914–15: During the First World War *Kasagi* was assigned to the First Fleet, and participated in the Tsingtao operation from August to October. She escorted Army transports and searched for the Austrian merchant ship *Theresia* that escaped to Shanghai.

1916: On her way back to Yokosuka from Vladivostok, *Kasagi* ran aground in the Tsugaru Strait on 20 July. With her bottom heavily damaged she became a total constructive loss and was stricken on 5 November.

Chitose

Chitose was designated No 2 Protected Cruiser in the Ten-Year Naval Expansion Programme and funded under FY 1896. She was built at the Union Iron Works of San Francisco. She and her sister *Kasagi* were built to the same design, but there were numerous differences in construction. Difficulties were experienced in adapting US shipyard practices to British-type structure and fittings. There were also differences in the construction schedule between the two ships, and delivery was delayed

A port broadside view of *Chitose* shortly after her arrival in Japan. She was completed on 1 March 1899, delivered to the IJN and sailed on the 21st without her armament. The guns, which were imported from Armstrong Elswick, were fitted at Yokosuka Navy Yard. The photo may have been taken either at Shimuzu or Kobe. Note that *Chitose* had only a single chrysanthemum emblem one at the bow, whereas her sister *Kasagi* had the emblem on either side. (NHHC, NH74388)

Kasagi at anchor in the port of Kobe from 13 to 16 June 1899 before entering Yokosuka. The open casemates had sliding shutters to protect the guns from the elements. The sponsons for the 4.7in and 12pdr guns fore and aft were more prominent in the two US-built ships than in the Armstrong-built *Takasago*. (Hans Lengerer collection)

by about four months even though both hulls were launched at about the same time. *Chitose* was armed at Yokosuka NY with the same guns mounted in *Takasago* and *Kasagi*.

1899: Left San Francisco on 21 March and entered Yokosuka naval port on 20 April. *Chitose* then embarked the guns imported from Armstrongs, and was assigned to the Standing (Permanent) 1st Fleet on 31 October.

1900: [As *Kasagi*]

1903: Assigned, together with *Yoshino*, to the Standing Fleet commanded by Rear Admiral Ijuin Gōrō.

1904–05: Shortly before the outbreak of the RJW she was assigned to the 3rd Division of the First Fleet (see *Tasakago* above) as the flagship of Rear Admiral Dewa Shigetō, participating in the same operations as *Kasagi*. She was damaged and suffered casualties in the Battle of the Yellow Sea on 10 August 1904. During the battle the Russian cruiser *Novik* escaped to the North, but was discovered off the island of Sakhalin on the 20th by the cruiser *Tsushima*. Both ships were damaged, but on the 21st *Chitose* encountered *Novik* and drove the heavily damaged cruiser ashore off Korsakowa port, where *Novik* was captured (July 1905 – she was later enrolled in the IJN as *Suzuya*). At the Battle of Tsushima *Chitose* suffered light damage: one of her main guns was put out of action; casualties were six men dead and wounded.

1907: The tricentenary of European immigration to Jamestown in Virginia (USA) was celebrated with a naval review. The IJN was represented by *Chitose* and the first major warship of Japanese construction, the 1st class cruiser (later 'battle cruiser') *Tsukuba*. An additional aim of the cruise was to support Japanese immigrants in the USA, and it was for this reason that the US-built *Chitose* was added as companion to the flagship. The ships left Yokosuka on 21 February under the command of Vice Admiral Ijuin Gōrō, the C-in-C of the 2nd Fleet, returning nine months later on 16 November. At that time the Panama Canal did not yet exist, so the ships had to pass through the Suez Canal and the Straits of Gibraltar during their passage to the East Coast. They entered Hampton Roads on 6 May and were welcomed by the US Atlantic Fleet – this was the first visit of Japanese warships to the USA since the Battle of Tsushima, and the rising sea power in the Far East attracted much public attention. The review took place on 13 May. The ships left New York on 19 May and entered Sheerness (UK) on 2 June. After embarking weapons and ammunition they sailed on the 19th and anchored at Kiel from the 22nd to the 28th to participate in Kiel Week (*Kieler Woche*). They then visited Vlissingen (Netherlands) and Ostende

Kasagi at Kobe during the latter half of 1900 or early in 1901. Sails were no longer used for cruising to save coal, and their deployment in this photo was probably for training purposes. At right in the background is a ship of the *Empress* class of the Canadian Pacific Steamship Ltd, Vancouver. Note the prominent shuttered casemates forward. (NHHC, NH74390)

(Belgium). and entered Portsmouth on 12 July, followed by Plymouth. There were also port visits to Portugal, Spain, Italy, and Yugoslavia. The European leg of the cruise ended in mid-September and both ships returned home. During the cruise there were port visits to ten countries in Europe and Asia, and 30,000 nautical miles were covered. Vice Admiral Ijuin had met the US President, the King of Great Britain, the German Emperor, and the Kings of Spain and Portugal – a remarkable diplomatic result.

1914–15: *Chitose* participated in operations against Tsingtao as part of the 2nd Fleet, and subsequently operated off the West Coast of America in company with the armoured cruiser *Tokiwa*. When the armoured cruiser *Asama* ran aground when entering San Bartolomeo Bay (Mexico) on 31 Jan 1915, *Chitose* was despatched to support the salvage operation. *Asama* was finally refloated on 8 May and towed to the distant Canadian port of Esquimalt by the *Kantō Maru*, where she was docked and repaired sufficiently to enable her to steam under her own power. She sailed on 23 August for Yokosuka, escorted by *Kantō Maru* and *Chitose*, arriving via Hawaii on 18 December.

1916: *Chitose* kept a watch on Vladivostok and was again despatched to the US West Coast in January. She returned to Yokosuka on 8 April. Her base port was changed to Kure, where she anchored until 1 May. She then embarked engineer cadets for a training cruise.

1917: On 13 March *Chitose* entered Dairen (Dalny) and sailed for Hong Kong and Bako (Pescadores). There were reports that German armed merchant cruisers were operating in Australian waters, and *Chitose* was despatched together with the ships of the 4th Division to guard British East India.

1918: Operated in the South China Sea and off Singapore.

1921: Classified as 2nd class coast defence ship on 1 September.

1924: The cylindrical boilers were replaced by the Kampon small watertube type, but *Chitose* retained her original main engines.

1928: Stricken on 1 April and became No 1 decommissioned ship on 6 July.

1931: Sunk as a target ship for naval guns and aerial bombs at Saeki Bay on 19 July.

THE ITALIAN NAVY AND THE BATTLESHIP IN THE 1930s:

THEORY AND PRACTICE

Michele Cosentino looks at the studies for battleships of moderate displacement undertaken by the *Regia Marina* during the early 1930s.

The long process of modernisation and upgrading of the Royal Italian Navy (*Regia Marina*) after the end of the First World War was marked by the construction of several classes of major warship, culminating in the design and construction of the battleships of the *Littorio* class, which were widely employed during the Second World War.

Until the beginning of the 1930s this process was influenced by two principal political-diplomatic factors, the first being Italy's accession to the Washington Treaty for the limitation of naval armaments signed in February 1922 by the five great naval powers: Great Britain, the United States of America, Japan, France and Italy. The second was the intense preparatory activities undertaken for the participation in similar and subsequent negotiations concerning the limitation of naval armaments.

The keystone of Italian naval policy during this period was Italy's aspiration to parity with France. This dictated foreign policy, which was focused on consolidating national interests in the context of the geopolitical scenarios that emerged from the First World War. However, these ambitions were overshadowed by the precarious situation of Italian finances in an era that was difficult for all Europe.

The design path that led to the *Littorio* class included a number of feasibility studies for battleships of around 25,000 tons, and British proposals for reductions in displacement and gun calibre were to provide the impetus for a further study, dating from the mid-1930s, for a battleship with a displacement of 26,500 tons.

The Washington Treaty and the Modernisation of the Italian Fleet

According to plans drawn up prior to the First World War, by the 1920s the Italian Navy was to have completed ten new battleships, including the 381mm-gun *Caracciolo*s, which were duly laid down in 1914–15, and a comparatively small number of minor warships. However, Italy's entry into the war forced her to abandon these ambitious plans: only six battleships were completed (*Dante Alighieri, Giulio Cesare, Conte di Cavour, Leonardo da Vinci, Andrea Doria* and *Caio Duilio*), while priority was given to building warships

better suited to naval operations in the Adriatic: destroyers and torpedo boats.

Six battleships and armoured cruisers were lost during the Great War, all but one of which were nonetheless obsolescent. After the end of the conflict only one of the new battleships, *Francesco Caracciolo*, was launched (12 May 1920). She was to have been the lead ship of a class of four: construction of *Cristoforo Colombo, Marcantonio Colonna* and *Francesco Morosini* had been suspended shortly after their keels were laid in 1915. On a displacement of 34,000 tonnes they were to be armed with eight 381mm (15in) 40-calibre guns and protected by a 300mm (12in) armoured belt; speed was to be an impressive 28 knots. The design anticipated the concept of the fast battleship: in effect, the *Caracciolo*s combined the armament and protection of battleships with the high speed of battlecruisers.

However, while the Italian military authorities were focused on learning lessons from the First World War, the political authorities were dealing with its grave financial and social consequences. In late 1919 Senator Carlo Schanzer, Italian Minister of Finances and future head of the Italian delegation at the Washington conference, presented a report to Parliament on the Navy budget for July 1920–June 1921.[1] In his discussion of the status of the Italian fleet, Schanzer highlighted the uncertain fate of the battleship *Caracciolo* and outlined the decisions already undertaken by the *Marine Nationale* and the Royal Navy. The French had decided against the completion of the five battleships of the *Normandie* class, while the RN had decommissioned its oldest and least useful warships. Taking into account the status of the major combatants then in commission or under construction by the principal maritime powers, Schanzer affirmed that:

> ... we must therefore, without increasing the size of the fleet, limit ourselves to increasing the number of torpedo boats, hasten the construction of scouts already in the shipyards, replace as soon as possible the four ships of the *Vittorio Emanuele* class,[2] which, as mentioned, represent only a semblance of firepower ... and adequate speed.

The only progress in new Italian shipbuilding was in minor combatants; financial difficulties prevented the replacement of larger warships, thereby postponing the construction of new battleships for better times. *Caracciolo*'s hull would remain incomplete and the programme was eventually cancelled.

The Washington Treaty established a fixed maritime hierarchy among the five major naval powers, allocating to each of them a displacement tonnage cap for battleships and aircraft carriers. France and Italy were each permitted a total tonnage of 175,000 tons 'standard' (177,800 metric tons) for battleships. This was a success for Rome, whose aim at the conference was to secure at least an 8:10 ratio with Paris. Furthermore, the maximum displacement for a replacement battleship under the Treaty was 35,000 tons standard (35,560 metric tonnes), while large-calibre guns could not exceed 16in (406mm).

From this point on parity with France, especially in naval matters, became the central element of Italy's military and naval policy until the Second World War. Italy's position was informed by two additional factors: the ten-year 'battleship holiday' decreed by the Washington Treaty, and the avowed intention of the signatory nations to continue along a path of arms control, if not disarmament, that would involve further international conferences, some of which took place under the aegis of the League of Nations. Consequently, Italian shipbuilding policy in the years after Washington was defined in accordance with a strict adherence to the Treaty. It was also heavily constrained by a military budget that, quite apart from naval expenditure, had to deal with the modernisation of the Italian Army and the requirements of the newly-formed *Regia Aeronautica*. As for naval

The battleship *Dante Alighieri*, the first Italian dreadnought, entering Mar Piccolo, Taranto, in 1918. (INHO)

doctrine, progress and developments in the underwater and naval air domains posed an increasing threat to the deployment of large, costly battleships in modern maritime warfare.

During the early 1920s, the Italian Navy therefore decided to limit its ambitions to the completion of the minor vessels planned during the Great War. The lack of financial resources forced the temporary suspension of the battleship replacement programme, and the limited funding available was used to begin the construction of the first major warships of postwar design, the cruisers *Trento* and *Trieste*, laid down in 1925. They would later be classified as 'heavy cruisers' but were characterised by an imbalance between firepower and speed on the one hand, and protection on the other. During the same period, in order to rationalise the management of the fleet, the *Regia Marina* decided to decommission all of its older battleships (*Dante Alighieri* and the four ships of the *Vittorio Emanuele* class), while the four more recent dreadnoughts of the *Cavour* and *Doria* classes were temporarily placed in reserve and used in training roles; *Leonardo da Vinci*, which had been salvaged after capsizing following a magazine explosion in 1916, was scrapped. These decisions drove the Italian Navy to base its blue-water component mainly on 'treaty' cruisers and led to the construction, under the five-year naval programme drawn up in 1928, of the four units of the *Zara* class (*Zara*, *Pola*, *Fiume* and *Gorizia*). Their design was more balanced than that of *Trento* and *Trieste*, with much thicker protection, but it was decided at the same time to complete a second three-ship cruiser division with an improved *Trento*, the fast, lightly-armoured *Bolzano*.

The International Conferences and the Barberis Study

Within the *Regia Marina*, discussions on new battleships resumed at the end of the 1920s. The 'battleship holiday' decreed by the Washington Treaty was due to expire, and a new multi-year shipbuilding programme was required. In addition to maintaining parity with France,[3] this programme would allow the fleet to be modernised in a systematic and economically sustainable way. In addition to the *Zara*s, the 1928 naval programme also included the construction of three battleships. The preliminary concept embraced two alternative design configurations, with size and displacement driven by the quantitative limitations enshrined in the Washington Treaty.[4] The first configuration was based on a ship of 23,000 tons standard displacement (for three ships of 69,000 tons), armed with six 381mm guns in three twin turrets and with a speed of 28 knots; the second called for a ship of 35,000 tons standard (two ships of 70,000 tons), with six 406mm guns and a speed of 29–30 knots. In both cases, protection was to be proportionate to displacement and armament, but this was very difficult to achieve in the first configuration due to the size limit.

Two conferences held in 1924 and 1927, in Rome and Geneva respectively, which aimed to extend the agreements reached in Washington to other categories of

The pre-dreadnought *Regina Elena*, seen here at full speed in 1907, was one of the older Italian battleships decommissioned in 1927. (Bonfiglietti Collection)

The heavy cruiser *Trieste*. She and her sister *Trento* were the first Italian major surface combatants built after the First World War. They influenced some of the fast battleship designs sketched by Barberis. (INHO)

warship, ended in failure. France declined to accept the proposed quantitative limitations on the newly-agreed categories of 'cruisers', 'destroyers' and 'submarines' at a conference held in London in early 1930, and the Italian delegation followed the French lead in withdrawing from discussions on this part of the treaty, leading to a British proposal to chair further negotia-

tions between Italy and France on naval arms limitation. Hopes of a subsequent agreement between Rome and Paris were encouraged by a subtle improvement in relations between the two nations.

Meanwhile, Germany was back on the European naval scene. In February 1929 the 'armoured ship' *Deutschland* was laid down, armed with six 280mm guns and the first

From right to left, the cruisers *Fiume*, *Zara*, *Pola* and *Gorizia*, moored at Naples in 1938. Their design was a more balanced development of the *Trento*s, with reduced speed but heavier protection. (INHO)

major German vessel built within the constraints of the Versailles Treaty. In response, the French Navy first planned a class of 23,330-ton battleships armed with eight 305mm guns and a speed of 30 knots. After a series of heated parliamentary debates, they finally decided on a larger, more powerful ship, *Dunkerque*, which had a standard displacement of 26,500 tons, eight 330mm guns, a speed of almost 30 knots and protection sufficient to sustain an engagement with *Deutschland* and cope with foreseeable air and underwater threats.

The decision on *Dunkerque*'s displacement was influenced by a British proposal, formulated prior to the London naval conference, to limit the displacement of newly-built battleships to 25,000 tons. During the long and arduous preparatory discussions for the international disarmament conference scheduled for Geneva by early 1932, the British government firmed up this proposal, which was further modified with an increase to 26,000 tons and a main armament to match.

The British proposal and its implications for potential new shipbuilding programmes for Italian battleships were carefully assessed by the *Regia Marina*. A vigorous exchange of letters took place between the Treaties Office (a department of the Minister's Cabinet) and the Operations Office (a department of the Naval Staff), which was supported by the Technical Departments of the Italian Navy.

In the light of the French decision, a memorandum of the Operations Office on displacement and armament limits stated: '... When we define the characteristics of our future battleships we cannot ignore the types of warship built by our possible adversary ....'[5] Information from France on *Dunkerque* was accurate regarding her displacement, while the main armament calibre was assumed to be 340mm (as in the *Bretagne* and *Normandie* classes). It was also expected that the French Navy would build four 26,000-ton ships, the total tonnage of 105,000 being equivalent to three ships of the maximum 35,000 tons permitted under Washington.

The memo went on to say that Italy no longer needed to take full account of the Washington Treaty constraints, because '... there is very little chance of it being renewed ...', demonstrating some scepticism within the *Regia Marina* regarding the future of international naval arms limitations. Therefore, in order to counter the new French ships: '... it would certainly be better to exceed 26,000 tons to build a battleship well protected against artillery and underwater attack, and able to steam at 28–30 knots'.

The memorandum closed by stating that if France actually built a 26,000 tons battleship it would be desirable, during the negotiations in Geneva, to propose a displacement of about 28–30,000 tons and a maximum gun calibre of 381mm. If, on the other hand, the French programme did not materialise, it would be '... desirable [from an Italian point of view] to support the lower proposal [28,000 tons] but not the abolition of battleships, because they alone can fight ... only they are useful for naval warfare'.

The Treaties Office replied to the Operations Office,[6] challenging on the one hand the assessments regarding the legal and material validity of the Washington Treaty and, on the other, supporting the construction of new battleships because '... a Mediterranean competition would lead to an equal starting point for both powers, which is advantageous for us'. The document closed with two proposals. The first was to limit the displacement of each new Italian battleship to a sub-multiple of the maximum tonnage granted to Italy at Washington (175,000 tons). The second suggested the adoption of a displacement in a range with two extremes (19,000 and 35,000 tons), so as to build a battleship suitably protected and capable of engaging similar French vessels in combat.

During this exchange of letters, the then-Chief of Staff of the Italian Navy, Vice Admiral Gino Ducci, entrusted General Luigi Barberis, Naval Engineering Corps, with a study of the displacement limitations for new battleships.[7] In order to measure the military value of a warship, and assuming that this increased with displacement, Barberis at first examined several British, French and German designs. He then began a pre-feasibility design phase based on several configurations of

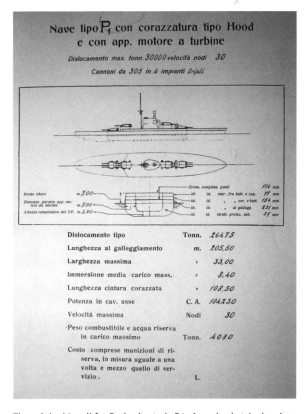

The original 'card' for Barberis study P1. A crude sketch showing the general configuration and the layout of the main armament was accompanied by a midship section illustrating the protection scheme. Other data such as dimensions, the length of the armoured citadel, horsepower and speed were recorded using hand-written entries in a standardised table beneath the sketch. (INHO)

warships having in common a '*Hood*-type' protection system and steam turbines.

Barberis elaborated three groups of design sketches, here referred to as 'cards', and each related to different displacement ranges.[8] The first group of cards, numbered from A1 to E5, were for a ship with a maximum full load displacement of 14,000 tonnes, a length (wl) varying from 147m to 205m, and a main armament of 203mm or 305mm guns in twin or triple turrets. Speed was between 28 to 36 knots. The full load displacement was calculated starting from a minimum value corresponding to specific linear dimensions, and increasing these to correspond to the increase in calibre of the main guns.

The second group comprised cards numbered from F1 to M3, and related to units with a maximum full load displacement of 20,000 tonnes, length between 169m and 228m, and an armament comprising six 305mm (12in) guns in two triple turrets or eight guns of the same calibre in four twin turrets. Speed was as in the first group.

The third group comprised the cards numbered from N1 to S4 – the letter 'O' being omitted to avoid confusion. This group is certainly the most important because the ensuing preliminary designs revolved around a displacement close to the 26,000 tons standard discussed by the Italian Naval Staff. In the N1-N8 cards, Barberis worked to a displacement of 27,066 tons, a waterline length of 190m, a 35.8m maximum beam, and a 8.56m draught. The common elements of the 'N' series of designs were turbine machinery to deliver 85,680shp for a maximum speed of 28 knots, and 3,525 tonnes of oil fuel and boiler feed water. The variants, which had a full load displacement of about 30,000 tonnes, differed in the thickness of their protection and their main armament layout, the latter varying from 305mm (12in) in triple turrets to 406mm (16in) guns in twin turrets.

The S1–4 group of cards, two of which are reproduced here, featured a full load displacement of 30,000 tons and a maximum – and arguably excessive – speed of 36 knots. Waterline length was 257.5m, while maximum beam was 25.9m. S4 had a main armament that comprised two 406mm triple turrets, and featured an unusually long central deckhouse with funnels at either end. The maximum speed of 36 knots required a huge propulsion system, able to develop not less than 212,000shp.[9]

An interesting feature of the Barberis study is that

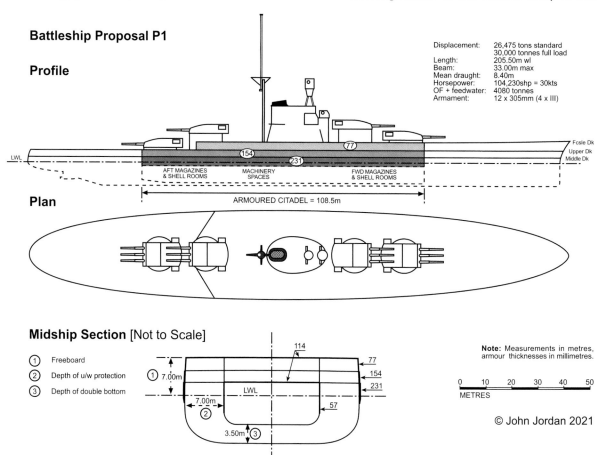

Battleship Proposal P1

Profile

Displacement:	26,475 tons standard
	30,000 tonnes full load
Length:	205.50m wl
Beam:	33.00m max
Mean draught:	8.40m
Horsepower:	104,230shp = 30kts
OF + feedwater:	4080 tonnes
Armament:	12 x 305mm (4 x III)

AFT MAGAZINES & SHELL ROOMS — MACHINERY SPACES — FWD MAGAZINES & SHELL ROOMS

ARMOURED CITADEL = 108.5m

Plan

Midship Section [Not to Scale]

① Freeboard
② Depth of u/w protection
③ Depth of double bottom

Note: Measurements in metres, armour thicknesses in millimetres.

0 10 20 30 40 50
METRES

© John Jordan 2021

A reworking of card P1 of the Barberis study: a sketch of a fast battleship displacing 26,500 tons standard. The main armament comprises twelve 305mm (12in) guns in four triple turrets, two forward and two aft. Maximum speed was to be 30 knots, to be achieved with 105,000shp. (Redrawn by John Jordan using Card P1)

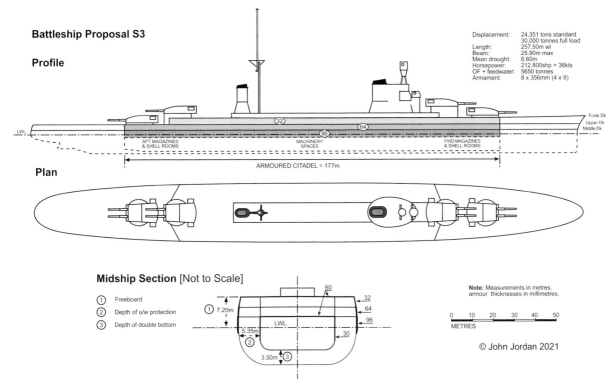

Battleship Proposal S3

Profile

Displacement:	24,351 tons standard
	30,000 tonnes full load
Length:	257.50m wl
Beam:	25.90m max
Mean draught:	8.60m
Horsepower:	212,800shp = 36kts
OF + feedwater:	5650 tonnes
Armament:	8 x 356mm (4 x II)

Plan

ARMOURED CITADEL = 177m

Midship Section [Not to Scale]

① Freeboard
② Depth of u/w protection
③ Depth of double bottom

Note: Measurements in metres, armour thicknesses in millimetres.

© John Jordan 2021

A reworking of card S3, for a battleship with a waterline length of just under 258m and eight 356mm (14in) guns in four twin turrets. A high length/beam ratio (10:1) plus an extraordinary 213,000shp would have been required to achieve the designed 36 knots. This, combined with the comparative light protection, would arguably have placed these ships in the 'battlecruiser' category. (Redrawn by John Jordan using Card S3)

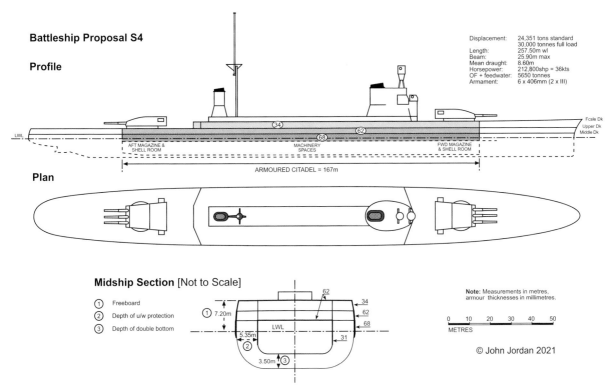

Battleship Proposal S4

Profile

Displacement:	24,351 tons standard
	30,000 tonnes full load
Length:	257.50m wl
Beam:	25.90m max
Mean draught:	8.60m
Horsepower:	212,800shp = 36kts
OF + feedwater:	5650 tonnes
Armament:	6 x 406mm (2 x III)

Plan

ARMOURED CITADEL = 167m

Midship Section [Not to Scale]

① Freeboard
② Depth of u/w protection
③ Depth of double bottom

Note: Measurements in metres, armour thicknesses in millimetres.

© John Jordan 2021

In card S4, the main armament comprises two 406mm (16in) triple turrets, a calibre not generally favoured by the *Regia Marina*. The long central deckhouse could have been used for a hangar and catapults. (Redrawn by John Jordan using Card S4)

The battleships *Cavour* and *Cesare* moored in Genoa during the late 1930s. Built during the Great War, they were modernised from 1933 to 1937. (Giorgio Alfano collection)

381mm (15in) guns were not considered for the main armament, although this calibre was discussed in meetings of the Naval Staff. Instead, a 356mm (14in) calibre was considered, possibly in response to the 330mm installed in the *Dunkerque*s.[10] It is also noteworthy that, apart from the gun calibre, the proposed layouts for the main armament included both twin and triple turrets. The most unusual factor of the Barberis study is protection: apart from the graduated thickness of the side protection – a feature of battleships designed before Jutland – the cards reveal a sort of double hull for all design sketches. The inner hull would house all vital systems and was separated from the outer hull by a 5-metre cofferdam. There was also a 3.5m-high triple bottom.

In his conclusions, Barberis listed the advantages and disadvantages of a large displacement, which he considered to be more efficient in terms of the 'military value' of a warship and better suited '... to ensure effective horizontal and underwater protection'. Furthermore, Barberis assessed that Italy had the '... industrial capacity to build even very large battleships'. As for disadvantages, a large displacement would mean, due to the quantitative limitations established by the Washington Treaty, the construction of fewer vessels, thereby hindering the development of a battle fleet of suitable size. Additionally, a large displacement would result in less flexible naval planning and compel the *Regia Marina* to devote large sums to '... equip naval bases'. Vice Admiral Ducci agreed with Barberis, and decided that it was convenient for Italy to accept an upper limit of 25,000 tons for future battleships. Indeed, if a future international agreement led to further limitation, Italy should not go below 25,000 tons, so as to have '... at least two divisions of battleships, each of two

or three units, plus one or two reserve units'.[11] For example, if 175,000 tons was confirmed for Italy, the *Regia Marina* could build seven 25,000-ton or six 29,190-ton battleships. If a new treaty reduced this figure to 125,000 tons, there was sufficient flexibility for five battleships each of 25,000 tons.

The conclusions of Vice Admiral Ducci were submitted and approved by the then-Navy Minister, Vice Admiral Giuseppe Sirianni. During the 1932 conference at Geneva, France and Japan supported the British proposal to reduce the maximum displacement and gun calibre of battleships, a position opposed by the United States. In this scenario, the Italian delegation at the Conference asked Sirianni for '... a new assessment, which took into account future political developments ...', as it was thought possible that Britain would probably postpone this issue to the conference planned for 1935.[12]

However, the 1932 Geneva Conference likewise ended in failure. In this phase of uncertainty in international politics, in 1933 the Italian Navy decided to respond to the construction of *Dunkerque* with the reconstruction of the two elderly dreadnoughts of the *Cavour* class, in order to have a minimum number of battleships with overall characteristics that were sufficiently balanced. However, this was a temporary solution to the problem of fleet renewal, because in the meantime the political mood favoured a dialogue between Rome and Paris, precisely focused on naval parity and begun on the sidelines of the Geneva talks. France proposed an agreement, binding until the end of 1936, that set at 26,500 tons the standard displacement of new battleships and included other limitations for light surface ships and submarines. Paris would cancel the construction of its battleships if Rome limited itself to building only a single ship, within a scheme potentially acceptable to both parties because it

Close-up of the main tower of *Cavour* (Genoa 1938), with the bridge tower, the main and secondary fire control directors and the two forward 320mm turrets prominent. (INHO)

did not make explicit the number of vessels allocated to each nation.

The proposal was favourably received by Italy and developed in discussions with France in such depth that a final agreement was drawn up in December 1933. However, the text presented by France for signature was different from that agreed by the naval delegates. It stated that Italy and France could each build one 26,500-ton battleship in addition to *Dunkerque*, which had already been laid down. Such a scheme was unacceptable to the Italian side because it would have sanctioned a disparity of two to one in favour of France, and this questionable behaviour would result in the failure of the negotiations. Its consequences could have been mitigated if, in the meantime (early 1934), Paris had not decided, in response to the latest reports from Germany, to build a second *Dunkerque*, later laid down as *Strasbourg*.

In Italy the French decision, together with other disturbances in the European political-military balance, paved the way for the formalisation of the design of two battleships of the *Littorio* class, which followed a heated exchange of views between the Ministry of the Navy and that of Foreign Affairs.[13] In this dialogue, a key role was played by Vice Admiral Domenico Cavagnari, who in November 1933 had been appointed as Under-Secretary of the *Regia Marina*. In June 1934, he would become Chief of Naval Staff, thereby combining political and operational functions in a single office.

The two new Italian battleships, *Littorio* and *Vittorio Veneto*, were laid down in November 1934. It had been agreed at the 1930 conference that a second naval arms limitation conference would be held in London in late

1935 to review the current Washington Treaty provisions, and it was known that the British would continue to push for reductions in the displacement and main armament of future battleships.

Aerial view of the battleship *Vittorio Veneto* steaming at speed in the Mediterranean. The red and white diagonal recognition bands on the forecastle were painted after Italy entered the Second World War. (INHO)

Studies for a Battleship of 'Moderate Displacement'

In the light of the new British proposals for the conference, the Regia Marina launched a preliminary study for a battleship defined as of 'moderate displacement' (Italian: *medio dislocamento*). The term translated into a standard displacement of 26,500 tons and a main armament of 305mm or 320mm guns.[14] Design work was mainly carried out by the Ship Design Committee (Italian acronym: *Maricominav*), at that time chaired by the Inspector General, Naval Engineering Corps, Umberto Pugliese, who was responsible for the design for the two battleships of the *Littorio* class, and also involved the high-ranking flag officers of the *Regia Marina*.

Maricominav commenced its work using some general indicators needed to define the characteristics of the 26,500-ton battleship, and then elaborated a number of possible configurations. General Pugliese illustrated the first results of this phase using nine coloured plates, each comprising a profile and plan.[15] Besides noting gun calibre, each plate showed a different possible configuration of the main armament, with twin, triple and quadruple turrets. A calibre between 130mm (5.1in) and 140mm (5.5in) was considered for the secondary battery, while air defence would be provided by

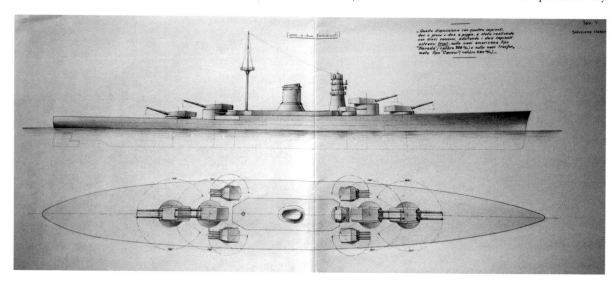

Plate 1 from the *Maricominav* series of sketches. This was defined as the 'standard solution' and claims to be inspired by the turret layout of the US *Nevada* class (with 356mm guns) and the *Cavour* class battleships (320mm guns), although it is noted that both these types had triple turrets in 'A' and 'Y' positions for a total of ten main guns. The notes also state that this solution could have one or two funnels. (INHO)

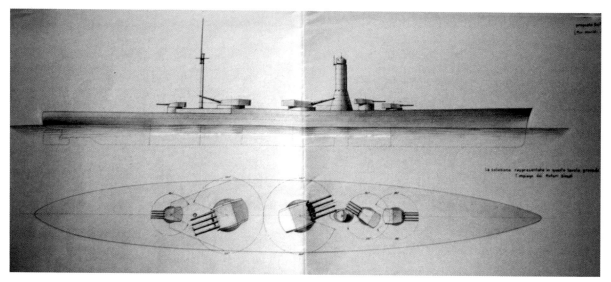

Plate 4, illustrating a layout proposed by Vice Admiral Vincenzo de Feo. There are two quadruple turrets on the centreline amidships, with the secondary turrets fore and aft. This arrangement had the advantage of placing the main magazines in the broadest part of the hull, but was otherwise problematic. The machinery was to be all-diesel with underwater exhausts, thereby maximising the firing arcs of the main turrets. (INHO)

100mm HA guns – the same calibre that currently equipped cruisers and destroyers.

As for machinery, the 26,500-ton battleship was to be able to achieve 30 knots, a speed matching that of *Dunkerque* and thus requiring steam turbines and boilers. If a large cruising radius was required, Pugliese was prepared to consider the adoption of a hybrid system that combined steam turbines with high-power diesel engines. However, he was sceptical about the outcome of the experiments then underway at Fiat to develop the latter.

Almost all the different configurations proposed by Maricominav had either one or two funnels – only one was shown in the drawings – whereas in the sketches made by Barberis there was a fairly precise distinction between solutions with one or with two funnels, the latter being adopted if high speed was required. In his documents, Pugliese did not provide precise information on the power needed to achieve 30 knots, as required by the Navy Staff for the preliminary studies. In fact, power calculations were still in at a very early stage and would have been firmed up in a subsequent phase of the design. However, it is safe to assume an approximate figure of 110,000shp, for which a machinery layout with two funnels would probably have been required.

As for protection, Pugliese stated: '… there is no doubt that it is advisable to defend the ship as much as possible against the torpedo, the big bomb, … and the gun of existing ships of moderate displacement (330mm in the *Dunkerque*s)'. Pugliese also urged the Naval Staff to make a choice of calibre (305mm or 320mm), number of

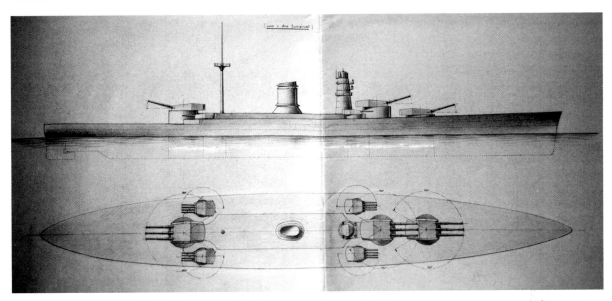

Plate 5, in which the layout of the main armament duplicated that of the *Littorio* class, albeit with 320mm guns instead of 381mm guns. The 320mm gun would have used the same ammunition as the modernised battleships of the *Cavour* class. This design proposal was arguably the most balanced and was the solution favoured by Pugliese. (INHO)

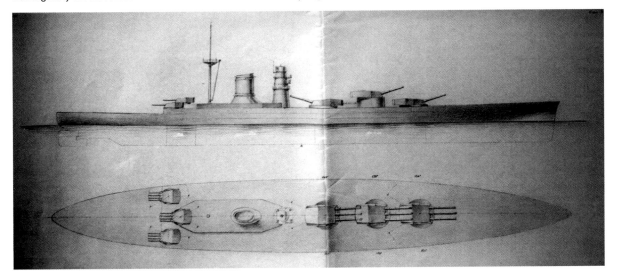

Plate 7, with three 320mm triple turrets in a 'pyramid' forward and the secondary guns aft,. The arrangement of the main guns was inspired by the British battleships of the *Nelson* class. (INHO)

guns and turret layout. This would help to define more precisely, within the displacement limit, other elements of the design.

As for the layout of the main turrets, that proposed by Fleet Admiral Vincenzo De Feo, then responsible for newly-built warships, comprised two quadruple turrets placed amidships. However, this was a somewhat problematic layout. The plate related to this configuration clearly indicates the use of diesel engines, while the absence of funnels suggests an underwater exhaust, an impractical solution if one considers the power needed to achieve high speeds. Two out of the nine proposed configurations for the 26,500-ton battleship featured a main armament concentrated forward, in a layout similar to those of the French *Dunkerque* class and the British *Nelson* class, which had two quadruple and three triple turrets respectively.

Pugliese's recommendations and all the coloured plates were sent to the fourteen flag officers who were responsible for the ashore and afloat commands of the *Regia Marina*.[16] With a view to securing a consensus, Cavagnari asked each admiral to 'briefly indicate the reasons that led you to express a specific opinion on each subject, adding any observations that you consider appropriate to clarify concepts and preferences, and formulate a summary conclusion on the organic set of characteristics to be achieved' for the 26,500-ton battleship.

General Pugliese assembled the views and comments in a large table and analysed them under several headings, but focusing mainly on the large-calibre guns.[17] However, since different opinions emerged for each topic, Pugliese tried to synthesise and hone them. He concluded that the 26,500-ton battleship was to be armed with nine 320mm guns in three triple turrets: two forward and one aft – a layout identical to that of the *Littorio*s. The secondary (anti-destroyer) battery was to comprise either twelve or sixteen 130/140mm guns in quadruple or triple turrets, while air defence would be provided by twelve 90mm guns in single enclosed mountings and numerous light guns. Requirements for maximum speed (30 knots) and endurance (4,000nm at 20 knots) would almost certainly have been met by the adoption of steam turbine machinery, but Pugliese did not provide any definitive information on horsepower.

Pugliese stated that these characteristics were 'harmonious and homogeneous' with those of the *Littorio*s, but would nevertheless lead to a standard displacement of 30,000 tons, with a 'tendency to exceed even this in order to provide ... effective protection, thus probably increasing displacement to 38,500 tons', as in the *Littorio*s.

Therefore, to limit the standard displacement to within 27,000 tons and maintain a protection scheme similar to the *Littorio*s, Pugliese first suggested accepting an armament layout similar to the

A close-up of *Vittorio Veneto* taken at La Spezia in March 1943, with the bridge tower, FC directors and 90mm HA guns prominent. Had they been pursued, the designs for 26,500-ton battleships drawn up by Pugliese would undoubtedly have had similar features. (INHO)

*Dunkerque*s – ie two quadruple turrets – and reducing maximum speed to 28 knots. However, several admirals were opposed to the quadruple turret, arguing that the concentration of the main guns in two turrets would have represented a limiting factor in firepower if one of them was damaged in combat. To enhance protection, it is also possible that Pugliese had in mind the installation of the watertight shock-absorbing cylinders that he had patented and had been adopted for the *Littorio*s. Although *Maricominav*'s papers did not mention the linear dimensions of the 26,500-ton battleship, a comparison with the displacements considered in the Barberis study suggests a length of about 245 metres and a beam of about 25 metres, sufficient for the installation of the aforementioned cylinders. Furthermore, since the Pugliese system would be included in a new design, its size could be conveniently harmonised with the width of the hull. This would undoubtedly achieve greater effectiveness than that obtained with the installation of the same system on the four older battleships of the *Cavour* and *Duilio* classes.

Pugliese carried out a comparative analysis between the *Deutschland*s and the *Dunkerque*s and concluded his report by stating '… it would seem more advantageous for our Navy … that no restrictions were accepted for the characteristics of battleships that might prevent us from continuing freely with the construction of additional *Littorio*-class battleships'. In a nutshell, either the *Regia Marina* had to accept the general limitations imposed by a limited displacement – which would be reflected in armament and protection – or the *Littorio* programme would have to be continued.

Considering the ongoing shipbuilding programmes of France and Germany and the evident impossibility of accepting proposals for limitations deriving from agreements no longer appropriate to the international situation, it was therefore clear that the design concept for the 26,500-ton battleship was now no longer valid, and that the modernisation of the Italian battle fleet would follow another path.

Endnotes:

[1] Italian Navy Historical Office (INHO), General collection, folder 1504.

[2] These were four old pre-dreadnought battleships (*Vittorio Emanuele*, *Regina Elena*, *Roma* and *Napoli*) commissioned in early 1900s.

[3] French naval shipbuilding was governed by the 1924 *Statut Naval*, a bill discussed in Parliament that projected a future fleet based on a total tonnage of 750,000 tons. Unlike most naval laws, the *Statut Naval* did not determine a precise programme of fleet development, but defined its total size and left the approval of funding for naval shipbuilding to each annual budget. The French Parliament never formally approved this 1924 *Statut Naval*, but the French Navy used it as a planning tool to submit its annual funding requests.

[4] Due to the lack of recent construction, France and Italy were each permitted to lay down two new 35,000-ton battleships, in 1927 and 1929 respectively, before the expiry of the 'battleship holiday'. As a concession to France, the total tonnage could be used as preferred, to build either four ships of 17,500 tons, three of 23,333 tons, or two of 35,000 tons. Under the Washington Treaty, a further 35,000-ton ship could be laid down in 1931 by each of the two nations following the end of the 'holiday'.

[5] INHO, General collection, folder 3211, Captain Wladimiro Pini, 'Limitazione del tonnellaggio massimo delle navi di linea e del calibro del loro armamento principale', 14 December 1931.

[6] INHO, General collection, folder 3286, Captain Paolo Maroni, 'Osservazioni dell'Ufficio Trattati al promemoria del Reparto Operazioni', 20 December 1931. Captain Maroni would later become the head of the naval section in the Italian delegation that attended the Geneva Conference.

[7] INHO, General collection, folder 3286. This document is undated but the study was carried out during December 1931–January 1932.

[8] Each card listed the main features of the sketch, a profile and a plan and a midship section with a schema of the protection system (see the accompanying image of the original card for P1). Each card also had a 'cost' line, but this was never filled in.

[9] Some authors consider these 36-knot designs to be 'battlecruisers' – see Willam H Garzke & Robert O Dulin, *Battleships: Axis and Neutral battleships in World War II*, US Naval Institute Press (Annapolis, 1980). The Italian Navy and the national shipbuilding industry considered this type of warship during the preparatory talks for the Geneva conference, but their design evolution was halted to concentrate intellectual and material resources only on battleships.

[10] Note that the 14in calibre was also favoured by the Americans and the Japanese; this would be the 'compromise' calibre agreed between Britain and the USA at the 1935–36 London conference.

[11] INHO, General collection, folder 3286, Office of the Chief of Staff, n. 8 RR, dated 10 January 1932.

[12] INHO, General collection, folder 3211, General Conference for Disarmament, Italian delegation, Naval section, 'Proposta britannica di limitazione del tonnellaggio e dell'armamento delle navi da battaglia', n. 419 CO, dated 30 April 1932.

[13] Italy was permitted to lay down battleships with a total displacement of 70,000 tons before the expiry of the Washington Treaty on 31 December 1936. However, the unit displacement of 35,000 tons, while permitted by the treaty, could be considered excalatory given that *Dunkerque* and her projected sister had a displacement of only 26,500 tons standard.

[14] The 320mm calibre had been already chosen for the modernisation of the battleships of the *Cavour* class, which had their original 305mm guns bored out.

[15] INHO, General collection, folder 2675, 'Progetto di corazzata da 26500 T. circa', n. 21095, Maricominav, dated 25 November 1935.

[16] INHO, General collection, folder 2675, 'Corazzata da 26500 T.', n. B.8739, Cabinet of the Minister, dated 2 December 1935.

[17] INHO, General collection, folder 2675, 'Progetto di corazzata di medio dislocamento: Sintesi dei giudizi formulati dagli Ammiragli', n. 302, dated 6 February 1936.

POSTWAR ELECTRONIC WARFARE SYSTEMS IN THE ROYAL NAVY

In this latest in a series of articles on technical developments in the Royal Navy during the postwar era, **Peter Marland** describes the evolution of electronic warfare.

Previous articles published in *Warship* have chronicled the development of fire control, weapons, command & control, sonar and radar in the postwar Royal Navy. The present article describes the development of the electronic warfare (EW) systems used by RN surface ships across the postwar period. It complements the earlier articles and builds on the excellent work of Kingsley,[1] who documented the wartime development of systems to detect German (and Japanese) radars, to deny enemy coastal surveillance by noise jamming and the use of chaff from aircraft, plus jammers to counter the guidance signals used by Hs 293 and FX 1400 guided bombs.

Production radar direction finding (DF) equipment only became available after the war had concluded. Kingsley also covered the corresponding development of high-frequency radio DF (HF/DF), which is now described as Communications Electronic Support Measures (CESM).[2] This article brings all these aspects forward to the turn of the 21st century.

Electronic Warfare is described using a number of acronyms, and is also referred to as Electronic Surveillance (ES) or Electronic Support Measures (ESM). Decoys and jammers are part of Electronic Counter Measure (ECM) systems closely interrelated to EW (see Fig 1).

A key factor in ESM is the 'range advantage' it generates, because two-way propagation losses mean that signals can be detected at up to twice the range that the originator obtains their first returning echo. This gives the ESM system a primary warning function that allows for tactical decision-making and deployment of countermeasures. Classification of the intercept may allow identification of the unknown contact, thus making a very significant contribution to situational awareness (SA).

It should be noted that there has been a change in the radar band descriptions from the immediate post-war system to the current designations used by the

---

Electronic Surveillance (ES) or Electronic Warfare (EW)

Electronic Support Measures (ESM)
    Radar ESM (RESM)   } Interception, DF and exploitation of opponent's transmissions
    Communications ESM (CESM)

Electronic Counter Measures (ECM)
    Electronic Counter-Counter   } Jamming, decoys, or deception of opponent & measures against his jamming
    Measures (ECCM)

Fig 1: Electronic Warfare Terminology (Graphic by John Jordan using material supplied by the author)

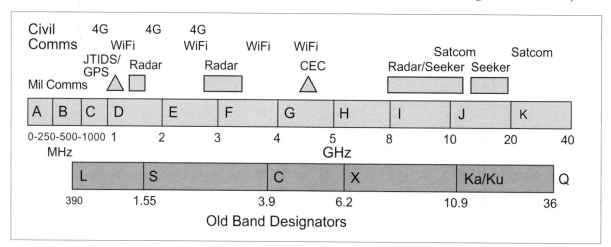

Fig 2: Electro-Magnetic Spectrum: Radar & Comms Bands (Graphic by John Jordan using material supplied by the author)

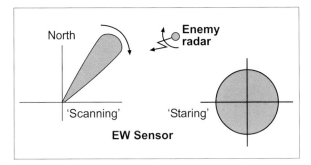

Fig 3: EW Sensing: Scanning and Staring (Graphic by John Jordan using material supplied by the author)

International Telecommunications Union (ITU) and NATO (see Fig 2). The Figure also illustrates the encroachment of modern civil comms equipment into formerly military allocations of the spectrum.

In the immediate postwar period, EW systems were either of the 'scanning' or 'staring' type. Scanning systems generally used rotating aerials; the higher gain could detect a radar emitter farther away. However, since both the radar and the EW system were rotating, the transmission and reception antennae had to be lined up to make a detection. This gave an overall 'low probability of interception', but better range and higher bearing accuracy. In contrast, a 'staring' system looked all-round at lower gain (and therefore lesser range), but with a 'high probability of interception' of the enemy radar – see the schematic in Fig 3.

Scanning was typified by the USN SLR and WLR-1

systems, while the equivalent UK system was the staring UA3. Scanning & staring technologies apply equally to both the frequency and spatial (bearing) domains. Scanning often appears in CESM systems because voice or data transmissions are longer and therefore more amenable to detection by a scanning system compared to pulsed radar transmissions.

Radar ESM

The initial postwar equipment was the RU1-4 family, which used a scanning aerial. However, a pre-production system trial in mid-1947 gave such disappointing results that this was shelved and EW effort switched to the UA1/2/3 series, which used fixed antennae as a 'staring' system. There were four distinct generations of postwar maritime Radar Electronic Support Measures (RESM) equipment.

Royal Navy involvement began with the widespread fitting of Outfit UA3 to escorts. This was triggered by the discovery of periscope radar during the postwar exploitation of German research, and the system used four directional horns for each band to give a general warning capability. The system was augmented by additional horns in later life to give some a J-band capability. UA3 was fitted in all early escorts up to the 'Tribals' and the early *Leanders*, *circa* 1962, and persisted in the *Rothesay* class (Type 12) until the late 1980s.

The second generation arrived in the early 1960s as UA8/9/10. This was a much more sophisticated and very sensitive system, with separate DF and Frequency

One of the last pair of frigates of the Type 12 *Leander* class, HMS *Ariadne* has the UA13 'Dunce's Cap' and 'Christmas Tree' antennae at the head of the foremast. She is seen here at the Silver Jubilee Fleet Review in June 1977. (C & S Taylor)

Measurement channels. Detection of a signal on the frequency display allowed the superhetrodyne bearing receivers to be mechanically tuned to the desired target frequency for a fine bearing measurement in the 3–5 degree class.

UA8/9/10 went into 'County'-class destroyers and 'Battle'-class conversions (from 1962 onwards), Type 61 AD frigates on refit, and then into all the later *Leander*s. Both UA3 and UA8/9/10 were manual systems fitted in an EW Office remote from the Operations Room. With the associated Type 667/668 jammers they typically required 3–5 racks of display, backed by a further 2–4 racks in the equipment room.

Another contemporary system in place of FH5 was UA13, covering from the HF communication band upward into low-band radars (25MHz to 1.4GHz). This was essentially the Signaal SPR-02 system, but it proved difficult to calibrate or maintain and was short-lived in RN service. UA15 was a J-band extension to UA8/9 and was introduced from 1975 to cover units not benefiting from UAA(1).

The third generation of RESM was UAA(1) 'Abbeyhill', delivered from 1978 to later Type 21 frigates and Type 42 destroyers, then all Type 22 frigates and *Invincible*-class CVS, plus *Bristol* and Batch 3 Seawolf *Leander*s at refit. This was a quantum leap in capability,

with five-band coverage from 1–18GHz, DF based on eight bearing channels in each band, separate instantaneous frequency measurement (IFM) aerials, and an integrated single panoramic display showing frequency against bearing. Direction finding was in the 2–3 degree class. There was a limited automatic threat warner, and when the operator selected a contact using a cursor it was compared to the library held on mylar tape. The signal sorter technology was also exploited in older UA8 and UA9 as Outfit YAG(1), the Selective Automatic Radar Identification Equipment (SARIE).

UAA(1) required less hardware than the previous generation, and used special-purpose (*ie* hard-wired) digital electronics, being updated post-Falklands as (2); both were semi-automatic systems. The UAA(1) console was fitted in the Operations Room, where the operator was an integral part of the Command team, calling 'Zippo'[3] alerts to warn of inbound attacks, and contributed to wider picture compilation by classifying unknown contacts on the parent Action Information Organisation (AIO) system. UAA(1) was fully integrated with the command system, and was able to generate EW bearing lines into ADAWS or CAAIS (see the author's article in *Warship 2016*), exported via Links 10, 11 or 16.

The current generation is UAT, though this system

The Type 21 frigate HMS *Ambuscade* on 1 September 1989, with UAA(1) 'Abbeyhill' ESM mounted on the foremast, and radars Types 992Q and 1006 at the masthead. The conical antennae near the base of the mast were for the ship's recreational TV system. (John Jordan)

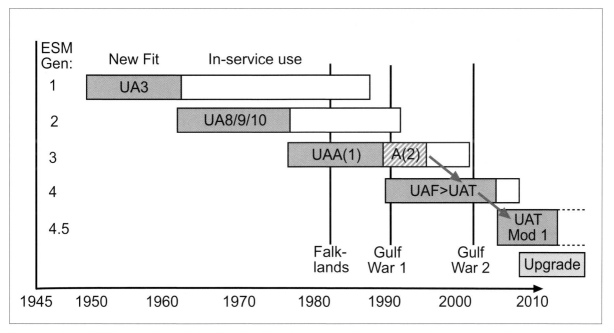

Fig 4: Overview of RESM Generations with Timeline (Graphic by John Jordan using material supplied by the author)

evolved via UAF (the initial ESM system in Type 23 frigates in 1990). The system is based on general-purpose digital computing to provide the de-interleaving. UAF proved to have an inadequate central processor, and was superseded by Outfit UAT (which retained the UAF aerials) from 1993. Escorts with UAA(2), particularly Types 22 and 42, were then updated with UAT(5), which married the UAT below-decks equipment with the existing UAA(2) aerial. Both UAF and UAT are fully automatic systems, and UAT added separate additional Channelised Receivers (CRx).

Figure 4 shows the timescales involved. Table 1

Table 1: **Generations of RESM Equipment and Associated/Peripheral Items**

Gen	System	Band Cover	Notes (aerials and associated items)
1	UA3	E/F band 2.5-4.1GHz	Original aerials: AYC (E/F band), AYD (G/H band), AYE (I band).
		G/H band 4.1–7GHz	AYK added for J band, and I band aerial (AYE) replaced by AXO; YAF analyser.
		I band 7–11.5GHz	
		J band 11.5–18GHz	
2	UA8	E/F band 2.5–4.1GHz	Bearing aerial for all three sets (UA8/9/10) covers all three bands.
			Physically: AYJ to support 992Q radar, or AYL with FH4 or 5 above, or AYM with URN-3 TACAN above.
			IFM Omni aerials: AYR E/F band, AYQ I band, AYT G/H band.
			All sets use YAZ pulse analyser, YAK/YAW bearing re-transmission units, and YAG SARIE.
	UA9	I band 7–11.5GHz	UA9 I band single fit with AYQ omni, and AYS bearing aerials.
	UA10	G/H band 4.1–7GHz	UA10 used UA8 or -9 display, *ie* not fully independent.
	UA15	Extends UA8/9 to J band 11.5–18GHz, aerials cover full 7–18GHz	UA15 with AXR IFM-omni plus AXQ for DF. These replace older UA-9 aerials – serves UA-9 equipment (7–11.5GHz) via diplexer.
	UA13	A/D band, 25 MHz to 1.4GHz	UA13 with AYU aerial, derived from Signaal SPR-02. In four B2/B3 *Leander*s, in lieu of FH5.
3	UAA(1)	5 bands (1–18GHz):	AYV
		Band 1 1–2GHz	Band 4 and 5 in all units, plus one band kit from other three bands (1-3).
		Band 2 2–4GHz	During later life, run-down in numbers allowed all units to have all bands.
		Band 3 4–7.5GHz	
		Band 4 7.5–12GHz	
		Band 5 12–18GHz	
4	UAF/UAT	5 bands (0.5 to 18GHz) but 0.8–18GHz with UAA(2) aerial	UAT has replaced UAF, though using the original JANE aerials, except in UAT(5)/(6) where the original AYV(2) is used.

Table 2: Summary of Key Differences between Generations of RESM

Generation	1	2	3	4
Equipment	UA3	UA8-9-10	UAA(1)	UAT
Bands	3	1, 2 or 3	5	5
Receiver Technology	Crystal Video (CVR)	Mechanical Superhet, IFM and bearing	Special purpose hard-wired digital	General purpose digital, plus Channelised Receiver (CRx)
User Interface	Manual	Manual	Semi-automatic	Automatic
Operators	1	2–4	1+1 EWD	1+1 EWD

summarises these 'generations' of equipment and their peripheral or associated items. The graphic shows that the Falklands (Operation 'Corporate') was fought with UAA(1) – two thirds of units – and UA3–10 (the remaining third). The First Gulf War (Operation 'Granby') was mostly fought with UAA(1), while the Second Gulf War ('Telic') was almost exclusively a UAT campaign. Table 2 summarises the key differences between the various generations of RESM.

Warner channels are those directly recognised 'alerts' available to the user, while a full library search allows a wider range of threats to be identified, albeit in slower time due to the processing involved. Libraries contain multiple entries against a single specific radar, with each

The 'Leander Seawolf' conversion HMS *Jupiter* in February 1989. She has UAA(1) 'Abbeyhill' ESM and radar Type 967/678 at the masthead, and antennae for the Type 670 Short Term jammer, installed in a number of units following the Falklands Conflict, are fitted near the base of the mast. (John Jordan)

'mode line' reflecting a particular permutation of pulse length, pulse type and repetition frequency.

Development Narrative

RU1–4: The handbook for RU4, dated 1946, identifies a 2–6GHz intercept system with twin (sided) rotating aerials Outfit AHD and a CRT-based visual display (BR2022). This looks quite similar to the German wartime *Naxos* FuMB24, or the later USN 'spinning dish' systems.

There are also three references to RU1–4 at TNA Kew, in ADM220/295, /594 and /1960. The earliest covers the trials in HMS *Saltburn* in February–March 1945 in the Forth area. This was an 'X' (*ie* experimental) model based on lab components, and had rotatable aerials but not the full servo-controlled scanning system. Trials were one-on-one against an escort destroyer, then against a bomber aircraft. These produced good results with ranges from beyond the horizon out to 90nm against the bomber at height. The paperwork makes clear that RU1 and RU4 were very similar, with RU1 aimed at V/UHF-band radars, and RU4 at S-band radars.

The second report looked at the search strategies, recommending that targets were first searched for in azimuth (since RU4 scanned at up to 120rpm), and then looked at in frequency, which was tuned via a motor drive (the VHF receiver was being tuned at only 5.5MHz per second).

The final report was the sea trial of a representative complete ('Z' model) RU4 in HMS *St James* (a 'Battle'-class destroyer) July–August 1947. This tested the equipment in a deployed force setting, and the operators found the system almost unusable due to mutual interference from other S-band radars in the force and from the ship's own search radar. When the *St James* radar (Type 293) was Emcon (Emissions control) Silent things improved, and when the ship was detached from the main body it could take accurate bearings on the other ships in the main body. What is evident is that there was no pulse synchronisation or interference suppression, hence the drop in usefulness compared to the early *Saltburn* trial.

Although RU1-4 had been slated for the new *Daring* class, at some point after the trial report the Admiralty cancelled RU4, but learning from the episode moved across to the UA1-3 series of 'high probability of inter-cept' systems. Lt-Cdr TJ Bird's article 'Passive Electronic Warfare Systems' (NER Oct 1970, Vol 24 No 2, 6–19),

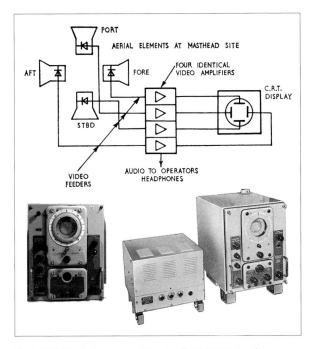

Fig 5: UA3 Block Diagram and Display (NER Vol 24 No 2)

described first and second generation EW techniques and outlined what was planned for the third generation.

First Generation: This was triggered by the discovery of periscope radar during the postwar exploitation of German research. Early systems (UA1/2) had fewer bands, but (UA3) covered all three (X, S, C bands). Four individual antennae (port & starboard, fore & aft) with crystal video receivers (CVR) fed four channels to give bearing of the intercepted signal to ±10°. Each horn covered a single band and was wide open to any signal in the band; this gave a high probability of interception and approximate bearing, but could not measure the signal frequency.

UA3 was usually manned by a radio operator RO(W), who manually assessed the detected radar's rotation rate by stopwatch and was able to aurally recognise some pulse styles or pulse repetition frequency (prf). The system included limited recording, plus training tapes for the operators to practise recognition of threat signals. Later additions were an Outfit YAF analyser, and Outfit RFP (REB) for recording and detailed fingerprinting analysis.

Second Generation (UA8/9/10): This was a much more sophisticated and very sensitive system with separate DF and Frequency Measurement channels. The operator detected signals on a frequency display and selected them by cursor, which mechanically tuned the four superhet bearing receivers (fed by a four-port DF aerial in each band) to the desired target frequency, for a fine bearing measurement in the 3–5 degree class. The key development was the Instantaneous Frequency Measurement (IFM) receiver, fed by an omni aerial and able to show

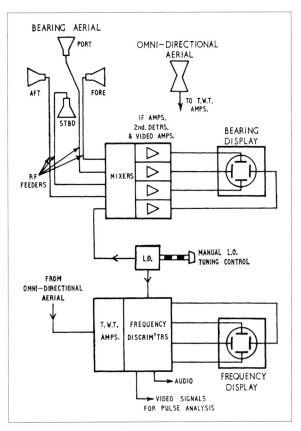

Fig 6: UA8/9/10 Block Diagram
ASWE outsourced the development of the IFM receiver as Project 'Pendant'. Peter East identifies SJ Robinson at Mullard Research Laboratories who led development of IFM technology using coaxial hybrid discriminators (later stripline & microstrip) between 1954 and 1957.

These went into UA8-10 ('Porker') from 1962, fed by the omni (IFM) antenna and allowed the operator to align a cursor with the selected signal. This tuned the associated superhet bearing receivers to provide the bearing of the selected target signal, with other parts of the set allowing more detailed analysis using Outfits YAF-YAW-YAZ. UK IFM technology was widely copied by the US and formed the basis of much of the postwar Allied EW effort. This analogue IFM was updated as Digital IFM (DIFM) from 1967 onwards. (NER Vol 24 No 2)

the received signals by frequency. UA8–10 had a more elaborate analyser YAW/YAZ.

The matching Type 667-8 jammer had trainable (sided) aerials, and included a separate receiver to 'set on' the jammer for frequency and bearing, using noise jamming (or spin modulation against conical scan fire control radars). Figure 7 shows the five consoles involved in a full fit of UA8/9/10 in a missile destroyer.

Third Generation (UAA1): This was a quantum leap in capability, with five-band coverage from 1–18GHz, DF based on eight bearing channels in each band, separate instantaneous frequency measurement (IFM) aerials, and an integrated single panoramic display showing contacts frequency against bearing. There were two parallel

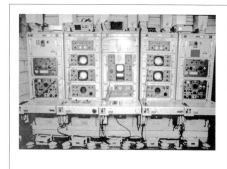
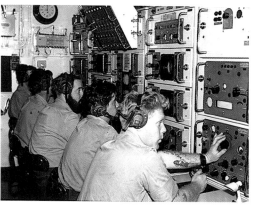

Fig 7: UA8-9 Display
The EW office of the missile destroyer HMS *Devonshire* in late 1962, and the crew operating UA8 and UA9. The nearest operator is LRO(W) Jim O'Halloran, controlling the Type 667 S-band jammer, which was also part of the EW suite. (John Wise)

processing channels: omni/IFM and bearing; signals detected in bearing (X axis) then gated the IFM data to show the matching frequency on the Y axis.

There was a limited threat warner, programmed for immediate threats by punched card. The operator could select any signal from the main display, using a cursor moved by roller ball; these were compared to the analyser library held on mylar tape via a rapid reader. The operator also had a manual pulse analyser, and the console was fitted in the operations room (rather than a remote EW Office), where the operator was an integral part of the Command team. UAA(1) included better end-to-end test equipment, and provided DF in the 2–3 degree class.

Fig 8: The UAA(1) console in the Ops Room of HMS *Bristol* (Peter Marland)

SARIE (Outfit YAG) was derived from the UAA(1) library/fast tape reader, and applied to UA8–9.

UAA(1) required less hardware than the previous generation (a rack at the mast head, two in an equipment space and a single console in the Ops Room). It used special-purpose hard-wired digital electronics, and though it carried out a degree of de-interleaving it was not based on a general-purpose digital computer with an externally loadable programme. Capitalising on experience from the Falklands, the system was updated as UAA(2), including an expanded Insight warner with additional channels, a hard drive-based digital signal sorter, plus display expansion of I band coverage. UAA(1) and (2) were essentially semi-automatic systems.

The Abbeyhill prototype was trialled at sea in summer 1967 as an in-house ASWE-developed 'bread-board' system using bought-in DIFM components (IFM2, covering 2–4GHz and contracted by the Royal Aircraft Establishment in 1965, was borrowed from Mullard Research Laboratories for the trial). Production was let to Thorn EMI, and the system entered service from 1970. Mullard Research Laboratories became Mullard Equipment Limited (MEL) at Crawley (owned by Phillips, but taken over by Thorn EMI in 1989, then by Thales). The other UK source of ES systems is Selex (formerly Marconi MSDS) at Stanmore.

Abbeyhill was a very capable ESM set that contributed wider situational awareness, as well as immediate threat warnings and 'zippo' responses. The author was in a destroyer in the North Sea for air defence exercises during which UAA(1) was able to hear the raid aircraft warming up their radars before they left their home airfields ashore. Figure 9 shows the aerials involved.

UAA(1) and (2) used Format A, then Format S for warner and signal sorter. UAT was initially on Format S, but has now moved to Format P. This issue is strongly linked to library structures ashore, with RNEWOS and then the wider Defence EW database.

Surviving UAT in Type 23 frigates and Type 45 destroyers have been brought up to a common standard as UAT Mod 1. This retained the existing front-end receiver and antenna, but introduced an entirely new de-

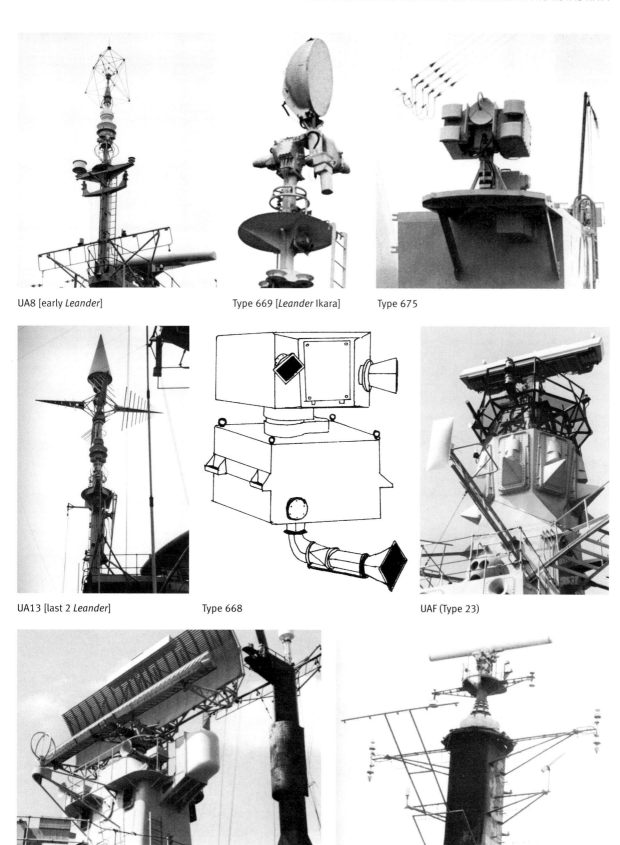

UA8 [early *Leander*]

Type 669 [*Leander* Ikara]

Type 675

UA13 [last 2 *Leander*]

Type 668

UAF (Type 23)

Type 670 [Type 42]

UAA(1) [Type 42]

Fig 9: Aerials (some from HMS *Collingwood*, courtesy of Clive Kidd)

interleaving and emitter identification architecture using the Minerva GTPA (Graph Theoretic Processing Algorithm) signal processor, and an emitter library matching system based on the Palantir technology demonstrator and Format P. The changes introduce flat-panel displays (*vice* the original CRTs), and the operator interface now uses a Windows-based Human Computer Interaction (HCI).

The principal benefits of this upgrade are: better de-interleaving and library identification performance, and commonality of both training and data support. However later programmes have struggled due to cost and the need to include the cost of re-lifing or replacing the inventory of decoy rounds.

ECM: Jammers and Decoys

By the end of the Second World War the British fielded the following jammers against German threats: Type 91 was used at Dover and in some large ships against deci-metric (90-600MHz) radars; Types 650 and 651 were widely deployed to jam guided bombs (±50MHz). Parallel work included FH3 and FH4 HF/DF to intercept communications from U-boats, and the 'Headache' receiver plus the FV3 VHF DF set were used against E-boat comms in home waters.

The initial thrust of UK naval ECM in the early 1960s was radar jamming, using the Type 667 (two bands: E/F and I) and Type 668 (I band only) that were part of the UA8/9/10 suite, and for each band a single trainable jammer (via dual-sided aerials) was provided. These delivered noise jamming for self-screening, and spin modulation to break the lock of a conical scan fire control radar that had acquired the ship. A prototype high-power I-band amplifier (Outfit WBZ) was trialled in HMS *Hermes* in 1969 to deliver 2–4kW jammer power, but was not taken forward.

The RN had introduced two forms of chaff. Chaff C, or 'Charlie' for confusion, via Radar Echo shells in I or J band (RE/I or /J), was fired from 4.5in guns; this was intended to confuse enemy targeting by adding additional contacts to his surveillance picture. The second form was Chaff D or 'Delta' for distraction, to counter an inbound missile; this had become necessary as the Soviet Union began to deploy anti-ship missiles. Chaff S or 'Sierra' for seduction is a later variation, covering cases where a seeker had already locked on its target.

The attack on the Israeli destroyer *Eilat* with SS-N-2 'Styx' missiles in 1967 reinforced the urgency of pre-existing plans to introduce the Knebworth Corvus 3in Mk 4 rocket launcher. Initially there were 6 barrels on each trainable launcher, loaded with N1, N2 and N3 rockets for separate frequency-band coverage against the radar homing heads of Soviet missiles such as 'Styx' and the over-the-horizon SS-N-3 'Shaddock'. This was later revised when the N4 broad-band chaff round became available, and two extra barrels were added to give eight per side. The other solution was the 'Bexley'

The CVS HMS *Illustrious*, seen here on 5 May 2009, has the distinctive UAT ESM array on the mainmast, below Type 996. (John Jordan)

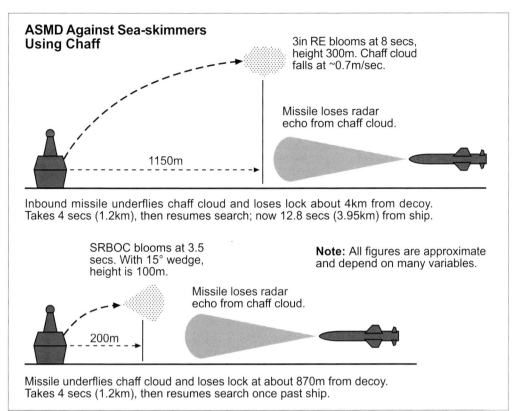

ASMD Against Sea-skimmers Using Chaff

3in RE blooms at 8 secs, height 300m. Chaff cloud falls at ~0.7m/sec.

Missile loses radar echo from chaff cloud.

1150m

Inbound missile underflies chaff cloud and loses lock about 4km from decoy. Takes 4 secs (1.2km), then resumes search; now 12.8 secs (3.95km) from ship.

SRBOC blooms at 3.5 secs. With 15° wedge, height is 100m.

Note: All figures are approximate and depend on many variables.

Missile loses radar echo from chaff cloud.

200m

Missile underflies chaff cloud and loses lock at about 870m from decoy. Takes 4 secs (1.2km), then resumes search once past ship.

Fig 10: ASMD Defence against Sea-skimmers (Graphic by John Jordan using material supplied by the author)

repeater jammer (Type 669) that relied on reflecting the received and amplified missile transmission back off the water, to give a stronger target aim point short of the ship in order to seduce a two-axis (azimuth & elevation) seeker. The system proved difficult to maintain, and was withdrawn when the balance shifted towards sea-skimmers such as Exocet that flew at a height set by a radar altimeter and that homed only in azimuth. Finally, a 'Honeydew' IR hotspot decoy 81mm mortar round was developed against SS-N-7/SS-N-9 submarine- and FPB-launched missiles, but was not taken through to service use.

Anti-Ship Missile Defence (ASMD) Tactics

A key aspect of ASMD is where to put the decoy, because this depends on the scan pattern of the incoming missile for its effectiveness. The goal is to have the decoy out and successfully 'bloomed', allowing it to be detected before the defended ship. Thus a missile scanning down, and from left to right, required a decoy behind and to the left of the real target, while one scanning 'out' would need a decoy placed in front of the ship. Early tactics used plastic 'widgers' to help ships' staff point the trainable 3in launchers and select a decoy barrel, while later tactics used all the decoys at the same time to cover all eventualities.

The next major revision of RN ASMD tactics was triggered by the Falklands in 1982. While Chaff D with 3in RE N4 BBC was effective, the conflict sparked renewed interest in countering an inbound Exocet that underflew

the 3in chaff cloud and then carried out a new search that might re-acquire the targeted ship.

Innovations included:

– the addition of the US SRBOC launcher with wedges to reduce the chaff bloom height, and thus the chance of a missile underflying the chaff and going into a reacquisition mode.
– helicopter-mounted jammers, able to exploit logic in the seeker and then climb to avoid the incoming missile.

The airborne jammers (DLQ-3B in Lynx and Sea King) were used to force the missile into a 'home-on-jam' mode, at which point the jamming aircraft could climb to a safe altitude. As part of the longer-term package, 'Yellow Veil' (a derivative of AN/ALQ-167) was acquired in place of the *ad hoc* Lynx fit, and the Short Term Jammer (Type 670, derived from Decca's RCM2) was added to many destroyers and frigates, with proper Range Gate Pull-Off (RGPO) modes to dump the attacking missile onto a decoy chaff bloom. Types 667/668 were declared obsolete about 1987, although 670 continued until 1994.

Post-Falklands, the emphasis shifted to 'breaking the lock' of a missile that had acquired its real target, and dumping the seeker onto a chaff cloud or floating decoy as the missile tried to reacquire the defended unit.

It should be noted that the above is a late 20th century view of ASMD, against missile seekers with known scan patterns. It is now more difficult, with Digital Multiple

Range Gate seekers able to 'map' using a single scan and chaff discriminators. This leads to a bias towards active decoys, coherent replica targets, plus more emphasis on 'hard kill' using short-range missiles such as CAMM/Sea Ceptor, or with CIWS such as Phalanx or Goalkeeper.

For the Type 23 frigate onwards, the ship's Radar Cross Section (RCS) area became an issue, with the design featuring an inclined outer hull and superstructures to minimise any reflected signal by avoiding perfect corner reflectors, or by treating external surfaces with Radar Absorbent Material (RAM) or similar sheet coatings (RASH). The German MEKO frigates and French *La Fayette* class introduced boat bays covered by 'stealth screens'.

Force Defence

In parallel, MoD developed jammer Type 675(2), which was a reduced-capability version of the original 'Millpost' requirement (NSR7337). 'Millpost' was primarily a force protection measure, generating sufficient high-fidelity false targets in a surveillance picture to prevent the enemy from correctly targeting missiles against the defended ships. Targets were Soviet surveillance aircraft such as the Tu-142 'Bear', and the Radar Ocean Reconnaissance Satellite (RORSAT). Received radar pulses were saved and re-injected into the surveillance radar via sidelobes with a sequence of delays, thereby creating a grid of realistic targets to mask the real high-value target.

Type 675(2) was fitted in some Type 22 frigates, most Type 42 destroyers and in the CVS, but was withdrawn from 1999 as an economy measure, leaving service by 2000. The scale of the equipment required can be gauged from Figure 11. Most of this was in a dedicated cabin with the antenna on top, with only the control console in the Ops Room, adjacent to the UAA(2) EW Operator's position.

Subsequent soft-kill has relied solely on decoys, particularly Chaff N4 or N5 from Seagnat or Shield launchers (DLB, DLJ, DLH), using combinations of both 104mm (3in N4) and 130mm (Seagnat) rounds, and Barricade in 'Hunt'-class MCMVs. The original 3in systems had hand-set time mechanical fuses and plug & socket firing

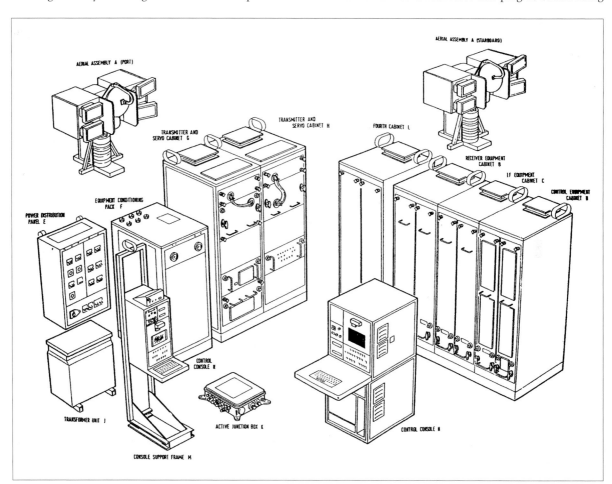

Fig 11: Type 675 Aerial Assemblies, Cabinets and Display Console
On the jammer head the horns on the left side are transmitters (upper CW, lower pulsed), while those on the right are the receivers, with 'squint' to DF monopulse radars. The central circular dish is for 'high gain' modes. Jamming modes included RGPO, AGPO, False Targets, and Intermittent CW with FM and/or AM background noise. (BR8331, HMS *Collingwood*, courtesy of Clive Kidd)

Table 3: **ECM Equipment and Associated/Peripheral Items**

Gen	System	Band Cover	Notes (aerials and associated items)
1	667	Both I band 7.45–10.45GHz and E/F band 2.5–4GHz	Aerial AYN (separate sided aerials for I band, and for E/F band jammers)
	668	I band 7.45–10.45GHz	Aerial AYO (sided aerials for I band jammer)
1.5	669	I band 7.8–9.6GHz	Aerials AYY (RX) and AYW (TX), 5MW
2	670	I–J band 7.7–15.3GHz	Aerial ABA: isd 1983, withdrawn 1994
3	675(2)	I–J band 7.5–15.3GHz	isd 1985, withdrawn 1999–2002

circuits, but the later systems have inductive coupling, and rounds can be programmed digitally while in the launcher. The newer decoys are the Mk 245 IR seduction, Mk 214 RF seduction and Mk 216 RF distraction rounds, and an RF payload (the Mk 251 Active Decoy Round) programmed by the parent ship's ESM system. Finally, the current passive floating decoy is Outfit DLF(3), sometimes known as 'Replica'.

Command Aids

As the complexity posed by threat missiles increased, the operators required 'widgers' or cursors for best placement of chaff blooms; this was elaborated in later Type 42 destroyers and the CVS as the Electronic Warfare Control Processor (EWCP) Outfit UCB, and the Captain's Combat Aid (CCA) Outfit JZZ. CCA was programmed in LISP, an early AI language. These sought to balance deployment of the Active Decoy Round (ADR) and the competing issues of weapon arcs (and ship signature) required for both hard- and soft-kill measures to be successful. Detailed EW database information was held on separate laptops.

Jammers were used significantly less than the parent ESM set due to security concerns – frequent use would have revealed their capabilities. This underuse (only in pre-planned exercises) led to support problems caused by condensation or 'poisoning' of the high-power microwave valves involved in the transmitters.

Research work on Maritime HF radar in the early 1980s was given a fillip by the Falklands, but was then overtaken by the introduction of a Sea King airborne early warning (AEW) variant. HF radar was then exploited by Canada as a groundwave system for surveillance of its Maritime Economic Zone, and Australia (as Project JINDALEE) using skywave.

Fig 12: DLF(3) Floating Decoy
Also known as 'Replica', the DLF(3b) floating decoy is launched from a large horizontal tube (see close-up of HMS *Lancaster*, 13 May 2022). The RN trialled floating decoys in the mid-1980s, and 3b is the latest iteration. The floating decoys avoid the problem of an anti-ship missile underflying the chaff cloud, but are expensive and cannot deployed very far away from the defended ship, so are not a single solution to missile defence. (John Jordan/IrvinGQ)

Discussion

The UK approach to maritime EW is a story of contrasts; with consistently strong support for ESM via UA8/9 and UAA(1), followed by a 'wobble' with UAF caused by a Cardinal Point Procurement that was recovered as UAT. However there has been a swinging 'pendulum' of interest in jammers, as Types 667/8, 669, 670 and 675. In many cases, jammers were removed early as 'support savings' due to the cost of high-power RF components, and they never had the same degree of commitment as things that could be fired. The evidence shows relatively strong science support to DE&S, though spoiled by a fragmented logistics chain for items such as jammers, where it was less easy to prove effectiveness.

There are several other factors that have implications for the future. A US open report from 1994[4] predicted pulse densities in the Littoral rising from 40kpps in 1970–80, to 500kpps–2Mpps in 1980–90, and 1–10Mpps in 1990–2000 (an order of magnitude increase compared to the previous decade), cited by *Jane's Navy International*, 'RESM faces up to the Littoral Challenge' (10 Aug 2004). This is compounded by moves toward Low Probability of Interception (LPI) technology like the 'Scout' radar which uses low power and a FMCW waveform.

The problems of rising signal density, technical changes to the equipment, and organisation in the Ops Room all interact. Developments in equipment and procedures are as follows:

– There has been a progressive move away from raw displays to wholly processed formats. The ESM displays have developed from essentially sensor pictures to a tactical presentation of processed contacts. The quality of this is dependent on the classifier and library performance; there is less ability to interrogate unknown contacts. The result is more akin to the derided US AN/SLQ-32 user interface.

– The EW branch structure at the operator level has evolved across the period, from RO(W) to AB(EW) to the current OEM(EW). These changes have been combined with de-skilling due to savings taken against career and pre-joining training. Each generation of equipment has required fewer operators, down from 3–4 operators and a controller or supervisor in a separate EW office to the current manning of a single EW operator plus the EW Director (EWD), both in the Ops Room.

– The EW Op now has to manage a sizeable workload, and tends to focus on the equipment, rather than the external Ops Room environment. The Ops Room space is constrained (even though the jammer function has been removed), and the EWD now co-ordinates ASMD and soft kill with decoys. The EWD also has to handle a number of *ad hoc* Intel laptop fits; the interface between ESM and the Command System is therefore less productive than was hitherto the case.

CESM

The RN involvement with Communications Electronic Support Measures (CESM) has some early roots. During the First World War, this included Direction Finding (DF) and early code-breaking and traffic flow analysis, leading to the Naval Intelligence cell (Room 40), and indications and warnings of German High Seas Fleet movements. These were largely based on Medium Frequency (MF) communications and shore-based intercept sites. By the Second World War, the focus had shifted to High Frequency (HF) communications. The shore DF and extensive crypto-analysis organisation has been described by several authors in the context of Bletchley Park, Enigma and ULTRA. Although the UK achieved a large amount of intelligence from the decoded material, there was a significant 'timelate' element involved, which made the information more applicable to a strategic (rather than tactical) setting. Post-war, Bletchley Park was succeeded by GCHQ Cheltenham, and the remote monitoring and DF sites that remained were transferred to the Composite Signals Organisation.

In parallel, the UK led development of HF direction

The Type 23 frigate HMS *Richmond*, seen here on 15 May 2014, has the UAT ESM array below the Type 996 radar at the head of the foremast. Note the empty platform at the forward end of the bridge structure intended for the launch tubes for 'Replica' floating decoys. (John Jordan)

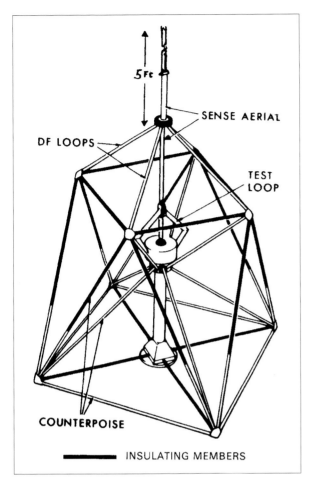

Fig 13: S25B HF/DF Aerial: Used in Both FH4 and FH5 (PE Redgment in Kingsley)

finding from ships, with the FH3 and FH4 systems deployed from 1941, which made a significant impact on ASW operations for the key convoy battles of 1942–43. These systems gave escort commanders early warning of enemy submarines operating in their vicinity by intercepting and direction finding the U-Boat's contact and homing reports, which were made on HF (1–24MHz band) within ground wave coverage (typically 30–150nm). Although operators afloat were not able to decrypt the morse intercepts, the contact reports had an identifiable (b-bar) prefix, and the ground wave coverage allowed commanders a degree of early warning outside the limited range of surface radar. This allowed informed decisions to deploy aircraft or detach an escort as a Surface Attack Unit. Taken together with the ULTRA intelligence, the combination of HF/DF with radar and aircraft facilitated the eventual success in the Battle of the Atlantic.

Postwar DF

FH4 was succeeded by FH5 with more modern electronics covering 1–30MHz and the same S25B frame aerial, but HF/DF continued to be fitted in virtually all UK escorts through Types 12, 14, 41, *Leander*, 21, 22 and 42 until the mid 1980s. FH5 was eventually removed as being obsolete and offering no capability against modern communications.

In the immediate postwar period, VHF/DF equipment was fitted, but was quickly retired as aircraft communications moved from VHF to UHF. This was succeeded by UHF/DF equipment, fitted to aircraft direction ships and aircraft carriers for control of friendly aircraft. The Royal Navy never made extensive use of TACAN in the same way as the USN for tactical aircraft control, and the requirement led to the lineal continuance of UHF/DF (as FU4) in the *Invincible*-class CVS. During the same period, MF/DF equipment was also fitted (FM16 covering the range 250–550kHz, and more recently SQB). This was used for routine navigation (taking bearings of MF beacon signals), and for maritime distress alarm signals made on 500kHz. This is now being superseded by the Global Maritime Distress and Safety System suite. Finally, some of the offshore patrol vessels involved in fishery protection have a VHF IMM-band DF system ('Polaris', as outfit AVV).

UA13 was introduced in 1975 using Signaal equipment in four Batch 2A and 3B *Leanders*, and covered 25MHz to 1.4GHz (with DF above 100MHz). The system was aimed at radar ESM against low-band systems, but proved difficult to calibrate and maintain; it was retired as the ships were eventually disposed of during the late 1980s and early 1990s.

Historically, ships have always had a general communications intercept facility. Initially, this was known as 'Searchbay'; this used manually tuned receivers and was in service until the early 1970s. It was updated as the Composite Reception Facility, hosting the Composite Reception Equipment (CRE) suite of receivers. This made use of spare aerials plus specialised 'walk-aboard' equipment fielded for intelligence purposes. All these systems were manned by RO(Special)s, who were transformed into the Communications Technician (CT) branch in September 1978 in order to increase status and reward. During the Falklands, these were able to give a running raid commentary of the Argentine pilots' radio chatter as they attacked the UK task force.

'Outboard'

Recent UK CESM experience is based on RN 'Outboard', a derivative of the USN programme known as 'Classic Outboard' (Ship HF/DF), working with 'Classic Bullseye' (Shore HF/DF) via the TACINTEL link as part of the overall 'Crosshair' DF network. This provided coverage against Soviet communications, and was complementary to the 'White Cloud' satellite network tasked against radars as the 'Classic Wizard' Ocean Surveillance Information system (OSIS). The rationale for 'Outboard' was protection of a carrier battle group, using two vessels per group in order to localise targets via crosscuts. The prime roles were: Signals Intelligence (SIGINT), early warning (I&W) against the Soviet Naval Air Force threat of manned bombers armed with air-to-surface missiles (ASM), and over-the-horizon detection and identification of surface ships for targeting of Harpoon and Tomahawk anti-ship missiles. Downstream reporting of contacts was via the Ocean Surveillance Information System, which has subsequently been updated via OSIS Baseline Upgrade (OBU) and the OSIS Evolutionary Development (OED).

'Outboard' was introduced in the US carrier escorts of the *Belknap* (CG-26) class in the 1970s, and UK involvement was initiated by First Sea Lord Admiral Ashmore in early 1974. In 1979, a bilateral memorandum of understanding (MoU) covered mutual support between USN and RN units. The RN 'Outboard' system was procured against SR(S)7373 and entered service in HMS *Boxer* (1984) and subsequent Type 22 Batch 2 class ships (six total), plus supporting communications infrastructure (RN INTEL), ancillary displays in command ships (CVS) and a training facility at HMS *Mercury*.

The original 'Outboard' system included several discrete equipments. The SLR-16 selected and acquired signals of interest in the HF band, and passed contacts to the SRD-19 for automatic direction finding/location. The SLR-23 carried out the same function at higher bands, and the SYQ-8 allowed precise analysis of the signals. The System Supervisor Station coordinated the process and communicated with other DF units via the INTEL network, and there was also a manual surveillance suite (UAD). RAF Edzell hosted the gateway between RN and USN units, and sanitised information was disseminated via Britmiss (the precursor to the Joint Operational Tactical System), or more recently by the RN's Command Support System (CSS).

The US 'Outboard' fit was subsequently broadened into the *Spruance* (DD-963) class and the nuclear cruisers, and this was followed by a more limited, smaller version initially known as 'Inboard' and now called Combat DF (AN/SRS-1), fitted in the *Wasp*-class LHD and later DDG-51 Flights. This was supported by a wider fit of the Ship Signals Exploitation Equipment (SSEE), via a number of incremental stages. The rationale was to provide Indicators & Warnings in ships that did not have a full 'Outboard' or Combat DF system, and SSEE Increment D was supplemented by the Transportable Radio Direction Finder (TRDF) system.

'Outboard' has subsequently been updated by a joint US/UK procurement programme for a Co-operative Outboard Logistic Upgrade (COBLU), with the memorandum of understanding (MoU) signed in July 1994. The COBLU programme was under SR(S)7395, which fitted equipment into Type 22 Batch 2 and 3 ships. The original configuration had effectively been replaced under this upgrade, which retained a similar aerial fit to the original system but replaced all the discrete below-decks equipment by racks and common operator workstations. Direct (over the air) interoperability with the US is not possible, and messages are interchanged via a shore gateway which subsumed the Edzell node following the closure of the latter site in 1997.

Jane's Defence Weekly has reported that COBLU has been replaced by a new system, initially known as 'Shaman' and more recently as 'Seaseeker', plus a more limited fit known as 'Hammerhead'.

Technical Aspects of CESM Equipment

Modern fits are characterised by a number of racks of digital receivers and the system software, plus user workstations. The change is the increasing degree of commercial off-the-shelf (COTS) content, at the expense of the bespoke hardware seen in legacy systems. This is likely to be supported by external communications and the DF aerials themselves. These usually include a VHF/UHF DF array, plus either a larger HF loop array or a series of distributed hull-mounted DF aerials. The distributed array potentially gives a longer baseline and better DF accuracy, offset by the greater influence of the ship's superstructure. Typical aerials are shown in Figure 14.

Discussion

The RN CESM capability is traceable back to the Second World War, and although there were some small breaks in continuity, these represent managed risk during the equipment succession process.

Most other Allied nations fit their escorts with a degree of CESM capability. In some cases this is no more than a Telegon equivalent, but is fitted on grounds of contributing to Situational Awareness, even without the

Fig 14: CESM Polemast and Deck Edge Aerials
Left: The AS-3112 SRD-19 DF antenna with its three-tier array; AS-3506 SRS-1 Combat DF was similar but had a two-tier array. (PE Law, *Shipboard Antennas*)

Right: The AS-420 TRDF; AS-420A was similar (MoD, Jane's IDR 17 June 2009).

Above: The original AS-3202 'Outboard' deck-edge aerial (MoD, Jane's IDR 17 June 2009).

cryptologic or exploitation content. Countries that have specialised electronic intelligence (ELINT) platforms still retain a CESM capability in escorts.

The Royal Navy's CRE offered a broadly similar capability to the US Navy's SSEE. The systems originally had a different rationale; however, with SSEE Increments D and E plus TRDF, the distinction between such systems and a full CESM outfit is becoming difficult to make. The degree of US Navy commitment to CESM can be gauged by the scale of the ship fit, including about one third of the large deck ships (LHD), a large percentage of the escorts (DDG-51 Flight 2/2A, and the remaining Aegis cruisers).

The pace of COTS development is faster than the regular procurement cycle. For example, COBLU had a Staff Requirement in 1989, was the subject of a UK/US MoU in 1994, and the equipment was in service by 2001. This has resulted in a need for regular technical refreshment. There is increasing commonality across programmes, leading to 'pick and mix' selections of software applications, hardware and aerials.

The move away from bespoke hardware and equipment is matched by a reduction in the size of the minimum viable CESM capability in each unit. As an example, the original 'Outboard' operator manning (thirteen, plus an officer, maintainers and any trainees) was driven by the number of separate equipments and the necessary linguistic skills, but newer systems may only require a team of three (or can operate while unmanned), but with greater dependence on reachback.

International Comparisons

In the period before the 'Five Eyes' (AUSCANZUKUS) group, the US was running on bilaterals, with the Office of Naval Research (ONR) in Europe and the residue of the UK Joint Mission to the US and with information sharing via the ACSIL structure. The UK shared its work on RU1-4, and this may well have influenced the US work on 'spinning dish' EW, as the Naval Radiation Laboratory (NRL) increased RU4's speed of 120rpm up to 250rpm (or in some cases 300rpm) – it should be noted that this was still a low-probability-of-intercept system.

It is ironic that the Americans often 'borrowed' or arrogated ideas from other countries, but then applied a predatory approach to intellectual property rights and patenting. Taken with their focus on precise measurement and instrumentation, this may have been their undoing for the first half of the postwar period given the relative impotence of their EW in the SLR and WLR-1 epoch.[5] US labs were good at 'polishing' their in-house technologies to enhance performance, but nowhere near as good at examining alternative options via Operational Analysis (OA), then re-directing their approach.

There were significant differences in the postwar approaches to EW. The US Navy only caught up with AN/SLQ-32 from late 1970's, and even then only as a warner function, not a fully-featured situational awareness tool.[6] SLQ-32 was based on dielectric lens technology (using a flat version of luneborg) as the beam former. The replacement AIEWS (AN/SLY-2) failed and is now an incremental Surface Electronic Warfare Improvement Program (SEWIP) – the similarity to the RN's UAT > MEWP initiative should be noted.

R&D and Procurement Issues

During the bulk of the postwar period, technical development was Government led, via a combination of research scientists (ASWE), procurement & development engineers (DGSW[N]), and serving RN staff as Naval Applicators (either user or technical). This was a creative partnership, responsible for most of the major improvements, typified by the quantum leap forward to UAA(1). In this era, ASWE-sponsored research led to an 'X', 'Y' or 'Z' model for sea trials; this was then 'production engineered' by a commercial firm before the main shipfitting programme could begin. As an example of timescales, sea trials of the initial 'X' model UAA(1) began in 1970 and development continued through to early 1973. The main production contract was let in May 1972 with delivery to shipbuilders and the refitting dockyards. However, build times and extended Part 4 trials led to it not being seen at sea until 1978–79. Factors in these timescales were resource limitations (a manpower ceiling) in research establishments, and cost-plus contracting of industry.

The change in the mid-1980s was the move to competitive tendering against a Cardinal Point Specification (CPS) in an attempt to shorten these timelines. CPS procurement was implemented by the DGSW(N) – then Dr Kiely – for the UAF and Type 996 procurements. The ethos of CPS was that industry 'knew best', and that provided MoD set the key parameters all would be well.[7] Hindsight has shown that this places a very high premium on the MoD setting the key user requirements (KUR) correctly (exemplified by the inadequate processor in UAF, and the support problems of Type 996). CPS led to a 'winner-takes-all' approach that ignored any desirable enhancements that emerged after the contract award. It also gave little emphasis to the more intangible aspects such as human factors, user friendliness and being 'jackproof', that had previously been the responsibility of Naval Applicators but whose input was now marginalised. The industry side included firms such as MEL, Thorn EMI, Siemens-Plessey and Racal, now consolidated to Thales alone. Both ASWE and RSRE retained small-scale production of specialist hardware until after the Falklands.

Conclusions

Electronic Warfare is the one postwar area at which the RN excelled, demonstrated by its:

– adoption of high-probability-of-interception 'staring' technology

– development of the Instantaneous Frequency Measurement receiver and the revolutionary panoramic frequency vs bearing display of UAA(1).

There were failures such as UAF and lukewarm support for jammers, but overall the combination of the RN, ASWE and their commercial suppliers delivered a series of world-beating capabilities.

Annex

Equipment nomenclature

For RN equipment, transmitters (radar, jammers and sonar) have a <u>Type</u> number, whilst the associated electronics have an <u>Outfit</u> title. The currently somewhat idiosyncratic scheme for identifying UK maritime equipment contains a number of different systems. Generally, older equipment was identified by two letters and a number but this evolved into the current three-letter Outfit title, with variants in parentheses, *eg* Outfit ABA(2), or in the case of radio, radar and sonar sets, by a Type number, *eg* radar Type 996. The scheme has no easily decodable structure (unlike the US system, where AN/SPY-1 explains the system function). Systems may also be known by their project open name or codeword (*eg* 'Orange Crop'), an abbreviation of their title; there are a few cases where the UK numbering scheme mirrors the equivalent US structure. Airborne systems tend to use both a codeword and an ARI (airborne radio installation) number.

Abbreviations

ACSIL	Admiralty Committee for Scientific Intelligence Liaison		HCI	Human Computer Interaction
ADAWS	Action Data Automation & Weapon System		HF	High Frequency
ADR	Active Decoy Round		HF/DF	High Frequency Direction Finding
AEW	Airborne Early Warning		I&W	Indications and Warnings
AGPO	Angle Gate Pull-Off		IFM	Instantaneous Frequency Measurement
AIEWS/SEWIP	(US) Advanced Integrated EW System/Staged EW Improvement Programme		IR	Infra Red
			ITU	International Telecommunications Union
AM/FM	Audio Modulation/Frequency Modulation		LFA	Radar Type 996 track extractor outfit
ASMD	Anti-Ship Missile Defence		MCMV	Mine Counter Measures Vessel
ASWE	Admiralty Surface Weapons Establishment, at Portsdown		KUR	Key User Requirements
			MEL	Marconi Equipment Limited
BBC	Broad Brand Chaff		MF/DF	Medium Frequency Direction Finding
CAAIS	Computer Assisted Action Information System		MoU	Memorandum of Understanding
CAMM	Common Airframe Modular Missile - Sea Ceptor		MRL	Marconi Research Laboratory
CESM	Communications Electronic Support Measures		NRL	(US) Naval Radiation Laboratory
			OA	Operational Analysis
CIWS	Close-In Weapon System		OB	Outboard
COBLU	Cooperative Outboard Logistics Upgrade		OBU	Outboard Baseline Upgrade
COTS	Commercial Off The Shelf		OED	OSIS Evolutionary Development
CPS	Cardinal Point Specification		OEM(EW)	Operator Equipment Maintainer (EW)
CRE	Composite Reception Equipment		ONR	(US) Office of Naval Research
CRF	Composite Reception Facility		OSIS	Ocean Surveillance Information System
CRT	Cathode Ray Tube		RAE	Royal Aircraft Establishment, at Farnborough
CRx	Channelised Receiver		RAM	Radar Absorbent Material
CSS	Command Support System		RASH	Radar Absorbent Sheet
CT	Communications Technician		RCS	Radar Cross Section
CVR	Crystal Video Receiver		RESM	Radar Electronic Surveillance Measures
CVS	(RN) Aircraft Carrier (*Invincible* class)		RF	Radio Frequency
CW	Continuous Wave		RGPO	Range Gate Pull-Off
DE&S	Defence Equipment & Support, based at Abbeywood		RO(S)	Radio Operator (Special) - later became CT branch
DF	Direction Finding		RO(W)	Radio Operator (Warfare) - original EW operator branch
DGSW(N)	Director General Surface Weapons (Naval). Predecessor to DE&S			
			RORSAT	Radar Ocean Reconnaissance Satellite
DIFM	Digital Instantaneous Frequency Measurement		RSRE	Radar Signals Research Establishment, at Malvern
ES	Electronic Surveillance			
ESM	Electronic Support Measures		SA	Situational Awareness
EW	Electronic Warfare		SARIE	Selective Automatic Radar Identification Equipment
EW Op	Electronic Warfare Operator			
EWD	Electronic Warfare Director		SIGINT	Signals Intelligence
GCHQ	Government Communication Headquarters		SRBOC	(US) Super Rapid Blooming Offboard Chaff
GTPA	Graph Theoretic Processing Algorithm		TACAN	Tactical Air Navigation

Project codewords

UA8–10 'Porker', 667/8 'Cookie', 669 'Bexley', FH5 'Dogma', UA13 'Dimple', UAA(1) 'Abbeyhill', YAG (SARIE) 'Tonga', 675 'Millpost', 670 'Heather', WBZ (high-power jammer amplifier) 'Handiwork', UAF 'Jane'. See Notes on Above Water Weapons in ADM 256/149, /158, /160, /165; 'Bexley' DEFE 69/492; UA9 ADM 220/1252, /2076.

Comment

Nomenclature for EW equipment is not a precise science. In the late 1950s Benjamin commented that a radar fingerprinting equipment was initially known as Outfit RFP, until someone thought this could be sensitive and it was changed to Outfit REB, because the tally could simply be put through the engraver again to amend strokes F>E and P>B.

Acknowledgements:

The following individuals significantly assisted in the preparation of this article: Peter East, Mike Keeping, Lt-Cdr Clive Kidd (until the *Collingwood* museum was closed in August 2021), Jon Sketchley, and John Wise.

Sources:

TJ Bird, Lt-Cdr, 'Passive Electronic Warfare Systems', *Naval Electrical Review*, Oct 1970, Vol 24 No 2.

PW East, 'Fifty years of instantaneous frequency measurement', *Radar, Sonar, Navigation*, Vol 6, IET (2012), 112–122. See also series of papers in *Electronic Support Measures*, *IEE Proceedings*, Vol 132 Part F No 4, July 1985.

LA Gebhard, 'Evolution of Naval Radio Electronics & the Contribution of NRL', NRL Report 8300, 1979.

DG Kiely, *Naval Electronic Warfare* Vol 5, Brassey's (London 1988).

TW Kimbrell, 'Electronic Warfare in Ship Defence', *NSWC Dahlgren Division Technical Digest*, Sept 1994, 80–87.

Preston E Law Jr, *Shipboard Antennas*, Artech House (Dedham MA, 1983).

JC Wise, 'The Navy is Listening', Vol 1 *Radio Warfare* (2019) & Vol 2 *Electronic Warfare* (2020); published privately.

Endnotes:

1 FA Kingsley, *The Applications of Radar and other Electronic Systems in the Royal Navy in World War 2*. The Naval Radar Trust & Macmillan, 1995. See Monograph 5: 'Electronic Countermeasures in the RN', 189–228.

2 There is a considerable technical overlap between RESM and CESM equipment, because newer 3/4G comms bands and WiFi run at up to 2GHz (higher than D-band air surveillance radars). However, RESM is looking for pulse transmissions with scan cycles, whilst CESM is usually tackling continuous CW for voice or data.

3 Also note that the comms bearers are often high-duty cycle or continuous wave (CW) signals rather than the pulse trains of conventional radars. This has the effect of increasing the background (or ambient) noise seen by military ESM equipment operating in the Littoral.

4 'Zippo' is a warning called by the EW Operator in response to an immediate threat such as a missile seeker; it uses a whistle to draw attention, and triggers a series of pre-planned responses by the ship's command team covering manoeuvre, decoy and close-in weapon system deployment.

5 TW Kimbrell, 'Electronic Warfare in Ship Defence', NSWC Dahlgren Division Technical Digest, Sept 1994, 80–87.

6 See Louis A Gebhard, 'Growth of Naval Radar & Electronics', NRL report 7600 June 76, via dtic.mil, 320ff.

7 The SLQ-32 Designed to Price EW System (DTPEWS) was modular: V(1) warner for SRBOC chaff, V(2) with SA, and V(3) with jammer.

8 DG Kiely, *op cit* – although the author was formerly DGSW(N), the book was written from a commercial perspective including the Cardinal Point procurement of Outfit UAF.

THE GERMAN FLAK SHIPS
PART I: THE GERMAN AND EX-NORWEGIAN HULLS

Aidan Dodson and **Dirk Nottelmann** outline the history of the first four of eight planned state-of-the-art anti-aircraft batteries converted from turn-of-the-century German and ex-enemy vessels by the *Kriegsmarine* during the Second World War. The remaining vessels are scheduled to be covered in next year's edition.

One of the many ways in which the Second World War differed from the First was in the significantly increased threat from the air. At sea, this was recognised in a number of navies by building or converting ships whose primary armament was directed skywards. Britain's Royal Navy had begun a programme of converting First World War-vintage light cruisers into ocean-going fleet and convoy escorts equipped with the latest AA weaponry and fire control systems. Such equipment was likewise installed by the German Navy in old hulls of similar size, but in this case primarily for the purpose of defending harbours from air attack from seaward rather than other ships at sea. As a result, self-propulsion was a secondary requirement, and of the eight such vessels projected only three were actually able to move under their own power, and then at a rather sedate pace.

In the Beginning

As early as 4 September 1939 the port of Wilhelmshaven, and the important fleet anchorage of the Schillig Roads

in the Jade Estuary that lay between it and the North Sea, had been subject to air attack by bombers of the Royal Air Force; countless more would follow before the end of the war. From the outset, the lack of seaward anti-aircraft defence for Wilhelmshaven, especially from the northeast and southeast, was recognised. In particular there were certain bearings which were difficult to cover by land-based heavy anti-aircraft (Flak) weapons, even when firing at the limits of their effective range.

To close these gaps, several proposals for floating batteries were discussed, each with particular reference to guns for both long-range and close-in defence. There

Arcona (above) moored at Swinemünde in 1938 and *Medusa* (below), at an unknown date, at Wilhelmshaven. Both hulls had been kept in good shape externally. (Dirk Nottelmann/Heidrich collection)

were also wider issues of the most effective positioning of the batteries, as well as how they should be integrated into the overall air defence network.[1]

One problem was the paucity of suitable hulls and, with few alternatives available, the Navy decided on the former small cruisers *Arcona* and *Medusa*, currently in use as accommodation hulks at Wilhelmshaven and Kiel.[2] Both were well suited to this conversion, as they had retained all of their structural strength-points for mounting medium-calibre guns, as well as magazines and ammunition hoists. While the ships retained their machinery, this had not been used since the 1920s (*Medusa* having even had her funnels removed – see photograph); this was not to be reconditioned, as it was deemed unnecessary for their intended harbour defence role.

Medusa had been launched in December 1900 as one of the third group of the *Gazelle* class, the first of the classic general-purpose small cruisers built by the German Navy up to the end of the First World War.[3] *Arcona* had entered the water in April 1902 as a unit of the follow-on *Frauenlob* class, and had been converted to a minelaying cruiser in 1912, serving as guardship in the Ems estuary throughout the First World War. She had remained in commission after the war as a minesweeper support ship and, following a refit, had served with the newly-established *Reichsmarine*[4] until paid off in December 1923. In contrast, *Medusa* had been laid up from 1908 to 1914, returning briefly to active service for second-line duties from 1914 to December 1916, when she became a training/accommodation ship at the principal naval school of Flensburg-Mürwik.

Medusa was subsequently recommissioned in July 1920 as the first major warship of the *Reichsmarine*, serving until September 1924. Although a major modernisation was briefly considered to allow her a further period of service, *Medusa* was never recommissioned; she was stricken in March 1929 in anticipation of the commissioning of her 'legal' replacement, *Karlsruhe* in November. Likewise, *Arcona*, which had served from 1921 to 1923, was stricken on 15 January 1930, the day her replacement *Köln* was commissioned. *Arcona* and *Medusa* were, however, retained as accommodation hulks. The former remained externally largely intact (save for the loss of her mainmast) while serving successively at Wilhelmshaven, Swinemünde and Kiel, but *Medusa*, which was used to accommodate the crews of destroyers and torpedo boats at Wilhelmshaven from 1927, was later stripped down to just her masts.

Arcona

Having been selected for conversion on 12 April 1940, *Arcona* was taken in hand at the Deutsche Werke at Kiel two days later, work being completed on 23 May. Her initial modifications were quite simple. The foremast was removed and the forefunnel was cut down to form the support for a 110cm searchlight; the second funnel was retained as an uptake for the remaining (after) group of boilers, which provided heating as well as steam for electrical power generation. Her outfit of guns would vary significantly over the coming years, with the full details not necessarily reflected in published sources. Other modifications would also be made (see below), with the vessel wearing various camouflage paint schemes during her Second World War career.

Four 10.5cm/45 HA mountings were initially fitted in the locations formerly occupied by the original main guns on the forecastle and poop. These required the addition of large sponsons protruding over the sides to provide sufficient space for the gun crews for all-round firing. For close-in defence the main battery was supported by single

Arcona in the spring of 1940, fresh from her reconstruction. She is wearing the first of her many different camouflage schemes (see below). Note the guardrail-lined sponsons for the 10.5cm guns, which would soon be closed by bulwarks. (Dirk Nottelmann collection)

3.7cm semi-automatic guns superimposed fore and aft, and six single 2cm guns forward, amidships and aft. A lattice-supported platform for a second searchlight was installed atop the engine casing, while fire control directors with 3-metre rangefinders were fitted fore and aft.

Arcona was rapidly brought into service, being

A set of images taken on board *Arcona* during 1940. Clockwise from the top right: view forward along the starboard side, with one of the 2cm AA guns in the foreground; crew members gather informally around the empty cradle for the motor launch; view from the quarterdeck towards the searchlight atop the former forefunnel; view from the bridge onto the forecastle, showing the remaining portside anchor cable. In this last image the strong current of the Jade is evidenced by the 'bow wave' of the mooring buoy. (Dirk Nottelmann collection)

anchored in the Schillig Roads some 19 kilometres north of the dockyard and linked to the wider local anti-aircraft network via a telephone buoy. From here she scored her first success against an enemy aircraft on the night of 20/21 July 1940. Initially she was moored in 13 metres of water, but concerns regarding her vulnerability to airborne torpedoes meant that her anchorage was later

moved 1.5 kilometres to the northeast into shallower (7-metre) water, the ship being declared operational in her new location on 27 December 1940.

On 7 January 1941, however, *Arcona* had to be temporarily withdrawn into the inner port of Wilhelmshaven due to strong icing within the Jade estuary. In the summer of 1941 she underwent a first

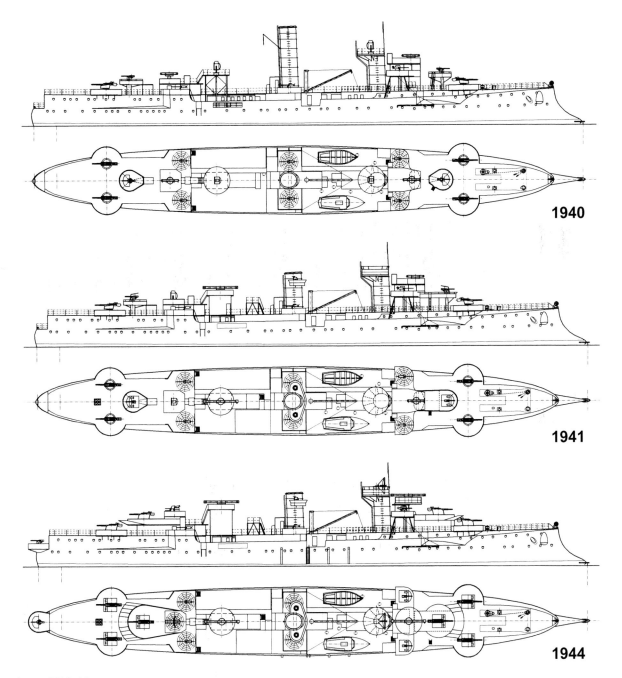

1940

1941

1944

Arcona 1940–44
As rebuilt, *Arcona* retained a single bower anchor (to port), unlike *Medusa*. After her first major refit in 1941, the most obvious change is the cutting-down of her second funnel, but other important changes include the 6-metre rangefinder aft and the fitting of splinter shields around the 37mm guns. In her final configuration in 1944, *Arcona* carries her final complement of guns, including one on the stern platform; both directors are fitted with 6-metre rangefinders, and there is a *Würzburg* radar antenna atop her former forward funnel. (Drawn by Dirk Nottelmann)

Arcona following her 1941 refit. (Aidan Dodson collection)

refit, during which the second funnel was shortened and fitted with a platform for two 90cm searchlights. A new fire control director with a 6-metre rangefinder was fitted aft, exchanging positions with the after searchlight. She would return to her former position at the end of August, but was again withdrawn into the inner port in January 1942 due to icing in the Jade. While in the dockyard in mid-February awaiting the March thaw, she and *Medusa* were put on high alert, owing to the presence of the battleship *Scharnhorst* in the dockyard for initial repairs following the 'Channel Dash'. *Arcona* left the dockyard on 17 March but, due to the continuing harsh winter, had to remain within the port for almost a further two months, albeit fully operational.

When she returned to Schillig Roads on 7 May, her berth was shifted 4.2 kilometres upstream. Towards the end of the year a further refit was carried out when a FuMG 39 TD (*Würzburg*) radar was installed. This was standard equipment for the Air Force and Army, and reflected the ship's integration into the shore-based air defences of Wilhelmshaven. It was fitted in the place formerly occupied by the searchlight (removed in anticipation in 1941) atop the former forefunnel; the radar became operational as of 1 November. Additionally, a fifth 10.5cm gun was added aft, and all mounts were now protected by splinter shields; the 3.7cm gun displaced by the new 10.5cm weapon was relocated to the former minelaying platform at the stern.

Having temporarily replaced *Medusa* on the south side of Wilhelmshaven during her half-sister's summer-1943 refit (see below), *Arcona* was once more refitted during the winter of 1943/44 to her final configuration. She received a sixth 10.5cm gun forward, supported by the replacement of the former 3-metre director atop the bridge with one equipped with a 6-metre rangefinder; a quadruple 2cm mounting (*Vierling*) was fitted aft in place of a single mount of that calibre that had replaced the after searchlight in 1943 (see camouflage graphic). On 22 July 1944 she moved permanently from her customary location at Wilhelmshaven North, being towed around to the Elbe estuary in front of the Kiel Canal locks at Brunsbüttel. Here she relieved *Ariadne* (see below) in

Medusa during the second half of 1941 after her first minor conversion, which included the mounting of splinter shields on the 3.7cm guns and the partial enclosure of the searchlight platforms. (Dirk Nottelmann collection)

German Flak Ships: Characteristics & Building Data

Arcona

Displacement:	2,657 tonnes
Dimensions:	104.4m (wl), 105.0m (oa) x 12.3m x 5m
Machinery:	Inoperative
Armament:	1940/42 – Four 10.5cm/45, two 3.7cm, six 2cm AA.
	1943 – Five 10.5cm/45, four 3.7cm, five 2cm AA.
	1944 – Six 10.5cm/45, three 3.7cm, eight 2cm (1 x IV, 4 x I) AA
Fire control:	1940 – Two directors (2 x 3m rangefinders)
	1941/42 – Two directors (1 x 3m, 1 x 6m rangefinders)
	1943 – Two directors (1 x 3m, 1 x 6m rangefinders)
	1944 – Two directors (2 x 6m rangefinders)
Radar:	1944 – One FuMG 39 TD (*Würzburg*)

Medusa

Displacement:	2,650 tonnes
Dimensions:	104.1m (wl), 105.1m (oa) x 11.8m x 5m
Machinery:	Inoperative
Armament:	1940/41 – Four 10.5cm/45, two 3.7cm, four 2cm AA.
	1942/43 – Four 10.5cm/45, two 3.7cm, six 2cm (2 x II, 2 x I) AA.
	1943/44 – Six 10.5cm/45, two 3.7cm, four 2cm AA.
	1944 – Six 10.5cm/45, two 3.7cm, eight 2cm (1 x IV, 4 x I) AA
Fire control:	1940 – Two directors (2 x 3m rangefinders)
	1943 – Two directors (2 x 6m rangefinders)
Radar:	1943 – One FuMG 39 TD (*Würzburg*)

Nymphe & Thetis

Displacement:	3,858 tonnes
Dimensions:	85.3m (pp), 92.7m (oa) x 14.8m x 5.4m
Machinery:	Three cylindrical boilers (two double-, one single-ended); 2-shaft VTE; 4,500ihp = 14 knots
Armament:	Six 10.5cm/45, two 4cm, six 2cm AA
Fire control:	Two directors (2 x 3m rangefinders)
Radar:	[*Nymphe* 1945: one FuMG 39 TD (*Würzburg*)]?

Building Data

Name	Built	Launched	Converted	Recomm
Arcona	AG Weser, Bremen	22 Apr 1902	Deutsche Werke, Kiel	25 May 1940
Medusa	AG Weser, Bremen	05 Dec 1900	Rickmers, Wesermünde	Aug 1940
Nymphe (ex-*Tordenskjold*)	Armstrong, Tyneside	18 Mar 1897	Kaldnes mekaniske verksted, Tønsberg	01 Feb 1941
Thetis (ex-*Harald Haarfagre*)	Armstrong, Tyneside	04 Jan 1897	Kaldnes mekaniske verksted, Tønsberg	01 Feb 1941

protecting the canal against attacks from seaward. Contrary to reports that she was scuttled in the II. Entrance at Wilhelmshaven on 3 May 1945, she was still there at the German surrender. Sometime during the six weeks that followed, she was towed to Wilhelmshaven and the crew discharged. It was believed she had shot down nineteen Allied aircraft during the war.

Medusa

Owing to a lack of dockyard capacity, *Medusa*'s rebuild was carried out by Rickmers at Wesermünde, from May to August 1940. Although the conversion was on the same lines as that of *Arcona*, as essentially a bare hull before conversion *Medusa* looked rather different. She had a slim new funnel and a mast supporting a derrick amidships, and lattice-supported platforms fore and aft each supporting a searchlight. As with *Arcona*, her armament evolved over the coming years (see above table).

On 13 August 1940, *Medusa* was towed out of Wesermünde and, on arrival at Wilhelmshaven, anchored in the Vareler Deep of Jade Bay, in a location six kilometres southeast of the dockyard. Connected like *Arcona* to the air defence network by a telephone buoy, *Medusa* was declared ready for action on the 22nd as part of *Marine-Flak-Abteilung* (Naval Anti-aircraft Division)

222, responsible for the defence of the southern side of the dockyard.

In July 1941 her gun barrels were replaced, and in October the ship underwent a refit that lasted a month. As with *Arcona*, the harsh ice of January 1942 forced *Medusa* to be moved into the dockyard, and while there she was badly damaged on 13 March when accidentally rammed by a tug while moored alongside, with damage on both sides of the ship. The four-week repair period included the stripping-out of the redundant forward boiler room (requiring the addition of concrete ballast to compensate for the lost boilers and ancillaries) and its conversion into a crew recreation space. The work was largely carried out by the ship's complement using equipment provided by the dockyard, as the dockyard's personnel could not be spared for a job of such low official importance.

When again withdrawn to the dockyard in the face of ice in January 1943, *Medusa* was docked and shields added to the 10.5cm guns, as had been done in *Arcona* a few months earlier. Further modifications were undertaken during a major refit that began at the end of July 1943, when two more 10.5cm guns were added and the rangefinders upgraded to the 6-metre type. In addition, the former after searchlight tower was moved forward to carry a *Würzburg* antenna. The tower was significantly heightened, and the funnel and derrick post were both cut down in order to give the radar uninterrupted all-round coverage. A pair of searchlights were mounted on the funnel and a light topmast on the derrick post. In October *Medusa* keeled over in dry dock due to poor bracing; she nevertheless completed the refit as planned at the beginning of November and returned to her customary station on 5 November 1943. During her refit, *Medusa*'s place in the Vareler Deep had been taken temporarily by *Arcona*.

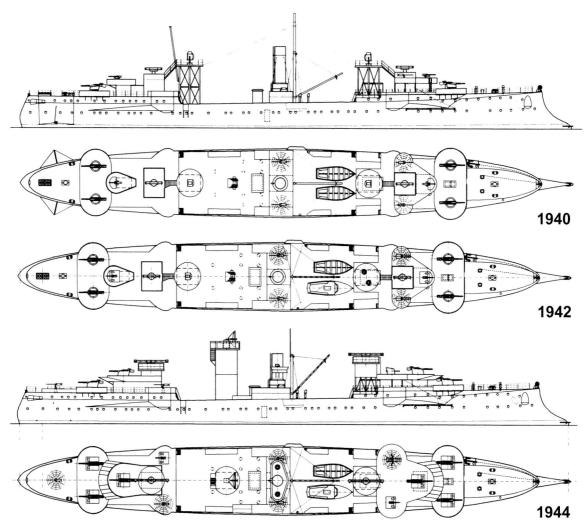

Medusa 1940–44

In her initial configuration in 1940, *Medusa* looked distinctly different from *Arcona*, especially with regard to her 'stovepipe' funnel amidships. By late 1942, a number of changes have occurred in her layout, prior to more radical changes during her 1943 refit. By 1944, she has shields for her guns, two 6-metre rangefinders, and a prominent *Würzburg* tower, raised above funnel height to avoid any danger of 'wooding'. (Drawn by Dirk Nottelmann)

The mild winter of 1943/44 did not require the Flak ships to take refuge in the dockyard, but on 15 February 1944 *Medusa* was accidentally rammed by a tug and had to be docked for repairs, the opportunity being taken to install a quadruple 2cm mounting (*Vierling*) on the port bridge-wing in place of the twin mount. The ship was back on station on 4 March.

Medusa was severely damaged in an attack by 14–16 fighter-bombers (including a number of De Havilland Mosquitos) around 14.30 on 19 April 1945, being hit by two bombs and suffering two near-misses, to port and starboard; casualties amounted to 22 dead and 41 wounded. She was, however, successfully towed into the dockyard by a pair of tugs, being secured in the Hipper (now-Großer) Hafen at 21.30, moored at the head of the Wiesbadenbrücke. As she was beyond immediate repair, four 10.5cm were removed for employment ashore on 22 April. The remaining two 10.5cm and one quadruple and four twin 2cm were ordered to be removed on the 25th, although this was not done. It had been planned to sink *Medusa* as a blockship outside Wilhelmshaven's III.

The forecastle of *Medusa* in 1944, with the shields added to the 10.5cm and 37mm guns and the forward 6-metre rangefinder prominent. (Dirk Nottelmann collection)

Entrance, but this was overtaken by the surrender of the port and she remained afloat, despite suffering extensive flooding.[5] Her remaining armament was removed on 31 August, and by 2 September she was moored along

A set of images taken on board *Medusa* early in her career in 1940. Clockwise from top right: the forward starboard 10.5cm HA gun, still unshielded; coaling on the quarterdeck – note the steam-operated cargo winch, added during her conversion; one of the diesel generators in a former machinery space, with the switchboard overhead; the ship's cutter and the after end of the bridge structure. (Dirk Nottelmann collection)

Arcona and the ex-Dutch conversion *Undine* (see Part II) in the winter 1945/46, in the lock at III. Entrance at Wilhelmshaven, accompanied by the tugs *Enak* and *Heros*. Both former Flak ships appear to be in good condition. (Dirk Nottelmann collection)

Arcona

1940/41

1941/43

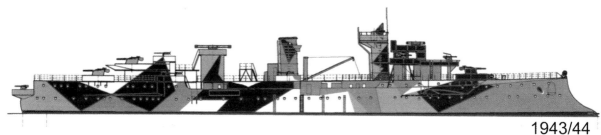

1943/44

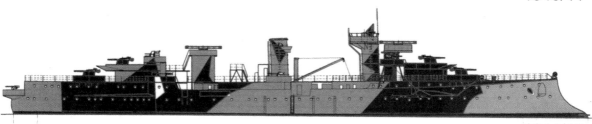

1944/45

A selection of the camouflage schemes worn by *Arcona*. (Graphic by Dirk Nottelmann)

with *Arcona, Ariadne* and *Undine* (for the latter two vessels see Part II), together with the small ex-Dutch survey vessel *Jever*, in the Nordhafen. An aerial photograph of 3 September 1945 shows either *Arcona* or *Medusa* moored inboard of one of *Ariadne* and *Undine* opposite IV. Entrance. During the winter, *Arcona* and *Undine* were photographed together in III. Entrance; this may have been in February 1946, when *Undine* was in transit to the Netherlands (see Part II). Most sources have *Arcona* and *Medusa* broken up during 1947–50, but one report has the remains of *Medusa* still present in the Nordhafen as late as October 1955, alongside those of the fleet tender *Hai* (ex-*Königin Luise*, ex-*F3*, sunk at Kiel[!] in 1945), a submarine and two merchantmen.[6]

The final fates of *Arcona* and *Medusa* are complicated by the fact that, while both vessels were afloat at the end of war, with *Arcona* (although not the bomb-damaged *Medusa*) seemingly in good condition, the Allies' Trinational Naval Commission (TNC), charged with surveying all German warships during the autumn of 1945,[7] noted both ships as 'wrecks'. This placed them in Category C, which mandated that they be destroyed no later than 15 August 1946. This was certainly what happened to all other significant vessels so classified. Ships still afloat were towed out into the Skagerrak and scuttled, and those resting on the bottom of the harbour were wrecked beyond hope of refloating by demolition

and depth charges, then scrapped *in situ*. For *Arcona* and *Medusa* to have been made exceptions would be contrary to the great care taken by the British authorities at Wilhelmshaven (and Kiel) to comply with the letter of inter-Allied agreements on the destruction of Category C vessels. The US authorities at Bremerhaven were equally scrupulous. However, the same cannot be said of the Soviets, who delayed taking action until 1947; although a considerable number of ships were then sunk, others were broken up afloat over a period of time.[8]

The ex-Norwegian Ships[9]

At the time of the German invasion of Norway in April 1940, the largest ships of the Norwegian Navy were four coast defence ships, built in pairs in the UK at the end of the 19th century.[10] Two, *Norge* and *Eidsvold* (1900), were sunk by German destroyers on the first day of the attack (9 April), but the other pair, *Tordenskjold* and *Harald Haarfagre*, were captured intact laid up at Horten Dockyard later the same day. Both were taken in hand for conversion to anti-aircraft vessels, but as their machinery was in good order both would be capable of self-propulsion, and would have perhaps the most prominent part in the war of all the conversions.

The ships had been laid down by Armstrong at Low Walker on the Tyne on 18 March 1896, and launched as

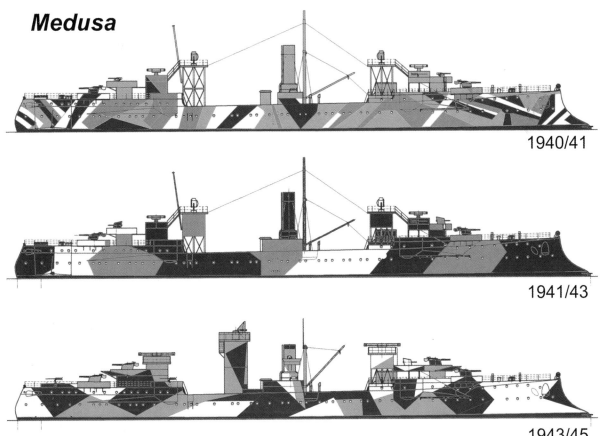

Medusa

1940/41

1941/43

1943/45

A selection of the camouflage schemes worn by *Medusa*. (Graphic by Dirk Nottelmann)

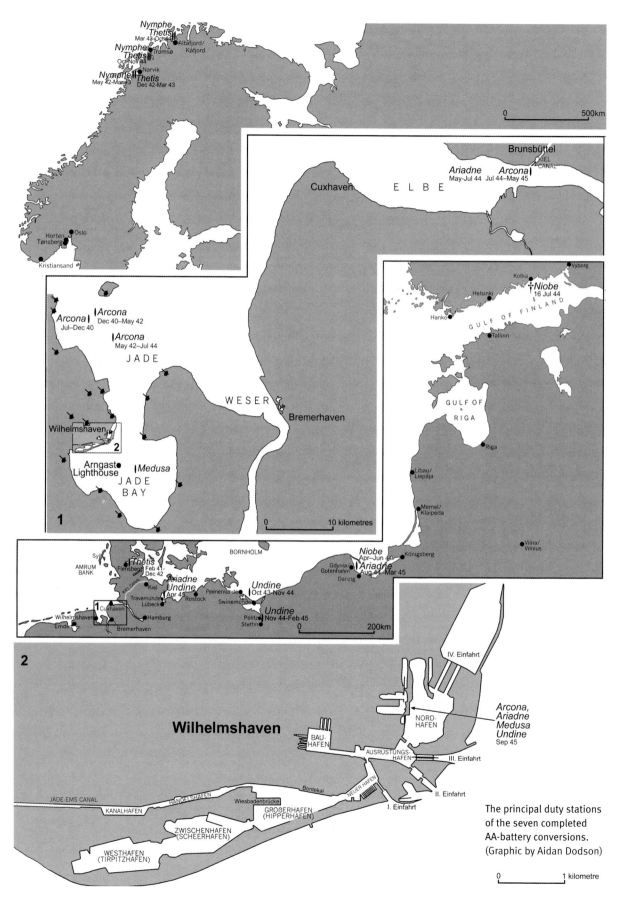

The principal duty stations of the seven completed AA-battery conversions. (Graphic by Aidan Dodson)

Harald Haarfagre at sea early in her career, with minimal bridgework. (Aidan Dodson collection)

Harald Haarfagre on 4 January 1897 and *Tordenskjold* on 18 March the same year. They commissioned on 18 December 1897 and 21 March 1898 respectively.[11] As built, the pair were armed with a 21cm/45 gun fore and aft and six 12cm/45 on the upper deck amidships, backed up by six 76mm/40 and six 1pdr weapons. By the 1930s, two 76mm HA guns had been added and four of the 1pdrs landed. Machinery comprised three cylindrical boilers (one single-, one double-ended), supplying steam for VTE engines rated at 4500ihp, giving a top speed of 16.9 knots.

Tordenskjold was employed with the fleet up to the First World War, but from 1917 operated primarily as a cadet training ship; she undertook annual cruises until 1934, and had her bridge greatly enlarged in support of this role. From 1934 she was an accommodation ship for

cadets at Horten. Like her sister, *Harald Haarfagre* had also been employed as a cadet training ship on occasion, in 1906, 1907, 1914 and 1920, as well as taking part in fleet exercises up to 1923. She was laid up by the late 1930s, becoming an accommodation ship for recruits at Horten in 1940.

Being virtually undamaged, the sisters were selected for conversion to Flak ships during the summer of 1940, with work beginning on 10 October. The surviving drawings suggest that *Tordenskjold*'s conversion served as the model for the conversion of her sister. The reconstruction was planned and executed by Kaldnes Mekanikske Verksted at Tønsberg, although guns and associated fittings were installed at the Deutsche Werke, Kiel.[12]

The sisters commissioned under the German flag on 1 February 1941, *Tordenskjold* becoming *Nymphe*, and

Two images of *Harald Haarfagre* during her conversion into *Thetis* at Kaldnes Mekanikske Verksted at Tønsberg. Structural work is complete but she still lacks her armament, directors and searchlights, which will be installed at Kiel. (Dirk Nottelmann collection)

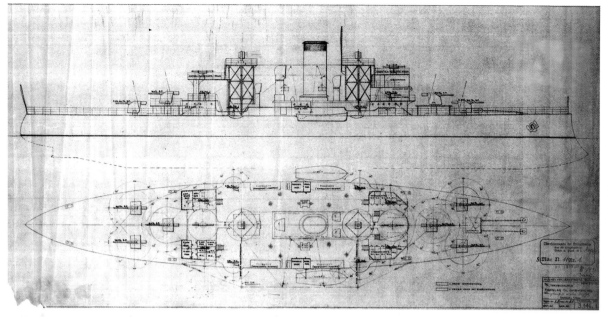

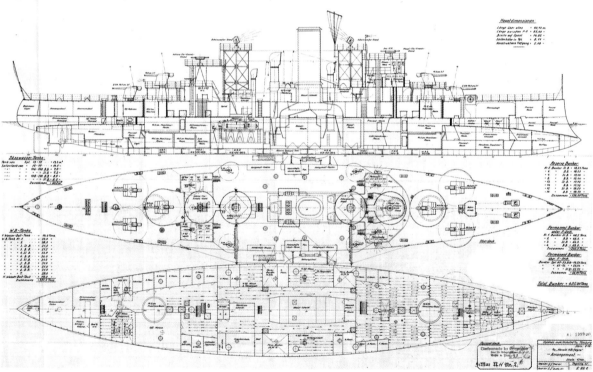

Plans for the Conversion of *Tordenskjold*
Two original plans for the conversion of *Tordenskjold* into *Nymphe* dating from December 1940. Unlike her sister, she did not have the shelter deck abreast the funnel built out to the sides. (Dirk Nottelmann collection)

Thetis on trials, shortly after completion of the conversion in February 1941, 1941, wearing a very elaborate camouflage pattern. She now has the tripod mast abaft her funnel that would serve to distinguish her from *Nymphe*. The guns are still without shields, as are the fire control directors. She has not yet been fitted with her deck-edge degaussing coil. (Dirk Nottelmann collection)

Thetis during the final stages of her fitting-out at Kiel. Her unique tripod mainmast has still to be erected. The photo gives an excellent view of the elaborate camouflage pattern with which she entered service. (Aidan Dodson collection)

Haarfagre taking the name *Thetis*; these names had both belonged to now-scrapped sisters of *Medusa*. This established a pattern of naming converted Flak ships after German small cruisers of the 1890s and early 1900s (see also Part II), implicitly placing them in a single class of vessel.

All existing armament was removed, and single 10.5cm/45 guns were paired on the forecastle and quarterdeck as in *Arcona* and *Medusa*. Being larger vessels, from the outset *Nymphe* and *Thetis* carried two more guns of this calibre in superimposed positions. According to the original plans, there were to be eight short-barrelled 4cm machine-cannon of unknown origin, four replacing the original corner 12cm weapons and four abreast the bridge, but in the event similar short-barrelled 2cm guns were planned to be substituted in all but two cases; this would be amended shortly afterwards to modern German AA guns of the same calibre. Directors with 3-metre rangefinders were to be fitted atop the original bridgework and on a platform on the cut-down mainmast. These were certainly fitted (with hoods) in *Thetis*, but photographs of *Nymphe* make it unclear whether she ever carried them. Tall lattice structures fore and aft of the funnel, which was shortened by some two metres, each originally supported a single searchlight, but

the forward model was later exchanged for a pair of sided smaller units in *Nymphe*, as would be done on *Medusa* for a while in 1942.

A major difference between the sisters as converted was that *Thetis* had a tripod mast installed aft of the funnel, a feature never present in *Nymphe*. Also, the latter did not have the shelter deck built out to the ship's sides abreast the funnel. In *Thetis* the shelter deck extension supported the ship's boats; in *Nymphe* these were

Thetis in the inner Kiel fjord in the autumn of 1942, painted in grey overall. Her forward searchlight appears to be covered by a tarpaulin, which renders it nearly invisible against the background. Hoods have been fitted to the directors, as well as splinter shields to the guns, and there is now a main topmast. Visible in the background are the hulked cruiser *Berlin* and the Hamburg-Amerika liner *New York*, both in use as accommodation ships. Shortly afterwards, *Thetis* would leave for northern Norway. (Dirk Nottelmann collection)

Nymphe in dry dock at Kiel, with her initial(?) camouflage pattern. Her degaussing coil is prominent; this was carried farther down the side of the hull than the deck-edge installation of *Thetis*. (Dirk Nottelmann collection)

By the time this photograph was taken in northern Norway, *Nymphe* had been repainted in a new scheme, and the forward searchlight had been replaced by two smaller units. (Dirk Nottelmann collection)

Thetis in northern Norway late in the war, in yet another camouflage scheme. She has received a topgallant mast on her forward signal pole, but her profile has otherwise been little altered. (Dirk Nottelmann collection)

Nymphe in northern Norway in May 1943, with the battleship *Scharnhorst* in the background. (Aidan Dodson collection)

Thetis at Tromsø in 1945, once again in overall grey, but (like her sister) now with a broad black top to her funnel. Modifications seem limited to a shortening of her topmasts. The forward searchlight is missing, possibly in preparation for the installation of *Würzburg*. (Aidan Dodson collection)

carried on davits. At the end of her career, *Nymphe* had her forward lattice structure significantly heightened, presumably to receive a *Würzburg* antenna, although it is uncertain whether this was ever installed. Her after lattice structure was shortened at the same time, probably as topweight compensation. These modifications were not carried out in *Thetis*, although the forward searchlight platform was empty at the end of the war.

Information on the careers of the two ships is incomplete, with some confusion regarding their individual histories. *Thetis* is generally reported to have joined *Marine-Flak-Abteilung* 709 based at Harstad/Norway from the outset but several images, taken at different times as indicated by changes in her camouflage scheme, contradict this. Most images instead show her at Kiel, while another source claims that she was employed at Flensburg from February 1941, protecting the naval academy as well as the town and local shipyard against air raids coming along the Flensburg fjord. This deployment seems to have lasted until December 1942 (with a confirmed brief stint at Kiel in October), when *Thetis* was reported to be located at Kristiansand, Norway, finally on her way north.

Nymphe is likewise reported to have initially joined *Marine-Flak-Abteilung* 214 at Kiel, suggesting a possible confusion of names. However, her transfer to Norway in May 1942, to join *Marine-Flak-Abteilung* 710 based at Tromsø, is confirmed. She would initially be deployed in the Ofotfjord off Narvik for the defence of the Bogen Bay anchorage. When the battleship *Tirpitz* moved her base from Bogen Bay to the new German fleet anchorage in the Altafjord/Kåfjord area in 1943, both *Thetis* and *Nymphe* were moved there to provide Flak protection. Their powerful anti-aircraft batteries would be crucial in

the seaward defence of the anchorage following *Tirpitz*'s extensive damage by British midget submarines in September 1943, which left much of the battleship's artillery out of order for a while due to shock damage. Following the loss of *Scharnhorst* in December 1943, *Thetis* was moored in the Skillefjord for a while, opposite Stjernsund, to allow her to employ her fast-firing battery against any small craft that might attempt to penetrate this narrow entrance to Altafjord. Eventually, both *Thetis* and *Nymphe* moved with the battleship to Tromsø in October 1944; however, they were unsuccessful in preventing the battleship's destruction by bombing on 12 November 1944.

Contrary to some published sources, the German surrender actually found both ships still in northern

Nymphe was run aground at Kunna, outside Svolvær, on 17 May 1945. She is shown here under salvage, with all significant fittings removed. An interesting detail is her heightened forward lattice structure, presumably intended to support a *Würzburg* antenna. Owing to her stripped state it cannot be verified whether this was ever fitted. (Aidan Dodson collection)

Norway. *Nymphe* was at Svolvær when she was ordered by the Norwegian authorities to sail to Narvik for the surrender of her German crew, together with some troops collected in the Lofoten islands. However, shortly after departing, on 17 May 1945, she had to be beached at Kunna, Meløy, after the (allegedly inebriated) former German crew had deliberately opened several seacocks. *Nymphe* subsequently sank in shallow water, her upper deck awash.[13] She was sold to the Stavanger firm of Brodrene Anda in 1948, refloated and broken up at Stavanger. An anchor from *Nymphe* is preserved outside the Lofoten War Memorial Museum at Svolvær. *Thetis* was successfully returned to Norwegian control, and after a short period as an accommodation ship was sold to Stavanger Skipsopphugging in 1947; she was broken up the following year.

Archival Sources:

Deutsches historisches Institut Moskau, *Akte 143. Anweisungen und Schriftverkehr des Oberkommandos der Kriegsmarine (OKM) und der anderen Marinebehörden über den Umbau der Beuteschiffe in die schwimmenden Flak-Batterien in der Zeit vom Juli 1941 bis September 1944*, Bestand 500 Findbuch 12453 - Oberkommando der Kriegsmarine (OKM).

Endnotes:

1   For a history of the air defence of Wilhelmshaven, see FA Greve, *Die Luftverteidigung im Abschnitt Wilhelmshaven 1939–1945: 2. Marineflakbrigade*, Hermann Lüers (Jever, 1999).

2   The two ships are covered in detail in Greve, *op cit*, 224–47.

3   For the evolution of the German cruiser down to 1918, see A Dodson and D Nottelmann, *The Kaiser's Cruisers 1871–1918*, Seaforth (Barnsley, 2021); see also Nottelmann, 'The Development of the Small Cruiser in the Imperial German Navy', *Warship 2020*, 102–18, and *Warship 2021*, 44–60.

4   Under the Treaty of Versailles and related agreements, the *Reichsmarine* was allowed up to six operational cruisers, with two more in reserve. As all the more modern vessels had been surrendered to the Allies in 1920 or scuttled at Scapa Flow in 1919, the only such vessels available to them were the surviving ships of the *Gazelle*, *Frauenlob* and *Bremen* classes, launched between 1899 and 1903. See Dodson, 'After the Kaiser: the Imperial German Navy's Light Cruisers after 1918', *Warship 2017*, 140–60.

5   For this and the immediately following, see G Koop, K Galle and F Klein, *Von der Kaiserlichen Werft zum Marinearsenal: Wilhelmshaven als Zentrum der Marinetechnik seit 1970*, Bernard & Graefe Verlag (Munich, 1982), 72–73.

6   *Op cit*, 78.

7   Dodson and Cant, *Spoils of War*, 186–88.

8   *Op cit*, 194–97.

9   Our thanks to Geirr Haarr for his comments on this section.

10   P Brook, *Warships for Export: Armstrong Warships 1867–1927*, World Ship Society (Gravesend, 1999), 205–210.

11   S Mo, *Norske Marinefartöy*, Bodoni Forlag (Bergen, 2008).

12   The latter accounts for the incorrect claim in a number of secondary sources that the reconstruction was undertaken at Kiel.

13   See www.myheritage.no – *Historier fra Ofoten*, 8.

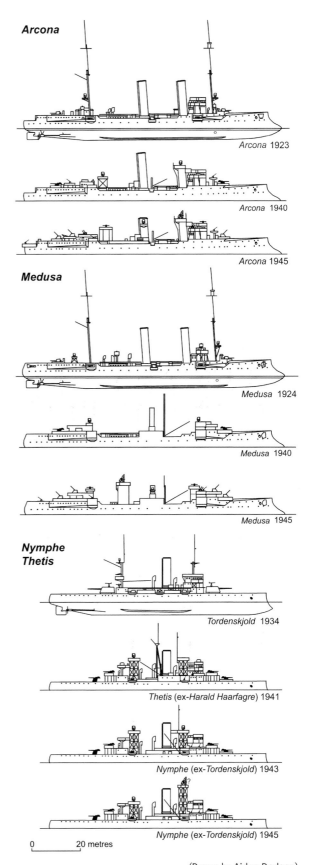

Arcona

Arcona 1923

Arcona 1940

Arcona 1945

Medusa

Medusa 1924

Medusa 1940

Medusa 1945

Nymphe Thetis

Tordenskjold 1934

Thetis (ex-Harald Haarfagre) 1941

Nymphe (ex-Tordenskjold) 1943

Nymphe (ex-Tordenskjold) 1945

0   20 metres

(Drawn by Aidan Dodson)

THE STRANGE FATE OF
GENERAL ALEKSEEV'S GUNS

In *Warship* 2021 **Sergei Vinogradov** described the unusual career of the Russian battleship *General Alekseev*. In this article he chronicles the even more surprising wanderings of her guns after the ship was scrapped. The text has been translated and edited by Stephen McLaughlin.

The battleship that eventually became known as *General Alekseev* was laid down in October 1911 as *Imperator Aleksandr III* at the Russud Shipyard in Nikolaev (now Mykolaiv, Ukraine). By the time the ship began her trials in July–August 1917 she had been renamed *Volia* ('Liberty') by the new revolutionary regime. Like all the Russian dreadnoughts, she was armed with twelve 12in/52 (305mm) guns manufactured by the Obukhovskii Works in Petrograd (as St Petersburg was renamed in September 1914), mounted in four triple turrets. Details of how the guns were transported across the 2,000km from the factory to the shipyard are lacking, but they were almost certainly delivered using the Imperial Navy's two specially-built 12-axle railway transporters, which were each able to carry a single gun. During the journey they would have been accompanied by a Naval Ministry official and a guard.

Volia test-fired her guns on 3/16 July 1917 during her passage to Sevastopol, but after entering service she went to sea for gunnery practice only once, on 13/26

Although not one of *General Alekseev*'s 12in/52 guns, this one is identical to those later mounted in the battleship. The guns were manufactured by the Obukhovskii Works, but several of the turrets were constructed by the St Petersburg Metallicheskii Works, which is where this photograph was taken in 1912. Note that the gun is at the full recoil position. (Sergei Vinogradov collection)

September 1917.[1] Her subsequent career would be marked by turmoil and sudden changes of fortune.[2] When Sevastopol was threatened by the German spring offensive of 1918, the Black Sea Fleet's most modern units, including *Volia*, fled to Novorossiisk on the Caucasian coast to avoid capture. The Germans forced her to return to Sevastopol in June, and she served briefly under their ensign. After the armistice of November 1918 she was taken over by the British, who in December took her to Ismid, Turkey, for safe-keeping. Eleven months later they turned her over to anti-Bolshevik White forces, who renamed her *General Alekseev* after an early leader of the movement. A year later she was forced to flee again when General Wrangel's White regime in the Crimea collapsed. She finally wound up in Bizerte in French Tunisia, along with other Russian refugee warships. Here the battleship's wanderings came to an end; taken over by the French government in October 1924, she was gradually scrapped in 1934–1937.

However, the odyssey of her twelve 12in/52 guns was just beginning. Along with their cradles they had been put in storage in the French arsenal at Sidi-Abdullah, and in the summer of 1939 the Finnish government expressed interest in purchasing seven of them (nos 91, 96, 113, 119, 121, 127 and 129). The Finns already had a number of identical guns in coast defence batteries, installed by the Russians during the First World War and taken over by Finland when it became an independent nation. In view of the USSR's increasingly threatening attitude, bolstering Finland's defences with this familiar type of gun was a logical move, and a steamer was sent to fetch the guns, but at the last minute the French government declined the sale.[3] However, after the Soviet invasion of Finland that began the Winter War (30 November 1939–13 March 1940) the French decided to donate the battleship's main and secondary batteries to Finland as military aid. An agreement was reached for the delivery of the guns on 4 January 1940.[4]

Table 1: *General Alekseev*'s 12in/52 Guns

Designation	12/52
Dates of manufacture	1914–1915
Manufacturer	Obukhovskii Steel-casting Works, St Petersburg / Petrograd
Bore	12in / 304.8mm
Weight incl breech	49.89 tons / 50.7mt
Elevating weight	82.87 tons / 84.2mt
Barrel length	624in / 15,850mm / 52 cal
Bore length	506in / 12,852mm / 42.2 cal
Rifled length	358.68in / 9,110.5mm / 29.89 cal
Length chamber	96.2in / 2,443.5mm
Volume chamber	224.6in^3
Number of grooves	72
Grooves	9.14mm deep x 2.28mm wide
Lands	4.15mm wide
Twist	30 cal
Pattern 1911 AP shell	
Weight	1,038lb / 470.93kg
Propellant charge	291lb / 132kg
Muzzle velocity	2,500ft/s / 762m/s
Maximum pressure	2,400kg/cm^2
Approx life	400 rounds
Range	25,600 yards / 23,410m at 25°
	128 cables at 25°

Sources:

L I Amirkhanov and S I Titushkin, *Glavnyi kalibr linkorov*, Gangut (St Petersburg, 1993), 20, 30.

A B Shirokorad, *Entsiklopediia otechestvennoi artillerii*, Kharvest (Minsk, 2000), 437–441.

A V Platonov, S V Aprelev and D N Siniaev, *Sovetskie boevye korabli 1941–1945 gg*, Tsitadel' (St Petersburg, 1997), 44.

The transfer was carried out without publicity, and three steamers were chartered to transport the guns. The first, *Juliette*, loaded four 12in guns and 1,000 tonnes of grain at Bizerte and put to sea on 29 January 1940. The

The twelve-axle railway transporter that was probably used to move the guns from the Obukhovskii Works in Petrograd to the shipyard in Nikolaev. The shack at the far end was for the Naval Ministry official who travelled with the gun. (Sergei Vinogradov collection)

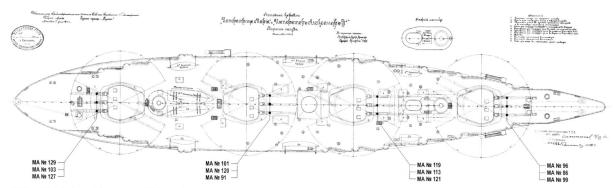

This official plan of *Imperator Aleksandr III* shows where each of the guns was mounted in the ship. 'MA' stands for *Morskaia artilleriia* = 'Naval Artillery'. (Sergei Vinogradov collection)

plan called for the ship to unload the guns in the Finnish port of Petsamo on the shores of the Barents Sea, but while she was on passage that port was occupied by the Red Army. The ship had to anchor at a nearby Norwegian port, biding her time until the end of the Winter War. Eventually she received approval from the Germans, who had in the meantime occupied Norway, to proceed down the coast to the Baltic. She arrived at the Finnish port of Turku on 8 September 1940. Soon after *Juliette* departed from Bizerte, a second steamer, *Karl Erick*, arrived and embarked another four 12in guns. She put into Goteborg, Sweden, and when the Winter War

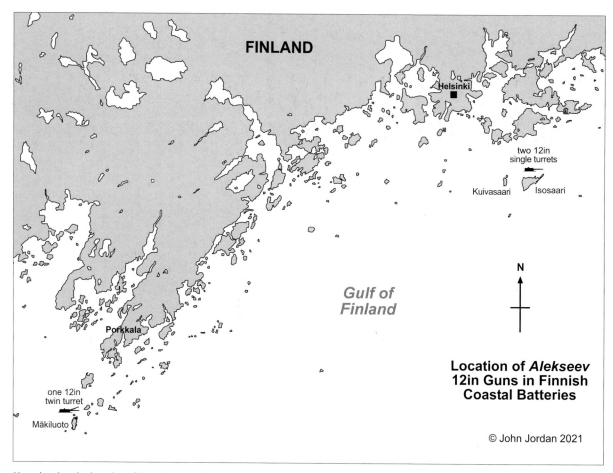

Map showing the location of Finnish coast defence batteries that used – or were intended to use – guns from *General Alekseev*. Two single turrets were completed on Isosaari, but one gun was destroyed in an accident in 1969; the other is now on display on the island. The incomplete twin turret on Mäkiluoto was destroyed by the Soviets after the Second World War, but the guns were salvaged by the Finns and are now displayed at Fort Örö, to the west of the area shown in this map. In addition to *Alekseev's* guns, Finnish defences included other Russian-made 12in guns at several locations, including Kuivasaari, Mäkiluoto, Örö and Ristiniemi, near the old border with the USSR. (Drawn by John Jordan from material supplied by the author)

Two views of a Finnish twin 305mm turret on Mäkiluoto Island. The photos are dated 30 September 1941, and the turret is therefore the one constructed in 1931–1933; the second turret, with guns from *General Alekseev*, would have been similar had it been completed. (SA-Kuva, Finnish Defence Forces)

A 12in APC shell in the Central Naval Museum, St Petersburg. This is the same type that would have been embarked on *General Alekseev*. Note the different metal of the ballistic cap and the two copper driving bands close to the base of the shell. (Stephen McLaughlin)

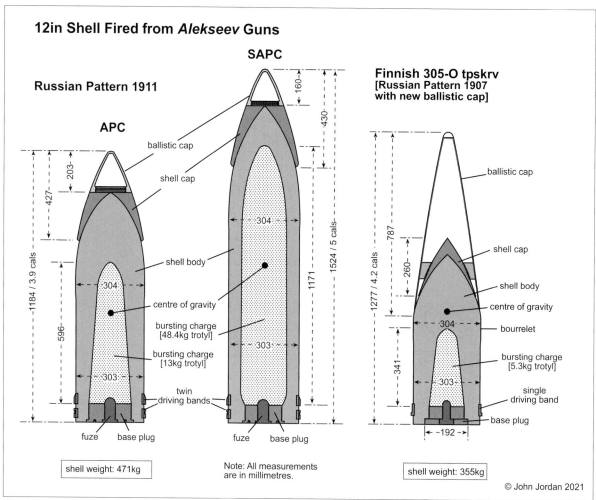

12in Shell Fired from *Alekseev* Guns

Russian Pattern 1911

SAPC

Finnish 305-O tpskrv
[Russian Pattern 1907 with new ballistic cap]

APC

ballistic cap

shell cap

160-

430-

304

1524 / 5 cals-

1171

ballistic cap

shell cap

shell body

787

centre of gravity

260-

shell body

427-

203-

1184 / 3.9 cals-

304

centre of gravity

bursting charge
[48.4kg trotyl]

bursting charge
[13kg trotyl]

596-

303

303

341-

1277 / 4.2 cals-

centre of gravity

bourrelet

304

bursting charge
[5.3kg trotyl]

303

twin
driving bands

single
driving band

fuze   base plug

fuze   base plug

base plug

← -192 →

shell weight: 471kg

Note: All measurements
are in millimetres.

shell weight: 355kg

© John Jordan 2021

A comparison of the original Russian M.1911 AP and SAP shells with a shell used by the Finns, modified from an M.1907 Russian AP shell. These older-pattern shells were used by the Russian predreadnought battleships and considerable stocks were probably left at Helsinki when the Russians evacuated the base in 1918. (Drawn by John Jordan from material supplied by the author)

Table 2: **12/52 Performance in Service**

Nation	Designation/	Shell Type	Shell Weight	Propellant	MV	Range / Elevation
Russia	12/52	Pattern 1911	470.93kg	132kg	762.5m/s	23,410m at 25°
Finland	305/52 O2	305-O tpskrv 3.9	470kg	146.8kg	778m/s	30,000m at 38°
		305-O t1/2pskrv	453kg	153kg	860m/s	41,000m at 38°
Finland	305/52 O	305-O tpskrv 4.1	355kg	137kg	900m/s	42,900m at 49°
Germany	30.5 cm	30.5cm Sprgr. L/3.8 Bdz.	405kg	140kg	825m/s	32,000m at 48°?
	Kanone 14(r)	30.5cm Sprgr. L/3.8 Bdz.	405kg	(Reduced)	?	28,000m at 48°?
		30.5cm Sprgr. L/3.6 Bdz.u.kz.m.H	250kg	140kg	1,020m/s	51,000m at 48°?
		30.5cm Sprgr. L/3.6 Bdz.u.kz.m.H	250kg	(Reduced)	?	38,000m at 48°?
USSR	TM-12-3	Pattern 1913	470.93kg	132kg	762.5m/s	28,600m at 50°
		Pattern 1928	315kg	140kg	950m/s	44,000m at 50°

Sources:

L I Amirkhanov, *Morskie Pushki na zhelsexhnoi doroge*, TMS (St. Petersburg, 1994), 61–62.

John Campbell, *Jutland: An Analysis of the Fighting*, Naval Institute Press (Annapolis, 1986), 342, 345.

Ove Enqvist, *Itsenaisen Suomen rannikkotykit 1918–1998*, Sotamuseo (Helsinki, 1999), 179.

Colin Partridge and John Wallbridge, *Mirus: The Making of a Battery*, Ampersand Press (Alderney, 1983), 21, 96.

A B Shirokorad, *Entsiklopediia otechestvennoi artillerii*, Kharvest (Minsk, 2000), 437–438.

ended these guns were also delivered to Turku. The careers of the last four guns, which never reached Finland, will be described below.

The eight guns that arrived in Finland (nos 86, 91, 96, 113, 119, 121, 127 and 129) were the same guns that had been selected in the summer of 1939, with the addi-

tion of no 86, which suggests that the Finns judged these guns to be in the best condition. In August–October 1940, Engineer-Captain J Salovius carried out a detailed survey of them and assessed their condition as good.[5] A March 1940 plan called for four of them to be mounted in coast defence batteries, while the remaining

12in SAPC shell being salvaged from the wreck of *Alekseev*'s sister ship *Imperatritsa Mariia* after she capsized and sank at Sevastopol in October 1916 following a magazine explosion. Note the much greater length of this shell compared with the APC round, evidence of the increased size and weight of the trotyl burster. (Sergei Vinogradov collection)

four were designated as spares. Guns 91 and 119 were earmarked for a twin turret on Mäkiluoto Island off the Porkkala Peninsula, about 40km southwest of Helsinki. There was already one twin 12in turret there, built in 1931–1933 using an incomplete 14in gun emplacement the Russians had started during the Great War. However, progress on the new turret was slow during the Continuation War with the USSR (June 1941–September 1944), and when Soviet victories forced Finland to accept an armistice the turret was still incomplete. The Porkkala region, including Mäkiluoto, was leased to the Soviet Union as a naval base, and by the time it was returned to Finland in 1956 the 12in gun emplacements had been destroyed, but the Finns were able to salvage the guns.[6]

Guns nos 113 and 121 were allotted to two single-gun turrets on Isosaari Island, south of Helsinki harbour.[7] The turrets were almost completed by September 1944, but under the terms of the surrender the Finns were forbidden to have any coast defence artillery larger than 120mm east of Porkkala, so the turrets were dismantled and removed. The restriction on gun calibre ended when the Paris Peace Treaty was signed in 1947, but it was only in 1959 that the Finnish government decided to reinstall the Isosaari turrets, the work being completed in 1962. One gun was destroyed in 1969 during experiments with 'super charges' and was replaced by one of the spares from *General Alekseev*. One of the turrets was scrapped in 1982, but the second still exists as a museum exhibit.

Russian Guns in a German Battery on British Soil

The last four of *General Alekseev*'s 12in guns, along with all eighteen of her 130mm secondary guns, were loaded aboard the third steamer, *Nina*, which arrived at Bizerte on 12 February 1940. She put to sea on 26 February, and on 11 March (two days before the signing of the treaty ending the Winter War) *Nina* arrived in Norwegian waters; she was still at Bergen when the Germans invaded Norway on 9 April 1940. They soon discovered the contents of her holds, and the ship and her cargo of Russian guns were seized.[8] The 130mm (5.1in) guns remained in Norway and were installed by the Germans in six three-gun batteries, at Kiby, Tana, Porsanger, Hammerfest, Alta and Rugsundøy; the latter battery fired 35 rounds at HMS *Kenya* during Operation 'Archery' on 27 December 1941, scoring three relatively inconsequential hits.[9]

Nina, with the four 12in guns (nos 99, 101, 103 and 120) still on board, was taken to Germany, and by May 1941 a design for single-gun installations (German designation *Bettungsschiessgerüst* C-40) had been developed for them. In October 1941 it was decided to install the guns at Guernsey in the Channel Islands, the only part of the British Empire occupied by German forces during the war. The construction of the battery was a massive undertaking, involving the use of 47,000 cubic metres of concrete to build the emplacements. Transporting the guns to the site was also a challenge. Along with their disassembled mountings they were shipped from St Malo in a river barge; upon arrival at Guernsey's St Peter Port they were unloaded by a Dutch-built 100-ton floating crane, the *Antee*, which had been specially moved there from Le Havre. The guns and cradles were then loaded onto one of the two low-load trailers (each with 48 steerable wheels) that had been brought to the island for this purpose. The trailers were towed by four 12-ton half-track prime movers at walking speed across the island

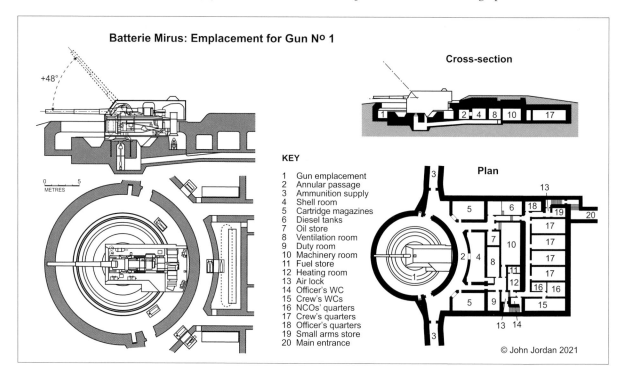

Batterie Mirus: Emplacement for Gun N⁰ 1

Cross-section

KEY

1. Gun emplacement
2. Annular passage
3. Ammunition supply
4. Shell room
5. Cartridge magazines
6. Diesel tanks
7. Oil store
8. Ventilation room
9. Duty room
10. Machinery room
11. Fuel store
12. Heating room
13. Air lock
14. Officer's WC
15. Crew's WCs
16. NCOs' quarters
17. Crew's quarters
18. Officer's quarters
19. Small arms store
20. Main entrance

Plan

© John Jordan 2021

along narrow roads.[10] Photographs of the guns being moved to their emplacements clearly show that, in addition to the barrels themselves, the Germans retained the original Russian cradles, slides, recoil and run-out cylinders, and mantlet plates – in other words, the entire elevating mass of the guns except for the loading mechanisms, which were replaced by counterweights. Once at the battery, the guns were shifted into position by two gantry cranes each with a lifting capacity of 73 tonnes.

The battery was initially named 'Nina' after the steamer in which the guns had been captured, but in August 1942 it was renamed in honour of Kapitän-zur-See Rolf Mirus, a prominent gunnery officer. He had been killed on 3 November 1941 during an inspection trip when RAF aircraft attacked and sank the boat carrying him from Guernsey to Alderney.

Gun No 1 of Batterie Mirus, camouflaged as a house. The armoured shield of the turret has been painted and a false structure has been built at the back. (Occupation Archive)

Foundation of Gun No 1 of Batterie Mirus as it appeared in the 1980s. (Stephen Dent)

The guns of Batterie Mirus were mounted in four single armoured turrets (150mm faces and roofs, 50mm sides) that could rotate through 360 degrees on a central pivot. They were installed in shallow concrete pits directly adjacent to their magazines and the quarters for the gun crews. Elevation and training were electrical, with manual back-up. The guns had elevation limits of –2 to +48 degrees, loading was manual at a fixed angle of 0 degrees, and the rate of fire was 1.5 rounds per minute at elevations up to +11 degrees, decreasing to one round/minute at the maximum elevation.

Lacking the original Russian ammunition, the Germans used First World War-era 405kg armour-piercing and high-explosive shells, with a muzzle velocity (MV) of 825m/s and a range of up to 32,000m (35,000 yards) at maximum elevation.[11] A lightweight 250kg high-explosive projectile was also developed; with a reported MV of 1,020m/s it had a range of 51,000m (55,775 yards).[12] However, in service the guns suffered several failures when firing at maximum elevation, possibly due to excessive stress on the recoil system, which had been designed for a maximum elevation of 25 degrees. Whatever the cause, reduced charges were adopted, decreasing the range to 28,000m (30,620 yards) for the heavy shells and 38,000m (41,560 yards) for the lighter ones.

The first test shot was fired by Gun No 2 on 13 April 1942, six months after the decision to erect the battery. It was only at the end of June, however, that all four guns were in service, and even then all operations still had to be done manually. Work on electrical systems was completed on 1 November 1942, but problems persisted: during a practice shoot on 13 April 1943 one of the mountings broke down.[13] A more serious incident occurred on 8 June 1943 when the battery went into action against naval targets detected by radar. Firing 250kg shells with reduced charges at an elevation of +31 degrees, one gun burst its trunnion ring after two rounds, another after three, while a third was put out of action when the recoil system failed.[14] These parts were replaced with ones from the former Russian 12in coastal battery on Wolf (Aegna) Island near Tallinn, Estonia. According to one source the battery became fully operational only in mid-1944.[15]

Despite these problems, Batterie Mirus did engage Allied ships on several occasions, but comprehensive data on firing, ammunition expenditure and damage inflicted on the enemy (if any) is lacking. However, the Allies generally showed a good deal of respect for the guns and stayed outside their range.

After the German surrender on 9 May 1945 the battery was transferred to British representatives of the Allied command, and in 1946 a Mr George Dawson signed a contract for dismantling the battery. He brought in Evans Welding Co and scrapping began on 23 June 1947, but only partial success was achieved: the largest and most massive parts of the installations – the gun barrels, mountings and armour plates – defied all efforts and the work was abandoned. In 1951 a new contractor, Iron

and Steel Disposals Ltd, was hired. Using oxyacetylene torches they were able to break up the armoured shields. As for the barrels of the 12in guns, they were first cut lengthwise into two halves, which were then cut into 5-ton chunks. These were transported by lorries to the port and sent to England to be melted down.

Soviet TM-3-12 Railway Mountings

The story of three of the guns the Finns had allocated as spares is the most surprising of all. It began in 1936, when the USSR began constructing three railway gun systems using available 12in/52 guns and cradles.[16] The transporters for the guns, designated TM-3-12, were manufactured by the Marti Works in Nikolaev and entered service between July 1938 and January 1939. Organisationally, they formed the Baltic Fleet's Separate Railway Artillery Battery (*Otdel'naia zheleznodorozhnaia artilleriiskaia batereia*, or OZhDAB) No 9. Although the transporter had two stabilising legs for firing from railway tracks, this was not their primary method of shooting. Having been designed for coast defence, they had to be able to traverse rapidly over large arcs to engage moving ships. Their main mode of operation was therefore from previously prepared positions built at various points around the Soviet Union's Baltic coast. These consisted of steel slabs with circular roller paths embedded in reinforced concrete foundations (16m x 16m x 3m). The gun transporter was towed onto the foundation along rails and fixed on a steel pivot in its centre, the bogies were then detached and rolled out, and the whole system was able to rotate and fire over a full 360 degrees.[17] The maximum elevation of the gun was 50 degrees and the range was 29,260m (32,000 yards) firing 470.93kg model 1911 naval high-explosive and armour-piercing projectiles. The total weight of the transporter was 340 tonnes; when emplaced on its concrete pad the rotating mass was 216.3 tonnes. The overall length of the transporter was 33.92m.[18]

On 30 November 1939, the first day of the Winter War, these guns opened fire on Finnish border guards and guns on Seskar Island, about 110km east of Leningrad (today St Petersburg), from fixed positions on the Kolgenpia Peninsula, almost directly south of the island. Over the next two months they fired on other Finnish military targets on several occasions, but their most important contribution came in February 1940 during the Red Army's offensive against the Karelian Isthmus. By the time they were withdrawn on 25 February the battery had fired 191 shells and earned the praise of the Soviet Army command for their very effective fire on Finnish fortifications.

The peace treaty between Finland and the USSR signed on 13 March 1940 stipulated that the Hanko (Hango) Peninsula would be leased to the Soviets for use as a naval base, and OZhDAB No 9 was transferred there in five echelons (a total of 103 railway carriages) from 2 to 7 October 1940.[19] Its guns, combined with coast defence guns now under Soviet control in Estonia, covered the

One of the Finnish railway guns in firing position. The bogies have been removed and, in the first photo, the roller path on the concrete foundation can just be made out. The stabilising legs used when firing from railway tracks can be seen in their stowed position under the rear overhang. The photos are dated 15 October 1942, so are of the first unit refurbished by the Finns, mounting gun no 127. (SA-Kuva, Finnish Defence Forces)

entrance to the Gulf of Finland. However, with the start of the Continuation War in June 1941 Hanko was cut off from the Soviet Union, and during its 160-day defensive battle (29 June to 2 December 1941) the three 12in guns, emplaced on their concrete foundations in the southern part of the peninsula, carried out 84 fire support missions against land targets and two at naval targets, expending a total of 625 shells.[20]

The order to evacuate Hanko came on 30 October 1941. The railway guns, which could not be transported by sea, were doomed. All their auxiliary rolling stock (ammunition waggons, workshops, power plants, as well as the multi-axle bogies of the transporters themselves) were driven into the sea by locomotives, which were then also sunk in Hanko harbor. The remaining 12in shells were buried and the propellant powder was spread on the ground and burned. The transporters themselves were disabled hurriedly on the last day of the evacuation. Only the barrels of the guns and their cradles were irreparably damaged, while the main structures of the transporters remained virtually intact. All the smaller gear – electric motors and auxiliary devices – were smashed with sledgehammers.[21]

After the Soviet departure, the Finns inspected the railway transporters and in July 1942 found their sunken bogies; having recovered them they decided to reconstruct these impressive artillery systems. Since there was

no question of repairing the guns, they used the spares from *General Alekseev* that had arrived in 1940 (nos 86, 127 and 129), which were identical.[22] Replacing guns and their cradles did not present any major difficulties: the transporters were brought by rail to the port, where their damaged guns were removed by a floating crane; the new ones, delivered by barge, were then put in their place. However, the electro-mechanical equipment and fire control gear, which had been almost completely destroyed, had to be manufactured virtually from scratch. Most of the work was done by the firm of Stremberg, a major electrical company. The total cost of their restoration amounted to about five million marks.[23]

On 15 October 1942 trials were conducted with gun no 127 mounted on a concrete foundation. Two rounds were fired with reduced charges, followed by three more the next day with full charges, the last being fired at the maximum elevation of 50 degrees.[24] In February 1943, another transporter, with gun no 86, was successfully tested. After that it was decided to reconstruct the third and most extensively damaged unit; the work was completed at the end of July 1943. The guns became the Finnish Army's 3rd Railway Battery, and on 29 November 1943 the Commander-in-Chief of the Finnish armed forces, Marshal Carl Gustav Mannerheim, visited Hanko and inspected this unique battery of captured guns.

One of the rebuilt Soviet TM-3-12 railway guns at Hanko, with its Finnish gun crew climbing aboard. The photo is dated 21 September 1943. (SA-Kuva, Finnish Defence Forces)

Two views of the railway transporter for Gun No 127, now on display at the Central Museum of the Great Patriotic War in Moscow. (Sergei Vinogradov collection)

Table 3: Fates of *General Alekseev*'s Guns

Number	Employment	Current Status
MA 86	Used by Finns to repair TM-3-12 railway gun at Hanko; ceded by Finns to USSR after the war.	In conservation at Fort Krasnaia Gorka, near St Petersburg.
MA 91	Intended for Mäkiluoto, mounting destroyed by Soviets; taken to Fort Örö as a spare.	On display at Fort Örö.
MA 96	Used as a spare.	On display at Fort Kuivasaari.
MA 99	Seized by Germans, installed at Batterie Mirus, Guernsey.	Scrapped by British after 1951.
MA 101	Seized by Germans, installed at Batterie Mirus, Guernsey.	Scrapped by British after 1951.
MA 103	Seized by Germans, installed at Batterie Mirus, Guernsey.	Scrapped by British after 1951.
MA 113	Intended for single turret at Isosaari, dismantled 1944–1945 under terms of armistice; reinstalled 1962.	On display at Fort Isosaari.
MA 119	Intended for Mäkiluoto, mounting destroyed by Soviets; gun taken to Fort Örö as a spare.	On display at Fort Örö.
MA 120	Seized by Germans, installed at Batterie Mirus, Guernsey.	Scrapped by British after 1951.
MA 121	Intended for single turret at Isosaari, dismantled 1944–1945 under terms of armistice; reinstalled 1962, damaged 1969.	Sold for scrap, 1970.
MA 127	Used by Finns to repair TM-3-12 railway gun at Hanko; ceded by Finns to USSR after the war.	On display at Moscow's Central Museum of the Great Patriotic War.
MA 129	Used by Finns to repair TM-3-12 railway gun at Hanko; ceded by Finns to USSR after the war.	On display at St Petersburg's Museum of Railway Engineering.

NOTES:

MA = *Morskaia artilleriia* (Naval Artillery)

Sources: In addition to data in the current article, information was also taken from CB Robbins, letter to the editor, *Warship International*, vol XXXII, no 4, 332, 334.

However the railway guns saw no action in the Continuation War, and in fact never left their base at Hanko. Under the terms of the September 1944 armistice, the former Soviet TM-3-12 guns were to be returned to the USSR. On 4 and 15 November 1944 they were thoroughly inspected by Soviet naval specialists, who assessed the guns as being 20–30 per cent worn; two of the transporters were combat-ready, while the third needed its ammunition supply and loading systems repaired. In addition to the guns, the Finns turned over 161 shells and 203 charges. On 25 December 1944 the guns were moved by rail from Hanko to the small border town of Vainikkala, where they were handed over to Soviet representatives.[25]

Immediately upon arrival in the USSR, the transporters were taken for repairs to the Leningrad Bolshevik Works – the former Obukhovskii Works, where the guns had been manufactured in 1914–1915. The refurbishment of the transporters lasted until June 1947. The guns were enrolled in OZhDAB No 294, which was assigned to coast defence duties at the naval base of Baltiisk (formerly Pillau), in the Soviet enclave at Kaliningrad. In the following years their crews periodically carried out gunnery exercises and practised moving the guns to Leningrad and back.[26]

On 15 January 1960 the battery, by now redesignated the 159th Separate Railway Artillery Division, was disbanded in accordance Nikita Khrushchev's programme for reducing the armed forces in order to boost the civilian economy. The guns became the 16th Battery in Conservation. On 5 May 1961 the artillery systems were transferred to the Krasnaia Gorka naval base near Leningrad for storage. Here they rested for forty years in sheds that had been built around them. In 1999 all three guns and transporters were earmarked for scrapping, but at the last moment the director of the Central Museum of the Great Patriotic War, V I Bragin, managed to get permission from the naval command to transfer one railway gun to his museum at Poklonnaia Gora, 12km west of the Moscow Kremlin. In June–September 2000 the transporter with gun no 127 was brought to Moscow with great difficulty; it now stands in the Museum's open-air display of naval equipment.[27] This successful undertaking served as an encouraging example, and helped prevent the two remaining railway guns from being scrapped. One gun (no 129) was transferred to St Petersburg and is now an exhibit of the Museum of Railway Engineering, while the third (no 86) remains at Krasnaia Gorka.

Conclusion

The odyssey of the 12in 50-ton guns of the former Russian dreadnought (and their 34-ton cradles) lasted almost a century. Manufactured in Petrograd, the capital of the Russian Empire, in 1915–1916 they were installed in the triple turrets of the *Imperator Aleksandr III*, later known as *Volia*. After fleeing to Novorossiisk in June 1918 the ship (and her guns) miraculously escaped being sunk on the orders of Lenin, who wanted to keep her out of German hands. Returning to Sevastopol, she was briefly under German control, then British. In

1918–1920 the dreadnought, now named *General Alekseev*, passed through the Bosporus three times, and at the end of 1920 she wound up in the French North African port of Bizerte. Although the ship was scrapped, her guns were put in storage, and in 1940 they were transported around Europe; four guns came under German control, while eight ended up in Finland. Of the latter, three guns on railway transporters were returned to the USSR at the beginning of 1945, where they served in the Soviet Navy. Placed in storage at Krasnaia Gorka near Leningrad in 1961, they remained there for forty years. Finally, in the early 2000s, two of the guns were transferred to museums in Moscow and St Petersburg, while the third gun remains at Krasnaia Gorka. In Finland, guns nos 91 and 119 are still preserved at Fort Örö, a third (no 113) is in a single turret on the island of Isosaari, while yet another (no 96) is at the nearby Kuivasaari Museum. So out of the twelve 12in guns of the Russian Empire's last dreadnought, seven barrels have survived to this day – a remarkable outcome!

Endnotes:

1   RGA VMF (Russian State Archives of the Navy), *Fond* 418, *Opis'* 1, *Delo* 2270, *List* 16; RGVIA (Russian State Military Archives), *Fond* 2003, *Opis'* 1, *Delo* 558, *List* 9.
2   For details, see Sergei Vinogradov, 'Refugee Battleship', *Warship 2021*, 183–187.
3   C B Robbins and Ove T Enqvist, 'The Guns of the General Alekseev', *Warship International*, vol 32, no 2 (1995), 185–193, at 186.
4   Colin Partridge and John Wallbridge, *Mirus: The Making of a Battery*, Ampersand Press (Alderney, 1983), 19.
5   V I Bragin, *Pushki na rel'sakh*, GUP Tipografiia Nauka (Moscow, 2006), 247.
6   Ove Enqvist, *Suomen rannikkotykit/Coastal Guns in Finland*, Moreeni (Vantaa, 2013), 174.
7   Robbins and Enqvist, 'The Guns of the General Alekseev', 187.
8   After Finland became a cobelligerent against the USSR the Finns pressed the Germans for compensation for the seized guns, and in 1944 the Germans gave them four identical 12in guns taken from coast defences in Estonia; see Enqvist, *Suomen rannikkotykit*, 174 and Ove Enqvist, *Itsenäisen Suomen Rannikkotykit 1918–1998*, Sotamuseo (Helsinki, 1999). These guns also had an interesting history: originally installed in Russian batteries during the First World War, they were inherited by Estonia when that nation gained independence in 1918. In June 1940 the Soviets seized them when they occupied the Baltic Republics. In the autumn of 1941 the Germans overran the region, and so the batteries fell into their hands. See Terry Sofian, 'Ex-naval Guns Used for Coast Defense Purposes. Soviet 12in/52 and 12in/56 Guns', *Warship International*, vol 37, no 1 (2000), 101–105, at 105.
9   Enqvist, *Suomen rannikkotykit*, 128; email, Dag Sundkuist to Stephen McLaughlin, 23 March 2021; TNA, ADM 234/444, 'HM Ships Sunk or Damaged by Enemy Action', courtesy of Vincent P O'Hara.
10   Partridge and Wallbridge, *Mirus: The Making of a Battery*, 22–33; there is a German propaganda film available at YouTube showing the transportation of the guns: https://www.youtube.com/watch?v=4oS_u0jQtOs.
11   Germany had been allowed to retain several 30.5cm guns for coast defence, along with a stock of shells for them; Sven Brummack, emails to McLaughlin, 31 March and 1 April 2021.
12   A ballistic analysis by William J Jurens indicates that the 51,000m range may be an exaggeration. email, Jurens to McLaughlin, 13 April 2021.
13   Partridge and Wallbridge, *Mirus: The Making of a Battery*, 80, 81.
14   This is according to Partridge and Wallbridge, *Mirus: The Making of a Battery*, 80. It seems unlikely that two of the massive trunnion rings should fail when firing light shells with reduced charges at modest angles of elevation. One possibility is that it was not the trunnion rings that broke, but the yoke to which the recoil piston tail-rods were attached. This was a known problem in Russian 12in/52 guns, and was eventually resolved by making the yokes more massive.
15   Sofian, 'Ex-naval Guns Used for Coast Defense Purposes', 105.
16   It has often been stated that these guns were salvaged from the battleship *Imperatritsa Mariia*, which sank after a magazine explosion in Sevastopol harbour in October 1916. In fact two of the three guns came from the fortress of Krasnaia Gorka and one from the battleship *Petropavlovsk*. After the Winter War with Finland, their worn guns were replaced by reconditioned barrels from the battleships *Sevastopol* and *Gangut*, and one from *Imperatritsa Mariia*. These were the guns later destroyed when Hanko was evacuated by the Soviets.
17   A B Shirokorad, 'Morskie zheleznodorozhnye ustanovki v Velikoi Otechestvennoi voine', *Morskoi Sbornik*, 2000, no 5, 53. A similar system of fixed positions was used for the American 14in M1920 railway gun; four of these were built, two each for the coast defences at Los Angeles and the Panama Canal Zone.
18   *Spravochnik po artillerii Voenno-morskogo flota Soiuza SSR*, part 1: *Material'naia chast' artilleriiskikh ustanovok*, Voenmorizdat NKVMF Soiuza SSR (Moscow, 1944), 32, 38.
19   A Volkov and A Voronov, 'Istoriia odnoi baterei', *Fotomaster*, 2004, no 3, 41.
20   Iu G Perechnev, *Sovetskaia beregovaia artilleriia: istoriia razvitiia i boevogo primeneniia, 1921–1945 gg.*, Nauka (Moscow, 1976), 78, 88.
21   L I Amirkhanov, *Zheleznodorozhnaia artilleriia forta Krasnaia Gorka*, OOO ITs Ostrov (St Petersburg, 2019), 129.
22   Bragin, *Pushki na rel'sakh*, 228, 248.
23   Volkov and Voronov, *Istoriia odnoi baterei*, 45.
24   Bragin, *Pushki na rel'sakh*, 253.
25   Bragin, *Pushki na rel'sakh*, 282.
26   Bragin, *Pushki na rel'sakh*, 350, 351.
27   Bragin, *Pushki na rel'sakh*, 370, 373, 376.

THE BATTLESHIP *MASSÉNA*

The battleship *Masséna* was the fourth ship of the five units of the 1890 programme that made up the so-called 'Fleet of Samples' (*Flotte d'échantillons*). Like her half-sisters *Charles Martel* and *Carnot* she never fired a shot in anger. **Philippe Caresse** looks at the rationale for her construction and her subsequent career, which ended with her employment as a breakwater at Gallipoli.

On 28 January 1891, a ministerial dispatch announced that the 1892 budget envisaged the laying down of two battleships based on *Charles Martel* or *Lazare Carnot* (subsequently renamed *Carnot* – see the author's article in *Warship 2021*), incorporating modifications currently being studied at Gâvres, the French Navy's proving ground. Four naval architects duly submitted their proposals: Bertin, Berrier-Fontaine, Huin and de Bussy. The Bertin proposal, which introduced a novel system of protection incorporating a cellular layer, was rejected out of hand. The services of Charles Huin, who had been responsible for the design of the first ship of the series, *Charles Martel* (see *Warship 2020*), were retained for *Bouvet*, while *Masséna* was allocated to the distinguished naval architect Louis de Bussy, who had recently been responsible for the design of the world's first modern armoured cruiser, *Dupuy-de-Lôme*. Construction of the two battleships was to proceed in parallel.

The design of *Masséna* would be unusual in that, like de Bussy's armoured cruiser, the ship would have three engines and three propeller shafts, a proposal approved by the *Conseil des Travaux* at a meeting on 31 July 1891. Also, the platform deck would be reinforced to 40mm to protect the machinery spaces and the magazines. Both ships were otherwise to have similar characteristics to the first three units of the series. However, on 26 May 1893, the *Conseil des Travaux* decreed that the single Mle 1887 305mm and 274mm guns would be replaced by guns belonging to the new 1893 series, which had more advanced construction and superior ballistics. The four 65mm light guns of the first three ships were also to be replaced by eight 100mm guns of a new QF model (Mle 1891).

Masséna was originally to have been fitted with six torpedo tubes: four above water and two submerged. On 3 August 1893 it was decided that two of the above-water tubes were to be replaced by submerged tubes, but these were ultimately suppressed altogether, leaving two above-water tubes forward and two submerged tubes aft (see below). De Bussy adopted a similar hull-form to his *Dupuy-de-Lôme*, with pronounced tumblehome forward combined with a prominent ram bow; this made the fitting of modern Marrel anchors problematic, and the two bower anchors had to be handled by cat-davits located on the forecastle that obstructed the arcs of fire of the forward turret.

As with *Jauréguiberry* (see the author's article in *Warship 2022*), the construction of the new ship was assigned to private industry. The constract for *Masséna* was duly signed on 18 May 1892 with the Société des Ateliers et Chantiers de la Loire (ACL) of Saint-Nazaire. As the shipyard was unable to supply armour plates, these were sub-contracted to various companies. The author has been unable to determine the precise date when the first frames and plates were assembled on the slipway, but this seems to have occurred during September 1892.

The Battleship *Masséna*

The construction of *Masséna* was supervised by Engineer Wohl of ACL. The weight of the hull was 3,744.48 tonnes. For the key dimensions and other characteristics see Table 1. Bilge keels would be fitted to subdue the ship's roll in February 1902 (see below).

The armour plates for the belt, which were of homogeneous steel, were supplied by Schneider and Saint-

Table 1: Hull & General Characteristics

Length oa	117.12m
Length wl	116.79m
Length pp	112.65m
Beam (wl)	20.28m
Depth of keel	7.73
Draught	7.03m fwd, 8.17m aft
Freeboard at bow	5.51m
Normal displacement	11,848 tonnes
Full load displacement	13,404 tonnes
GM	0.925m (normal displacement)
Surface of underside	3,750m^2
Complement	734 officers & men
Protection	
Main belt	450mm (250mm bottom edge); 2m high fwd/amid, 1.65m aft
Upper belt	100mm; 1.2m high
Armoured deck	70mm (extra-mild steel)
Splinter deck	40/30mm steel
Main turrets	370mm sides, 70mm roof, 60mm floor, 320mm barbette
138.6 turrets	100mm sides, 70mm roof, 60mm floor, 100mm barbette

Masséna: Profile & Plan

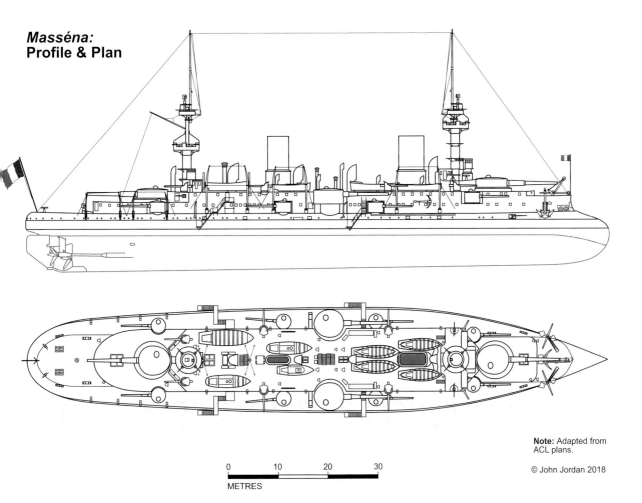

0   10   20   30
METRES

Note: Adapted from ACL plans.

© John Jordan 2018

GA Plans

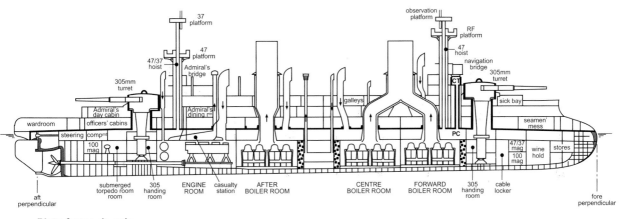

37 platform

47 platform

47/37 hoist

Admiral's bridge

305mm turret

Admiral's day cabin

officers' cabins

Admiral's dining rm

wardroom

steering compmt

100 mag

observation platform

RF platform

47 hoist

navigation bridge

305mm turret

CT

sick bay

galleys

seamen' mess

47/37 mag

100 mag

wine hold

stores

PC

aft perpendicular

submerged torpedo room room

305 handing room

ENGINE ROOM

casualty station

AFTER BOILER ROOM

CENTRE BOILER ROOM

FORWARD BOILER ROOM

305 handing room

cable locker

fore perpendicular

Plate-forme de cale

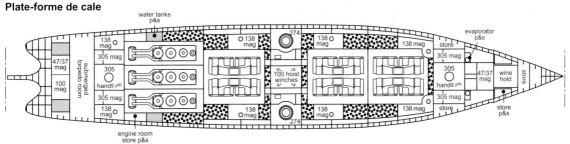

water tanks p&s

47/37 mag

100 mag

submerged torpedo room

138 mag

305 mag

305 hand⁹ rᵐ

305 mag

138 mag

138 mag

100 hoist winches

138 mag

274

274

138 mag

138 mag

evaporator p&s

138 mag

305 mag

305 hand⁹ rᵐ

305 mag

47/37 mag

wine hold

store

store

store p&s

engine room store p&s

143

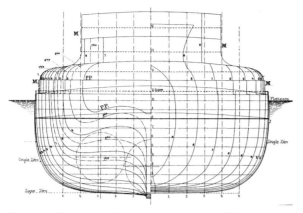

Body plan of *Masséna*. Note the pronounced tumblehome above the waterline. (Philippe Caresse collection)

Chamond. They were 450mm thick amidships, reducing to 350mm at the bow and the stern. The belt had a maximum height of 2 metres forward and amidships, of which 0.5 metres was above the waterline, and 1.65 metres aft. Schneider also supplied the upper belt (*ceinture mince*), which was 100mm thick and had a height of 1.2 metres.

The plates for the main armoured deck were of 70mm extra-mild steel (*métal de Saint-Jacques*), secured to a double layer of 10mm mild steel (total thickness: 90mm), and were ordered from Châtillon & Commentry; the deck was 0.50 metres above the waterline. The splinter deck below, covering the machinery spaces and the magazines, comprised two layers of 20mm mild steel (total thickness: 40mm) and was 1.5 metres below the waterline. The armoured coamings for the boiler uptakes and the main passageways had 350mm bases and were of forged steel; they were supplied by Saint-Chamond. The total weight of armour was 3,993.58 tonnes.

Masséna: Midship Half-Section

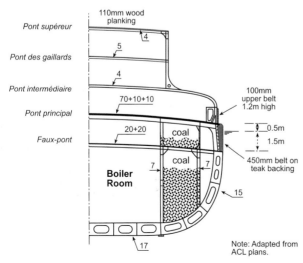

Note: Adapted from ACL plans.

© John Jordan 2018

Masséna: Sections

Frames 43/44 (from aft)

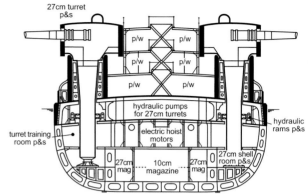

Note: Adapted from ACL plans.

© John Jordan 2018

Frame 87 (from fwd)

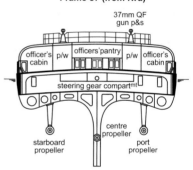

The conning tower, which weighed 32.22 tonnes, had a 330mm face and side walls 280mm thick, and the communications tube was protected by hoops of 200mm steel down to the main deck. When the ship was first completed, the navigation bridge was mounted atop the conning tower. In 1903 it was enlarged, and in April of the same year an admiral's bridge was constructed on the after superstructure.

Armament

Masséna was armed with two 305mm 45-cal guns Mle 1893, mounted in fully-enclosed turrets fore and aft, and two 274.4mm 45-cal guns, also Mle 1893, in wing turrets.

The gun mechanisms were supplied by Schneider and the armour for the 305mm turrets, including the sighting hoods, by Marrel; the armour for the 274.4mm turrets and barbettes was supplied by Châtillon & Commentry. The 305mm and 274.4mm turrets had identical protection: 370mm plates of special steel on the walls of the gunhouse with 70mm for the turret roofs and sighting hoods, the barbettes being protected by 320mm plates of special steel. Although in theory these guns had a rate of fire of one round per minute, the 1898 *devis de campagne* of the ship gave a figure of only one round every three minutes. New sights would be fitted in March 1906.

The mechanisms for the 138.6mm guns were supplied by Marrel and the armour for the turrets by Châtillon et Commentry. There were 100mm plates of special steel on the turret walls, with 20mm plating on the roofs and 100mm on the barbettes. New sights were installed in the turrets between September 1906 and November 1907, and Germain hydraulic order transmission for the guns was fitted between June and August 1907.

The gun armament was completed by a combination of 47mm QF and 37mm QF and revolver cannon for anti-torpedo boat work. The official plans show two 47mm Mle 1885 guns and two 37mm revolver cannon on the bridge structure, and two 47mm guns in the after super-structure with a further two revolver cannon on the stern. The two military masts were each to have mounted four 47mm guns on the lower platform and four 37mm QF guns on the upper platform. During trials, in May 1887 the CO requested the suppression of the 37mm guns on the upper platform of the foremast to create sufficient space for an experimental rangefinder. Photos of the ship in service generally show all the 47mm and the four 37mm revolver cannon in place but only 2/4 37mm QF guns atop the upper mainmast platform.

Masséna's armament was completed by two trainable above-water 450mm torpedo tubes and two fixed submerged tubes. The above-water tubes were suspended from the upper deck forward of the pivot for the forward 305mm turret. The height of command was 2.26 metres, and training arcs were between 80 and 170 degrees. The two submerged tubes were in a large athwartships torpedo room on the lower platform deck abaft the pivot of the after 305mm turret; they were perpendicular to the ship's axis and were 2.62 metres beneath the waterline

Table 2: **Armament**

Two 305mm 45-cal Mle 1893 BL guns in two single turrets
Two 274.4mm 45-cal Mle 1893 BL guns in two single turrets
Eight 138.6mm 45-cal Mle 1888–1891 QF guns in eight single turrets
Eight 100mm 45-cal Mle 1891 QF guns in open single mountings
Twelve 47mm 40-cal Mle 1885 QF guns in open single mountings
Five 37mm 20-cal QF guns in open single mountings
Three 37mm revolver cannon
Two a/w, two sub 450mm torpedo tubes

Calibre	Shell weight	Muzzle velocity	Firing cycle
305mm	292kg CI	815m/s	1rpm
	340kg APC	780m/s	1rpm
274.4mm	216kg CI	815m/s	1rpm
	255kg APC	780m/s	1rpm
138.6mm	30kg CI	770m/s	3rpm
	35kg APC	730m/s	3rpm
100mm	14kg CI	740m/s	6rpm
	16kg APC	710m/s	6rpm
47mm	1.5kg	650m/s	9–15rpm
37mm	0.5kg	435m/s	20–25rpm

CI   cast iron
APC   armour-piercing, capped

Calibre	Angle of elevation	Range
305mm	+14°/-5°	12,500m
274.4mm	+14°/-5°	11,600m
138.6mm	+15°/-10°	9,700m
100mm	+20°/-10°	9,500m
47mm	+20°/-20°	4,000m
37mm	+12°/-30°	2,000m

Masséna: Submerged Torpedo Room

Cross-section from Forward

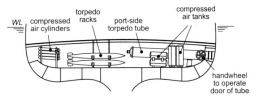

Plan View

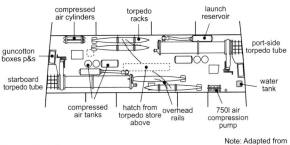

Note: Adapted from ACL plans.

0 1 2 3 4 5
METRES

© John Jordan 2018

Masséna steams with the Squadron. In the foreground is the starboard after 138.6mm turret; note the armoured sighting hood and the access door in the rear of the turret, directly behind the breech of the gun. (Author's collection)

A view of the upper deck of *Masséna* in 1899. On the right is one of the shielded 100mm QF guns. Note the wooden deck planking amidships. (Author's collection)

(see drawing). The sights for the torpedo tubes were a large Pampelonne model. Electric bells were used to cue the firing of the torpedoes. The two above-water tubes would be disembarked in March 1906.

The Mle 1892 torpedo had a length of 5.05 metres and had an all-up weight 501kg that included a 75kg warhead. When completed *Masséna* carried a total of ten combat and two exercise torpedoes. Three Thirion pumps supplied the compressed air for the torpedoes and the tubes.

Finally, there were two 65mm field guns Mle 1881 for the landing party; these were stowed between decks.

In July 1907 a Barr & Stroud rangefinder was temporarily installed atop the navigation bridge. Two of these rangefinders were in place by 1912; the starboard R/F was raised to clear the R/F to port.

Machinery

Steam for the the propulsion machinery was supplied by 24 Lagrafel & d'Allest large watertube boilers built by

ACL at their Saint-Denis works. They were distributed between three stokeholds designated Forward, Centre and After Boiler Rooms (see Hold in GA Plans), the Centre and After Boiler Rooms being separated by the magazines, shell rooms and handing rooms for the wing turrets. Each of the boilers had a single furnace and an operating pressure of 14kg/cm^2; they were first lit on 19 December 1896 under the supervision of Engineer Bosquillon de Frescheville.

The first funnel, which combined the uptakes for BR1 and BR2, had a cross-section of 9.42m^2, while the smaller second funnel, which housed the uptakes for BR3, had a cross-section of only 4.39m^2. The tops of the funnels were 20 metres above the gratings.

The boilers supplied steam for three vertical triple-expansion (VTE) engines built by AC Loire at their Saint-Denis factory. The four-cylinder engines were in three independent engine rooms located side by side (see GA plans). *Masséna* was the first French battleship to have three shafts. At the meeting of the *Conseil des Travaux* on 31 July 1891 in which this arrangement was

A fine overhead view of *Masséna* alongside at Brest with the *contre-torpilleur Baliste* alongside. Note the circular configuration of the turrets for the main guns and the flat turret roofs. (Author's collection)

discussed, the advantages were stated to be as follows:

– The engines would be located in three compartments (vs two), so there was a reduced danger from flooding on one side of the ship.
– The engines were not as high, making it possible to reinforce the protection of the platform deck above.
– The arrangement made possible the adoption of faster, lighter engines.
– The ship could cruise on the centre shaft, thereby reducing coal consumption.

There were three three-bladed propellers of special bronze; the centre propeller had a diameter of 4.5 metres, the propellers for the wing shafts 4.2 metres. The portside and central propellers turned to the right, the starboard-side propeller to the left. The immersion of the upper blades of the propellers at a draught of 8.43 metres was 2.70 metres for the wing shafts and 3.25 metres for the centre shaft. The turning circle at 8 knots was calculated as 690 metres; at a speed of 10 knots with 20 degrees of rudder, the angle of heel was between 3 and 5 degrees.

For damage control *Masséna* was equipped with four pumps rated at 600 tonnes per hour, five Thirion pumps rated at 30t/h, a Stone manual pump with four pistons rated at 20t/h, three 5t/h hand pumps and three 640-

Table 3: **Machinery**

Boilers	24 Lagrafel & d'Allest
Engines	three 4-cylinder VTE built ACL
Propellers	three 3-bladed 4.20m/4.50m
Rudder	non-balanced, 24.93m²
Designed power	13,352CV
Maximum speed	17.07 knots
Coal	638 tonnes normal
	1,081 tonnes full load
Endurance	1,860nm at 14kts
	1,370nm at 15.5kts
	970nm at 17kts
Equipment	
Searchlights	six 60cm Mangin 45/70A projectors
Boats	two 8.9-metre steam pinnaces
	one 7.6-metre White steam launch
	one 11-metre pulling pinnace
	two 10-metre pulling cutters
	two 9-metre pulling cutters
	four 8-metre whalers
	two 5-metre dinghies
	one 3.5-metre punt
	two 5.6-metre Berthon canvas boats
Anchors	two 14.45-tonne bower anchors
	two 3.67-tonne stock anchors

tonne service engines. There were two large 350mm drains in the double bottom, one on each side of the ship.

The six ventilators for the boiler rooms, which featured inclined cylinders, had a unit output of 60,000m³. The three ventilators for the engine rooms, which operated on the same principle, were each rated at 30,000m³. Electricity for the ship was supplied by four Sautter & Harlé 600A dynamos feeding an 83-volt circuit.

Equipment

There were six Mangin 60cm searchlight projectors: two atop the military masts (*ligne haute*) and four on the lower level (*ligne basse*). When not in use the latter were stowed within the hull and superstructures on trolleys with electric controls. One was located on the middle deck in the bow, another on the quarterdeck abaft the 305mm turret, and the remaining two on either side amidships, immediately abaft the 274.4mm guns. All were operated remotely using an electro-mechanical linkage.

The 11-metre pulling pinnace could be armed with a 37mm QF cannon. The 10-metre and 9-metre pulling cutters could likewise be equipped with a 37mm cannon, and the former could also embark spar torpedoes. The larger pinnaces and cutters were handled by six pairs of large davits amidships; four pairs of smaller, simpler

davits for the whalers were located on the quarterdeck. The larger davits were powered by two Bossière & Samson two-cylinder steam winches with a 3,000kg capacity.

The chain cables for the main anchors had a diameter of 62mm and a length of twenty-six 30-metre shackles. The main capstan was a two-cylinder steam-powered model from Caillard Bros (the capacity is not given in the ship's legend, the *devis d'armement*). Besides the two main anchors there were two 3.76-tonne stock anchors, equipped with four shackles of 30mm cable.

Provisions could be stowed sufficient to sustain a crew of 734 men for 45 days at sea. Twenty cubic metres of wood were embarked to fuel the galleys, stowed in the wine hold. The heating system for the living spaces was from Gravelle & Anquebourg, and gave complete satisfaction.

The Early Years

Masséna was launched at Saint-Nazaire on 24 July 1895. A correspondent of the magazine *Le Yacht* reported the event as follows:

On Wednesday Ateliers & Chantiers de la Loire launched the first class battleship *Masséna*, for which the contract was signed on 18 May 1892. The plans of the ship were

The battleship *Masséna* shortly before her launch at Ateliers & Chantiers de la Loire at Saint-Nazaire. The main armour belt has yet to be fitted. Note the prominent 'plough bow'. (Author's collection)

drawn up by Monsieur de Bussy, retired Général du Génie Maritime, member of the Académie des Sciences, and eminent naval architect who designed the *Dupuy-de-Lôme*. The ship will cost 27,438,230 francs [equivalent to £1.1m sterling in the currency of the day]. According to the contract, she is due to be delivered on 6 March 1897. She will then be transferred from Saint-Nazaire to Brest where she will undergo her acceptance trials. It is therefore anticipated that the ship will join the fleet during 1897.

However, the hull of the ship could not be docked that same day because she grounded in the Loire during the night. On the morning of the 25th, the tugs attached to the port were unable to refloat the *Masséna*, and tugs from Lorient had to be summoned for assistance. The battleship was at last able to enter the dock on the evening tide. There was found to be light damage to the after part of the hull, with some of the outer plating deformed.

During fitting out, it was decided to replace the planned above-water torpedo tubes on the main deck with tubes suspended from the deck above; the tubes came from the torpedo sloop *D'Iberville*.

The first static machinery trials were carried out between 9 November and 19 December 1896. On 17 April 1897, *Masséna* left Saint-Nazaire for Brest, arriving the following day; the main guns were yet to be fitted. Sea trials took place between 23 and 30 April, during which a marked tendency to veer to starboard when steaming straight ahead was noted. In order to remedy this defect the original rudder, which had a surface area of 18.94m^2, was replaced by a larger model with a surface area of 24.93m^2. The ship also had problems attaining the anticipated 17 knots. Despite these disappointments, following a ministerial dispatch dated 16 May the battleship was commissioned (*armement définitif*) on 24 May 1898.

On 7 June Vice Admiral Barrera, commanding officer of the Northern Squadron, hoisted his flag in *Masséna*. In June and July she visited Douarnenez, Quiberon, Houat, and Belle Ile, and during August there were port visits to Cherbourg, Le Havre, Saint-Malo and Dunkirk. In September, following the Fashoda Incident, the composition of the squadrons was radically modified, and it was decided to base all the new battleships of the *Flotte d'échantillons* in the Mediterranean. Admiral Barrera left the ship on 14 October and *Masséna* sailed from Brest the following day, arriving at Toulon on the 22nd. During the crossing the ship ran into bad weather in the Bay of Biscay. The watertight seals on the turrets were damaged, some of the lamps and a whaler were swept away, the bulkhead of the sick bay was stove in, and the 138mm and 274mm magazines were partially flooded. .

On arrival at Toulon *Masséna* was integrated into the 1st Battle Division with *Brennus* (VA Fournier) and *Bouvet*; the 2nd Division comprised *Charles Martel* (CA Roustan), *Carnot* and *Jauréguiberry*. Successful exercises followed at Les Salins d'Hyères and, in February 1899, the squadron was at anchor in

The battleship during fitting out. Some of the turrets are in place, but the guns are yet to be fitted. (Author's collection)

Villefranche roads. On 9 April, the ships visited Cagliari, where they were hosted by an Italian squadron. On the 12th, the ships of both squadrons joined together for a naval review in the presence of the Italian King and Queen. The French ships returned to Toulon on 20 April.

Following these sorties, the following evaluation of the qualities of the ship appeared in the captain's 1899 *devis de campagne*:

Masséna steers a steady course and manoeuvres well. She has a slight or negligible roll and a gentle pitch. Overall she is therefore a good sea-boat. However, the configuration

Masséna at anchor with boat booms deployed. (Author's collection)

of the bow is very unsatisfactory. At higher speeds the prominent plough bow throws up huge quantities of water as high as the raised forecastle, floods the flat part of the hull on either side amidships, and flows around the midship turret groupings.

The boilers and engines are robust and have proved more than satisfactory. However, the internal decks suffer from excessive temperatures.

There is much to say about the ship's military qualities. The rate of fire of the heavy guns is far too slow: one round every three minutes means that they cannot be used as they should be. The medium 138.6mm guns, which are in enclosed turrets, are more flexible in operation and have a good rate of fire, but there is one serious defect: the access doors to the turrets are on the axis of the guns, which means that the gun crew has to embark via the flat part of the hull (*les boulevards*), which is not always easy in heavy seas.

The conning tower is far too small: it can accommodate only half the personnel essential for combat situations. It should be modified or replaced as soon as possible.

In summary, *Masséna* could have been a formidable combat unit, and should be able to engage with every chance of success any foreign battleship that has been in service for seven or eight years.

This report highlighted the conceptual defects of the ship, defects that would not be erased over the course of time. In addition, it would prove impossible to flush out the water that regularly flooded the armoured deck, and the upper edge of the thick armour belt was far too close to the waterline. In order to lighten the ship the *Conseil Supérieure de la Marine* (CSM) recommended the removal of the wooden deck planking fore and aft, the suppression of the military masts, modification of the hawsepipes, and disembarkation of the third anchor carried on the forecastle, which was difficult to deploy, and of the above-water torpedo tubes. It also recommended replacing the torpedoes manufactured at Toulon with torpedoes built at Fiume. Needless to say, none of these recommendations were implemented at the time.

However, these technical issues did not prevent *Masséna* from resuming her activities. In July diplomatic missions took her to Spain, and in October there were port visits to Piraeus, Beirut, Tripoli, Alexandretta, Rhodes, Smyrna and Salonika.

A fine stern quarter view of *Masséna* in 1899. Note the slim second funnel, which served only the after boiler room. (Author's collection)

Return to the Northern Squadron

With the entry into service of the new battleships *Charlemagne* and *Gaulois*, *Carnot* and *Masséna* were again assigned to the Northern Squadron. On 4 January 1900, the latter two ships left Toulon for Brest. Shortly after their arrival, the battle divisions were constituted as follows:

1st Division: *Masséna* (VA Ménard), *Carnot*, *Amiral Baudin*
2nd Division: *Formidable* (CA Touchard), *Amiral Duperré*, *Redoutable*

Having transferred part of their crews to *Charlemagne* and *Gaulois*, *Masséna* and *Carnot* were placed in reserve with a reduced complement. Because of this there were only brief sorties to the Ile d'Aix or Quiberon. However, on 29 June the entire Northern Squadron set sail for the summer manœuvres that saw the junction of the Northern and Mediterrean Squadrons off the coasts of Spain. The two squadrons then headed for a spell of leave at Brest, arriving on 9 July, and the following day *Masséna* left for Cherbourg. She was followed there by the remainder of the ships on the 13th, and a review took place in the presence of President Emile Loubet. On 21 July the two squadrons returned to their respective bases, and *Masséna* resumed her normal activities.

On 18 and 21 January 1901, *Masséna* conducted wireless telegraphy trials with the armoured cruisers *Dupuy-de-Lôme* and *Bruix*. The summer manoeuvres began on 22 June and, after a port visit to Vigo in northwest Spain 24–26 June, the Northern Squadron was directed to enter the Mediterranean. After coaling at Tangier, the manoeuvres began officially on 3 July. *Masséna* anchored at Ajaccio (Corsica) on the 8th and 9th, arriving at Toulon on the 11th. In the presence of President of the Council Waldeck-Rousseau and Minister of Marine Lanessan, who were embarked on *Bouvet*, firings were carried

Masséna in the port of Brest. In the foreground is the former American monitor *Onondaga*, which was sold to the French following the Civil War and served as a coast defence battleship until 1903. The original battery of 8in Parrot rifles and 15in Dahlgren smoothbores was replaced by French-pattern 24cm rifled guns. (Author's collection)

out at Les Salins followed by a virtual attack on Ajaccio.

On 1st August the Northern Squadron headed back to Brest, arriving on the 12th. On the 15th the Squadron was at Dunkirk to greet the arrival of Tsar Nicholas II, leaving on 21 September and returning to Brest two days later. On 20 October Admiral Ménard left his command, and *Masséna* was assigned to the Reserve Division of the Mediterranean Squadron. She left Brest on 20 February 1902 and arrived at Toulon on the 26th, replacing *Amiral Baudin* in the division.

There remained a number of problems to be resolved on board *Masséna*, of which the most pressing were the poor ventilation of the internal spaces and the replacement of the hydraulic rammers of the main turrets, which were responsible for the slow rate of fire – more than three minutes per round. The solution was to instal manually-operated rammers, which had already been trialled in 1899 in the forward 305mm turret. The 305mm turrets were duly modified in that same month of February 1902, and the refitting of

Masséna at her moorings in the anchorage at Brest. Note the clumsy anchor-handling arrangements forward. The starboard anchor is suspended from one of the two cat-davits. (Author's collection)

the 274.4mm turrets would follow from May onwards.

In April *Masséna* conducted firing practice at Porquerolles, with port visits the following month to Golfe-Juan, Villefranche and Les Salins. It was during this period that the ship was fitted with bilge keels. On 4 July the summer manoeuvres took place with the participation of the Northern Squadron. The ships visited Algiers, Bougie, Philippeville, Bône and Tunis. The Squadron returned to Toulon on 28 July and for the remainder of the year *Masséna* made only brief sorties to Les Salins d'Hyères.

On 21 January 1903, the ship again headed for Brest, and Vice Admiral de Courthille hoisted his flag in her on 1st April. On 2 May the Northern Squadron was at Cherbourg to welcome King Edward VII, who was making a courtesy visit to France.

During the night of 4/5 June, in the anchorage at La Pallice, Admiral de Courthille suffered a stroke; he would be replaced on 1st July by Vice Amiral Caillard. On 17 August Minister of Marine Camille Pelletan, who had little enthusiasm for the battleship as a type, asked to attend firing trials against the forward 305mm turret of the new battleship *Suffren*. Moored to four buoys facing the Ile Longue, *Masséna* fired two 305mm rounds against a 400mm armour plate secured to the turret. The firings, which were conducted at a distance of 100 metres, were completely satisfactory, but a shell splinter weighing 50kg fell only a few metres from the Minister.

On 21 June, the Squadron was at Cherbourg for the launch of the armoured cruiser *Jules Ferry*.

An Undistinguished Career

In early 1904, the press was surprised to note the immobilisation of *Masséna* in the dockyard. In truth, although the ship did not participate in any of the Squadron's sorties, she profited from her inactivity to have her hawsepipes modified and the drive shaft for her rudder replaced.

On 8 April the torpedo boat *Corsaire*, which was underway in the anchorage at Brest, collided with one of *Masséna's* pinnaces and cut it in two; happily there were

no casualties. On the 19th the battleships and destroyers headed for Concarneau, mooring in a single line comprising the coast defence battleship *Henri IV* (replacing the docked *Formidable*), *Jauréguiberry*, *Masséna*, *Bouvines* and *Amiral Tréhouart*. The following day, the ships were off Quiberon, where they were joined by the armoured cruiser *Jeanne d'Arc*. Torpedo firing exercises followed in these waters, and the Squadron moored off Belle Ile on the 28th. On 9 May the Northern Squadron was at its moorings between La Pallice and Ile de Ré, returning to Brest on 17 May. Following gunnery practive against some decommissioned torpedo boats in the vicinity of the Minou lighthouse, the Squadron headed for Cherbourg, arriving in early June. The ships returned to their base at Brest on the 17th. In July there were exercises with submarines, and in August the ships again moored off La Pallice. In October *Masséna* entered the dockyard for maintenance.

In late May 1905, the Northern Squadron visited Cherbourg to welcome a Spanish naval formation and, on 4 June, ships of the Royal Navy were hosted at Brest. On 9 August Admiral Caillard was at Portsmouth, where a Franco-British fleet was reviewed by King Edward VII. The King was then hosted on board *Masséna* with all the honours due to his rank. On 16 September, Vice Admiral Caillard assumed command of the Northern Squadron and, on 19 June 1906, the ships headed south, entering the anchorage at Mers el-Kebir on the 25th. On 6 July they would be at Algiers, where they would meet up with the Mediterranean Squadron, The summer manoeuvres took the two Squadrons to Bougie, Bizerte and finally Toulon on the 26th. The Northern Squadron cast off on 30 July and headed for Marseille, returning to Toulon on 3 August. It then headed west along the coast to Grau-du-Roi on the 10th, visited Tangier on the 15th, Royan on the 21st, Ile d'Aix on the 24th, and returned to Brest on the 28th. In September, *Masséna* underwent a refit in which the two above-water tubes were disembarked.

Shortly after that, in conformity with the *Entente Cordiale*, all the French battleships were to be concentrated in the Mediterranean; only the armoured cruisers remained at Brest. On 16 January 1907, Rear Admiral

Masséna at Spithead in August 1905. Admiral Caillard hosted King Edward VII during the visit and the ship took part in a major naval review. (Author's collection)

The washing is hung out to dry in this view of *Masséna*. (Author's collection)

Kiesel hoisted his flag in *Masséna* and at the same time assumed command of the 2nd Battle Division of the Mediterranean Squadron; *Masséna*'s *divisionnaires* were the battleships *Carnot* and *Jauréguiberry*. Arriving at Toulon on the 13th, *Masséna* immediately entered Missiessy Dock No 3. On 15 February the division was renamed *Division de réserve de l'Escadre de la Méditerranée*. *Masséna* was undocked on 11 March, the

other two Missiessy docks (Nos 1 & 2) being currently occupied by the battleships *Suffren* and *Iéna*. The following day, the latter ship was devastated by an internal explosion that resulted in 112 deaths.

On 1st April the Reserve Division was redesignated the 3rd Division. The summer manoeuvres began on 27 June, and *Masséna* made port visits to Mers el-Kebir, Philippeville and Les Salins d'Hyères. In July a

A swimming lesson takes place in front of the battleship *Masséna*. (Author's collection)

A fine view of *Masséna*. Four 37mm QF guns are visible on the upper mainmast platform. (Author's collection)

Masséna departing Toulon. She received a new livery of uniform blue-grey in 1908. (Author's collection)

Barr & Stroud rangefinder was mounted experimentally atop the navigation bridge. On 5 October Rear Admiral Chocheprat took command of the 3rd Division and *Masséna* made only brief visits to Villefranche, Golfe-Juan and Les Salins. On 18 April 1908 the battleship had her complement reduced and was assigned to the Gunnery School (*Ecole de canonnage*). On 1st October Rear Admiral Chocheprat was replaced by Rear Admiral Le Bris on board *Masséna*, and the ship participated only in formation exercises in Toulon roads. Nevertheless, on 26 June 1909 she conducted firing practice against the torpedo boat *Lévrier* using 100mm shells with a melinite burster.

The year 1910 was relatively uneventful, although on 5 November, at about 2100, lightning struck *Masséna*'s mainmast. Apart from the blackening of the paintwork on the mast, the only damage was to throw all the ship's compasses out of alignment.

Despite this inactivity and the monotony that accompanied the ship's reduced status, an important event would again place *Masséna* at the centre of things. On 4 September 1911 there was a major naval review in the Vignettes roads off Toulon, for which the French assembled no fewer than nineteen battleships, nine armoured cruisers and 24 destroyers. *Masséna* was selected to host President Armand Fallières, President of the Council Joseph Caillaux, Minister of Marine Théophile Delcassé, as well as a host of political and military personnages. On 20 October, after the celebrations were

concluded, Rear Admiral Bouxin assumed command of the Schools Division.

On 1st January 1912, *Masséna* was placed in Normal Reserve. On 10 March she was recommissioned with a reduced crew and was slated to replace her half-sister *Charles Martel* in the 3rd Squadron based at Brest. She left Toulon on the 26th and arrived at her destination on 2 April. Two days later, Rear Admiral Adam hoisted his flag in her. There followed a number of sorties with port visits to Cherbourg, Le Havre, Quiberon, Morgat and Dunkirk. In October the 3rd Squadron was again assigned to the 3rd Maritime Region, in accordance with the Franco-British agreements. The formation left Brest on 16 October, called in at Mers el-Kebir on the 22nd, then proceeded to Algiers where it remained from 24 October to 6 November. *Masséna* arrived at Toulon on the 9th and was placed under the orders of Vice Admiral Boué de Lapeyrère, who commanded the recently-created *Armée Navale*. On 21 December Admiral Adam was replaced by Rear Admiral Ramey de Sugny and, on 6 January 1913, *Masséna* was due to sail for Bizerte where she was intended to undergo a major refit.

A Fatal Breakdown

Casting off from her moorings, *Masséna* headed for the pass, but when passing Les Vignettes a steam collector in the forward boiler room exploded. Jets of steam invaded the stokehold, killing eight stokers and injuring eight

Masséna in the anchorage at Toulon. Note the position of the hawsepipes, which caused the anchor cables to chafe against the lower part of the bow. (Author's collection)

Masséna played a prominent part in the Great Naval Review of 4 September 1911, when she hosted President Armand Fallières and Minister of Marine Théophile Delcassé. (Author's collection)

The wing 274.4mm and 138.6mm turrets are prominent in this view of *Masséna* dating from 4 September 1911. The turrets are mounted on a flat area of deck informally referred to as the *boulevards*. (Author's collection)

On board *Masséna* on 4 September 1911: on the left of the photo is future President Raymond Poincaré, and on the right Rear Admiral Pierre Le Bris, who commanded the Gunnery School division. (Author's collection)

others. The collector was quickly isolated but one of the forward boilers overheated, damaging the funnel uptakes. The battleship dropped anchor while it attempted to control the damage, but managed to return to Toulon with only the boilers in the after room lit.

Masséna was then surveyed at the dockyard, and the authorities estimated repair costs at 70,000 francs. However, there were now questions about whether it was worth repairing such an elderly and dated vessel. On 19 June *Constructions Navales* reported:

> We have examined the repair dossier for the *Masséna*, and the dockyard has estimated an expenditure of 98,000

Masséna on her return to Toulon l6 January 1913. Note the blackening of the fore-funnel, caused by the explosion of a steam collector. (Author's collection)

Commanding Officers

CV Juhel	19 Apr 1897 – 6 Aug 1908
CV Kiesel	6 Aug 1898 – 24 Dec 1899
CV Marquer	24 Dec 1899 – 15 Jan 1900
CV De Fauque de Jonquières	15 Jan 1900 – 20 Oct 1901
CV Le Léon	20 Oct 1901 – 1 Apr 1903
CV Lormier	1 Apr 1903 – 1 Jul 1903
CV Saint Paul de Saincay	1 Jul 1903 – 16 Sep 1905
CV Gauchet	16 Sep 1905 – 16 Jan 1907
CV Aubry	16 Jan 1907 – 5 Oct 1907
CV De Bon	5 Oct 1907 – 18 Apr 1908
CV Girard de la Barcerie	18 Apr 1908 – 27 Oct 1909
CV Lacaze	27 Oct 1909 – 20 Oct 1911
CV Morin	20 Oct 1911 – 1 Jan 1912
CF Le Blanc	1 Jan 1912 – 3 Apr 1912
CV Fournier	3 Apr 1912 – 21 Dec 1912
CV Bernard	21 Dec 1912 – 18 Mar 1913
CV Delahet	18 Mar 1913 – 11 Jul 1913
CV Saunier	11 Jul 1913 – 1 Mar 1914

Flag Officers

VA Barrera	7 Jun – 14 Oct 1898
VA Ménard	15 Jan 1900 – 20 Oct 1901
VA De Courthille	1 Apr 1903 – 6 Jun 1903
VA Caillard	1 Jul 1903 – 15 Sep 1905
VA Gigon	16 Sep 1905 – 15 Jan 1907
CA Kiesel	16 Jan – 4 Oct 1907
CA Chocheprat	5 Oct 1907 – 18 Apr 1908
CA Lebris	1 Oct 1908 – 19 Oct 1911
CA Bouxin	20 Oct – 31 Dec 1911
CA Adam	4 Apr – 20 Dec 1912
CA Ramey de Sugny	21 Dec 1912 – 1 Mar 1913

Notes:

VA	*Vice-Amiral*		Vice Admiral
CA	*Contre-Amiral*		Rear Admiral
CV	*Capitaine de Vaisseau*		Captain
CF	*Capitaine de Frégate*		Commander

francs to carry out full repairs to the vessel, and 70,000 francs simply to restore the steam pipework to normal operating conditions.

On 7 July the commanding officer of *Masséna* concluded:

> Even if *Masséna* were to become a school ship, a number of repairs would be essential ... To sum up, *Masséna* would be out of service for several months ...

During the same month Captain Saunier submitted a further report on the state of the ship:

> The trim tanks are no longer watertight. All the ship's boats are in poor condition. The after 30cm turret is immobilised, and the submerged tubes often cause damage to the torpedoes on launch. *Masséna* is essentially worn out. It would take a considerable investment of labour and funding even to permit her to sail independently as a gunnery school ship. She would not be able to deploy as a first-line fleet unit. She has no value either as a ship or as a military unit.

The wreck of *Masséna* at Seddul-Bahr after the war. On the right can be seen the hull of the former liner *Saghalien*. (Author's collection)

Masséna was provisionally placed in Special Reserve on 1st March, and it was formally announced on 1st April 1914 that she would be decommissioned on 25 June. She was immobilised in an anchorage in the depths of the dockyard, and the guns were disembarked together with all other recoverable materiel. The superstructures and funnels were cut away, leaving an empty hull devoid of all equipment. Soon, preparations for war would completely eclipse any concerns regarding the fate of *Masséna*. However, the ship would come to play a minor role in this terrible conflict.

At the Dardanelles, the failure of attempts to force the straits on 18 March 1915 had led the respective General Staffs to set in train a landing operation on the Gallipoli Peninsula. The French forces were assigned a zone west of the fort at Seddul Bahr, near Çanakkale. In order to resupply the expeditionnary corps with men and equipment, it was decided to scuttle two old ships to form a breakwater for the bay. The final destiny of *Masséna* was thus announced. She left Toulon for Bizerte on 23 August under tow from the tugs *Samson* and *Vigoureux*. This small formation reached its destination on the 31st, and the hull of the battleship remained immobilised in Tunisia until 5 September. On that date, the tugs *Atlas* and *Vigoureux* again took her under tow and headed for Mudros, where they arrived without incident on the 12th. Eleven days later, when she was still in the anchorage, *Masséna* broke her moorings and grounded on Veruli Point. Refloated, the old battleship threatened to founder at any moment, so on 9 November she was towed for the last time and sunk, under the direction of CF Bréart de Boissanger, at Cape Helles, thereby closing

off part of the anchorage of Seddul-Bahr. Her neighbour was the former Messageries Maritimes passenger liner *Saghalien*.

These provisions proved their efficacy when there were severe gales on 27 November. The British installations suffered severe damage, whereas the French arrangements were more resistant to the huge seas whipped up by the storm.

In 1917 the two 305mm guns disembarked from *Masséna* were installed on Batignolles mountings and were assigned to the Heavy Railway Artillery (*Artillerie Lourde sur Voie Ferrée*, or ALVF). On 4 December of the same year, the 274.4mm guns were installed on Schneider sliding mountings and assigned to the 20th Battery of the 7th Group of the 77th Heavy Artillery Regiment.

After the war, a Marine Paris report dated 11 August 1919 stated:

> Work to refloat the *Masséna* would require extensive preliminary studies with investigations carried out by divers. In the absence of military divers, costs are estimated at 10,000 francs. Refloating would only be a viable option if the Turks were to oppose the sale of the wreck in its current situation.

In the event, the wreck was sold for breaking up in March 1923 to a certain Monsieur Jost.

Editor's Note:

This article was translated from the French by the Editor. The drawings are based on the official plans of *Masséna* held at the Centre d'Archives de l'Armement.

THE DEVELOPMENT OF YOKOSUKA NAVY YARD

In the second part of his article on Yokosuka Navy Yard, **Hans Lengerer** looks at the development of the facility after 1868.

Yokosuka Shipyard, still incomplete at the time of Meiji Restoration, passed through two serious crises during the civil war (*Boshin Sensō*). The first was the fear that the hired Frenchmen would become entangled in a fight between Bakufu troops and those of the new government, bringing with it diplomatic complications; the second, even more serious, was the danger that the French bank to which it had been mortgaged as security to obtain credits might take possession of the shipyard.

At the beginning of 1868 the army of the last Tokugawa Shogun, Prince Yoshinobu, was defeated at Fushimi (27 January), Toba (29 January) and Osaka (2 February), and he withdrew to Edō. At the end of February an 'Imperial Army' advanced to Edō, utilising the Tōkaidō and Nakasendō roads, and took up quarters at Sumpu (5 March) to prepare for the assault on Edō. Naturally, neither the Bakufu nor the new government had the time to manage the Yokosuka Shipyard, and it was feared that the French might become involved in the domestic conflict. In the circumstances Hattori, the highest financial official of the Bakufu at Yokosuka, advised Verny to stop work and to withdraw to Yokohama, which offered better protection for foreigners. However, Verny refused on the grounds that the repair of the foreign ships could not be halted. Also, the French Ambassador argued that the establishment of the shipyard was the responsibility of the French government, and pointed out that the Bakufu's loan of $500,000 was to be paid within seven months, otherwise the Yokosuka plant would be sold. In the event there was a pause of only a few days, and in anticipation of possible aggressions a French warship was ordered to anchor in Yokosuka Bay to protect the Frenchmen working in the shipyard.

Dr PAL Savatier, the French doctor at Yokosuka, wrote in April 1868: '... We are now in the midst of revolution in Japan ... but do not know how the revolution will turn out ...'[1] In reality, this statement related to the fear of a British plot to take France's position in the new government, rather than imminent danger for the French employees.

On 16 April 1868 Yokosuka Shipyard was also put under the jurisdiction of Kanagawa Law Court, as was the Yokohama Works, and the French engineers and workmen were allowed to return to Yokosuka from Yokohama, where they had been taken for their own

François Léonce Verny (1837–1908), the designer and technical adviser for Yokosuka Shipyard. Verny remained in Japan until the beginning of 1876 following his release as Head of the Shipyard at the end of 1875. (Lars Ahlberg collection)

protection the previous month. The new government was well aware of the importance of the shipyard, and its policy was to continue the work started by the Bakufu. There were delays due to financial and other difficulties, but in general the work progressed despite the disorder caused by the civil war.

On the previous day (15 April) the government official in charge of the iron works (*Seitetsushō*), Kawakubo Chubei, and other officials were appointed and superseded the former Bakufu retainers. The change of administration did not affect the rights of Verny, but when submitting proposals to the government he now had to deliver them in advance to the overall controllers, Terajima and Iseki.

Three months later, Yokosuka Shipyard faced its most serious crisis as it had been offered as security in a contract between the Bakufu and France for the purchase of weapons arranged by the French Ambassador Léon Roches. Furthermore, the building of the shipyard had been made possible by a loan of $450,000 from the Comptoir National de Paris, Yokohama Branch, but the entire shipyard had had to be mortgaged to the Société Générale in order to guarantee the loan. The deadline for repayment had already elapsed, and it seemed inevitable that the shipyard would fall into the hands of the French when, in July of 1868, Okuma Shigenobu, Foreign Minister of the new Meiji govenment, ordered councillors Higashikuze, Terajima, Komatsu and Iseki to negotiate a foreign loan. After consultation with the British Minister Sir Harry Parkes, the British Oriental Bank Corporation (*Tōyō Ginkō*) at Yokohama advanced $500,000 to the Japanese representatives; a bill for the total amount owing was requested from the local branch of the French bank, and on 26 July the sum of $470,000 was repaid.

Administrative Changes

In March 1869 the government decided to invite the senior French naval engineer Jules Thibaudier to Japan and drew up a contract. He worked as assistant to Director Verny and became head of the French workforce. In October of the same year, the shipyard was removed from local jurisdiction and placed under the newly-established Finance Ministry (*Okurashō*). On 25 November the later Viscount Yamao Yōzō was ordered to take over the management of the plant and this was implemented on 13 July 1870, when it was transferred to the Traffic and Communications Ministry (*Mimbushō*).

On 4 April 1870, three months after the foundation of the Navy Department (*Kaigunshō*), the Yokosuka Works was brought under its jurisdiction and attached to the Ishikawajima Ship Administration Bureau. The later Baron and Vice Admiral Akamatsu Noriyoshi, at that time a civil officer in the IJN corresponding to captain in rank (*Daijō*), was appointed head of the shipyard, but this was primarily an administrative post as Verny, assisted by his deputy Thibaudier, continued to assume responsibility for the building work. The appointment was necessary because Verny had been given six months leave, on half salary, to recruit new employees, but an additional factor was to ensure that the Japanese took on more of the workload, thereby reducing the financial burden. At the same time the name *Yokosuka Seitetsushō* (Iron Works) was changed to *Yokosuka Zōsenshō* (Shipyard) to reflect the true character of this shipbuilding and repair enterprise.

In October 1870 the Industry Ministry (*Kobushō*) was established specifically for the promotion of industry in Japan, and the Yokosuka Works was transferred to this

Hida Hamagorō (1830–1889) in the Netherlands. He was an engineer and bureaucrat in the Tokugawa and Meiji eras. He became chief engineer aboard *Kanrin Maru* and later designed the steam engine for *Chiyodagata*. In 1864 he was despatched to the Netherlands to buy machine tools for Ishikawajima Shpipyard. He was then sent to Paris, where he had a disagreement with Verny concerning tools for Yokosuka Navy Yard. He died after trying to jump on a train at Fujieda Station, an incident that even Rudyard Kipling recorded. (Lars Ahlberg collection)

organisation in April 1871. In July of the same year Hida Hamagoro was appointed chief of the shipbuilding and production sections, and he occupied this post from 15 August. However, the repair work and shipbuilding required the skill of the French instructors, and at the end of that year (12 December 1871) about half of the original group, twenty-five Frenchmen, were still employed. Director Verny resumed management of the shipyard after returning from leave, but now had to take into account the views of Yamao, then Akamatsu and Hida. Nevertheless, Verny was highly regarded by the Japanese and his decisions accepted.

In mid-October 1872 Yokosuka Shipyard, which was the largest and most advanced government shipbuilding undertaking in Japan, was transferred from the civilian Industry Ministry to the Navy Ministry,[2] which now became responsible for the wages of the French and Japanese workers. These administrative moves from the

- The repair and building of hulls and engines of domestic and foreign ships needed the authorisation of the Navy Minister (article 1).
- Design and construction schedules would be decided at a meeting between the head of the yard and Verny, then submitted to the Navy Minister (article 2).
- Verny would be responsible for all technical aspects such as the construction and repair of ships, engines and buildings (article 3).
- The head of the shipyard would handle all financial and administrative matters such as purchases, recruitment and contracts (article 4).
- The French officials and others were to assist the domestic officers, foremen and workers, and questions from the Japanese contingent were to be treated with respect (article 6).
- The domestic technical officers should have overall control, from the register of workers to storage of materials, and related financial matters (article 7).

This considerably weakened Verny's authority, but he left Japan not in anger but with the conviction that he had performed his task well. The Japanese rated his services highly and accorded him the utmost respect, both at the time and in subsequent evaluations of his work.

Verny's assistant Thibaudier continued as head of the French workers, but the management of the yard had passed into Japanese hands. The employment of foreign personnel was wound down, and the last of them left in August 1877, to be replaced by Japanese workers.

Extension and Completion of the Plant

When the Yokosuka Works was transferred to the Meiji government, No 1 graving dock and two berths were nearing completion. The completed shops had an area of approximately 12,900m²;[4] those under construction 6,600m². Eight vessels had already been completed, eleven more were building. Yen 600,000 were requested to complete the shipyard.

In May 1869 the wrought-iron shop (108 workmen, 14 machines, steam power 10hp), in December the boiler shop (90 workers, 15 machines, steam power 10hp), and in September 1870 the casting shop (97 workmen, steam power 10hp) were completed. The workforce had increased from 422 in 1867 to 960 by the end of 1869.

On 7 April 1871 the Yokosuka Shipyard was formally opened. According to a note by Verny the shipyard occupied 16.5 hectares, the stores and accommodation 9.5 hectares, for a total of 26 hectares (equivalent to 65 acres). The total expenditure to 19 February 1871 amounted to $1,470,431. The construction of the second dock, together with various arrangements for the building slips and quays, offices and stores, still remained to be executed in accordance with the programme agreed in 1865. The harbour had a surface area of 11 hectares and was dredged to a depth of 9 metres, but had still to be protected against the north-easterly swell by a break-water with a length of 180 metres. About 1,400

Akamatsu Noriyoshi (1841–1920). He was appointed Head of the Shipyard in 1870 with the rank of captain. It was an administrative post only, as Verny retained his senior position. (Lars Ahlberg collection)

Kanagawa Local Law Court (15 April 1868) to the Finance Ministry (18 October 1869), the Traffic and Communications Ministry (13 July 1870), the Industry Ministry (7 April 1871) and finally the Navy Ministry (8 October 1872) not only illustrate the rapidly-changing organisation of the government agencies after the Meiji restoration, but they also demonstrate that the huge sums involved in building the Yokosuka Shipyard could only have been financed by the state.

Following the transfer of Yokosuka Shipyard to the Navy Ministry the transition to Japanese management and a Japanese workforce was intensified, but Verny remained in overall control until his retirement on 31 December 1875, despite a compromise arrangement adopted during his final year.[3]

On 20 May 1875 Hida Hamagoro proposed a new standing order, which was authorised by Navy Minister Kawamura Sumiyoshi. The proposal comprised eight articles that considerably restricted Verny's rights in favour of the (Japanese) head of the shipyard. In addition, the process of hiring Frenchmen and drawing up their contracts was to be transferred to the Japanese from 1 January 1876, Verny being involved only as a consultant. The key clauses were as follows:

workmen were employed in the workshops and, remarkably, they received the same wages as their European counterparts. In October 1871 the total number of machines was 116, steam power totalled 180hp, and 50 furnaces for casting and forging had been installed. A total of ten steam ships, dredgers, lighters and crane ships, displacing a total of 740 tons and powered by a total 76hp, were utilised by the yard .

According to a description published in *La Revue Maritime et Coloniale* in May 1873,[5] among the Japanese personnel there were a number of commissioned and non-commissioned officers who had been assigned to the shipyard for two years and had replaced their French counterparts in the management of the shipyard and the workshops.

There were now three departments: accounting, repair and construction (for the IJN), and hydraulics (this department dealt with civilian and naval construction carried out by domestic enterprises). There was also a large number of factories, workshops and warehouses for shipbuilding materials, the latter being supervised by Japanese officers. The workshops were managed by a head of administration and a foreman in charge of technical work and assigned as replacement of the French foreman. In addition to the workshops already in operation at Yokohama, such as the machine shops and smithy, there were: several carpentry shops (sawmill, boat building, joinery, model shop, and pulley shop); a ropery, housed within a building 270 metres in length and equipped with machines purchased in Cherbourg; large and small smithies, together with a locksmith's workshop in two buildings with 130 employees; and a copper smithy divided into three workshops (a smithy and a machine shop with a boiler fitting shop between them). Among the factories the most notable was the iron foundry, which had an average capacity of 120 tons of iron and 10–12 tons of bronze per month, and had 47 employees.

The repair slips were constructed as simply as possible. There were rails with toothed wheels and safety catches between them, and the ships were hauled onto the slipway using two winches. The building slips were likewise simply constructed to minimise expenditure; they were initially employed only for the construction of small ships.

Graving dock No 1, opened in April 1871,[6] was built by taking advantage of the geographical and geological conditions; length (from sill to sill) was 114.30m, width at the entrance (floor) was 25m, and depth 11m. The depth of water was between 7.10m and 6.50m depending on the tide. The caisson for the dock was built in France, transported to Yokosuka, and mounted in position. Four centrifugal pumps, made by Kent & Dumont and driven by 24hp steam engines, were able to pump out the dock within 8 hours.

Dock No 2 (later No 3) was begun in 1871 and completed in January 1874. It was smaller than No 1, measuring 85m x 12.5m with a depth of water between 5.6m and 6.0m. It was similarly constructed but the depth of the base was increased near the dock gate to facilitate removal of the rudder once the dock had been pumped out.[7]

The Achievement of Verny

Verny occupied the position of Head of Yokosuka Shipyard for more than ten years and played a leading role in the modernisation of Japanese shipbuilding technology. In addition to the building of the industrial plant at Yokohama and Yokosuka, he had been responsible for the construction of ships, lighthouses, agricultural and mining machinery, and especially the repair of foreign and domestic ships, the latter amounting to 205 vessels prior to his retirement.[8] He designed (and partially supervised the construction of) the armed Imperial yacht *Jingei* and the warships *Seiki* and *Amagi*, designed and built *Komei Maru*, *Yokosuka Maru*, *Soryu Maru*, *No 1* and *No 2 Tone Maru* (ex *Tonegawa Maru*), two 10hp ferry boats, various types of small steamer, steam dredgers, a crane ship, and stone transporters. He had also supervised the construction of three building berths, two docks, No 3 lighthouse at Kannonzaki, No 4 lighthouse at Shinagawa, No 4 lighthouse at Jogashima, No 1 lighthouse at Nojimazaki and others, and built roads and houses for bureaucrats.

Early Shipbuilding

As with Yokohama Iron Mill the construction of ships began before the official opening of the yard. In 1869 the Imperial yacht *Sōryū Maru* was laid down, followed by the paddle wheel-driven small *No 1* and *No 2 Tone* (ex-*Tonegawa*) *Maru* in 1871 and 1872 respectively. In the same year *Sōryū Maru* was begun, and Verny completed the lighthouse at Kannonzaki (designed by two French engineers), the first modern lighthouse in Japan. The first armed ship of the paddle-wheel type was the Imperial yacht *Jingei*, which was laid down on 26 September 1873 but not completed until 5 January 1881 due to problems with her machinery. She was armed with guns and was later used for torpedo training. (Despite this, the author hesitates to classify her as a warship, as most Japanese sources do, and prefers the term armed Imperial yacht.)

Warship building began in 1873 when the sloop *Seiki* was laid down on 20 November. In contrast to the former ships she was driven by a conventional propeller, but she was still rigged as a three-masted barque. Before her completion on 21 June 1876 the sloop *Amagi* had been laid down on 9 September 1875, followed by the gunboat *Banjō* and the sloop *Kaimon* in 1877. The final ship of Yokosuka's series of wooden steam-propelled warships, rigged as three-mast barques for auxiliary propulsion (even though they were regarded primarily as sailing ships), was the sloop *Tenryū*, laid down on 9 February 1878.

Up to *Amagi* the designs were drawn up by Verny, but from *Banjō* Akamatsu Noriyoshi was responsible, assisted by Verny's former deputy Thibaudier.

All of these designs drew heavily on those of the

preceding ships. With regard to the supervision of construction it is difficult to assess the relative contributions of the French or Japanese personnel, but it is reasonable to conclude that from *Kaimon* the Japanese were preeminent.

Change of Construction from the French to the British Type

On 2 October 1870 the government decided that the IJN should be developed on the British model, and in 1873 a British naval mission was invited to teach the design and construction methods employed by the Royal Navy. At the Yokosuka Shipyard the French system was firmly embedded from its inception, but it proved inconvenient to use different systems, and there were demands for simplification and uniformity. It was therefore logical that once the French departed in 1878 preparations began for the move to British construction methods.

One of the key reasons for the change was the construction of the warships *Fusō, Kongō,* and *Hiei* in British shipyards and the subsequent visit of their designer and supervisor of construction, Sir Edward Reed, in 1879. These ships were transferred to Japan by British crews and arrived in 1878, in June, March, and May respectively. A few technicians from the temporary crews were hired to give introductory training in British shipbuilding technology. Also on board these three vessels were nine Japanese students who had completed their studies in Britain.

On 21 June of that year Yokosuka Shipyard submitted a request to the Navy Ministry requesting a move from the French to the British system, beginning with the teaching of the English language,[9] but emphasising that this change needed to be gradual and carefully managed 'because it is not easy to make the improvement immediately.'

One of the problems was the change in the system of measurements implied. In November 1878 Yokosuka shipyard had been ordered to use imperial measurements instead of the metric system, but insisted in a report submitted on 29 January 1879 that the metric system was to be retained for ships currently in design/build due to the possibility of errors being committed in the conversion process.

In order to realise the change from the French to British construction methods the Navy Ministry hired the British naval architect Francis Elgar as adviser for shipbuilding from 3 January 1880 to 25 June 1881.[10] He was assisted by a British technician, and by an engineer who had come to Japan on board *Fusō* in 1878.

Torpedo boat No 4 in 1887. (Lars Ahlberg collection)

Elgar was responsible for the torpedo boats *TB-1* to *TB-4* (built by Yarrow & Co, Poplar, shipped in broken-down condition to Japan in 1880), and for the reassembly of these boats at Yokosuka. The British engine worker A Broadmeyer and shipwright W Banten, both employees of Yarrow, were hired on 9 April. They left London on 12 April,[11] began the supervision of the assembly of *TB-1* on 9 July 1880 and that of *TB-2/3/4* on 19 February 1881, but work was suspended when the government was unable to pay the supervisors. Their contract ended on 30 June 1881 and they returned to England.

The complete change from the French to the British type from about 1883 was due to the requirement to build iron-framed and armoured ships. It was reported in *Yokosuka Kaigun Senshō Shi* on 25 June 1883 that:

> ... previously, *Shusenkyoku* [predecessor of the NTD] discussed with us preparations for iron-framed and armoured ships, in line with world naval trends. Today, we concluded the contract to invite Henry Lewis and David Nicholas, shipwrights at Pembroke Royal Dockyard, England, to work on ships of this type ...[12]

Both had been invited by Lt-Cdr Sasō Sachū, who was to become Japan's senior naval architect from before the Sino-Japanese War to shortly before the Russo-Japanese War and arrived in Japan on board the unprotected cruiser *Tsukushi* on 20 September 1883. They worked there until 18 September 1889, during which time the iron-and-wood composite sloop *Musashi*, the steel-and-iron composite gunboat *Atago* and the cruiser *Takao* of the same type were completed, and the steel despatch boat *Yaeyama* was launched. Subsequent ships were built exclusively of steel, thereby completing the change from composite to uniform construction material. Even though *Yaeyama* was designed by the famous French naval architect Louis-Emile Bertin, it appears that Lewis and Nicholas fulfilled their task, as this ship was launched on 12 March 1889 and nearing completion when they left Japan. Following their departure, with few exceptions, design and construction were executed by Japanese naval architects, engineers, technicians and workmen.

Extension of the Shipyard and The Move from Iron to Steel

When shipbuilding was well underway, the extension of the shipyard was also progressed. In 1878 construction of dry dock No 3 (later re-numbered No 2) was begun, but it could not be completed before June 1884 because of ongoing financial problems. With a length of 142 metres it surpassed the two earlier docks, but the method of construction (stone blocks fitted together with sand and clay) remained the same.

Development was not limited to administrative changes, the extension of facilities and the installation of superior equipment, but also covered shipbuilding techniques associated with the change from iron to steel. While Yokosuka was under construction, the series of wooden three-mast sailing ships with auxiliary steam power had been superseded by iron-framed vessels fitted with single screw propellers. On 17 February 1881 Yokosuka Shipyard submitted a report to the Navy Ministry in which it pointed out the necessity of adopting iron framing due to a shortage of high quality timbers, which needed to be stored and seasoned for seven years before use. The head of the yard pointed out that they were now compelled to use timber after only three/four years, resulting in the expenditure of large sums on repair and delays in construction. He proposed replacing the wooden framing by iron framing for three/four years and building 'composite' ships, beginning with the small 40hp ship currently planned. His submission was accepted, and the Navy Ministry's permission was obtained on 10 March.[13]

The decision meant that Yokosuka Shipyard, hitherto exclusively engaged in building wooden hulls, had to provide the facilities for working iron, such as shops with machinery for bending, shaping, and piercing iron plates, a larger pattern and forging shop, plumbers' shops etc. In response to this decision the installation of three 12-ton steam hammers and a 5-ton iron smelting furnace was agreed in September and December respectively of that year. In addition, the personnel had to be trained in composite shipbuilding, as working with iron required different skills.

Due to the magnitude of this change, no new warship was laid down from February 1878 to November 1882, and following the laying down of the sloop *Katsuragi* on 25 December more than two years passed before *Musashi*

was laid down on 9 March 1885. Both were iron/wood composite vessels, the model for their construction being the corvettes *Kongō* and *Hiei* built in Britain and delivered in 1878. The construction work was planned and supervised by Lewis and Nicholas, who had been hired especially for this purpose.

With the construction of *Katsuragi* the hitherto simple method of concentrating the weight of the hull upon a single row of stocks in the middle of the building berth was changed, with two rows of stocks parallel to the keel in order to reduce the loading on each row by 50 per cent. This method was retained for the following ships.

Ship construction proceeded even as the shipyard continued to develop, and the Navy Ministry recognised the danger that this process would be hindered by the additional use of Yokosuka as an operational naval base, and established Tokai (East) Naval Station (*Chinjufu*) at Yokohama in 1876. Yokosuka now became Japan's centre for repair and shipbuilding. However, in 1884 the Tokai Naval Station at Yokohama was abolished. Everything was transferred to Yokosuka Naval Station, and from this date Yokosuka Shipyard was controlled by this organ and Yokosuka became the IJN's first complete base for naval operations.

Table 1 provides a survey of the works organisation, disposition of engines and labour power in 1886, some twenty years after the laying of the foundation stone on 27 September 1865.

In the meantime the superiority of steel over iron became well established. Steel was used for framing and other items from around 1885, but production methods

The sloop *Musashi* following her launch at Yokosuka on 30 March 1886. Note that the early-model camera used has been unable to cope with the movement of the smaller craft. (Lars Ahlberg collection)

The gunboat *Atago* at Yokosuka on 17 June 1887. (Lars Ahlberg collection)

had not yet developed sufficiently to permit the use of steel for shell plating. On the other hand, better-quality iron could be produced, and this brought about another type of composite construction with steel framing but iron plating. The gunboat *Atago* (one of the four ships of *Maya* class) and the cruiser *Takao* were built using this system; they were laid down in July and October 1886 and completed in March and January 1889 respectively.

Technological progress was rapid, and within a few years the quality of the steel was improved to such an extent that it could also be used for the outer plating, and this provided a number of advantages compared to the composite ships. Thus, after the construction of four 'composite' ships, two of iron/wood and two of steel/iron, Yokosuka Shipyard laid down its first all-steel warship, the despatch boat *Yaeyama*. Designed by the French aval architect Bertin, she was powered by an engine manufactured in England by Hawthorn, Leslie & Co but assembled and installed at Yokosuka, giving her the extraordinary speed of 20 knots. *Yaeyama* was laid down on 7 June 1887 and completed on 15 March 1890.

The extension and upgrading of the facilities needed to

Table 1: Yokosuka 1886

The following table provides a survey of the factory organisation, disposition of engines and labour in 1886, or roughly 20 years after laying of the foundation stone (27 September 1865).

Shops	No of Workers	No of Engines	Horsepower
Building berth	822	6	74hp
Dock	440	11	103hp
Rope	98	1	6hp
Saw and Plane	23	1	20hp
Machine tooling	169	1	30hp
Forging	151	1	10hp
Casting	111	1	10hp
Boiler	327	1	30hp
Building	136	1	30hp
Ship tooling	84	–	–
Fabrication	148	–	–
Drawing	42	–	–
Repair	167	–	–
Transportation	159	–	–
Others	17	–	–
Total	2,894	25	296hp

Source: *Yokosuka Kaigun Senshō Shi*, Vol II, 362–63.

The cruiser *Takao* in 1890–1891. (Lars Ahlberg collection)

be ongoing in order to keep abreast of the rapid progress in metallurgy, manufacturing and construction methods. In 1886 the interior of a former shipbuilding berth was changed to a smithy to extend the facilities necessary for building iron vessels, and in 1887 a 500kg steam hammer was installed in the forge; a 7hp locomotive punching machine in the dockside workshop, drilling machines in the boiler shop, and a 60-ton steam crane completed the facilities for building iron ships. In the following year a drawing office (detailed design and working drawings) and a wrought iron shop were newly erected, while improved machines and machine tools were installed in the various workshops. The equipment of the building

berths was also upgraded: in 1889 a 22-ton steam hammer was installed in the wrought iron shop; the shipbuilding shop received five new multiple drilling machines, the boiler shop new boiler flange machinery, and new equipment for the engine shop included a 12hp locomotive punching and numerous other machines. This trend continued in 1890 with the installation of a 30-ton crane and other equipment in the boiler shop, and a large (15in) slotting machine in the machine shop. A new boiler was installed in the shipbuilding shop to provide steam for the increased power of the machinery. Electric lighting was greatly expanded – the first generator had been installed in 1882 – to facilitate evening and night work.

The above data illustrate the constant struggle for improvement, despite a tight budget. The change from manual to mechanical work, unavoidable in the case of iron and steel shipbuilding, not only meant improvements in the production system and the technical skill of the employees, but served to increase shipbuilding and engine production capacity.

The move from iron to steel during the 1880s was accompanied by major developments in propulsion machinery with a view to obtaining higher speeds.[14] Table 2 illustrates the key changes, which were as follows:

– Engines of the horizontal return type were superseded first by the two-cylinder compound (double expansion) type, then by the vertical triple expansion (VTE) three-cylinder type.

The cruiser *Niitaka* dressed overall at Kōbe on 8 March 1906. (Lars Ahlberg collection)

Table 2: **Ships Completed at Yokosuka 1885-1912**

Completion	Name	Material	Type of Engine	Type of Boiler	HP	Speed
Early Period						
5 Mar 1885	Tenryu	wood	1 x horizontal, return-acting two-cylinder, double expansion	4 x iron cylindrical	1,162hp	12 knots
4 Nov 1887	*Katsuragi*	iron/wood	1 x horizontal, return-acting two-cylinder, double expansion	6 x iron cylindrical	1,404hp	12 knots
9 Feb 1888	*Musashi*	iron/wood	1 x horizontal, return-acting two-cylinder, double expansion	6 x iron cylindrical	1,830hp	12 knots
2 Mar 1889	*Atago*	iron	2 x horizontal, direct-acting two-cylinder, double expansion	2 x steel cylindrical	970hp	10.25 knots
16 Nov 1889	*Takao*	steel/iron	2 x horizontal, direct-acting two-cylinder, double expansion	5 x steel cylindrical	2,350hp	15 knots
15 Mar 1890	*Yaeyama*	steel	2 x horizontal, three-cylinder, double expansion	6 x steel cylindrical	5,500hp	20 knots
Later Period						
27 Jan 1904	*Niitaka*	steel	2 x vertical, four-cylinder, triple expansion	16 x Niclausse large watertube	9,400hp	20 knots
25 Mar 1910	*Satsuma*	steel	2 x vertical, four-cylinder, triple expansion	20 x Miyabara single-ended large watertube	17,500hp	18.25 knots
31 Mar 1912	*Kawachi*	steel	2 x Kawasaki Curtis turbines	8 x Miyabara single-ended, 8 x Miyabara double-ended watertube	25,000hp	20 Knots

The battleship *Satsuma* on the slipway at Yokosuka on 2 November 1906. (Lars Ahlberg collection)

The launch of the armoured cruiser *Kurama* at Yokosuka on 21 October 1907. (Lars Ahlberg collection)

– Boilers of the high-cylinder type made of iron were superseded by the steel low-cylinder type, operating at higher pressures, and the steam generated by a single boiler doubled (sufficient steam for 2,000hp).

The ships built after *Yaeyama*, such as the coast defence vessel *Hashidate*, showed a major increase in displacement; that of *Hashidate* was 4,277 tons, and she was the largest warship constructed in Japan until the building of first class cruiser *Tsukuba* in 1905. The cruisers *Akitsushima, Suma, Akashi, Niitaka, Otowa*, the despatch boat *Chihaya*, the battleships *Satsuma* and *Kawachi*, the first class cruiser *Kurama*, the battle cruiser *Hiei*, and smaller types of vessel were built exclusively of steel. The type of engine changed to the vertical triple expansion type with either three or four cylinders, and in the last ship of the period under consideration to the steam turbine. During this later period armoured ships were generally fitted with the locally-developed Miyabara watertube boiler, while smaller ships continued to trial foreign models.

Extension 1895–1904

During the Sino-Japanese War (1894–95) the Shipbuilding Division worked in two shifts: day and night. The number of workers increased rapidly, and more than 1,300 were dispatched aboard repair ships to Kure, Sasebo, Port Arthur and Weihaiwei.

From 15 August 1894 until 4 January 1895 the building and repair of foreign vessels was halted, and in 1899 the repair of foreign and domestic civilian ships was abandoned in recognition that civilian shipbuilding had been developed to a level permitting the construction of modern merchant vessels. This followed the promulgation of the shipbuilding and navigation (shipping) 'encouragement laws' after the SJW and resulted in the abolition of Yokosuka's supplementary role in support of the civilian shipbuilding industry in order to focus on work for the IJN.[15] After the war Japan embarked on a major expansion of the Navy using a large part of the Chinese war indemnity, and factories and their equipment were further improved and expanded where necessary.

On 30 September 1897 the name was changed to Yokosuka Navy Shipyard (*Yokosuka Kaigun Zosenshō*)[16] and on 5 November 1903 the shipyard was united with the Yokosuka Naval Arsenal (*Yokosuka Heikishō*) and received its final designation, namely Yokosuka Navy Yard (*Yokosuka Kōshō*). At the same time the commander of the Navy Yard was given control of all the other factories and workshops belonging to the naval station. The organisation was as follows:

1 Shipbuilding and Repair Division (*Zōsenbu*)
2 Engine Manufacturing Division (*Zōkibu*)
3 Weapon Manufacturing Division (*Zōheibu*)
4 Accounts Division (*Kaikeibu*)

Following the expansion of armament facilities after the SJW, the first two and last divisions covered more than 70 acres of ground, including four docks – one of which was under construction – and building berths, numerous factories, workshops and warehouses. These three divisions were located at Yokosuka, while the ordnance division, with factories, workshops and warehouses covering a further 60 acres of ground, was located in nearby Nagaura Bay. The factories and workshops had been increased in size and number, supplemented with new equipment – the largest steam hammer in one of the forging shops was rated at 20 tons – and newly-erected shops such as the brass foundry to create a modern shipbuilding facility. Everything was now directed towards a possible future war with Russia.

The number of workmen varied from 4,000 to 6,000 depending on the work being carried out, and in the years after the Russo-Japanese War the number rose to roughly 16,000 on account of the conversion and repair of captured ships that had to be executed over and above new construction and the routine refit and repair of vessels of IJN origin.

In 1899 the Navy Artillery Training Station (*Kaigun Hojûtsu Renshujō*) was established in Koumi, but moved to Taura the following year. In September 1901 the new building for the Navy Machinery School (*Kaigun Kikan Gakkō*) was completed, and in Shiodane the Navy Engineering Training Station (*Kaigun Kikan Gijutsu Renshujō*) for warrant and petty officers was established.

The Shipbuilding School to which reference was made in Part I as an off-site technical education facility reopened on-site as soon as the Yokosuka Shipyard came under the jurisdiction of the IJN (1872), and 'on the job' training was continued to provide skilled workers. The former school (under different names) educated engineers from 1866 to 1878, then from 1889 engineering and naval shipbuilding technicians (during the years 1879–1888 the school was closed). 'On the job' training was executed in the foreman school from 1872 onwards as a 'lower' education facility. There was considerable fluctuation in the intake cohort, and trained workmen were disseminated to other, mostly civilian shipyards; this had the salutary result of raising the general skill level in the shipbuilding industry.

The *History of Japan's Modern Shipbuilding: Meiji Era* has the following evaluation:

> It should be pointed out that the high standard of technical education has contributed much to the remarkable development of the Japanese shipbuilding industry, irrespective of the poor natural resources that compelled Japan to import nearly all its raw and construction materials.

Education was the key to successful industrialisation, and was indispensable for closing the gap between Japan and the countries which had experienced the Industrial Revolution. The dispatch of workers and engineers abroad (to France, Britain, Germany, and the USA) to learn new or particular manufacturing processes was continued, but on a relatively small scale because of the high cost involved. Other means of obtaining information were foreign publications and the exchange of experience between the military and civilian shipbuilding industries. The years 1896–1903 are widely acknowledged as the peak in this respect, as the expertise gained in these years laid the ground for the domestic building of armoured ships and improvements in all fields of shipbuilding.

The workload of the dockyard increased substantially during the Russo-Japanese War, but everything went well and Yokosuka carried out support of the fighting troops in the hinterland.[17]

Independent Construction of Capital Ships

The preparation of the ships for the RJW, the repair of the battle-damaged ships and the adaptation of the Russian war prizes to the IJN's requirements occupied a

Kawachi docked in Dock No 4 of Yokosuka Navy Yard. She had recently been completed at the fitting-out pier, and the photo shows her on 13 January 1912, seven days before she began trials, having just been repainted in her grey livery. The dock, completed in September 1905, was subsequently enlarged several times. Dock No 5 can be seen under construction on the left of the photo; it would be completed ten years later in preparation for the building of the capital ships of the Eight-Eight Fleet. Note also the excavation work proceeding on the hills in the background to provide space for the erection of factories and the enlargement of the docks. (Lars Ahlberg collection)

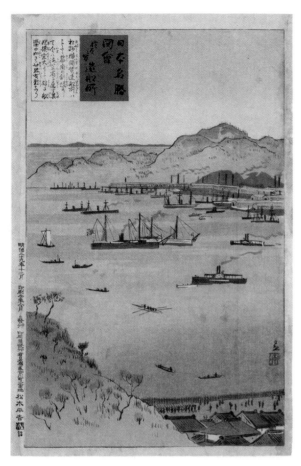

The Yokosuka Shipyard in 1896: a woodblock print from the series *Views of the Famous Sights of Japan* by Kobayashi Kiyochika. (Courtesy of the Lavenberg Collection of Japnese Prints)

growing proportion of capacity. In addition the size of the ships being built grew rapidly, and in May and August 1905 respectively the keels of the battleship *Satsuma* and armoured cruiser *Kurama* were laid, marking a new epoch in Japanese warship construction.[18] *Satsuma* was for a time the world largest warship, and the armoured cruiser *Kurama* was the predecessor of the later 'battle cruiser', combining the speed of a cruiser with the firepower of a battleship. Remarkably, the entire propulsion machinery of *Satsuma* was manufactured by the Engine Production Division, including all castings, all important forgings, the main engines and the Miyabara large watertube boilers, as well as most of the auxiliary machinery. *Satsuma* was launched 18 months and *Kurama* 13 months after the keels were laid, and these comparatively short building times attracted the attention of the advanced shipbuilding nations.

In 1905 the IJN's first five submarines, built by the American Fore River Yard and shipped to Japan in a broken-down condition, were assembled. In January 1906 No 4 graving dock, which had a length of 175 metres (later expanded to 226m) and a width of 26m was opened. It could accommodate all ships, including battleships requiring repair or reconstruction after the RJW, and those now in the design stage. The building of heavy oil tanks was also begun in 1906 at Azuma, and they were later supplemented by tanks captured during the occupation of the German stronghold Tsingtao in 1914.

The appearance of the Royal Navy's *Dreadnought*, the studies by naval architects for future battleships published in annuals such as *Jane's Fighting Ships*, and the naval arms race between Britain and Germany provided a clear indication of the trend towards increases in the size and number of capital ships, and in order to

Yokosuka Navy Yard in November 1896, looking onto the graving docks. The ship on the far right with the black-painted hull is probably the battleship *Fuso* (i). The other ship with a black-painted hull in the centre of the picture may be the protected cruiser *Takasago*. On the left is the cruiser *Akitsushima*, with two of the early torpedo boats in the foreground. Beyond the shed on the left can be seen the tripod mast of a ship of the *Matsushima* class. (*Sekai no Kansen*)

Another view of Yokosuka Navy Yard. in November 1896, showing the covered slipways with the shipyard workshops and the rope-making factory on the right. (*Sekai no Kansen*)

prepare for this situation the support infrastructure on shore needed to be expanded. This was done by either land acquisition or reclamation work, the latter being the main source for the expansion of the area of Yokosuka Navy Yard to around 335 acres in 1907. The latter work included preparations for the construction of a dry dock almost twice as large as No 4, capable of accommodating warships of the largest dimensions now afloat and also the ships which to be built under the IJN's ambitious 'Eight-Eight Fleet' programme.[19] The construction of this dock, with dimensions 312m x 34.8m, began in 1911.

Towards the end of the Meiji era, Japan's first naval aviation base was built on the beach of Oppama in Nagaura Bay.

The Yokosuka Navy Yard at the End of the Meiji Era

By 1912 four graving docks had been completed and the fifth was under construction; there were also five building slips. The drawing office comprised two buildings (main room and a store) and the shipbuilding facilities comprised the main factory, the first and second machinery shops, a bending slap, a forge and two yards

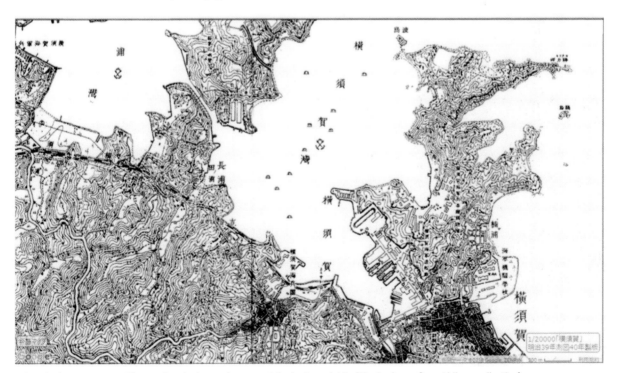

Yokosuka in 1906–1907. The graving docks can be seen at the bottom right of the harbour. (Lars Ahlberg collection)

where material was stored. The equipment shops included a mould loft and a machine shop, two iron working shops, a zinc plating shop, a nickel and silver plating shop, woodwork and pipework shops, a sawing and planing shop, an erecting shop and a hydraulics testing room. Among the ten buildings that constituted the ship repair facilities were a machine shop, a boat building shop, two woodwork mills, a caulker's shop and a forge. The riggers' workshop had one anchor shop and two anchor cable tester sheds in addition to the main factory. In addition to these main buildings there were numerous small attached or independent structures necessary for the maintenance of trouble-free operation.

The number of machines (dynamos and motors, pumps and hydraulic machinery, cranes, workshop machines, smithy furnaces and blowers) totalled 476, of which the majority (193) were in the equipment shops and 185 in the hull construction yard. The workforce was around 3,500 men, the majority of them ordinary workers while about 200 (including 130 apprentices) performed special duties.

Up to that date seventeen major warships, eighteen destroyers and eleven torpedo boats had been completed; others were under construction. The number of steamers, boats and miscellaneous vessels amounted to 530, making a grand total of 576.

At that time the former fishing and farming villages were accessible only by water, and a population of 3,422 in 1879 had grown to a town of more than 70,000 people covering the greater part of the Miura peninsula, with a complex modern infrastructure that included a branch railway line, streets, bridges, water supply and some electric lighting. This dramatic increase in population was due to the development of the shipyard, the selection of Yokosuka as the site of a naval station, the two major wars and the subsequent expansion of the Navy Yard, and the multiplication of officials, workmen, merchants and manufacturers.

The shipbuilding works belonging to the state were instrumental in the promotion of the civilian shipbuilding industry, with consequent impacts upon general industry, manufacturing, commerce, communication, and even social life. The Meiji Government continued to endorse the principle of 'independence in military equipment' formerly adopted by the Bakufu government, and industrial policy therefore encouraged the development of domestic production. However, before this goal could be attained model factories had to be built, entrepreneurs found and subsidies allocated, and the technical skills of the population had to be improved. The development of the Yokosuka Iron Mill into the Yokosuka Navy Yard is a prime example of these policies in action.

Endnotes:

1 Hazel J Jones, *Live Machines: Hired Foreigners and Meiji Japan*, 30.
2 On 4 April 1872 the former *Hyobushō* was abolished and the office divided into in two separate ministries, the other being the Army Ministry.
3 After retirement Verny worked as an adviser for a short time but left Japan on 13 March 1876 on board a French ship.

Before leaving, having fulfilled the terms of the contract under which he had agreed to build the Yokosuka–Yokohama complex, Verny supervised the construction of a simple water supply system to the shipyard from a spring 7km away. The system was greatly expanded to supply warships and the iron foundry in 1889, when a telephone system was installed within the yard. Verny's work is honoured by a monument at the centre of the park in Yokosuka, facing the sea, which has statues of Verny and Oguri side by side.

4 In October 1868 the plane machine factory (77 workmen, 19 machines, steam power 50hp) had been completed.
5 'Note sur l'Arsenal Maritime de Yokosuka'.
6 The work was begun in March 1867.
7 There was then a ten-year gap before the opening ceremony for No 2 dock in June 1884.
8 This figure makes it clear that the main purpose of the shipyard was initially repair, not construction, and the number of foreign ships exceeded that of domestic vessels mainly for financial reasons. By adopting this policy Verny not only reduced governmental costs, but also secured funding for the improvement of the infrastructure of the shipyard.
9 The hiring of a teacher of English had already been approved by the head of the yard on 18 June.
10 It appears that Elgar was involved in the design of new ships. The Imperial yacht *Jingei* had suffered extensive damage to her engine during the trial off Boshu on 21 February 1880, and much of Elgar's time was occupied with the inspection of this ship.
11 Yokosuka had planned to integrate the iron-made *No 1* torpedo boat in 1880 and to begin the integration of *Nos 2–4* at the same time, but this schedule was later changed for financial reasons. The material for the four boats arrived on 9 June 1880. The Japanese personnel had been selected in spring of that year.
12 The contract had been signed by Ambassador Mori in London and the men were hired to work in Yokosuka Navy Yard from 19 September 1883; they were accommodated in House No 11.
13 At that time the assembly of iron *TB-1* had been completed and that of *TB-2* to *TB-4* was underway. Broadmeyer and Banten were still in Yokosuka. There is no evidence that their work played an active part in the proposal, but they must have exerted some influence because they taught selected Japanese personnel iron shipbuilding.
14 There was parallel progress in gunnery, particularly the appearance of the quick-firing medium calibre gun in the latter half of this decade. From the mid-1880s specially-designed ammunition storage magazines were built at Taura and Azuma in 1889, and in 1890 an ordnance factory was completed.
15 It is generally stated that this supplementary role in support of the civilian shipbuilding industry continued up to the beginning of the First World War.
16 Previously, it had been under the jurisdiction of Yokosuka Naval Station as *Chinjufu Zōsenbu*, but this was revised to *Kaigun Zōsenbu* (own jurisdiction), and at the same time the ordnance facilities at Funakoshi were expanded, being upgraded to 'Arsenal' (*Heikishō*) in 1900.
17 Kōichi Takasu, 'Yokosuka Naval Base and Imperial Japanese Navy' in *Sekai no Kansen*, March 1993, 91.
18 The construction of armoured cruisers had already begun at Kure Navy Yard, which had now superseded Yokosuka in terms of size and workforce.
19 A huge naval expansion programme approved by the Emperor on 4 April 1907 – see the author's article in *Warship 2020*.

PREPARING FOR THE NEXT PACIFIC WAR:

THE US NAVY AND DISTRIBUTED MARITIME OPERATIONS

Conrad Waters examines how the US Navy is adapting to address the challenges posed by Chinese naval expansion.

The last decade has seen a major change in the global balance of naval power. The US Navy's worldwide supremacy – essentially unchallenged since the collapse of the Soviet Union – is increasingly being threatened by the rapid expansion of the Chinese People's Liberation Army Navy (PLAN), now numerically the largest navy in the world. While the US Navy retains a considerable technological edge, a new strategy is being evolved to counter China's naval modernisation. Known as Distributed Maritime Operations (DMO), the new concept envisages significant shifts in operational doctrine and fleet structure to ensure that the US Navy prevails in any new Pacific war.

Background

The United States emerged from the Second World War with an effective monopolistic hold over global maritime power. While this position was tested by the rise of the Soviet Navy, a new Forward Maritime Strategy imple-

The US Navy's carrier strike groups were able to project power from sea to land without serious opposition in the immediate post-Cold War era. This favourable situation has changed with the rise of China's maritime A2/AD capabilities. The photo shows the *Nimitz*-class carrier *Carl Vinson* (CVN-70) operating with the Australian frigate *Ballarat* in October 2021 during the course of a deployment to the Western Pacific and Indian Ocean. (US Navy)

mented under the Reagan presidency during the early 1980s ultimately saw off the threat. This new approach was largely based on an offensive posture that targeted the so-called 'bastions' – sea areas close to the Soviet land mass that housed the Soviet Union's all-important strategic missile submarines. This forced the Soviet Navy to focus on the defence of these critical seas, thereby reducing the threat to NATO's maritime communications. The Forward Maritime Strategy was supported by plans to rebuild fleet strength to achieve a 600-ship navy.[1] The subsequent break-up of the Soviet Union in 1991 allowed the US Navy return to the monopolistic position it had enjoyed immediately after the Second World War.

The aftermath of the Cold War saw the US Navy re-orientate itself towards the more uncertain strategic backdrop heralded by the collapse of the previous bipolar world order. While a reduction in fleet size was an inevitable part of the post-Cold War 'peace dividend', the Navy had a prominent part to play in the international stabilisation missions that characterised the new world environment. There was a dramatic shift from oceanic 'blue water' sea control towards projecting power from sea to land in coastal littoral regions, a shift that had been heralded by the Navy's important supporting role during the 1990–91 Gulf War. This new emphasis was reflected in the priority given to retaining naval assets such as aircraft carriers and their supporting shipping that were appropriate for these missions. Conversely, units such as anti-submarine frigates and strategic submarines that had been particularly relevant to the stand-off with the Soviet Union suffered disproportionate

reductions. The revised operating environment was also reflected in programmes for new naval construction. The land-attack focused *Zumwalt* (DDG-1000) class destroyers and *Freedom* (LCS-1) and *Independence* (LCS-2) classes of 'littoral combat ships' trace their origins to the importance assigned to littoral operations during this period.

The US Navy's period of re-orientation to meet the requirements of the post-Cold War environment coincided with an equally significant time of change for China's PLAN. The PLAN entered this period as a technologically backward fleet largely restricted to coastal operations. However, the country's rapid economic development – reflective of the wider shift in commercial power and influence to the Asia-Pacific region – facilitated a programme of investment that has progressively transformed China's fleet into a much more modern and capable force. The initial emphasis of this modernisation was the development of effective anti-access/area (A2/AD) capabilities in China's near seas. The priority assigned to this capacity may have reflected events during the 1995–1996 Taiwan Strait Crisis. This highlighted the PLAN's limited ability to deter a hostile presence in these waters when the US Navy deployed substantial forces in China's 'backyard' in response to Chinese sabre-rattling over the disputed island. Over time, the PLAN's A2/AD proficiency has expanded to the extent that it is regarded as being capable of holding American forces at risk over large areas of the Western Pacific.[2] The PLAN has also started to develop its own power projection capabilities in support of China's global trading interests. These are best represented by the Type 001 through to Type 003

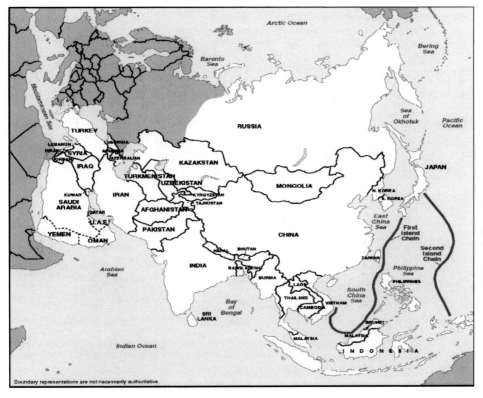

China has steadily increased its maritime A2/AD capacity to the extent that it is able to exert significant control over the waters contained within the First Island Chain and increasingly influence events as far as the Second Island Chain, depicted here in this US Department of Defense map. (US Department of Defense)

China's naval shipbuilding industry has out-built its American rival to the extent that it is now numerically the largest navy in the world. The Type 054A general-purpose frigates *Yangzhou* and *Huanggang*, seen here in 2017, form part of a class that is eventually expected to total at least 50 ships. (Crown Copyright 2017)

series of aircraft carriers and its Type 071 and Type 075 amphibious ships.

An important element of China's A2/AD strategy has been the acquisition of large numbers of anti-shipping missiles. The majority of these are land-based. At first,

many were sourced from Russian industry. However, they are now exclusively of local manufacture, sometimes as improved iterations of the original overseas designs. Examples include the YJ-18 'Eagle Strike' series of supersonic cruise missiles that are reportedly similar

Table 1: China's Expansion of the PLAN: 2000–2030: 'Battleforce Ships'[1]

Year	2000	2005	2010	2015	2020	2025	2030
Strategic Submarine (SSBN)	1	1	3	4	4	6	8
Attack Submarine (SSN)	5	4	5	6	7	10	13
Patrol Submarine (SSK/SS)	56	56	48	53	55	55	55
Major Surface Combatants (CV/DDG)	19	25	25	26	43	55	65
Other Surface Combatants (FFG/FF)	38	43	50	74	102	120	135
Other[2]	91	91	89	92	149	154	149
PLAN Total	210	220	220	255	360	400	425
US Navy Comparable[3]	318	282	288	271	297	n/a[3]	n/a[3]

Notes:

[1] Data is based on Congressional Research Service report RL33153: 'China Naval Modernization: Implications for U.S. Navy Capabilities – Background and Issues for Congress', which itself draws on unclassified ONI data provided in a report to the US Senate Armed Services Committee in February 2020. The 'Battleforce' designation is based on US Navy counting rules and excludes many non-blue water combatants, notably the PLAN's large number of missile-armed fast attack craft. No account is taken of the qualities of individual combatants.

[2] The 'Other' line has been derived by subtracting ONI data on specific ship types from their total figure for the year in question.

[3] This data is based on historical US Navy fiscal year end numbers. US fleet numbers were targeted to increase to an ultimate goal of 355 vessels under the 2016 Force Structure Assessment (FSA), but reports suggest this target has been increased to 373 units by 2045 in an updated and classified Battle Force Ship Assessment and Requirement (BFSAR) submitted to Congress in mid-2022.

to the Russian 3M-54 Kalibr as well as the indigenous DF-21D and DF-26 anti-ship ballistic missiles (ASBMs). The long-range ASBMs would likely be used in conjunction with hypersonic glide vehicles and broad-area maritime surveillance systems. They could potentially target US Navy carrier strike groups operating far from the Chinese mainland.[3]

The PLAN has also invested in a significant flotilla of modern, air independent propulsion (AIP) equipped submarines and an increasingly potent surface fleet. Modernisation of the latter has encompassed three strands: the Type 056/56A series of littoral corvettes; the Type 054A general-purpose frigates; and the Type 052C/D destroyers. All these warships have been built in considerable numbers. By 2020, the PLAN had overtaken the US Navy's previous numerical superiority in major surface combatants. Publicly-released US Navy intelligence assessments also suggest that PLAN design and material quality is often comparable with American warships, with areas of deficiency being progressively overcome. A case in point is the new PLAN Type 055 'Renhai' class destroyer. These state-of-the-art, 12,000-tonne cruiser-sized vessels are larger and more heavily-armed than the latest variants of the US Navy's *Arleigh Burke* (DDG-51) class, a design that traces its origins as far back as the late Cold War era.

The Origins of Distributed Maritime Operations

The US Military has not been blind to the changing balance of power in the Asia Pacific region. As early as 2006, the Quadrennial Defence Review saw a greater proportion of the US Navy's total strength devoted to Indo-Pacific operations in order to counter the rise of the PLAN. This was followed by the Obama presidency's announcement of the 'Pivot to the Pacific' in 2011 and by the official rollout of the Air-Sea Battle concept the previous year. The latter was an attempt to bolster the effectiveness of the American capacity to counter the A2/AD strategies being adopted by potential adversaries, of which China was the most prominent, by more effectively integrating naval and air force assets.[4] Other significant developments included attempts to arrest and ultimately reverse the steady post-Cold War decline in US Navy warship numbers as well as initiatives to enhance collaboration with regional allies such as Australia and Japan.

Despite these efforts, it has become increasingly apparent that the US Navy's advantage over the PLAN has been progressively eroded. The early stages of China's maritime rise coincided with the long war on terrorism heralded by the 9/11 attacks, inevitably reducing the focus on the potential threat posed by the emergence of a new 'near peer' competitor. Subsequently, American efforts to stabilise the government's financial deficit under the framework of the Budget Control Act of 2011 resulted in a tightening of defence funding. Against this backdrop, the US Navy struggled to implement an

Attempts to increase the 'distributed lethality' of the US Navy's surface fleet – including equipping more vessels with surface-to-surface missiles – constituted one of the early stepping-stones towards the DMO construct. This picture shows the littoral combat ship *Gabrielle Giffords* (LCS-10) launching a Naval Strike Missile in 2019. (US Navy)

effective strategy to grow its fleet to counterbalance PLAN expansion. It was also evident that the fleet that had been restructured to support littoral power projection ashore in lower threat environments was less than optimally equipped to meet the threat posed by an increasingly proficient rival naval power. For example, the disposal of the US Navy's longer-range strike aircraft meant that its carrier air wings had to operate closer to their objectives to perform their missions. This made them more vulnerable to China's ASBMs and other A2/AD weapons systems. It was clear that a new naval strategy was required.

It is not entirely clear from published documents precisely when the US Navy decided to adopt Distributed Maritime Operations (DMO) as its overarching operational concept. Certainly, a number of distributed approaches to achieving control over the maritime battlespace were being actively explored as early as 2015. A key step in the process was the publication of 'Surface Force Strategy: Return to Sea Control' by the then-Commander, Naval Surface Force early in 2017.[5] This new strategy emphasised the concept of 'distributed lethality' as a means of allowing sea control to be achieved at a time and place of the US Navy's choosing. Distributed lethality was, in turn, to be implemented by '... increasing the offensive and defensive capability of individual warships, employing them in dispersed formations across a wide expanse of geography, and generating distributed fires'. Subsequently, in December 2018, the need to make progress with maturing the DMO concept was officially referenced in the then-US Chief of Naval Operations' strategic guidance paper 'A Design for Maintaining Maritime Superiority 2.0'. A shift to a more distributed fleet architecture has now become firmly embedded in current US Navy strategic planning.

The overall objective of the DMO concept appears to be to use the US Navy's technological leadership, particularly in the area of command and control, to defeat China's expanding A2/AD capacity in a 'high-end' war at sea. Essentially an operational concept, it is based on integrating the combined potential of geographically dispersed warships, aircraft and other assets to provide a synchronised warfighting effect capable of overwhelming a less coordinated enemy force. Key advantages of the revised strategy compared with the current carrier strike group-centric approach include:

– complicating China's targeting requirements by dramatically expanding the range of US Navy forces it needs to detect and monitor
– reducing the loss of overall capability resulting from the successful identification and engagement of specific US Navy units
– improving the fleet's manoeuvrability and flexibility to take advantage of enemy weaknesses
– maximising US advantages in areas such as communications, underwater assets and unmanned units.

The shift to a DMO construct involves a process of change that arguably surpasses the adjustments to the US Navy that followed the end of the Cold War. DMO requires both a radical rethink with respect to fleet struc-

ture – including a much greater focus on unmanned vehicles – and an acceleration of American leadership in fields such as command and control to achieve the required results. It also depends on effective coordination of efforts with other branches of the US Military – including its US Marine Corps sister service – for maximum effect. These areas are explored in more detail below.

Fleet Structure

The most significant implication of the adoption of DMO is the desirability of shifting the US fleet's current structure in line with a more distributed operational concept. In simple terms, this implies moving from a navy focused on large combatants to a force mix with a greater proportion of smaller warships contained in a more numerous overall total. Although the US Navy's large and expensive aircraft carriers might be considered vulnerable to pruning under this approach, there seems to be little appetite to reduce numbers from the currently mandated eleven-strong force or, indeed, a twelve-ship target.[6] Instead, it seems that the intention is to shrink numbers of large surface combatants – cruisers and destroyers – to assist funding a numerically stronger force of small surface warships. The Navy's most recently published Force Structure Assessment – released in 2016 before the advent of DMO – called for a 2:1 ratio of 104 large surface warships and 52 smaller vessels. There have been some suggestions that this ratio might be reversed in the future fleet. However, latest planning suggests a much more modest shift to a *circa* 3:2 large to small combatant mix, possibly because of technological factors explained below. Instead, this traditional fleet will increasingly be supplemented by large numbers of unmanned and/or optionally crewed platforms. These will rebalance the

Table 2: **US Navy Fleet Structure**

Planned Fleet Structure:	FSA 2016[1]	BFSAR 2022[2]	Current[3]
'Battle Force' Ships	(Pre-DMO)	(Post-DMO)	(Mid-2022)
Strategic Submarines (SSNBs)	12	12	14
Attack Submarines (SSGNs/SSNs)	66	66	54
Aircraft Carriers (CVNs)	12	12	11
Large Surface Combatants (CGs/DDGs)	104	96	93
Small Surface Combatants (FFGs/FFs/MCMVs)	52	56	33
Large Amphibious Vessels (LHAs/LHDs/LPDs/LSDs)	38	31	32
Small Amphibious Vessels (LAWs)	Nil	18	Nil
Auxiliary Vessels	71	82	63
Sub Total	355	373	300
Large Unmanned Surface & Sub-Surface Vessels	Not Stated	c 150	Nil
Total	Not stated	c 523	300

Notes:
[1] Numbers based on the Force Structure Assessment released in 2016.
[2] Numbers based on the classified Battle Force Ship Assessment and Requirement submitted to Congress in mid-2022 and summarised in the 'Chief of Naval Operations Navigation Plan 2022'. The US Navy would hope to achieve this force design by 2045.
[3] Based on information contained in the Naval Vessels Register as of August 2022.

Deployment of large numbers of large unmanned vessels under an approach referred to as 'Manned-Unmanned Teaming' forms a major part of the US Navy's efforts to expand the fleet to the size needed for the effective implementation of DMO. The trials vessels *Ranger* and *Sea Hunter* – seen here in the course of deployment to the RIMPAC 2022 exercise – provide an indication of the large unmanned surface vessels (LUSVs) and medium unmanned surface vessels (MUSVs) initially planned. (US Navy)

Ongoing experimentation with unmanned vehicles suggest that much of the enhanced intelligence capability required by DMO can be provided by small, expendable drones such as the Saildrone Explorer, which can be deployed from virtually any manned surface vessel. (US Navy)

fleet away from costly, manpower-intensive platforms to less-expensive but still lethal vessels.

Investment in unmanned warships is intended to dramatically increase the fleet's capacity for 'distribution', particularly by increasing its overall missile-carrying capacity and expanding its intelligence, surveillance and reconnaissance (ISR) capabilities. In essence, these unmanned units are to act as 'force multipliers' for their manned counterparts under an approach known as Manned-Unmanned Teaming. It was initially envisaged that the surface component of this new fleet would comprise flotillas of independently deployable unmanned surface vessels (USVs). These would be divided into two main types:

– **Large Unmanned Surface Vehicles (LUSVs):** The LUSV is anticipated to displace between 1,000 and 2,000 tonnes and have a length of between 200ft and 300ft. Prioritising endurance over speed, it will be equipped to embark a range of modular, containerised systems. Prominent among these will be vertical launch systems for anti-ship and land-attack missiles, thereby counter-balancing China's current numerical superiority in these weapons.

The planned 'Orca' extra-large unmanned undersea vehicle (XLUUV) – based on Boeing's Echo Voyager design – will supplement the US Navy's large fleet of nuclear-powered attack submarines in expanding the United States' dominance of the underwater domain. (Boeing)

– **Medium Unmanned Surface Vehicles (MUSVs):** Smaller than the LUSV, the MUSV concept is intended to displace around 500 tonnes and be anything from 45ft to 190ft in length. It is similarly optimised for endurance and focused on reconfigurable, modular payloads. However, the MUSV's primary mission will be to enhance the ISR capacity of the distributed fleet.

The US Military has been undertaking testing and trials of the forerunners of these planned vessels for a number of years. Most recently, prototype units of the newly established Unmanned Surface Vessel Division One undertook a high profile deployment to Hawaii as one element in the RIMPAC 2022 exercises. It seems that increasing practical experience with USVs is resulting in an evolution of previous plans, particularly with respect to the MUSV concept. Notably, good results have been achieved by performing ISR missions achieved from smaller, even more cost-effective unmanned vehicles that can be deployed from pretty much any manned vessel. This suggests that the need for the MUSV may no longer be as important as first anticipated.

The underwater arena is one area where the US Navy retains a significant advantage over its PLAN rival. This is largely based on its large fleet of stealthy and sophisticated nuclear-powered attack submarines. The United States anticipates leveraging this leadership under the DMO concept by maintaining previous plans to grow submarine numbers and increase their overall missile-carrying capacity. The latter will be achieved by installation of the Virginia Payload Module – a hull plug fitted with additional missile launchers – in the latest iterations of the *Virginia* (SSN-774) class. This will expand total

missile numbers by 28 per unit, an uplift of approximately 75 per cent. However, extra-large unmanned undersea vehicles (XLUUVs) are also intended to form part of the submersible mix.[7] These will supplement the manned submarines, particularly in higher risk environments. One widely anticipated use is to deploy the new Hammerhead mine, which is tethered to the seabed and armed with a torpedo in similar fashion to the Cold War-era CAPTOR. Five prototype 'Orca' XLUUVs based on Boeing's Echo Voyager UUV design are currently being acquired. Around 50 tonnes in weight and 51ft long, they are capable of being fitted with an additional modular internal payload section of up to 34ft in length that has 2,000 cubic feet of volume. The 'Orca' will also be able to deploy additional externally-carried equipment.

One additional consequence of the shift to DMO will be the need to expand the size and capabilities of the fleet's support train to sustain the greater requirements of a distributed force for logistical support, particularly in terms of fuel. The relatively low profile area of naval logistics has arguably been an area that has suffered from a lack of post-Cold War era investment in many fleets, and the US Navy has been no exception to this tendency. While serial construction of the new *John Lewis* (T-AO-205) class fleet oilers will go some way towards meeting the requirement, a next-generation logistics ship programme is also envisaged to boost overall support capacity. These planned vessels are likely to follow the trend for smaller, cheaper vessels inherent in projected procurement of surface vessels. They will probably be built to a series of different designs optimised to support the various warships that will comprise the distributed fleet. Unit cost is currently estimated

The lead *John Lewis* (T-AO-205) class fleet oiler departs San Diego in the course of sea trials in February 2022. The distributed fleet envisaged by DMO will require a much greater logistical support capacity, resulting in plans for a new class of smaller and cheaper next-generation logistics ships. (General Dynamics NASSCO)

Efforts to expand the US Navy's distributed strike capabilities include development of a new generation of hypersonic missiles. The *Zumwalt*-class destroyer *Michael Monsoor* (DDG-1001) will be one of the first American warships to be equipped with these weapons, losing her twin Advanced Gun Systems in the process. (US Navy)

at US$150m, only around a fifth of that of the T-AO-205 oilers.

Technology

It will be readily apparent that the DMO concept is highly dependent on the successful development and effective implementation of a wide range of new technologies. This is particularly the case in terms of the command and control systems that will be required to ensure that the various elements of a distributed naval force can be linked together to form a cohesive whole. The US Navy has historically been a world leader in such systems, initially through the introduction of tactical data links during the 1950s. These allowed sensors deployed on various warships and other units to be linked together to form a consolidated picture of the operational theatre. A further advance was achieved with the introduction of cooperative engagement capability (CEC) from the mid-1990s onwards. This improved the quality of the combined picture to the extent that the sensors and weapons of suitably-equipped units within line of sight of each other could be networked to work as an integrated system. At the current time, only a handful of navies worldwide have matched this achievement. None of these have deployed CEC to anything like the extent seen in the US fleet.[8]

In spite of this undoubted leadership, the demands of DMO will require the US Navy to make further technical advances. As currently configured, CEC is most useful in enhancing the anti-air warfare performance of the units of a naval task force, such as a carrier strike group, operating in relatively close proximity. Combining the sensors of the much more geographically dispersed fleet envisaged by DMO will be a greater challenge, requiring CEC to function at much longer range than hitherto. Some progress has already been made in this direction, notably through the Naval Integrated Fire Control - Counter Air (NIFC-CA) programme. This provides an over-the-horizon engagement capability through integration of CEC capacity into aircraft such as the E-2D Advanced Hawkeye and F-35 Lightning II. More broadly, DMO is likely to necessitate improvements beyond fire control integration to allow overall command functions to be exercised in a timely and accurate fashion over units that are likely to be dispersed over the full extent of an operational theatre. Technological advances in areas such as artificial intelligence (AI) are likely to be helpful in this regard. The US Navy is already working on the top secret Project Overmatch to help develop the required capacity, but little detail has entered the public domain. Nevertheless, it seems that fielding an appropriate command system to allow DMO to achieve maximum effect will only emerge a considerable time into the future.

DMO also requires a significant uplift in the offensive lethality of the individual warships that will now be dispersed throughout the theatre of operations. The post-Cold War era saw this offensive 'punch' heavily skewed towards the carrier strike groups and largely focused on the coastal land attack mission, an emphasis also replicated in the priority given to the Tomahawk Land Attack Missile (TLAM) deployed on board the US Navy's large surface combatants and submarines. The new strategic environment in the Pacific region means that anti-shipping missiles have now gained greater importance in order to ensure sea control. This leaves the US Navy exposed to lack of recent investment in this area. In the immediate term this deficiency is being made good by acquisition of the Norwegian Kongsberg Naval Strike Missile (NSM) for service aboard the fleet's littoral combat ships and future *Constellation* (FG-62) class frigates. NSM is a stealthy, high subsonic missile with a publicly-quoted range of over 100 nautical miles. It is being manufactured locally by Raytheon under the RGM-184 designation. NSM arguably provides a more potent anti-shipping capability compared with the modernised RGM-84 Harpoon series of missiles deployed on board some destroyers and cruisers.

In the longer term, the US Navy will probably need to make further progress to counterbalance the very large numbers of surface-to-surface missiles that form a key part of China's A2/AD posture. One line of development encompasses hypersonic weapons: missiles that can fly at speeds greater than Mach 5 within the earth's atmosphere. US Navy efforts are currently focused on the Conventional Prompt Strike programme. This is developing a boost-glide hypersonic missile that will share a Common Hypersonic Glide Body with the US Army's similar Dark Eagle system.[9] In a Pacific War context, the new weapons would likely be used to undertake rapid strikes against key elements of Chinese A2/AD infrastructure. They are to be deployed on board the *Virginia*-class submarines and converted *Zumwalt*-class destroyers. The

latter ships will lose their 155mm Advanced Gun Systems originally intended to provide naval gunfire support against shore base targets as part of their modification –a further indication of the lower priority now being assigned to littoral warfare.

The Conventional Prompt Strike missiles will make relatively large demands on a vessel's internal volume. This may partly explain the unexpectedly high proportion of large surface combatants maintained in the latest force mix devised to implement DMO. Another influence may be the continued importance of surface warships in performing anti-ballistic missile and area air defence missions. These roles are increasingly reliant on the use of the new generation of SM-3 and SM-6 Standard Missiles and the latest iteration of the Aegis combat management system in conjunction with the modular AN/SPY-6 active phased array radar.[10] More challenging air defence requirements demand use of the largest and most power-hungry variant of SPY-6, emphasising the advantages of a larger hull. In the longer term, the US Navy is also pursuing the widespread use of directed energy weapons. These are also dependent on the greater power generation capacity typically found in a large surface warship.

The importance of large, unmanned vehicles in the US Navy's future force construct has already been referenced. At least initially, these will either be optionally crewed or at least subject to remote operator control, thereby retaining some human interface in the command

The *Arleigh Burke*-class destroyer *Chafee* (DDG-90) launches a Standard series surface-to-air missile during the RIMPAC 2022 exercise. The size and power demands of the new generation of radars used to support air and missile defence may be one of the reasons the US Navy continues to retain considerable numbers of large surface vessels in its latest fleet plans. (Royal Canadian Navy)

Boeing's MQ-25 Stingray, an aerial refuelling drone that is currently undergoing prototype testing, holds out the prospect of extending the range and flexibility of the US Navy's carrier strike groups. (US Navy)

loop. However, the US Military has long recognised the potential advantages of achieving full autonomy through the use of advanced AI. These include the freedom from reliance on potentially vulnerable communications links that this would provide. Various trials have been undertaken by the US Defense Advanced Research Projects Agency (DARPA), the Department of Defense and the US Navy in developing maritime autonomy. These have progressed to the extent that test vessels have safely undertaken voyages of several thousand nautical miles in autonomous mode. Nevertheless, considerable technical and ethical challenges need to be overcome before the full benefits of autonomy are likely to be realised.[11]

Naval aviation, which will retain its importance under the DMO concept, is also likely to be increasingly impacted by the unmanned systems revolution. Unmanned aerial vehicles (UAVs) were already a fundamental part of the US Navy's plans before the decision to shift to a distributed force, particularly in terms of performing ISR missions. These ranged from the 'high end' MQ-4C Triton reconnaissance drone, which is designed to undertake persistent surveillance over broad areas of the ocean, to lower-cost lightweight systems such as the RQ-21 Blackjack that are deployable from a wide range of surface vessels. Small UAVs are likely to be particularly valuable in extending the reconnaissance envelope of a dispersed force. They offer considerably greater range and endurance than, for example, the manned helicopters typically deployed on surface

combatants. Meanwhile, the US Navy's counter-A2/AD capacity will also be considerably enhanced by current efforts to introduce a new generation of unmanned carrier aircraft. The pioneer in this regard is Boeing's MQ-25 Stingray, an aerial refuelling drone that is currently undergoing prototype testing. Its deployment at sea will help extend the range of the US Navy's comparatively short-range strike fighters, increasing the flexibility and resilience of the carrier force. In time, it seems likely that a process of spiral development of such aircraft could see them play an important part in the long-range strike role. The US Navy is also beginning to deploy the AGM-158C LRASM (Long Range Anti-Ship Missile) on both carrier- and shore-based aircraft as a further step towards improving its anti-shipping capabilities.

Expeditionary Advanced Base Operations

An important factor that will determine whether or not DMO will achieve its full potential is the extent to which the concept can be integrated with the plans of other branches of the US Armed Services, as well as with America's network of allies across the Pacific. Perhaps unsurprisingly, an early supporter of DMO has been the US Navy's sister service, the US Marine Corps (USMC). Its shift towards more distributed operating concepts was heralded by a new 'Marine Corps Operating Concept' published in 2016.[12] Among other initiatives, this resulted in the development of the Expeditionary Advanced Base Operations (EABO) operational concept, which was signed off early in 2019.

EABO is primarily based on utilising highly mobile light forces to achieve a forward presence in the relevant theatre of operations. In the context of a Pacific War against China, this would include the deployment of USMC forces within the Chinese A2/AD defensive shield. The approach, therefore, has echoes of the Forward Maritime Strategy of the 1980s. However, in this instance the aim is to disrupt the freedom of movement enjoyed by hostile forces and reduce the overall effectiveness of any anti-access 'umbrella'.

EABO is envisaged as taking many forms. In addition to providing ISR, potential missions for USMC formations could involve the rapid establishment of transient launching sites for precision strikes by the M142 High Mobility Artillery Rocket System (HIMARS) or truck-mounted NSMs. Trials have also been carried out to assess the effectiveness of creating forward refuelling and rearming points for F-35B Lightning II STOVL aircraft similar to the original operating concept for the Harrier jump-jet. A common theme is the utilisation of relatively agile and, if the worst comes to the worst, expendable formations that can be deployed within high risk areas that would be off-limits to more traditionally structured units. The use of light, manoeuvrable forces also lessens the dependency on fixed bases such as ports and runways, and large amphibious ships that would be prime targets for enemy attack.

Just as DMO is significantly impacting the structure of the US Navy, EABO is producing changes to the shape of the USMC and its supporting shipping. One notable consequence is the corps' reduced emphasis on deploying heavy equipment such as tanks. As a result, some of the large amphibious ships built to carry these systems have less relevance than in the past. This is being reflected in accelerated retirement of the *Whidbey Island* (LSD-41) and *Harpers Ferry* (LSD-49) dock landing ships that previously played a key part in transporting a Marine Expeditionary Unit's heavy vehicles, and in some curtailment of plans for replacements. Large amphibious ships will, however, still have a part to play in future USMC operations. In addition to their current role as a key element of the amphibious ready groups, this will include undertaking new missions. A good example is the ability of the large-deck amphibious assault ships to contribute to distributing naval air power through their secondary 'Lightning Carrier' role. Additionally, the needs of the distributed USMC units will be served by a new class of light amphibious warship (LAW). This will be a shallow-draft vessel capable of inshore operation that seems to have much in common with the landing ships of old. Published requirements suggest a displacement of around 4,000 tonnes and an ability to transport at least 75 marines and supporting equipment over distances of up to 3,500 nautical miles.

Although the USMC has clearly bought into the DMO concept, the extent of the Navy's conceptual alignment with other branches of the US Armed Forces is unclear from publicly-available documents. There are certainly increasing efforts to integrate units across the military into early trials of the DMO concept. At the time of writing, the most recent – and ambitious – of these was Exercise 'Noble Fusion', which was conducted in February 2022. Involving the US Air Force's 18th Wing and Japan's Maritime Self Defence Force in addition to the US Navy and USMC, this encompassed a series of high-intensity training missions across a wide extent of the First Island Chain.[13] More broadly, the longer-term ability of the different branches of the US Armed Services to operate in combination should be assisted by progress with the Joint All-Domain Command and Control (JADC2) project. This is an embryonic attempt to connect sensors across all the military services into a combined command and control network. The results of

The US Marine Corps is reconfiguring itself around lightweight and manoeuvrable forces that will, *inter alia*, be able to conduct precision strikes within China's A2/AD cordon. This will include use of the High Mobility Rocket Artillery System (HIMARS), which has already demonstrated its potential in the Russo-Ukrainian war. (US Marine Corps)

the Navy's Project Overmatch will feed into this combined effort.

Implementation and Challenges

The adoption of DMO as the US Navy's overarching operational concept is a clear response to the rise of China, particularly the PLAN, as a near-peer competitor after a period of unchallenged American supremacy in the post-Cold War era. It appears to be based on a realistic assessment of the difficulties posed by China's growing A2/AD cordon to the successful conduct of naval operations in the Western Pacific. It also takes a relatively hard-headed approach to the United States' inability simply to 'buy' itself out of the problem given its shrinking economic leadership, and seeks to leverage areas where America retains a technological advantage. At the same time, DMO remains very much work in progress.

Perhaps most obviously, DMO is predicated on a radical restructuring of the fleet from that configured to meet the different requirements of the post-Cold War era. It was initially suggested that a shift towards a larger number of smaller, less expensive vessels would make this transition affordable. However, latest plans suggest there is a reluctance to trim major elements of the current fleet, particularly the expensive nuclear-powered carrier-focused strike groups.[14] As a result, the planned increase in smaller manned and unmanned combatants will essentially be additional to the current fleet structure, resulting in higher capital and operating costs. It is not at all clear that the US defence budget will be sufficient to pay for this navy. There are also questions as to whether a weakened American industrial base will be able to build and sustain it.

DMO also requires an expansion of US technological leadership, particularly in the areas such as command, control and autonomy, to be made to work effectively. Positively, American industry has a track record of considerable achievements in this area, providing solid foundations from which to make the required leap. However, the technical hurdles in linking the disparate elements of a distributed fleet to function as a cohesive whole are huge, particularly given the likelihood that hostile forces will do their upmost to disrupt the necessary connectivity. There are also unanswered questions as to how the capabilities of the US Air Force and US Army will be integrated into the DMO concept. These questions are also applicable to America's regional network of Allied fleets. It remains to be seen to what extent they will be allowed – and be able to afford – access to the technology that will underpin the DMO approach.

Finally, it remains to be seen whether China will provide the US Navy with the space it needs to bring DMO into full effect. The speed at which the PLAN has

A F-35B Lightning II fighter aircraft with Marine Fighter Attack Squadron 121 refuels at a temporary Forward Arming and Refuelling Point during simulated Expeditionary Advanced Base Operations (EABO) in 2019. The use of light, manoeuvrable forces under EABO facilitates deployment in higher risk areas and also lessens dependency on fixed bases. (US Marine Corps)

The US Navy *Nimitz*-class carrier *Ronald Reagan* (CVN-76) operating with the Japanese destroyer *Onami* (DD-111) in the Philippine Sea in August 2022. Large aircraft carriers remain an important part of the US Navy's fleet structure, but unwillingness to trim numbers to help pay for a larger fleet may make the DMO concept unaffordable. There are also questions as to how America's regional naval partners will be integrated into DMO. (US Navy)

been able to erode previous American technical leadership has been something of a surprise. It would be naïve to assume that it will simply stand by and allow DMO to be implemented without adopting counter strategies of its own. There is also a concern that China will seek to leverage its current strengths by staging an 'incident' before the new concept can rebuild America's past advantage. In this regard, the US Navy's current plans to retire large numbers of 'legacy assets' to help finance DMO creates a window of vulnerability. While the author believes a Chinese provocation is unlikely due to both economic and operational factors, the risk cannot be entirely discounted.

All in all, DMO represents a considered and practical attempt to maintain the maritime supremacy that the US Navy has enjoyed for much of the last century. Its implementation will, however, need to overcome significant challenges if it is to achieve the operational benefits that the US Navy envisages.

Acknowledgement:

The author acknowledges with gratitude the assistance provided by Sidney E Dean in commenting on an early draft of this chapter. All errors remain the author's own.

Sources:

This article has been primarily researched from published US Navy planning documents, as well as from the ever-informative reports produced by the Congressional Research Service. All of these are accessible by means of a straightforward internet search. The most important of these, as well as a number of useful secondary sources, are listed below.

Berger, David H, 'Commandant's Planning Guidance', US Marine Corps (Washington DC, 2016).

Eyer, Kevin, 'Distributed Maritime Operations: Implication and Challenge' in Waters, Conrad (ed) *Seaforth World Naval Review 2021*, Seaforth Publishing (Barnsley, 2020), 180–191.

Haddick, Robert, *Fire on the Water: China, America, and the Future of the Pacific*, Naval Institute Press (Annapolis MD, 2014).

Gilday, Michael M, 'Chief of Naval Operations Navigation Plan 2022', US Navy (Washington DC, 2022).

Lehman, John F & Wills, Steven, *Where are the Carriers? US National Strategy and the Choices Ahead*, Foreign Policy Research Institute (Philadelphia PA, 2021).

Neller, Robert B, 'Marine Corps Operating Concept', US Marine Corps (Washington DC, 2016).

O'Rourke, Ronald, 'China Naval Modernization: Implications for U.S. Navy Capabilities: Background and Issues for Congress' (RL33153), Congressional Research Service (Washington DC, 2022).

O'Rourke, Ronald, 'Navy Force Structure and Shipbuilding Plans: Background and Issues for Congress' (RL32665), Congressional Research Service (Washington DC, 2022).

O'Rourke, Ronald, 'Navy Large Unmanned Surface and Undersea Vehicles: Background and Issues for Congress' (R45757), Congressional Research Service (Washington DC, 2022).

Richardson, John M, 'A Design for Maintaining Maritime Superiority 2.0', US Navy (Washington DC, 2018).

Rowden, Thomas S, 'Surface Force Strategy: Return to Sea Control', US Navy (Washington DC, 2017).

Yoshihara, Toshi & Holmes, James R, *Red Star over the Pacific*, Naval Institute Press (Annapolis MD, 2010).

Endnotes:

1   The 600-ship fleet was never fully achieved, numbers peaking at a maximum 594 ships at the end of FY 1987.

2   China's maritime strategy has often been somewhat simplistically described as being initially focused on achieving effective sea control over the waters enclosed by the First Island Chain, the line of islands that run from the Kuriles through the Japanese archipelago, the Ryukyus, Taiwan and the Philippines and finishes in Borneo. This area includes the East and South China Seas, which are considered key areas of Chinese economic and strategic interest. Over time, the PLAN's capacity has extended to exert meaningful A2/AD potential within the Second Island Chain, which runs from the Kuriles through Japan, the Bonins, the Marianas, Guam and Palau to end in the western part of the Indonesian archipelago (see map).

3   It should be noted that the much-hyped maritime capabilities of China's current generation of ballistic missiles are somewhat speculative, with the weapons reportedly first being tested against a moving ship as recently as the second half of 2020. The likely success of such weapons in overcoming American ballistic missile defences and probable countermeasures against their targeting systems is questionable.

4   The Air-Sea Battle had echoes of the Air-Land Battle concept of the 1980s, which relied on greater coordination of US Army and US Air Force capabilities to defeat any Warsaw Pact invasion of Western Europe. A modified version of the Air-Land Battle was used to good effect during the liberation of Kuwait in the 1990–91 Gulf War. The Air-Sea Battle nomenclature was dropped in 2015 in favour of the less snappily-named Joint Concept for Access and Maneuver in the Global Commons, reflecting the need to integrate US Army forces into the collaborative approach. There is ongoing debate about how effective the US Military has been in developing an effective joint operational concept.

5   Some commentators believe that a decisive shift to DMO was heralded by the first iteration of the strategic guidance 'A Design for Maintaining Maritime Superiority', which was released early in 2016. This emphasised the return to great power competition with China and Russia, as well as the impracticality of simply buying a way out of the challenges this presented. While a new way of thinking was called for, there was, however, no specific mention of the DMO concept.

6   The US Navy is mandated by law – 10 U.S.C. 8062(b) – to maintain a force of no fewer than eleven operational aircraft carriers. This force currently comprises ten *Nimitz* (CVN-68) class vessels and the first unit of the new *Gerald R Ford* (CVN-78) class. There have been various proposals to move away from the current focus on large, nuclear-powered carriers. These include construction of a new series of conventionally-powered, medium-sized vessels and utilisation of the flexibility inherent in the F-35B short take-off vertical landing (STOVL) variant of the Lightning II strike fighter as the basis of a new fleet of 'Lightning Carriers'. The latter concept has been trialled on board the large-deck amphibious assault ships that support US Marine Corps' operations. However, it is currently seen as a supplement rather than a replacement for the aircraft carrier force.

7   The US Navy defines the XLUUV as a UUV with a diameter of more than 84 inches, meaning that it would be too large to be housed in the standard launch tubes of a manned submarine.

8   The US Navy describes CEC as a real-time sensor netting system that enables high-quality situational awareness and integrated fire control by combining geographically dispersed sensors to provide a single integrated air picture among units equipped with the system. CEC's two major system functions consist of a Cooperative Engagement Processor (CEP) for sensor networking and a Data Distribution System (DDS) for real-time communications among co-operating units (CUs). Sensor data from individual units are transmitted to other units in the network via the real time high-quality, anti-jam-capable line of sight DDS. Each CEC-equipped unit uses identical sensor data processing algorithms resident in its CEP, meaning that each unit has the same display of air tracks. CEC gives an individual ship the capability to launch anti-air weapons at hostile aircraft and missiles within its engagement envelope based on remote sensor data provided by the CEC sensor network. More than one hundred US Navy units are currently fitted with CEC.

9   A boost-glide hypersonic missile typically uses a rocket to carry its boost-glide vehicle into the upper atmosphere and accelerate it to the required speed. It then glides down to its target.

10 The AN/SPY-6 family of radars – initially known as the Air and Missile Defence Radar (AMDR) – is starting to supplement the veteran AN/SPY-1 in US Navy service. It is comprised of 'building blocks' of self-contained radar modular assemblies (RMAs) that can be stacked together to match the specific sensor requirements of the host ship. The latest, Flight III iteration of the *Arleigh Burke* class destroyer is equipped with the SPY-6(V)1 variant, incorporating four fixed arrays that each comprise 37 RMAs. By contrast, the SPY-6(V)3 system used, *inter alia*, in the *Constellation*-class frigates utilises three fixed arrays each with nine RMAs.

11 Experiments to date have focused on navigational autonomy, with weapons release still being under the control of human operators.

12 It should be noted that the USMC's shift towards distributed operational concepts predates the adoption of DMO by the wider US Navy. It should also be noted that EABO also interfaces with a number of other new operational concepts, including Stand-In (essentially forward-deployed) Forces and Littoral Operations in a Contested Environment.

13 It is clear that the US Air Force is considering the relevance of distributed operations to a conflict with a rival great power such as China. It commissioned a Rand Corporation consultancy report on the subject in 2019 entitled 'Distributed Operations in a Contested Environment'. This highlighted the vulnerabilities of the current network of large air bases to focused attacks and/or communications interference. However, the dispersal of aircraft across a wider network of bases would trade efficiency for survivability. It would also create political challenges in negotiating access rights to suitable sites.

14 The US Navy's reluctance to reduce its carrier strike groups is understandable given the flexible and hugely potent striking power they provide. This remains relevant under the DMO concept. Large aircraft carriers also have considerable utility in supporting American interests in scenarios falling short of all-out conflict with a near-peer rival. It is ironic that many of the warships now being decommissioned to help pay for DMO comprise the small and relatively cheap littoral combat ships, which might appear to be well-suited to distributed operations. Their withdrawal is seemingly based on a lack of survivability and, particularly, lethality. These assertions are contrary to the optimism once expressed in the modular capabilities of the LCS design.

WARSHIP NOTES

This section comprises a number of short articles and notes, generally highlighting little known aspects of warship history.

'HIDDEN IN PLAIN SIGHT'

Ian Sturton writes about the proposed conversion of the two-decker HMS *Duncan* to a breastwork monitor on the lines of HMS *Devastation*.

The coming of the ironclad saw the Royal Navy's considerable fleet of complete and incomplete screw line-of-battleships valued at many millions of pounds summarily rendered obsolete. A number of proposals were put forward for the conversion of the old type to the new.

Seven incomplete two-deckers were cut down by one deck and completed as broadside ironclads ('ironclad frigates'); three of the seven were additionally lengthened with engine power doubled. The three-decker *Royal Sovereign* was cut down by three decks for the trial installation of four Coles turrets. A distinguished naval

architect, John Henwood, outlined the conversion of two- and three-deckers to fully-rigged low freeboard ironclads with two or three Coles turrets. However, in the Commons the Secretary of the Admiralty had to point out that an 1866 two-turret Henwood proposal worked out in detail would have a freeboard of only a few inches when fully equipped.

In February 1867 Chief Constructor EJ Reed prepared drawings for converting the two-decker *Duncan* to a two-turret breastwork monitor, a much enlarged version of the small turret ship (the eventual *Cerberus*) sought by the Government of Victoria for the defence of Melbourne and Port Phillip. He was unenthusiastic about the task: the converted ship, like all the conversions, would roll badly, and the strains imposed by heavy guns and thick armour on a wooden hull, however braced and rein-

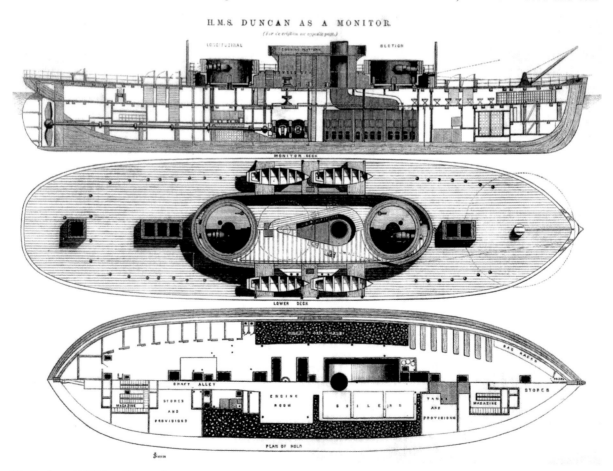

(*The Engineer*, Vol XXIX, 4 Feb 1870)

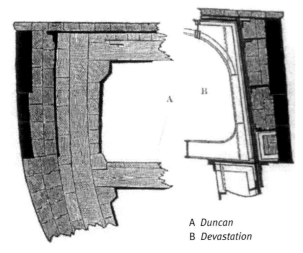

A *Duncan*
B *Devastation*

(*The Engineer*, Vol XXIX, 4 Feb 1870)

Characteristics

	Duncan as illustrated	*Devastation* and *Thunderer*
Length pp	252ft 0in	285ft 0in
Breadth, extreme	63ft 0in	62ft 3in
Draught fwd	25ft 1.5in	25ft 9in
Draught aft	25ft 4.5in	26ft 6in
Tonnage, BM	3,727	4,406
Horsepower (nominal)	800hp	800hp
Speed	12.5 knots	12.5 knots
Armament	4 –12in MLR	4 – 12in MLR
Weight of broadside	2,400lb	2,400lb
Height of monitor deck above water	4ft 0.5in	4ft 6in
Height of command of guns	13ft 0in	13ft 6in
Complement	250	250

As regards armour on the belt amidships, taking ⅛ of an inch of iron to equal 8in of solid wood in resistance:

– in *Duncan*, there were 10.5in armour, 18in teak (equivalent to 2.25in iron), an inner skin 1.5in iron and finally 10in wood (equivalent to 1.25in iron) for a total of 15.5in solid iron
– in *Devastation*, the figures were 12in armour, 18in teak (equivalent to 2.25in iron), and an inner skin of 1.5in iron for a total of 15.75in solid iron

forced, would mean a short, troubled life (seasoned timber was likely to be in short supply). Reed emphasised carefully that his conversion would be only for a national emergency; normally, iron-hulled new construction would be infinitely preferable.

By 1870 the purpose-built turret ships *Devastation* and *Thunderer* were well over the horizon. In reviewing the various conversion proposals, Oscar Parkes (*British Battleships 1860–1950*) remarked that it was with great regret that the search for plans of the *Duncan* to *Devastation* conversion had had to be relinquished without result, as such a metamorphosis would have been well worth recording. However, apparently unknown to Dr Parkes, the elusive plans were described and illustrated in the 4 February 1870 issue of the journal *The Engineer,* which on pages 64–65 published an elevation, two plans, cross-sections and data comparing the proposed conversion with *Devastation* as built; these have been in the public domain for a century and a half, largely ignored.

The writer of the *Engineer* article, seemingly not a Reed fan, selected the broadside ironclad *Ocean* for discussion. If she were converted to a breastwork

monitor, the complete 4.5in belt might be replaced by a belt of three times the thickness and one-third the height without affecting the draught. For a given draught, the smaller the area to be protected meant the thicker the armour. So much was self-evident. The writer failed to take into account the additional horizontal armour that would be essential for a low hull or to consider the effect of the armour changes on the ship's centre of gravity and consequent behaviour at sea. He furthermore claimed that the converted broadside ironclads were steady ships whereas, as Reed had pointed out, they actually rolled badly.

Note: The Brass Foundry outstation of the NMM has conversion proposal drawings for *Duncan* in Box ADRB1557.

PATTERNS OF POLITICAL NOMENCLATURE IN THE RUSSIAN AND SOVIET NAVIES

Kenneth Fraser continues his series on warship names.

Warships have often been given names with political significance, but if the constitution of the state changes these names may also need to change. In the Russian and Soviet states over the last hundred years they have altered to a degree unparalleled elsewhere.

The watchwords of the late 19th century Russian Empire were 'orthodoxy', 'autocracy' and 'nationality', and these principles were reflected in the names given to most of its battleships and cruisers. They might be named after saints of the Orthodox Church, members of the

imperial dynasty and its predecessors, military and naval commanders of the past, or after the victories they had won. The smaller vessels, on the other hand, usually had names not politically inspired: destroyers, for example, were often given adjectival names or those of animals and birds. Nevertheless there were exceptions, such as the destroyer *Emir Bukharski,* so named because that semi-independent potentate had paid for her construction.

By the early 20th century, signs of serious political unrest were appearing. When these took the form of naval mutinies, the authorities, wishing to avoid reminding people of them, sometimes changed the name of the ship involved. Thus after the mutinies of 1905 the famous battleship *Potemkin* (strictly *Kniaz Potemkin Tavricheskii,* or Prince Potemkin of Tauris) became

Panteleimon (a saint's name) while the cruiser *Ochakov* became *Kagul*.

Then came the revolutions of February and October 1917. Russia was declared a republic, and it became necessary to change the names of the ships named after the Romanovs. Thus the battleship *Imperator Pavel* became the *Respublika* and the *Tsessarevich* the *Grazhdanin* ('Citizen'). On the Black Sea the dreadnought *Imperatritsa Ekaterina Velikaia* became the *Svobodnaia Rossiia* ('Free Russia'), while the *Imperator Aleksandr III* became the *Volya* ('Freedom'). The ships that had mutinied regained their original names, as the mutinies were now considered precursors of the Revolution. The *Potemkin* however was soon renamed *Borets za Svobodu* ('Fighter for Freedom').

When the Bolsheviks came to power they required much more radical changes. Not only did they denounce monarchy, but they regarded the saints as relics of superstition, the generals and admirals as minions of tyranny, and their victories as battles in imperialist wars. Practically every significant ship had her name changed – although, curiously, it has not been recorded that this ever applied to the battleship *Andrei Pervosvanni* (Andrew the First-called), which was sunk in 1919.

During the ensuing Civil War a few ships had their names changed when they came under the control of the White Russians. *Volya* was renamed *General Alekseiev* after a recently deceased White commander (see pages 128–141), and *Ochakov* became *General Kornilov* after another. Both ships eventually left Russian waters, never to return.

By the end of the Civil War, many major warships had been lost or were not worth refitting. The principal ships inherited by the Soviet Navy were the Baltic dreadnoughts. Of these *Gangut* was renamed *Oktiabrskaia Revolutsiia* ('October Revolution') and the now-immobile *Poltava* the *Frunze*, for a recently deceased commander of the Red Army. The other two ships commemorated earlier revolutions which the Bolsheviks considered forerunners of their own. Thus *Sevastopol* became the *Parizhkaia Kommuna* ('Paris Commune') and *Petropavlovsk* the *Marat*, for the most radical leader of the French Revolution.

The perceived need to rename ships wholesale in the first decade of Communist power was met in several different ways. Destroyers were usually named after revolutionary heroes (not always Russian); many of these had died in the Civil War or had been assassinated. Marx and Engels were commemorated, as was Spartacus. The German Communist martyr Karl Liebknecht was also honoured (but not his fellow sufferer Rosa Luxemburg, who had disagreed with Lenin). However, in giving ships the names of living Communist leaders, it was not foreseen that some would eventually be denounced as traitors. Replacements had then to be found for the names of Rykov and Zinoviev (executed), Trotsky (exiled and assassinated), and Petrovsky (sidelined, but survived).

When the former imperial yacht *Shtandart* was converted to a minelayer, she was renamed in honour of

André Marty, the seaman who had led a mutiny in the French squadron that had intervened in the Black Sea during the Civil War. In 1952, however, he was to be expelled from the Communist Party, whereupon the ship was again renamed *Oka*.

Communist icons of one kind or another were a useful source of names. These might be emblems, as with the gunboat *Krasnoe Znamia* ('Red Flag') or the transport *Serp i Molot* ('Hammer and Sickle'), places (the depot ship *Smolny*, named after Lenin's HQ in October 1917), or dates, (the minelayer *Pervoe Maia* ('First of May').

Communist organisations might also be honoured in this way. For instance, the cruiser that had been laid down as the *Svietlana* emerged as the *Profintern*, named after the Soviet-sponsored international trade union organisation.

An original style of names was devised for submarines, which previously had taken the names of animals but were now renamed for types of revolutionary worker, such as *Tovarishch* ('Comrade'), *Rabochii* ('Worker'), or *Krasnoflotets* ('Sailor of the Red Fleet').

Geographical names were often prefixed with 'Red', and these names were bestowed on three cruisers laid down before 1917. The *Profintern* was later renamed the *Krasni Krim* ('Red Crimea') while a sister ship became the *Krasni Kavkaz* (for the Caucasus); *Chervona Ukraina* had, uniquely, her name expressed in Ukrainian rather than Russian.

The expansion of the Navy in the late 1920s led to a change in naming policy; it seems to have been accepted that there would not be sufficient political names to meet every need, and there was a return to names that were more traditional or neutral. A series of gunboats were named after storms and winds, a large class of destroyers took adjectival names of the kind used before 1917, and the large flotilla leaders of the *Leningrad* class (see *Warship 2022*) were named after major cities. However, the new cruisers of the *Kirov* class took the names of Communist leaders, three of them deceased but two (Molotov and Voroshilov) still living. The exception was the *Maksim Gorkii*, named in honour of the famous writer.

At about this time a problem arose with the names of submarines. The previous system had been continued and even extended to followers of earlier revolutionary movements, in France *(Yakobinets)*, Italy *(Karbonari)*, and even Britain *(Chartist)*. Now the same principle was applied to followers of Soviet leaders, whether dead *(Sverdlovets)* or alive *(Stalinets)*. But in the 1930s, living Soviet leaders might suddenly fall from favour. It was proposed to name a submarine *Yezhovets* ('Follower of Yezhov', head of the secret police), but not long afterwards he was executed. Who might be next? From 1938 onwards, numbers were used for submarines, but not before three had been named for the Party newspapers *Pravda*, *Izvestiia*, and *Iskra*, a choice of names unparalleled elsewhere.

The cruiser programme continued with the *Chapaev* class; the majority were never completed, but most of them would have been named after Communist person-alities (all dead at the time). The exception was the revo-lutionary hero Zhelezniakov who had actually been an anarchist; Chkalov had been a famous aviator. There was to have been an *Avrora*, named in honour of the ship that had fired the first shot in October 1917.

A number of large capital ships was also under construction, none of which would ever be completed. The first was to have been the *Sovietskii Soiuz* ('Soviet Union') and the other three would have honoured the three largest constituent republics, *Sovietskaia Rossiia*, *Sovietskaia Ukraina*, and *Sovietskaia Belorussia*. It is believed that a fifth was ordered, named *Sovietskaia Gruziia* for Stalin's homeland of Georgia. However, the projected battlecruisers (referred to as 'heavy cruisers') would have had the town names *Kronstadt* and *Sevastopol*; the third might have been named *Stalingrad*. A similar principle was followed when the British battle-ship *Royal Sovereign*, lent to the Soviets in 1944, was named *Arkhangelsk*, and a few years later, when the former Italian battleship *Giulio Cesare* became the *Novorossiisk*.

A further change took place in 1941, when the German invasion of the USSR induced Stalin to recall Russian nationalism and the memories of its military and naval heroes to the aid of the Soviet Union. One sign of this was that the old battleships *Petropavlovsk* and *Sevastopol* reverted to their original names – *Poltava* was by now immobile, and it was unthinkable to rename a ship that honoured the October Revolution. Only after the war was the first ship named after a Tsarist hero, when the former German cruiser *Nürnberg* became the *Admiral Makarov*. At about the same time the former Finnish coast defence ship *Väinämoinen* was renamed *Vyborg*; in this case the geographical name was actually political, as that city had been annexed from Finland.

After the Great Patriotic War, great efforts were made to expand the Navy. Battlecruisers were again laid down, but would never be completed. They would have been named *Stalingrad* and *Moskva*. The third might have been given the name *Arkhangelsk* or *Kronstadt*. However, the names of the cruisers demonstrated a different approach to their pre-war counterparts. Of a total of 21 (including those never completed) only five were named after prominent Communists, whereas nine would have had the names of military and naval heroes of the past, six the names of cities, and one, *Varyag*, was a traditional name (commemorating the Varangian Guard of the Byzantine Emperors). The numerous destroyers continued to have adjectival names, while frigates often had names derived from the natural world.

Even in the 1950s, however, previous 'political' names occasionally created a problem. When Stalin was denounced, several of his surviving acolytes fell from favour, and the names of the corresponding ships had to change. Thus *Kaganovich* became the *Petropavlovsk* (the old battleship having gone) and *Molotov* the *Slava* ('Glory' – an old Tsarist name). A few ships had been named after cities that themselves had been named after politicians, and they too were changing. Thus *Molotovsk* became the *Oktiabrskaia Revolutsiia*, while *Stalingrad* (formerly the Italian cruiser *Emanuele Filiberto Duca d'Aosta*) became the *Kerch*.

In the final stage of Soviet nomenclature, from the 1960s onwards, while the fleet expanded rapidly, the use of overtly political names declined, and it would be rare to name a ship after a political leader – those chosen were now invariably deceased. Ship types were also changing. Destroyers, as before, had adjectival names, but the larger vessels must have been considered cruisers, and often had the names of prominent towns, some of which, like *Sevastopol* or *Ochakov*, repeated pre-revolutionary names. There was also a new *Krasni Kavkaz*, a *Krasni Krim*, and (much later) a *Chervona Ukraina*; the Soviet Navy was now old enough to have its own traditional names. Ships often bore the names of admirals, few of whom were chosen from historical periods, although the names *Admiral Nakhimov* and *Admiral Makarov* were revived. Among the fairly numerous Soviet admirals commemorated, those who had held high rank during the Great Patriotic War had had little opportunity to win remarkable victories, while others had held it only in peacetime.

In a rather haphazard fashion, political names arose now and again, often commemorating anniversaries with somewhat cumbersome results, as with the submarine *Shestidesiatiletia Velikogo Oktiabria* ('Sixty years of Great October') so named in 1977. However, the most numerous in the political category were those connected with the Communist Youth League (the *Komsomol*). In 1933 a submarine had been named *Komsomolets* because the Young Communists had raised the funds to pay for her; and from about 1960 to the end of the Soviet period we find about 70 vessels named at various dates, and apparently for the same reason, in honour of the Komsomol of a particular town (*Yaroslavskii Komsomol*) or even of a whole republic (*Komsomol Kazakhstana*). These were usually submarines, frigates or corvettes, but there is no obvious pattern in their selection. When a ship went out of service, another might be given the same name; and according to A S Pavlov, there were even cases when two vessels had the same name at the same time: he records an 'F' class and a 'W' class submarine both being named *Vladimirski Komsomolets* in 1967.

The Soviet Navy acquired helicopter carriers and aircraft carriers rather late in the day, and gave them the names of major cities. However, when it built the large cruisers of the 1980s, it reverted to the practice of an earlier era by naming them after prominent Communist leaders. Three of the names had been used before, but the final ship was the *Yuri Andropov*, whose namesake had died only a few years previously.

By this time the Communist system was in difficulties, which occasionally affected even the names of ships. The aircraft carrier laid down under the name of *Riga* was renamed *Leonid Brezhnev* shortly after the death of that long-serving leader. But as the reformers gained ground, his memory was no longer regarded with favour and the name was changed to *Tbilisi* in 1987. When Georgia began to show signs of nationalist unrest, that name in turn was deemed unsafe, and the ship emerged as the *Admiral Kuznetsov* – her sister ship, eventually sold to China, was another *Varyag*. At about the same time, and for similar reasons, the carrier *Baku* became the *Admiral Gorshkov*. In other respects the usual Soviet naming systems continued to the end; for example, a cruiser to be named *Oktiabrskaia Revolutsiia* was laid down but never completed.

The sudden break-up of the Soviet Union in 1991 once again made some names inappropriate. Among the first to be changed, in 1992, were those of the big nuclear-powered cruisers, three of them taking the names of pre-revolutionary Admirals while the fourth became the *Petr Velikii* ('Peter the Great'), the first ship since 1917 to be named after a former Tsar. The extent of renaming was in general rather limited. The most obviously Communist names had to go, and the 'Komsomol' names were discarded in favour of more neutral geographical or adjectival ones. Some ships had the names of places in Soviet republics which had seceded: for example the cruiser *Simferopol* became *Severodvinsk*. However, the numerous ships named after Soviet military and naval leaders remained undisturbed.

The fall of Communism allowed the new regime a wider choice of names when it came to new construction. However, on the whole there have been few radical departures. A good many recent ships have geographical names, as have most submarines (now once more named rather than simply numbered). An unusual case is the 'Kilo'-class submarine *Sviatoi Nikolai Chudovorets* (St Nicholas the Miracle-worker), named after the patron saint of seamen; one or two other saints have also been commemorated. The two most recently built classes of frigate have been given the names of admirals, the majority from the Soviet period but a few from earlier, including the (previously uncommemorated) First World War, during which Admiral Grigorovich was the last Imperial Minister of the Navy. Perhaps the most signifi-

cant names are those of the new ballistic missile submarines. It might have been the influence of the US *George Washington* class that caused them to be named after national heroes. Thus far, most of these have been from the mediaeval period (*Yuri Dolgoruki, Aleksandr Nevskii*), but one or two are from more recent times, such as *Generalissimus Suvorov*. Nearly all these people had had ships named after them before 1917, and two are particularly interesting: *Imperator Aleksandr III* commemorates an Emperor who won no great victories and was noted for his unflinching autocracy, while *Kniaz Vladimir* honours the 10th century Prince of Kiev who was canonised for his adoption of Christianity, but for the same reason is equally revered as the patron saint of Ukraine. The conflict of ideas implied in that choice of name may help to explain the crisis of 2022.

Sources:

Anthony J Watts, *The Imperial Russian Navy*, Arms and Armour Press (London 1990).

Jürg Meister, *The Soviet Navy* (2 vols), Macdonald (London, 1972).

A S Pavlov, *Warships of the USSR and Russia 1945–1995*, Chatham (London, 1997).

Eric Wertheim, *The Naval Institute Guide to Combat Fleets of the World*, 16th ed, Naval Institute Press (Annapolis 2013).

Jane's Fighting Ships, 1920, 1931, 1943–44, 1986–87, 1993–94, 2011–12.

V V Jarovoj and René Greger, 'The Soviet cruisers of the *Chapaev* and *Sverdlov* classes', *Warship* 1994, 147–58.

Stephen McLaughlin, 'Project 69: the *Kronstadt* Class Battlecruisers', *Warship* 2004, 79–117.

Stephen McLaughlin, 'Project 82: the *Stalingrad* Class', *Warship* 2006, 102–123.

Stephen McLaughlin, 'Stalin's Super-battleships: the *Sovietskii Soiuz* class', *Warship* 2021, 9–28.

Vladimir Yakubov and Richard Worth, 'The Soviet Project 7/7U destroyers', *Warship* 2008, 98–114.

http://www.rusnavy.com.mes/kalanst8.htm

http://www.navypedia.org/ships/russia

HMS *PIONEER*, 1945

Kenneth Fraser has sent in an interesting and recently re-discovered photograph of the former light fleet carrier, which originally came into his possession some 60 years ago.

HMS *Pioneer* was laid down in December 1942 at Vickers Armstrong's Barrow shipyard as the light fleet carrier *Mars* of the *Colossus* class, and was launched under that name in May 1944. In July that year she was renamed *Pioneer*, and was completed as an aircraft maintenance ship in February 1945; her role was to carry out minor and medium-scale repairs to aircraft and their engines. This photograph shows her at Manus Island, forward base of the British Pacific Fleet, where she was employed in repairing aircraft between July and

September that year. After deployment to Hong Kong following the Japanese surrender, she returned to the UK via a repatriation passage to Sydney and was placed in reserve early in 1946. She was sold for scrap in September 1954, having never been recommissioned.

The photograph appears to have been taken either early in the morning or in the evening, evidenced by the long shadows. The aircraft visible on deck are Grumman Avengers and Chance Vought Corsairs, which would have been embarked by crane. They were transferred from and to carriers or ashore by lighters lowered into the water by crane and stored on deck when not in use. The structure right aft on the upper deck (former flight deck) is an aircraft engine test bay and is surrounded by spare engines stacked up in their crates. Further testing of aircraft and their equipment could also take place on the former flight deck, though

for full flight-testing the machines had to be taken ashore by lighter.

The photograph itself has two stamps on the back; 'P. & F.' and 'For Herbert Cowan' but it is not clear if either of these refer to the photographer, a crew member, or someone else entirely.

Thanks to David Hobbs and Sandra Lowe for help with producing this Note.

[*Warship* is always pleased to hear from readers with unusual or interesting photographs, especially if they have an accompanying story.]

'ZOMBIES' IN WARSHIP HISTORY

In the first of a new series, **Aidan Dodson** looks at some of the 'zombie facts' that continue to stalk histories of the world's warships.

Once something appears on the printed page (or, increasingly these days, on the internet) it tends to acquire the status of a 'fact' – even more so if the source in question is part of what becomes regarded as a 'standard reference'. Thereafter it can find itself repeated without the need for further verification. However, for the historian, almost everything is a work in progress, and it is often the case that claims made in secondary sources need to be investigated. A 'fact' frequently turns out have been based on a misinterpretation of inadequate data, and the appearance (or reinterpretation) of new primary material can literally 'change history'.[1] Sometimes this is only a matter of detail, but sometimes it is far more fundamental. Yet such re-evaluations may long remain deeply buried in specialist periodicals, the 'standard' works rarely being revised to reflect new versions of reality.[2] Thus, the history of warships, like other branches of the historical disciplines, has long been stalked by 'zombie facts' that have proved difficult to kill.

Indeed, it should be noted that back in the very first volume of *Warship*, John Campbell had occasion to highlight 'persistent errors' regarding ships' armaments.[3] This series of Warship Notes is therefore intended to highlight a few examples concerning vessels' origins, fates – or indeed their very existence!

Phantom ships

Perhaps the most pernicious 'zombies' concern wholly-non-existent warships. Particularly prominent has been

the Ottoman battleship '*Reshad-i-Hamiss*'. According to *Brassey's Naval Annual*s for 1910–12, two battleships were ordered in 1911: one from Armstrong (*Reshad-i-Hamiss*) and one from Vickers (*Mehmid Reshad V*, later *Reshadieh*, later HMS *Erin*), the former being suspended in 1912 and subsequently cancelled in the wake of the Balkan Wars. However, Armstrong's records[4] show that only one ship was ordered – from Armstrong, to an Armstrong design and with an Armstrong armament – but actually to be built by Vickers. This was clearly at the root of the confusion in *Brassey's*, compounded by no one noticing that the alleged 'Armstrong ship' had the same name as the Vickers one: 'Hamiss' (more correctly *ḫâmis*) is simply the Osmanli (Ottoman court language) writing of the Turkish 'Reshad' (*reşat*) – the epithet of Sultan Mehmed V, for whom the ship was named. A sister to *Reshadieh* did exist, to be named *Fatih Sultan Mehmed*, but she was not ordered until 1914, and although laid down in June by Vickers, work was halted in August and the material cleared from the slip.[5]

The late 19th-century Chinese Navy was particularly

Erin during 1917-18; she was one of seventeen battleships of the Grand Fleet fitted to operate a kite balloon to extend the ship's vision at sea. (NHHC NH 89154)

The Chinese cruiser *Nan Thin* or her sister *Nan Shui*. (Dirk Nottelmann collection)

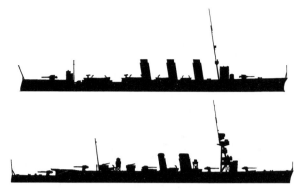

Comparison of the silhouettes of the Turkish scouts and HMS *Centaur*. (Author's graphic)

prone to 'zombies': the difficulty in obtaining reliable information and the assorted ways in which Chinese names may be transliterated into the roman alphabet left plenty of scope for misunderstandings. A good case study concerns the programme for five generally similar 'fast' cruisers initiated in 1881.[6] Three, *Kai Chi* (1883), *King Ching* and *Huan Tai* (1886), were built in China and had composite hulls, but the remaining pair, with steel hulls (but without the armour deck alleged by *Jane's Fighting Ships 1900*), were ordered from Howaldt at Kiel, *Nan Thin* [*Nan Chen*] being launched on 12 December 1883 and *Nan Shui* [*Nan Rui*] on 8 January 1884.

Although these ships completed the programme, contemporary western sources conjured up a series of Chinese-built copies, allegedly named '*Hi Ying*', '*Yung Pao*', '*Foo Sing*' and '*Fu Ch'ing*'. The latter's existence as a sister of *Nan Thin* and *Nan Shui* was maintained not only by *Jane's 1900* but also into the 1970s by *Conway's All the World's Fighting Ships 1860–1905*.[7] In reality, *Fu Ch'ing* was a 1,000-ton torpedo gunboat, probably laid down under the name *Kuang Ting*, and launched in 1893.[8]

Phantom designs

While the ships actually existed – or would have done, had they not been cancelled in the wake of the Washington Treaty – the design universally published for the four Japanese battleships of the *13* class never seems to have been official. Like so much information on the Imperial Japanese Navy, the information derives from the works of Fukui Shizuo (1913–1993), who presents them as 30-knot, 47,500-ton vessels armed with 18in guns. However, more recent archival work in Japan has indicated that this design was actually a personal study by the Japanese naval architect Hiraga Yuzuru (1878–1943), rather than one produced for the Navy's capital ship construction programme.[8] Rather, the *13* class was to be built to the same basic design as all the post-*Kaga* class capital ships of the 8-8 plan and beyond, and data would have replicated that of the *Amagi* class (41,000 tons, 30 knots, ten 16in).[9]

Disputed origins

The pre-First World War Ottoman naval procurement programmes have been a fertile breeding ground for

'zombies'. One long-current example concerns the two light cruisers of the *Centaur* class, launched by Armstrong for the Royal Navy in 1916, which early sources claimed were begun for Turkey and completed 'to a design slightly modified to meet British requirements'.[10] This was by no means the case, as while the *Centaur*s completed to the very latest variant of the 'C' class design, the Ottoman ships had been totally different vessels. They were to have had a distinctly archaic appearance, with a raised poop, closely resembling *Hamediye* and *Mecidiye*, launched in 1903 – and also *Drama*, launched in 1912, but requisitioned as the Italian *Libia*: clearly the Ottoman navy was looking for uniformity in profile among its cruising vessels.[11]

The fact that the Ottoman ships had the yard numbers 877 and 878, while the *Centaur*s were 888 and 889, made it quite clear that they were different vessels, although built on the same allocated slips using some previously-gathered material. However, while recognising the difference in design, some works have gone as far as to state that this material included the original Vickers-built machinery.[12] While the Ottoman vessels had eleven mixed-fired boilers supplying steam for 3-shaft direct-drive turbines of 24,000shp, the *Centaur*s had six oil-fired boilers and 4-shaft geared turbines of 40,000shp. Again, the fact that Vickers allocated the numbers 461 and 462 to the Ottoman machinery and 476 and 477 to that of the *Centaur*s should have given the game away.[13]

Another 'zombie' related to material appropriated from a foreign contract at the outbreak of the First World War concerns the machinery of the German minelaying cruisers *Bremse* and *Brummer*. Published Western sources appear to be unanimous that these ships were built around turbines being built by AG Vulcan at their Hamburg workshops for the Russian battlecruiser *Navarin*. However, the specifications of the battlecruiser make it clear that this re-purposing would have been impossible. *Navarin* was to have 4-shaft turbines of the Parsons reaction type, while the 2-shaft installations in *Bremse* and *Brummer*s were of the very different Curtis impulse type. It is also clear from Russian official records that the engines for *Navarin* were ordered from the Franco-Russian Works at St Petersburg on 22 April 1913![14]

Nevertheless the engines of *Bremse* and *Brummer did* in fact come from machinery building for Russia, but comprised the 4-shaft Curtis-turbine installation intended for the light cruiser *Svetlana*, building at the Russo-Baltic Shipyard at Reval (Tallinn),[15] with the engines subcontracted to AG Vulcan. At the end of August 1914, Vulcan offered to build a pair of destroyers around these turbines, which clearly would not be delivered to the now-hostile Russia.[16] However, the Construction department of the German Naval Office preferred to use the machinery to build fast minelayers, a type currently lacking in the fleet. After some discussion, a formal order was placed with Vulcan's Stettin yard on 23 December, the ships being completed in 1916, although in the event little used in the minelaying role.

Disputed detail

There are frequently differences of opinion between reference works on the armament of vessels – including on occasion the very calibre of their main batteries. One example concerns the Russian coast defence ships of the *Admiral Seniavin* class, for which the standard sources are all-but-unanimous in ascribing an armament of four 9in guns in twin turrets fore and aft to the first pair (*Admiral Seniavin* and *Admiral Ushakov*), but three 10in – the after turret being a single – in the final ship, *General-Admiral Apraksin*.

However, all three vessels had 10in guns on completion, *Apraksin* having had her number of guns reduced in 1895 in view of the overweight state of her sisters.[17] The confusion had its origin in the fact that the original specification for the class *did* include 9in guns, but when development of the intended weapon was dropped in 1892, the armament was switched to a new lightweight 10in gun – which proved a failure. Thus a heavier gun of that calibre was

General-Admiral Apraksin in drydock at Kronstadt in 1901, showing her single after 10in mounting. (Author's collection)

substituted, furthermore mounted in an enclosed turret instead of the originally-planned hooded barbettes. This all contributed to the first pair being 16 per cent overweight; *Apraksin*'s loss of a gun reduced the excess to 'only' 7.5 per cent. However, it was the armament of the original design that found its way into *Jane's Fighting Ships* from the outset. Combined with a general assumption that *Apraksin*'s reduction in barrel numbers was to accommodate a larger calibre on the same displacement as four 9in, this was created a most enduring 'zombie'.

Phantom fates

Erich Gröner's *Die Deutschen Kriegsschiffe*, with a number of editions published since 1936,[18] has long been the baseline reference source for German warships. However, among a number of its errors are a swathe concerning the fates of submarines surrendered at the end of the First World War. In particular a dozen were listed in its first edition as 'run aground' or 'sunk' on the way to the breakers in 1921, with the gloss 'on the East Coast of Great Britain' having been added to these entries by the time the 1991 English edition was produced.

In fact, *none* of the boats in question suffered this fate. Six of them were actually scuttled in the English Channel, south of the Isle of Wight, by the Royal Navy in the summer of 1921, while another of the boats had been sunk in the Solent as a target the previous year. Others alleged by Gröner to have been 'scrapped' or 'expended' in France had actually foundered or been wrecked in the English Channel *en route* from the UK. Furthermore, a group of submarines alleged by a number of sources to have been 'blown ashore in a storm' at Falmouth had actually been purposely dumped on the beach following damage in Royal Navy explosives trials. Further confusion in the standard secondary sources has been caused by misprints or misunderstandings of *U-* versus *UB-* numbers in contemporary and later sources, leading to vessels' fates being confused or even conflated.[19]

The errors in Gröner have likewise impacted on the identification of extant wrecks, as in the case of the remains of three First World War German submarines that still lie in the Medway estuary. Two have long since been reduced to their bottom frames and are visible only at very low tide, but one is still in fair condition. The latter is currently enshrined in Google Earth as '*UB122*', but *UB122* was actually scuttled in the English Channel on 30 June 1921 at 50° 11'55 N, 1° 10'09 W. This is made clear by an Admiralty list dated 19 July 1921 of boats sunk in compliance with inter-Allied agreements for the disposal of ex-German assets.

The question of the identification of the three Medway wrecks is in fact straightforward: the British Admiralty Sales Ledger, held by the MoD Naval Historical Branch, states unequivocally that the hulls of *UB144*, *UB145* and *UB150*, purchased by M Lynch & Son in 1920 and initially moored in the Medway at Rochester, were 'dumped' in 1922 – something not found regarding any other ex-German submarines in the ledger. All three were of the UB-III type, which perfectly matches the size and

The wreck of a German submarine of the UBIII type (one of *UB144, UB145* or *UB150*) off Danhead Creek in the Medway estuary. (Historic England 27196.026)

form of the Medway wrecks.[20] However, which wreck is which remains – and probably will forever remain – obscure.

[*Warship* would be pleased to hear from any readers who can add to this list of 'zombies'. The annual can be contacted at the usual address.]

Endnotes:

1 See, for example, the Assistant Editor's Warship Notes on the loss of HMS *Curacoa* in *Warship 2012* and *Warship 2014*.

2 As an example. in recent years Seaforth Publishing has produced beautifully re-set, and sometimes re-illustrated, versions of classic works (*eg* RA Burt's *British Battleships* series), yet with no attempt at significant textual revision, leaving them as repositories of 'zombies'. A further factor is the issue of the 'respected' or 'distinguished' author, whose errors are preferred to new research by 'lesser' individuals.

3 NJM Campbell, 'Persistent errors in descriptions of ships' armament', *Warship* Nos 1/2 (1977), 62–63.

4 Investigated by Peter Brook, *Warships for Export: Armstrong warships 1867–1927*, World Ship Society (Gravesend, 1999), 143–44.

5 For the full story of *Reshadieh/Erin* and *Fateh*, see A Dodson, *Windfall Battleships* (Seaforth Publishing, Barnsley, forthcoming).

6 RNJ Wright, *The Chinese Steam Navy 1862–1945*, Chatham Publishing (London, 2000), 55–57; see also A Dodson and D Nottelmann, *The Kaiser's Cruisers, 1871–1918*, Seaforth Publishing (Barnsley, 2021), 170.

7 R Gardiner, R Chesneau and EM Kolesnik (eds), *Conway's All the World's Fighting Ships 1860–1905*, Conway Maritime Press (London: 1979), 396.

8 A Endo, 'Japanese Battleships (INFOSER Question No. 10/99, W.I. No 1, 1999, 90)', *Warship International* XXXVI/4 (1999), 322.

9 *Amagi, Akagi, Atago, Takao, Kii, Owari*, 11–16; *Kii* and later vessels would have slightly thicker belts than the first four.

10 'Origin of HM Cruisers CENTAUR and CONCORD', *Warship International* VIII/3 (1971), 295–96.

11 The first drawing of these vessels to be published appeared in P Brook and I Sturton, 'Armstrong Portfolio Number Four', *Warship 2001–2002*, 155.

12 D Morris, *Cruisers of the Royal and Commonwealth Navies*, Maritime Books (Liskeard, 1987), 148; R Gray, *Conway's All the World's Fighting Ships 1906–1921*, Conway Maritime Press (London, 1985), 60; the latter also wrongly states that the ships were built by Vickers (who only built the machinery), rather than Armstrong.

13 All this was pointed out as long ago as 1972: see A Smith, 'Re: The Turkish Scout Cruisers of 1914', *Warship International* XXX/1 (1972), 5–6.

14 S McLaughlin, *Russian & Soviet Battleships*, US Naval Institute Press (Annapolis, 2003), 253.

15 For full details, see A Dodson and D Nottelmann, *The Kaiser's Cruisers, 1871–1918*, Seaforth (Barnsley, 2021), 190–93.

16 Replacement turbines were ordered by the Russians from the UK.

17 For the full story, see S McLaughlin, 'Armament of the Russian *Admiral Senyavin* class coast defence ships', *Warship International* XXXVI/1 (1999), 103–4; for a complete treatment of the ships, see S McLaughlin, 'The Russian Admiral Senyavin Class Coast Defence Ships', *Warship International* XLVIII/1 (2011), 43–66; L Ahlberg, '*Admiral Seniavin* and *General-Admiral Apraksin* in Japanese Service', *Warship International* XLVIII/1, 67–75.

18 First published as *Die Deutschen Kriegsshiffe 1815–1936*, JF Lehmanns (Munich and Berlin, 1937), updated as the two-volume *Die Deutschen Kriegsshiffe 1815–1945*, JF Lehmanns (Munich and Berlin, 1966–68), with an eight-volume revised edition by Deiter Jung and Martin Maas published in 1982–93 by Bernard & Graefe (Koblenz), and a partial English translation in 1991 as *German Warships 1815–1945*, Conway Maritime Press (London, 1983); the latter is replete with misprints and flawed translations.

19 For a comprehensive treatment of the fates of surrendered vessels and issues concerning them, see A Dodson and S Cant, *Spoils of War: The Fates of Enemy Fleets after the Two World Wars*, Seaforth Publishing (Barnsley, 2020).

20 For a detailed assessment of the alleged '*UB122*', see KE Walker and SJ Webster, *Strategic Assessment of Submarines in English Waters*, Cotswold Archaeology (Cirencester, 2014), 109; a pre-1939 photograph of one of the other hulks is published by P O'Driscoll, 'WW1 Medway U-boats', *After the Battle* 36 (1982), 39. The failure of previous researchers to make this identification may be due to the fact that the key document, the disposals ledger, is in the Naval Historical Branch, rather than the more easily accessed National Archives.

A's & A's

A SERIES OF UNFORTUNATE EVENTS: THE LOSS OF HMS *AUDACIOUS* (*WARSHIP* 2023)

Due to an oversight on the part of the Editor, the two tables supplied by **John Roberts** to provide an overview of the disposition of the Grand Fleet during the period in question were not included with the article. They are reproduced below:

Table 1: Battleships and Cruisers of the Grand Fleet and Northern Patrol in Northern Waters 16th October 1914

GRAND FLEET

Fleet Flagship
Iron Duke (operated with 4th BS, attached ships cruiser *Sappho* and destroyer *Oak*)

1st BS: *Collingwood, Colossus, Hercules, Marlborough* (VA), *Neptune, St Vincent* (RA), *Superb, Vanguard*

2nd BS: *Ajax, Audacious, Centurion, Conqueror, King George V* (VA), *Orion* (RA), *Thunderer* (attached cruiser *Boadicea*)

3rd BS: *Africa, Britannia, Commonwealth, Dominion, Hibernia* (RA), *Hindustan, King Edward VII* (VA), *Zealandia* (attached cruiser *Blanche*). Ships of 6th BS attached to 3rd BS: *Albemarle, Duncan, Exmouth, Russell* (RA)

4th BS: *Agincourt, Bellerophon, Erin, Dreadnought* (VA), *Temeraire* (attached cruiser *Blonde*)

1st BCS: *Lion* (VA), *New Zealand, Queen Mary*

2nd BCS: *Invincible* (RA), *Inflexible*

2nd CS: *Achilles, Cochrane, Natal, Shannon* (RA)

3rd CS: *Antrim* (RA), *Argyll, Devonshire, Roxburgh*

1st LCS: *Falmouth, Liverpool, Lowestoft, Nottingham, Southampton*

NORTHERN PATROL

10th CS: *Crescent* (RA), *Dryad, Edgar, Endymion, Gibraltar, Grafton, Hawke, Theseus* + AMCs *Alsatian, Teutonic*

VA: flag of Vice Admiral
RA: flag of Rear Admiral
AMC: Armed Merchant Cruiser

Note: Ships absent and not listed above were *Monarch* (2nd BS), returning from docking at Portsmouth; *Princess Royal* (1st BCS), returning from Atlantic escort duty; *Drake* and *Mantua* (10th CS), detached to Archangel; *Birmingham* (1st LCS) and *Bellona* (cruiser attached to 1st BS) docking at Devonport; *Royal Arthur* (10th CS) docking at Haulbowline.

Table 2: Location of Grand Fleet Battleships and Cruisers 22–26 October 1914

Lough Swilly
Iron Duke, 1st BS and *Liverpool* of 1st LCS (temporarily attached in place of *Bellona*), 4th BS + *Blonde, Birmingham* (sailed on 25th to re-join 1st LCS at Scapa on 26th).

Loch na Keal
2nd BS (less *Conqueror*) and *Boadicea*.

At sea
3rd BS, *King Edward VII* class and *Blanche* patrolling to the westward of Shetlands and Orkneys in support of the blockading cruisers of the 10th CS and 3rd CS. *Russell* and *Duncan* patrolling off northwest coast of Ireland. *Albemarle* and *Exmouth* patrolling area of Stanton Banks to southwest of Tiree.

1st BCS and 1st LCS (less *Birmingham* and *Liverpool*) sweeping North Sea from Orkneys to the Skagerrak until 25th, then retired to Cromarty (1st BCS) and Scapa (1st LCS).

2nd BCS sailed from Cromarty on 22nd to support the Harwich Force during an operation against the Cuxhaven Zeppelin Sheds. It returned to Cromarty on 25th.

2nd CS patrolling to westward of Hebrides; *Sappho* cruising to westward of Fair Isle.

THE GENESIS OF YOKOSUKA NAVY YARD (*WARSHIP 2022*)

Author Hans Lengerer has written in to point out that there is a missing digit in the table on page 141 of *Warship* 2022. The Total should read: 1,769,026 Ryō.

BOOK REVIEWS (*WARSHIP 2021*)

Jon Wise has written to point out an error in the publication details given at the head of his book review on page 213 of *Warship* 2021. These should read:

Stephen C Ellis
The Russian Baltic Fleet: In Time of War and Revolution 1914-1918: The Recollections of Admiral S N Timirev.
Seaforth Publishing, Barnsley 2020; hardback, etc.

NAVAL BOOKS OF THE YEAR

Chris Baker
What Happened to the Battleship: 1945 to the Present
Seaforth Publishing, Barnsley 2022; 304 pages, 170 photographs; price £30.00.
ISBN 978-1-3990-7008-9

Most histories of the battleship tell a simple tale following the end of the Second World War: an almost immediate, wholesale disposal of the older vessels, followed by a twilight existence for the more modern ships that came to an end around 1960. The subtext is that the battleship was all but dead in the wake of the war and that its disappearance was inevitable. This book, however, makes it clear that things were by no means as straightforward as the standard narrative implies, with lack of government finance actually being the key driver rather than matters of doctrine, technology or strategy.

The book begins with an overview of late-Second World War battleship activity, culminating in the signing of the Japanese surrender on 2 September 1945 on board USS *Missouri*, in the presence of HMS *Duke of York* and eight other battleships. There follows a summary of the battleships (and battlecruisers) extant at that date. Bizarrely, this includes capsized sunken wrecks such as *Utah*, *Bretagne* and *Cavour* and the US Navy's *Alaska* class (explicitly classified as cruisers), but not the Swedish coast defence battleships. There are also numerous inaccuracies concerning the fates of the non-UK and non-US ships.

The second chapter relates the activities undertaken by US, UK and French battleships during the months immediately following the end of hostilities, ranging from American ships' troop transport roles to *Richelieu*'s firing of some of the first shots in what would be the long-drawn-out conflict in Indochina. The account of the RN vessels' service draws heavily on the logs and other documents held in the UK National Archives, which endows it with particular authority.

The next chapter looks at how the battleship fitted into the postwar naval planning of the UK, the USA and France. All initial plans were over-optimistic as to what was possible in light of reductions in funding and personnel. In the USA and the UK only the post-1930s ships and the fully-modernised older vessels were retained, and the majority were in reserve or on training duties; the remainder would be disposed of, and this process is detailed in Chapters 4 and 5.

Chapters 6 and 7 describe respectively British, French and US battleship operations up until the end of the 1940s, by which time only *Vanguard*, *Missouri* and *Richelieu* remained active, while Chapter 8 recounts how funding issues and chronic personnel shortages ended the UK's plans to retain ships older than the *King George V* class.

Stalin's attempts to revive the Russian capital ship programme that had been derailed by the Second World War are the subject of the next chapter, together with the absorption of the ex-Italian *Cesare*. Focus then moves on to the Korean War, which resulted in the reactivation of the *Iowa*s. The retirement of most of the surviving battleships is covered in Chapters 11 and 12; by 1976 only the *Iowa* class remained on a navy list anywhere in the world. Two chapters are then devoted to the deployment of *New Jersey* off Vietnam during 1967–69, and the reactivation of her three sisters between 1982 and 1992; the last two ships of the class were declared surplus to requirements only in 2009. The final chapter considers the broader story of the preservation of battleships as museum ships and highlights the difficulties of maintenance.

The book ends with an Epilogue, a Bibliography (with a number of misprints), and an extensive set of endnotes. Regrettably the author often shows a preference for established, dated works over more recent articles based more directly on primary sources that resolve some of the points of disagreement he highlights.

An excellent selection of images is included, some of which are new to the reviewer. *What Happened to the Battleship* breaks new ground in fleshing out the story of the last decades of the service of the battleship, demonstrating that the story was far more complex and nuanced than is often implied, and is highly recommended.

Aidan Dodson

Alan Smith
Balchen's *Victory*: The Loss and Rediscovery of an Admiral and his Ship
Seaforth Publishing, Barnsley 2022; hardback, 256 pages, 3 maps, 11 B&W illustrations and 20 colour photographs; price £25.00.
ISBN 978-1-3990-9412-2

This book sets out to recover the memory and exploits of one of the Royal Navy's least-known professionals, a man generally remembered only for his loss at sea with his ship and all hands. The story first came to this reviewer's attention as the result of a political dispute over the ownership of a newly-discovered wreck in the Western Approaches, the *Victory*. The firm Ocean Odyssey had already acquired a reputation among historians for 'treasure hunting' under the guise of archaeology and there was concern that it had been handed this wreck without due process – a decision that appeared to go against all the rules for shipwreck ownership and treatment of war graves.

After all the fuss had died down and the wreck returned to government ownership, the reviewer was approached by Greenwich University to help them with a project from the then-National Maritime Museum to try and establish why the *Victory* sank. The results of this were published at a RINA conference and get a mention here in Chapter 4.

Also included here are some insights not available to the Greenwich study, in particular the extensive reconstruction of *Victory* in 1737, some seven years before her loss. Given the way the dockyards worked in those days, she would effectively have been a new ship. It appears that there had been Admiralty pressure to reduce the height of ships, and local pressure to add a further deckhouse caused some conflict for the shipwrights. This may have been why there were four tiers of windows, while a model of the ship suggests that the lowest tier had been 'pushed down' somewhat to comply with the need to reduce overall height; this made them very close to the waterline. We did a study on the strength of Georgian glass that suggested that these windows were very vulnerable to green water pressures and might therefore allow the lower deck to flood, all of which seemed to bear out the last description of the ship as 'wallowing'.

Further chapters cover the family background, career and active service of Admiral Balchen. Much of this is little known today, despite his many years of dutiful service, possibly because he remained aloof from politics, unlike many of his contemporaries and successors. This book goes a long way to redeem his life story and is clearly the result of much research, acknowledged in the many appendices. The final chapter concludes with the current situation of the wreck and, perhaps more importantly, some thoughts on the unstinting service that Balchen gave to the Navy and Britain, setting standards of duty that were an inspiration to many of his better-known successors.

WB Davies

Christopher M Buckey
Genesis of the Grand Fleet: The Admiralty, Germany and the Home Fleet, 1896–1914

US Naval Institute Press, Annapolis 2021; hardback, 364 pages, 32 B&W photographs, bibliography and index; price £41.95. ISBN 978-1-682475-81-2

The theme of this book is the evolution from 1902 of the Royal Navy's home fleets into the Grand Fleet of 1914–1918. Topics include: Fisher's reorganisation of the fleets and his building programme; exercises and manoeuvres; war plans; unbuilt design projects; the Fisher-Beresford confrontation; the characters and contributions of the First Lords and First Sea Lords; the 'Great Gunnery Scandal'; the unbuilt Canadian dreadnoughts; 'flotilla defence'; and the proposed substitution of torpedo craft for dreadnoughts in the 1914–15 programme. Christopher Buckey's text is firmly based on a wealth of archival research, and provides a useful survey of much recent scholarship on British naval developments in the prewar years,

The first Home Fleet was formed in 1902 from the commissioned and reserve ships in home waters. Then, at the end of 1904, as part of Fisher's redistribution of the fleets, the expanded Home Fleet was renamed the Channel Fleet while remaining under Sir Arthur Wilson's command. Next, in 1906, Fisher proposed forming a new Home Fleet from reserve units. However, when the fleet was established in 1907, its Nore Division comprised fully commissioned ships, including six battleships and the 5th Cruiser Squadron. Buckey rarely identifies individual ships and does not explain why *Dreadnought* was combined with a rather motley collection of predreadnoughts. Nonetheless, by March 1909 the division was transformed by the addition of both *Lord Nelson*s and all the *Invincible*s and *Bellerophon*s. In March 1907, Sir Francis Bridgeman took command of the Home Fleet while Lord Charles Beresford succeeded Wilson as C-in-C, Channel Fleet. Both Fisher and Beresford proposed at different times that the Channel and Home Fleets be merged and this eventually took place in March 1909, with Sir William May as C-in-C Home Fleet. The first two divisions corresponded roughly to the previous Home and Channel Fleets, each with a battle squadron, a cruiser squadron and a destroyer flotilla.

By 1912 the strategic focus was entirely on the North Sea. The Atlantic Fleet was abolished and all ships in home waters were reorganised into three Home Fleets – a term which Buckey fails to use in its plural form – under one C-in-C, Sir George Callaghan. Each of its four 'squadrons' comprised a battle squadron of battleships and a cruiser squadron. Buckey asserts that these battleship-cruiser squadrons never became official, yet they do appear in 1912 *Navy Lists*; however, by 1913 they had been dropped so that the First Fleet comprised four battle squadrons, a battle cruiser squadron, two cruiser squadrons and a light cruiser squadron. From 1912 the four destroyer flotillas of the First Fleet came under the Commodore (T) while the submarines and the older destroyers were commanded independently by the Admiral of Patrols. In August 1914, this same organisation was retained: the Home Fleets became the Grand Fleet (a term that had been in intermittent use since 1912) with the First Fleet renamed the Battle Fleet. Thus it seems that the genesis of the Grand Fleet was a process of progressive merging of all the fleets in home waters, rather than the Home Fleet alone being its 'direct ancestor' (page 248).

This reviewer can only applaud Buckey's discussion of the Dreyer/Pollen controversy over fire control, not least his use of new sources in the Mountbatten Papers, while disagreeing with his conclusion that 'any further investigation of which system was technically superior may be a blind alley' (page 185). Arguments put forward by certain naval historians during the 1990s that British ships had paid a severe penalty at Jutland because they were not equipped with the supposedly superior Pollen/Argo system were based on a flawed technical comparison of the rival systems. The battlecruiser losses at Jutland were due not to technical inferiority but to poor tactical leadership.

With a book of this scope, there are bound to be a few contentious points. Hoists of just a few signal flags were fully capable of ordering manoeuvres in real time. Some comparisons of British and German building programmes would have been helpful, as would more details on the organisation within the fleets of older predreadnoughts and armoured cruisers. But Buckey firmly rejects revisionist theories of short battle ranges, flotilla defence and substitution. All in all, his book is a welcome new study of the prewar Royal Navy.

John Brooks

John F Lehman with Steven Wills
Where are the Carriers? US National Strategy and the Choices Ahead

Foreign Policy Research Institute, 2021; paperback, line drawings by AD Baker III plus a few B&W photos, maps and graphics; price $20.00 (as donation to FPRI).
ISBN 978-0-910191-17-3

John F Lehman was Secretary of the Navy under the Reagan administration and is the Chair of FPRI's Program on National Security; Steven Wills is a Research Analyst for the Center for Naval Analysis. Together they have renewed the long-running debate about the utility of the aircraft carrier.

Many of the arguments in the book have been stated at various points since 1945 and focus on the need for a sufficient number of large flight decks and suitable (ideally long-range) aircraft for power projection. However, the authors clearly feel that the US Navy is at a cross-roads, with the capability of the carrier arm threatened by a decline in the number of hulls, aircraft with insufficient range and penetration to be used for land attack against a 'peer-level' adversary (Russia/China), and the rocketing costs of new hardware. The crisis has been prompted by the technical problems experienced with the new 'supercarrier' *Gerald R Ford*, the in-service date of which has been subject to constant delay, with costs rising from an initial estimate of $3.3 million to a current estimate of $17.8 million, almost three times the cost of the last CVN of the *Nimitz* class. The decision to incorporate so much new and untried technology into a single ship is now viewed as a serious error, and problems with the electromagnetic catapults, which are incapable of maintenance during flight operations, have yet to be resolved.

Even if it is assumed that these problems will eventually be ironed out, the *Ford*-class carrier is clearly unaffordable in the numbers that Lehman and Wills consider necessary in order to implement and support US foreign policy, and the authors look at a number of possible alternatives. The Royal Navy's *Queen Elizabeth* type is not favoured because of the limited range and capabilities of the aircraft that can operate from its flight deck using the ski-jump-assisted STOVL mode. The US Navy's 'Lightning Carrier' concept, involving the operation of the same F-35B aircraft from an LHD/LHA-type ship, is disliked on the grounds of its small air group and vulnerability to fire and action damage. The authors therefore propose the construction of a '*Midway*-sized medium aircraft carrier' with a traditional 'three-dimensional' air wing, a speed of 30 knots and the survivability of a *Nimitz*. Such a carrier, they argue, could be built in at least four US shipyards, thereby avoiding the uncompetitive costs of the single yard currently building the *Ford*s, Newport News.

It could be argued that the authors fail to engage fully with the challenges of the technological features associated with such a carrier. Electronic, cyber and kinetic defences get a mention, along with armour, full watertight compartmentation and the latest firefighting technology. But would the new carriers have EMALs, or would they revert to conventional steam catapults (which would have implications for their propulsion system)? What sort of long-range strike aircraft – presumably with the latest 'stealth' features to aid penetration –would they operate and how much would these cost? Lehman and Wills have attempted to set the parameters for the new debate, but one senses a hint of nostalgia for 'better times' in some of Lehman's arguments, and there can be little doubt that this debate will be prolonged and at times bitter, with some hard and painful decisions being required.

John Jordan

Guy Warner
Atlantic Linchpin: The Azores in Two World Wars

Seaforth Publishing, Barnsley 2021; 160 pages, numerous B&W photographs, appendices, notes, bibliography, index; price £25.00.
ISBN 978-1-3990-1090-0

The three island groups that make up the Azores lie far out in the Atlantic Ocean, more than 1,000 miles from Newfoundland to the west and some 800 miles from Caba da Roca, the most westerly point on the European mainland. The strategic importance of these Portuguese-owned territories was recognised in both world wars and is the subject of this book by Guy Warner, who was partly sponsored by the Azorean Institute of Culture to research and write an account of the aviation and naval activities that took place during this period. The author retains a special affection for what he describes as these 'remote and peaceful islands', and his familiarity with the topography is a special feature.

Germany declared war on Portugal in 1916 following a move by the latter, prompted by the British, to seize all German ships in Portuguese harbours. When the USA entered the war in 1917, she soon sought to exploit the islands as a staging post to and from Europe and as a seaplane base. Permission was granted by the Portuguese for an American garrison to be stationed on the islands, while the British established a wireless station. The resumption of unrestricted U-boat warfare in February 1917 resulted in a number of sinkings of Allied ships in the vicinity during the final 18 months of the war.

The author devotes a chapter to the interwar years, when the Azores were visited on numerous occasions by the ever-larger and more sophisticated flying boats of the leading nations that progressively made the aerial journey between the old and new worlds a reality – at least for the rich. The British Government, in 1941, recognising the geographical significance of the islands, negotiated with the neutral Portuguese to build an airfield. Permission to base aircraft on Terceira Island followed two years later, paving the way for the archipelago to become a key component of the Allied battle against the U-boats in the mid-Atlantic area during the remaining years of the Second World War; this enabled the British to introduce a more southerly routing for their transatlantic convoys.

Guy Warner uses a large number of personal recollections to give a flavour of life on the islands through the eyes of the servicemen and women posted there, and these memories are supported by numerous photographs, particularly of the aircraft involved that played such a key role. Frequently though, the recollections take the form of unnecessarily long quotations, some over a page in length. What is missing is a more detailed consideration of the wider strategic and political context. To give an example, we are told that the Portuguese cruiser NRP *Vasco da Gama* arrived at the port of Ponta Delgada with a senior officer on board in March 1918. One of the reasons given for the visit was that the Portuguese Government 'was wary of the American presence and did not wish to see a US annexation of the Azores'. Apart from learning that this diplomatic mission was not very successful, we are given no further information about what was a highly significant move on the part of the Portuguese.

Guy Warner's book draws welcome attention to an under-researched subject, and *Atlantic Linchpin* is a readable account of life for American and British service personnel stationed there during the two world wars. One hopes that a more thoroughgoing study of the wider aspects will follow, with greater attention paid to the role of the navies involved and also to the position of Portugal as an uneasy ally.

Jon Wise

David Hobbs
The Fleet Air Arm and the War in Europe, 1939–1945
Seaforth Publishing, Barnsley 2022; hardback, 340 pages, illustrated with numerous B&W photographs; price £35.00.
ISBN 978-1-5267-9979-1

In this masterly addition to his series on the Fleet Air Arm at war, David Hobbs addresses naval air operations in the Atlantic, the North Sea, the Arctic, and the English Channel. If some of the events may be familiar, the level of detail, depth of analysis and incisive conclusions transform the way we understand them. Successes and failures are analysed and explained with a naval aviator's insight, paying close attention to the historical record and to the voices of those who took part, many of whom were from the Commonwealth. The use of German records to check claimed enemy losses adds a new level of authority to the judgements.

The Fleet Air Arm had a serious lack of aircraft in service in 1939, a consequence of Treasury parsimony, Air Ministry hostility, and the lack of ambition in aircraft design. Aircrew and maintenance team numbers were similarly restricted; the loss of HMS *Courageous*, with all her aircraft and key personnel, within days of the outbreak of war had a major impact. Lacking a fighter fast enough to catch German medium bombers made operations off Norway difficult, while the loss of *Glorious* and dispatch of *Ark Royal* to Force H left the Home Fleet with limited aviation for air defence or carrier strike until mid-1941. In a sober account of the *Bismarck* chase Hobbs concludes that the torpedo bombers from *Victorious* scored no hits, but that evasive action by the German ship added to the damage caused by *Prince of Wales'* guns.

Central to the book is the heroic effort by six Swordfish of 825 Squadron to intercept three large German warships in the 'Channel Dash' of February 1942. A succession of failures by the RAF allowed the German ships to reach the Straits of Dover without being spotted. Instead of the intended night attack Eugene Esmonde and his men attacked in the afternoon, with inadequate RAF fighter cover; all six aircraft were shot down, no hits were made, and many of the aircrew were lost. Other shore-based operations in the Channel were far more successful: flying at night, Albacores denied the enemy the opportunity to move by sea, while FAA pilots provided gunnery spotting for D-Day and the subsequent operations off Normandy in 1944.

Scarce resources at home at the mid-point of war reflected priorities elsewhere, notably the Mediterranean, but the arrival of escort carriers, American aircraft and more aircrew boosted capabilities, notably for Arctic Convoy PQ18, where fighter defences and AA fire shattered the *Luftwaffe*'s torpedo bomber formations. The ability of Swordfish armed with 3in rockets to sink U-boats was a major boost in the attritional war that raged across the Atlantic and Arctic theatres down to the end of the conflict. Operation 'Tungsten', the Home Fleet carrier strike against *Tirpitz*, provides the final 'strategic' highlight. The German battleship was preparing for sea trials when Barracuda dive-bombers struck, inflicting heavy damage and significant casualties. Carrier strikes against U-boats and other German shipping off Norway continued to the end of the war, using escort carriers and ships working up for the Pacific.

The enduring theme is what might have been had the FAA been as well-resourced as its Japanese and American peers. New British carriers were well-designed and durable, but they lacked adequate numbers of planes and crew, long-range single-seat fighters and modern strike aircraft until American supplies arrived. Having ordered more fleet carriers than Japan or America up to 1939, the Navy and the Government failed to provide the men and aircraft to exploit them fully. That the FAA achieved so much despite those handicaps is a testament to the commitment and determination of those involved.

Andrew Lambert

Paul Stillwell
Battleship Commander: The Life of Vice Admiral Willis A Lee

Naval Institute Press, Annapolis 2021; hardback, 336 pages, 6 maps & 30 B&W illustrations; price £39.95/$37.95. ISBN 978-168-245-94-2

Paul Stillwell started work on this book over 40 years ago when, as the assistant Combat Information Centre officer on board the re-activated USS *New Jersey*, he began researching CICs, which soon led him to Willis Lee. For the rest of his career as an officer, and later an academic, Stillwell continued interviewing and researching, and this is the result.

Compiling evidence was not easy. Lee died only ten days after the end of the Second World War; he had consistently shunned the limelight and left no papers or memoir. Additionally, during the Pacific War, he had been 'type commander' of the fast battleships, overshadowed by aircraft carriers and relegated mainly to anti-aircraft defence and shore bombardment. Lee did lead battleships into battle when *Washington* and *South Dakota* sank *Kirishima* in November 1942, during the Guadalcanal campaign. Yet in 1944, during the Marianas landings, he declined to chase Japanese warships, judging that they posed no threat to the Saipan beachhead and that his own ships lacked the necessary tactical experience for a surface action. Later the same year his battleships were deprived of the opportunity to engage their enemy counterparts due to Admiral Halsey's poor decision-making at Leyte Gulf.

Stillwell's book takes the reader back to Lee's early life in rural Kentucky, where he developed his skills in marksmanship. Entering the Naval Academy, he graduated 106th out of 201 but was already a notable member of the Navy's shooting team, even shooting for the USA in the 1920 Belgium Olympics.

Lee's naval career included time serving afloat and ashore, in battleships, cruisers and gunboats. He commanded cruisers and destroyers, served with the Bureau of Naval Ordnance and developed a specialism in naval gunnery. He proved himself an excellent ship handler and an officer who inspired loyalty in both his subordinate officers and enlisted men. The year 1939 saw him in the Fleet Training Division, tasked with readying the US Navy for war. He liaised well with his British counterparts and in 1942, with the US now at war, Lee was appointed to command BatDiv Six, comprising the new fast battleships now joining the Pacific Fleet. Lee's

gunnery expertise led to him establishing an embryonic Combat Information Centre on his flagship, *Washington*, something that proved its worth in the sinking of *Kirishima*. Lee was also active in improving the effectiveness of the fleet's anti-aircraft defences, pressing for more 40mm and 20mm guns and the VT proximity fuze. Lee ended the war in Maine, using his expertise to develop tactics to counter Japanese *kamikazes*. It was here that he died of a heart attack.

Stillwell obviously admires Lee, whose 'folksy' manner and often dishevelled appearance hid a brilliant and analytical mind, and whose major contribution to the US Navy was in developing gunnery and tactics. This book is recommended to everyone with an interest in the Pacific war, and the role of an influential but little-known admiral in forming the fleet that fought it.

Andrew Field

Gérard Garier & Alain Croce
Les Cuirassés Echantillons Tome 02: *Jauréguiberry, Bouvet, Masséna,* et *Henri IV*

Editions Lela Presse, Le Vigen 2021; large format hardback, 432 pages, many photographs, maps, plans and drawings; price €55.00. ISBN 978-2-37468-037-8

The first volume of this work was reviewed in *Warship 2022*. Volume 2 adopts a similar approach but covers the later battleships of the series. The inclusion of *Jauréguiberry* is a slightly odd choice given that she belonged to the first group, which was armed with the older-model Mle 1887 guns and had only four 65mm QF guns rather than the eight 100mm QF of the later *Masséna* and *Bouvet*. Even more questionable is the inclusion of *Henri IV*, which was strictly a coast defence battleship (and designated as such on the early plans) and served as a demonstrator for the radically-different 'cellular' protection system being proposed by the naval architect Emile Bertin. A possible justification for her inclusion is that *Henri IV* is the only notable French battleship of the period that has not been covered in other books published by Lela Presse, but she was a very different ship to the others covered here. Her inclusion pushes the extent of the book to a massive 432 pages (66% more than for the first volume), but Lela have at least managed to cap the price at €55.00

The advantage of this volume over the first is that the *atlas de coque* for all four of these ships have survived. The plans are comprehensive, beautifully reproduced and, unlike some of those in Vol 1, appropriate; many of them (particularly those of *Henri IV*), were not available for download from the SHD website. The data, generally supplied in the form of tables, is likewise comprehensive, and ranges from the calibre, model, location and command of the guns to the height of the masts and provisions for the crew; it appears to be from primary source documentation (the official *devis*). However, armour thicknesses are given in metres rather than the usual millimetres, and this occasionally causes confusion (slippage of the comma separator for the main belt of *Bouvet* results in an armour thickness of 4.20 metres (13.8ft!).

As in the first volume, the official plans are complemented by line drawings (showing modifications) and artwork (colour schemes) by Gérard Garier and an excellent collection of photographs, generally contemporary postcards sold by local photographers in the French ports. The captions are admirably informative, and identification errors on the original postcards have been corrected. This is a flawed but impressive work, and a 'must' for those interested in the pre-dreadnought era.

John Jordan

Mark Lardus
B-25 Mitchell vs Japanese Destroyer: The Battle of the Bismark Sea 1943

Osprey Publishing, Oxford 2021; softback, 80 pages, with 56 photographs and 8 pages of full colour illustrations; price £13.99.
ISBN 978-1-4728-4517-7

This is one of a number of recent accounts of the Battle of the Bismark Sea (albeit including one that is a work of fiction), so the subject has been well covered. That said, the author has clearly done his research, particularly with regard to the apparent neglect of anti-aircraft protection in the Imperial Japanese Navy. Considering Japan's track record of successful aircraft attacks on warships, this seems rather a strange omission in what were in many respects otherwise successful designs.

The book is one of Osprey's 'Duel' series and has as its primary focus ships vs planes; it has a familiar layout, with text interspersed with photographs and specially prepared colour artwork. The combat description itself follows analyses of the men and materiel involved, taking the reader back to design origins and basic training through to the actual battle itself and its aftermath, the aircrews having learned how to deal with vessels that were poorly defended against air attack.

One small disappointment is that the customary double-page colour spread is given over to a Japanese Navy crew manning a 13mm machine gun in action; a wider view of the ship might have been better value for money, given the evident competence of artist Jim Laurier. However, this is a handy book packed with data that would be particularly useful to modellers.

WB Davies

John R McKay
Surviving the Arctic Convoys: The Wartime Memoir of Leading Seaman Charlie Erswell

Pen & Sword Maritime, Barnsley 2021; hardback, 182 pages, 1 map and 34 photographs; price £19.99.
ISBN 978-1-39901-303-1

In his acknowledgements author John McKay describes this book as a labour of love, arising from having met Charlie Erswell and been enthralled by his tales. Having

been brought up from an early age on such books as JPW Mallalieu's *Very Ordinary Seaman* and Nancy Spain's *Thank you Nelson* by parents who both served in the war, and then having a father-in-law whose early days in the RNVR were on HMS *Walker*, which took part in the same Arctic convoys, the reviewer appreciated the additional insights in this account.

It is set out in 22 shortish chapters, after an introduction, prologue and map, and is closed by an epilogue, all written in the first person as Charlie Erswell. The lack of an index is to some extent offset by the chapter titles. The first two chapters cover Erswell's upbringing in Berwick-on-Tweed and his work in London during the Blitz; the next 16 cover the titular topic, with the last four covering his career in the Merchant Navy and eventual retirement.

Erswell's introduction to the Navy followed closely that of the reviewer's father-in-law, including time at HMS *Ganges* and then at sea. The major difference, however, was that Erswell was never bothered by seasickness, whereas father-in-law was so sick that he soon found himself with a land job, taking apart unexploded mines for the rest of the war. The other thing that stands out is that Erswell seems to have been somewhat more aware of the wider war than many others, though whether this is the result of hindsight – after all he is narrating this sixty years after the event – or whether his captains were unusually forthcoming to their crews is not clear.

As a memoir of wartime life in the Royal Navy this is one of the better ones: being fairly upbeat in tone it makes for a less harrowing read than some others, and is highly recommended.

WB Davies

Martin Stansfield
Japanese Carriers and Victory in the Pacific: the Yamamoto Option

Pen & Sword Maritime, Barnsley 2021; 227 pages, 50 photographs, 13 tables, 2 maps; price £25.00.
ISBN 978-1-3990-1011-5

This book is predicated upon a 'what if': how might the Second World War have played out had Japan made different decisions over its naval planning in the years leading up to the conflict. It begins with an account of the sinking by internal explosion of the battleship *Mutsu* in 1943, but then goes on to speculate what effect this might have had in 1936. The author suggests that it might have discredited the battleship and resulted in the cancellation of the planned series of 'super-battleships' of the *Yamato* class, and the substitution of a large-scale programme of aircraft carrier construction. This programme, which would have more than doubled the number of carriers and aircraft available at the crucial points of the conflict, is dubbed the 'Phantom Fleet', and is the focus of the latter part of the book, where it is woven into an alternative history of the Pacific War.

Prior to this, the real history of the Imperial Japanese Navy is traced through the lens of the aircraft carrier, together with a discussion of the events that led up to the decision for war in 1941. A chapter then follows on what is dubbed Japan's 'Shadow Fleet', the series of vessels designed for service either as naval auxiliaries or commercial passenger liners with provision for easy conversion to aircraft carriers.

The focus then shifts to fleshing out the author's proposed 'Phantom Fleet', which is based on what might have been possible had the IJN diverted the resources that had been devoted from 1939 onwards to the construction and reconstruction of battleships and cruisers (and the conversion of liners to carriers) to the construction of aircraft carriers designed from the keel up. The analysis is not sophisticated, and there is little consideration of matters of logistics and infrastructure that would follow from a major increase in the numbers of carriers and the fundamental change in the balance of the fleet. In particular, the training and maintenance of air groups is barely touched upon, despite earlier comments regarding the difficulty of the latter in the context of the actual carrier fleet. The 'Phantom' ships are then fed into a detailed alternative history which concludes that, while not giving Japan victory, they might have enhanced the possibility of a negotiated peace settlement.

These speculations are not without merit. However, behind everything lurks the inherent unlikelihood that the IJN would ever have abandoned its long-term naval doctrine of the 'decisive [big gun] battle'. There are also stylistic issues, and one suspects that the excessively colloquial language reflects the author's background as a publicist. The book eschews any kind of referencing, or even a bibliography, in favour of a set of Acknowledgements, which names some sources but also cheerfully admits that one section of the book 'relie[s] entirely on internet surfing'. If one can tolerate the author's style the book is quite an enjoyable read, and where it deals with the real world gives a useful overview of events and their drivers. However, as a predictor of what *could* have been it does not convince.

Aidan Dodson

Stefan Draminski
Anatomy of the Ship: The Aircraft Carrier *Hiryū*
Osprey Publishing, Oxford 2022; large format hardback, copiously illustrated by CGI colour artwork and line drawings plus B&W photos; price £45.00.
ISBN 978-1-4728-4026-4

Stefan Draminski's latest 'Anatomy of the Ship' is similar in many respects to his treatment of the German battleships *Bismarck* and *Scharnhorst*, combining CGI colour artwork with conventional line drawings based on the official plans. The availability of plans of warships of the Imperial Japanese Navy is extremely patchy, with many lost to posterity; fortunately the full

set of builders' plans of the carrier *Hiryū* has survived, making this volume possible.

The book begins with the standard introduction, comprising a detailed technical history plus a full service history. It is illustrated by virtually all the surviving photographs of the ship, together with comprehensive data tables. The first page of this introduction repeats two errors that have become well-established in secondary sources. *Ryujo*'s defects, related in part to her lack of stability. were a *consequence* of the London Treaty of 1930, which prompted her redesign with a double hangar. And the G6 design of 1932 was for a fully-fledged aircraft carrier not, as the author states, for a 'flying deck cruiser', as after 1930 cruisers could neither exceed 10,000 tons nor mount 8in (20cm) guns. However, Draminski is on more solid ground when it comes to the design of *Hiryū*, and the remainder of his introduction cannot be faulted.

The main body of the book takes us from Primary Views, in glorious colour CGI (including a full complement of aircraft in their Pearl Harbor and Midway liveries), through the General Arrangements, Hull and Hangar Structure, Superstructure and Flight Deck, down to Armament, Fire Control, Fittings, Aircraft and Boats. The line drawings are of high quality, with the profiles showing an unpredented level of detail down to the shell plating. As in the earlier books, perspective fragments of the CGI models are often juxtaposed with the two-dimensional line drawings. Mostly this works well, although on occasions the fragments are on the dark side, and they can be overwhelming given the relatively light line weight of the drawings taken from the plans.

There is the occasional odd choice of terminology: 'Superstructure' for 'Island', 'Bottom/Tank/Lower Tank Deck' for 'Platform', 'Hold' and 'Double Bottom' respectively. However, this is otherwise a superlative piece of work, detailing everything you would ever wish to know about this influential aircraft carrier.

John Jordan

Aidan Dodson and Dirk Nottelmann
The Kaiser's Cruisers
Seaforth Publishing, Barnsley 2021; hardback, 320 pages, illustrated with 300 B&W photographs, maps, plans and drawings; price £35.00.
ISBN 978-1-5267-6576-5

The subject of this important book is the series of small cruisers (*Kleiner Kreuzer*) that were developed by the Imperial German Navy (IGN) up to the end of the First World War. It also traces the earlier history of the distinct classes of corvettes and *avisos* that began even before there was a *Kaiserreich*. This, the first book published anywhere on these topics, is evidently based on meticulous research. Its eleven historical chapters are followed by a comprehensive illustrated tabulation of characteristics. However, especially in the early chapters, even basic data like displacements are omitted from the text; thus the reader is obliged to keep turning to this tabulation.

At German unification in 1871, the new IGN possessed nine fully-rigged steam corvettes capable of world-wide cruising and three *avisos* intended mainly as fleet scouts. In the next two decades, the two types developed separately. However, after the accession of Kaiser Wilhelm II in 1888, their characteristics began to converge. In 1894 the then-Captain Tirpitz proposed that future needs could be met by a single design of small cruiser with sufficient bunkerage both for cruising and for sustained high speed while scouting for the fleet; the idea was supported by a visualisation sketched by the Kaiser himself. Once he became State Secretary Tirpitz preferred the single type as also simplifying negotiations with the *Reichstag*; small cruisers, usually two per annum, were stipulated by the Fleet Laws governing the future construction programme of the IGN.

The first all-purpose small cruiser was *Gazelle* (laid down 1897), with a protective deck and armed with ten 10.5cm/40 guns. However, she was a knot slower than the 21.5 knots of the following six of her class, while the final five introduced standardised Navy boilers (of the Schulz/Thorneycroft type). The succeeding classes retained the basic characteristics established by the *Gazelle*s but with gradually increasing displacement and speed; to improve seakeeping, the early ram bows became less pronounced. In the *Kolberg*s (1907–08), the main armament was increased to twelve 10.5cm guns.

In a radical development, the *Magdeburg* class were given longitudinal rather than transverse framing; the consequent weight saving allowed for an armoured belt and increased bunkerage. They also had a modern bow form with a straight stem. After several years of trial turbine installations, the *Karlsruhe*s (1911) were the first with standardised Navy turbines. Although there had been discussions on increasing the gun calibre to 15cm, front-line commanders continued to favour the 'hail of fire' delivered by the 10.5cm. Thus the final major development in German small cruisers did not come until 1913 when the *Wiesbaden*s were armed with eight 15cm.

In the earlier classes, the usual disposition of the main armament was two guns abreast on the forecastle and astern with the remainder on the broadside, with a consequent limit in firepower; but from the *Regensburg*s onwards the after pair were on the centreline and arranged for superfiring. An all-centreline disposition was adopted only for the four 15cm guns of the *Brummer* 'mine steamers' (1915); these also had mixed framing to simplify construction.

Two chapters cover the service of the cruisers during the War. The section on the Battle of Jutland is rather brief. While the night action demonstrated the effectiveness of the German 10.5in guns at short range, the crews of broadside guns were vulnerable to splinters from hits on the superstructure behind them. By 1918, the idea of the 'one size fits all' small cruiser was being questioned, smaller designs suited mainly to fleet roles being

preferred. Nonetheless, the classes actually built had proved invaluable in the War.

The authors of this excellent book have written a definitive account of the Kaiser's (and Tirpitz's) cruisers.

John Brooks

Matthew Wright
The Battlecruiser *New Zealand*: A Gift to Empire
Oratia Books, Auckland, and Seaforth Publishing, Barnsley 2021; hardback, 272 pages, illustrated in colour and B&W; price £25.00.
ISBN 978-1-5267-8403-2

This book in effect tells the story of the 'dreadnought era' through the history of one ship – albeit a slightly unusual ship, with an unusual story. It begins by recounting *New Zealand*'s genesis, which took place within the context of Anglo-German rivalry but which is given a different perspective by being seen from an antipodean viewpoint. It seems incredible today that New Zealand, then in the grip of 'social militarism', was once dubbed 'the Prussia of the Pacific'. Premier Joseph Ward was cut from a very different cloth to his modern counterpart, Jacinda Ardern and, while much-criticised and ridiculed both at the time and subsequently, he determinedly pursued the policy of buying a dreadnought, even though the machinations of the devious Admiral 'Jackie' Fisher meant it ended up as a battlecruiser rather than the '1st class battleship' that was intended.

If *New Zealand*'s origins were unusual, her initial career was hardly conventional either. Within three months of commissioning she was sent off on a global circumnavigation, a hugely expensive exercise in imperial PR which, nevertheless, seems to have been a great success. Wright notes that during this voyage *New Zealand* consumed more than her own weight in coal, while the lengthy stop-over in New Zealand itself saw around one third of the country's population visit her. It was here that she acquired the famous 'piupiu', the Maori flax skirt gifted to the ship's CO. The tale of the 'piupiu' turns out to be a lot less straightforward than legend might suggest, encompassing both the tangled racial and imperial politics of the period and the often unreliable nature of the historical record. Wright steers a careful path here, neither uncritically following contemporary attitudes that would seem antediluvian today nor indulging in too much judgemental revisionism. No sooner was the ship back home than she was off on her travels again, this time to St Petersburg as part of another highly successful mission, that of reinforcing the new *rapprochement* between Britain and Russia.

The account of Europe's gradual tumble into conflict, from the perspective of just one ship and those on board, is grimly compelling. After a pretty abject introduction to action at Heligoland Bight, *New Zealand* acquitted herself rather better at Dogger Bank, being responsible for the crucial round that disabled the unfortunate *Blücher*. Jutland was another matter. The narrative here, again from the viewpoint of one individual ship, gives the reader a clear idea of what it would actually have been like for those there at the time, with little of the wider picture evident. *New Zealand*'s performance was once again far from impressive: it appears that she fired more heavy-calibre shells than any other British dreadnought yet scored just four hits, all during the final, brief daylight encounter between the fleets.

Wright's book is not without faults. The whole of *New Zealand*'s career from Jutland to the Armistice is covered in a single short paragraph, while her important post-war second circumnavigation only gets a few pages. In contrast other subjects such as finance (presumably an interest of the author) receive very detailed treatment. There are a few typos and the occasional error – Bombay briefly becoming Mumbai 75 years too early! Moreover, the illustrations are not reproduced to best advantage, especially given that many are less-well-known views. However, the three contemporary coloured sketches of the view from the ship's conning tower during Jutland and Dogger Bank are striking, again for their sense of immediacy compared to the grainy and indistinct black-and-white photographs that have survived; that of the last moments of *Queen Mary* is particularly dramatic.

Overall, this is a fine book, carefully written and particularly evocative of the period. New Zealand's history, like that of every former part of the British empire, is not always an easy one to cover; this was a time when the world was changing, with the eponymous ship in many ways a relic almost before she was completed – and certainly by the time her short but eventful career was over.

Stephen Dent

Malcolm Cooper
The Ocean Class of the Second World War
Seaforth, Barnsley 2022; hardback, 210 pages, 278 B&W photographs; price £30.00.
ISBN 978-1-3990-1553-0

This book covers the little-known predecessor of the 'Liberty' ships, the 'Ocean' class. Many readers will be aware of the pre-Lend-Lease British Purchasing Mission in the context of aircraft such as the Mustang and Tomahawk, but less familiar with the merchant ship-building component of the mission, which resulted in the design and eventual order of the 60-ship 'Ocean' class of 10,000dwt cargo steamers. The design of these vessels would lead in turn to that of the 'Liberty' ships, which used much of the equipment designed for the 'Oceans'.

The book's seven chapters tell the story of a purchase of 60 ships by the British government from American yards that should in theory have been straightforward; in fact it was anything but, for a multiplicity of reasons. Firstly the very idea of *purchasing* something in which Britain led the world caused much heart-searching in the UK until wartime losses made it, in modern parlance, a 'no-brainer'. Secondly, no single US shipyard could

deliver the order, resulting in new yards being built. Thirdly, US yards had long since given up Scotch boilers and reciprocating engines, meaning that a whole new industry had to be set up to supply 'British' equipment. The latter two measures were to lay the foundations for the later 'Liberty' and 'Victory' programmes.

The book goes into great detail about these vicissitudes and about the resultant cost premium that had to be paid. It also covers the career of each ship, from launch through wartime use (including losses) to postwar disposals. As the ships entered service at the high point of U-boat activity, the fleet losses were quite high, but that is no criticism of the design, which itself was the result of much thought.

Well researched, well illustrated and well produced, this book fills a gap in the history of wartime ship-building.

WB Davies

Ben Warlow and Steve Bush
Pendant Numbers of the Royal Navy: A Record of the Allocation of Pendant Numbers to Royal Navy Warships and Auxiliaries
Seaforth Publishing, Barnsley 2021; hardback, 432 pages, illustrated with a 16-page B&W plate section; price £25.00.
ISBN 978-1-5267-9378-2

This book is a lot more interesting than its title (and the uninspiring cover illustration) might imply. As the some-what clumsy subtitle suggests, it is a comprehensive listing of the pendant numbers of Royal Navy ships from their introduction in the early years of the 20th century to the present day, but there is a good bit more, making this important new work of reference often a surprisingly good read.

The book begins with an explanation of the term 'pendant numbers', noting that both 'pendant' and the more recent 'pennant' are acceptable, while then sticking firmly with the former. There follows an introduction covering the story of the adoption of the system and subsequent modifications over the years, as well the use of other distinguishing insignia such as bands and – more recently – individual emblems on ships' funnels.

The following 280 pages give an alphanumeric listing of pendant numbers by 'flag superior', with the first chapter covering surface ships, the second submarines, and a third taking in the British Pacific Fleet of WWII, which adopted US Navy-style hull numbers. The bulk of the remainder of the book is taken up with a listing by ship name, followed by two appendices covering mercantile auxiliaries and the deck letters adopted as a means of identifying individual ships from the air, which are now ubiquitous.

These listings are enhanced by a number of short but often fascinating sections providing explanatory and/or background information (including pointing out the many areas where mystery or inconsistency exists). The story of why some submarines had numbers and others names is cited as an example of Churchill's genius, though it could equally well be viewed as showing his essential sentimentality. In addition many of the individual entries have further explanatory notes, and these are full of unexpected nuggets, such as US Navy ships with RN pendant numbers, 'dummy' numbers to confuse the enemy, and so on. The small selection of photos illustrates the variety of styles and uses, as well as highlighting some of the problems that can occur when attempting to use pendant numbers to identify a particular vessel.

Commendably, the authors make a point of noting where gaps remain in their research. They use as a device Donald Rumsfeld's oft-quoted aphorism about known knowns, known unknowns and unknown unknowns, hoping to place the first in the public domain, shed some light on the second, and at least stimulate discussion of the third.

For those who collect or do research using warship photographs, or are merely fans of masses of arcane data, this book is essential. However, it also contains much material of a wider, more general naval historical interest.

Stephen Dent

Premysław Budzbon
The Polish Navy 1918–45: From the Polish-Soviet War to World War II
Osprey Publishing, Oxford 2022; 48 pages, 34 photographs, 10 paintings; price £11.99.
ISBN 978-1-4727-4700-3

The end of the First World War brought into existence a range of new navies, one of the most interesting being that of Poland. Following the usual Osprey pattern of mixing archival photographs with modern colour illustrations, this slim volume aims to outline the first three decades of the force's existence.

It begins with the story of Poland's re-emergence as an independent state after a dozen decades of partition between the German, Russian and Habsburg empires, in the wake of their collapse in 1918. The Polish Navy was established at the end of November 1918, although access to the Baltic Sea was only secured through the Treaty of Versailles in June 1919. In the meantime, the new navy's Pińsk Flotilla had already been action on the inland waterways during the Polish-Bolshevik war that raged during 1919–20. An extensive account is given of this campaign, which ended with the Treaty of Riga in March 1921.

As far as a seagoing navy was concerned, major work was required: the coastline granted to Poland included only a pair of fishing ports, while the six torpedo boats ceded by Germany were without armament and in generally poor condition. A naval base had to be built from scratch at Gdynia, and the fleet gradually built up by refitting second-hand vessels and a new construction programme. This began with locally-built river monitors, and continued with submarines, destroyers and a minelayer, constructed in France. This reflected close political and financial links between Poland and France, but as these cooled during the 1930s the next pair of destroyers was ordered in the UK, with two submarines constructed in the Netherlands, and a class of minesweepers built in Poland. In 1939, two further destroyers were begun at Gdynia, and a pair of submarines ordered in France.

There was little that the Polish navy could do in the face of the German onslaught in September 1939, and all ships were lost except for three destroyers that had been sent to the UK and five submarines, two of which made it to Britain with three interned in Sweden. The vessels in the UK, augmented by a considerable number of units loaned by the British, fought alongside the Royal Navy through to 1945, suffering significant losses in the process. A detailed account is provided of the Polish Navy's exploits in both the North Atlantic and Mediterranean theatres, ending with the disbanding of the Polish Armed Forces in Britain in 1946. This followed the establishment of a Communist government in Warsaw which few personnel were willing to serve. The last image of the book is a melancholy view of the Polish Navy's ships laid up at Harwich in 1946, awaiting the reclaiming of loaned ships by the Royal Navy and the return of the remainder to Poland.

While technical and basic details are given of a number of ships and classes, a summary fleet list is lacking. Also, while the ex-German A-III type torpedo boats are dealt with in some detail (including a colour rendition), the more capable two *V105*-class vessels, acquired at the same time, are hardly given any substantive mention; *Mazur* (ex-*V105*) appears in two photographs and their captions only (plus an oblique reference in a table), while the second vessel *Kaszub* (ex-*V108*) is not mentioned at all. This is the more surprising since her loss by internal explosion in 1925 was a significant event in the early history of the Polish Navy. Nevertheless, this book is to be recommended as a handy summary of the history of a significant, but often overlooked, contributor to the Allied naval victory during the Second World War.

Aidan Dodson

John R Muir
Years of Endurance: Life Aboard the Battlecruiser *Tiger* 1914–1916
Seaforth Publishing, Barnsley 2021; hardback, 202 pages, 8 B&W photographs; price £12.99.
ISBN 978-1-3990-1720-6

John Muir was serving as a senior medical officer at Chatham on the outbreak of war in August 1914 and was heavily involved in the detailed work of mobilisation before being appointed to the new battlecruiser *Tiger* in October. He continued to serve in the Royal Navy after 1918, eventually retiring with the rank of Surgeon Rear Admiral, never losing his love of the sea. On the outbreak of another war in September 1939 he joined the RNVR as a Sub-Lieutenant after being told that he was too old and too senior to return to his former specialism, and was killed while navigating a patrol vessel off Portsmouth in June 1940. This title was originally published by Philip Allen in 1937, but Seaforth have re-published it to provide a remarkable description of the 1914 naval mobilisation, life in HMS *Tiger* and the Battle of Jutland as it was experienced by a principal medical officer and his small team. Value is added by a foreword written by Mike Farquarson-Roberts, a former RN Medical Director General who is now a medical historian.

The Australian naval historian James Goldrick wrote in his widely acclaimed book *Before Jutland* that, in general, we know more about how the ships of Nelson's navy were operated and fought than we do about the ships that fought at Jutland. Major works of naval history have barely mentioned the work of naval surgeons ashore or afloat and the part they played in action. Muir's book redresses this imbalance and, while detailed, its readable style brings an intensely interesting period of history to life as the story unfolds. The events he describes took place more than a century ago but, as Farquarson-Roberts points out, many of the problems he faced still have relevance today, for example in the period of mobilisation leading up to the first Gulf War. By then Farquarson-Roberts had others' considerable wealth of experience to fall back on, but in 1914 Muir had no recent precedents to guide him and he had to work out his own solution to every problem.

This book is far more than a description of Muir's medical duties; it gives a detailed account of a capital ship's organisation when she was straight out of the builder's yard with a scratch ship's company hastily assembled. He was obviously proud of his ship and its people and has left us with an intimate picture of life on board. *Years of Endurance* is a fascinating read and an outstanding description of a ship's operation during a period that should be better understood by today's generation. Thoroughly recommended.

David Hobbs

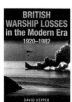

David Hepper
British Warship Losses in the Modern Era, 1920–1972

Seaforth Publishing, Barnsley 2022; hardback, 424 pages, illustrated with B&W photographs; price £30.00.
ISBN 978-1-3990-9766-6

This book completes a three-volume series covering all British and Commonwealth warship losses since 1650, exploiting official and other records to analyse the causes. Some of the findings will change the way we think about specific events; others enable us see them in their wider context. Then there are the distinct patterns of casualty: were ships sunk by other ships' guns, submarine torpedoes, by aircraft bombs, by mines or, from 1943, by guided weapons?

While this volume is necessarily dominated by the scale and intensity of British warship losses in the Second World War, it brings the story up to the Falklands conflict of 1982. Critically it is a record of how Britain has used its navy to secure the nation against invasion, protect the vital supply lines, secure or recover the overseas territories of Empire or Commonwealth, support allies, and project British and Allied land power onto hostile shores. Losses are the price that has been paid for taking ships to sea to engage the enemy; the only navies that do not lose ships are those that do not go to sea or fight. The list of landing craft, especially those used to provide inshore fire support lost during Operation 'Infatuate', which opened the Scheldt Estuary in late 1944, fills two pages.

One striking feature of the book is the large number of constructive total losses recorded from the middle of the Second World War, as American production and over-stretched ship repair facilities made it uneconomic, in time and manpower, to mend crippled escort carriers, frigates and older combatants. Mass production methods increased new-build levels to the point where there were more warships than crews.

The Falklands losses have been assessed using the relevant Board of Enquiry reports. *Sheffield* sank while under tow towards South Georgia; *Coventry*, *Ardent* and *Antelope* succumbed to bomb hits. This was a high-risk campaign entirely dependent on sea control to secure a beachhead, and support for the Marines and troops ashore involved risks that had numerous parallels with the Second World War.

There are some fascinating insights. Following the loss of the brand-new cruiser *Raleigh* in 1922, run aground on the rocky coast of Labrador due to basic errors of seamanship, the sight of the wreck so offended the C-in-C that he had it blown up to disguise its origins! When *Ark Royal* was hit, the fatal torpedo was one of four fired by a U-boat at HMS *Malaya*; all four missed due to operator error, the hit on the carrier being entirely accidental! The loss of three minesweepers to friendly fire from RAF Typhoons off the Normandy beaches on 18 August 1944 is traced back to the failure of the naval squadron commander to inform the relevant RAF headquarters – an oversight with serious consequences.

This is a work of reference that will be consulted for decades by every student of the past century of British (and Commonwealth) naval activity.

Andrew Lambert

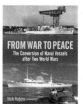

Nick Robins
From War to Peace: The Conversion of Naval Vessels after Two World Wars

Seaforth Publishing, Barnsley 2021; hardback, 192 pages, copiously illustrated; price £25.00.
ISBN 978-1-3990-0958-4

This attractively produced book covers a fruitful but previously unharvested field, that of conversions of naval vessels to civilian use after both world wars. Author Nick

Robins presents a valuable introductory commentary on the rationale for this process: naval vessels surplus to requirements were essentially cheap to purchase (although not necessarily to convert) and available more quickly than a new-build. Front-line warships with high-powered machinery, fine lines and extensive subdivision rarely made good candidates, but second-line vessels such as minesweepers and trawlers were often suitable. These considerations are well discussed, as are the technical issues involved, which sometimes included re-engining.

The book is mostly about former Royal Navy vessels, although there are sections on former US Navy, Canadian and German vessels. The largest ships reviewed are former escort carriers, but as most were designed originally as merchant ships reconversion was relatively straightforward, if costly and prolonged. Plenty of examples are given with subsequent histories: Victorian gunboats to salvage vessels, frigates to car carriers, sloops to coasters, corvettes to whale catchers (the 'Flower' class was derived from a whaler design in 1939), landing craft to ferries and motor launches to excursion vessels. Some types needed less conversion for civilian use, for example tank landing ships to roll-on/roll-off vessels, tugs and motor fishing vessels. Among the strangest conversions were the 1894 cruiser *Charybdis* to a passenger-cargo vessel for the Bermuda to New York trade in 1918, and some elderly German warships not interned in 1919 from coast defence vessels to cargo ships.

A good selection of photographs reveals some barely recognisable from their original appearance. Inevitably only a small selection of the thousands of vessels sold off can be covered in 176 pages, although the eight small WWI monitors converted to Shell tankers in the 1920s surely deserved a mention. It would have been impossible to list all the vessels sold off, but the author seems to have overlooked the comprehensive listing of tank landing craft Marks 3 and 4 in the World Ship Society's publication *Warships*. Also, disappointingly, quite a few proper names are misspelt. However, the book is otherwise a well-researched, worthwhile and readable contribution to a hitherto fragmented subject.

Ian Buxton

Admiral James G Stavridis, USN (Ret)
The Sailor's Bookshelf: Fifty Books to Know the Sea
Naval Institute Press, Annapolis 2022; hardback, 232 pages; price £23.50.
ISBN 978-1-68247-698-7

We all have our favourite books. Whenever a friend of this reviewer was feeling seasick, he would reach for a copy of Monsarrat's *The Cruel Sea*, his logic being that no matter how bad he felt, nothing could compare to the destructive power that emerges when the sea combines with war and is faced on an open bridge corvette – something Monsarrat captures so well. It is therefore pleasing to see this classic chosen by Stavridis to appear on *The Sailor's Bookshelf*, with a strong recommendation as the

book to read to understand the sacrifice of a captain in the worst of circumstances.

Stavridis is an eminent retired admiral and prolific author with a self-declared passion for reading. He advocates the ability of books to enrich readers' lives. Eager to inspire others, he has compiled a bookshelf of fifty of his favourite naval and maritime reads. However, this is so much more than simply a reading list or collection of book reviews. In choosing his titles he has selected a broad range of topics and styles to give a full appreciation of all that the sea and seafaring encompasses, balancing fiction and non-fiction titles and complementing the historical with some of the fundamental texts that help mariners learn and hone their craft: from understanding the essence of navigation, through Sobel's *Longitude*, to *Moby Dick*. He has chosen well, and everybody is likely to find something here to develop their perception and understanding of the sea.

Each title is introduced with the author's own personal reflection on its significance, and these reflections are enhanced with a selection of anecdotes, as well as 'bonus' recommendations to take the reader further. Not only is this unusual book an enjoyable read in itself, but reading all the recommended titles will help counter 'sea blindness' as well as presenting an exciting opportunity to broaden what for many is already a favourite subject.

Phil Russell

Paul Kennedy
Victory at Sea: Naval Power and the Transformation of the Global Order in World War II
Yale University Press, New Haven & London 2022; hardback, 521 pages with 54 colour paintings by Ian Marshall, numerous maps, tables and graphs; price £25.00.
ISBN 978-0-300-21917-3

The author of *Victory at Sea* was born in the UK and is now the J Richardson Dilworth Professor of History and Director of International Studies at Yale University. The book is described by the publisher as a lavishly illustrated history of the rise of American naval power during the Second World War. Kennedy sets out to achieve this by following three distinct strands: a narrative description of the war at sea, an analysis of how American industrial might made possible a vast expansion of the US Navy, and reproduction of a series of water colour paintings by the late Ian Marshall.

Marshall's paintings are an excellent way of illustrating the subject. He was a Fellow and past President of the American Society of Marine Artists and his pictures capture the atmosphere of their subject matter in a way that no photograph can. Their appearance is further enhanced by the high quality of the paper on which they are printed.

In terms of the analysis of the shift in global power balances, Kennedy's arguments are ably supported by coloured graphs. That on page 299 illustrates the dramatic rise of the US Navy after 1941 from just over two million tons, slightly less than the Royal Navy, to more than eleven million tons four years later, while RN tonnage remained more or less constant and the fleets of the Axis powers went into terminal decline. Kennedy highlights the overwhelming part played by American industrial expansion in gaining victory at sea. The USN's ability to recruit and train sufficient manpower to use its vast fleet effectively was another triumph, with many of the newly-trained personnel quickly becoming experts in the new form of warfare, especially naval aviation.

The third strand, a narrative description of key events in the war at sea, is arguably the book's weakest aspect. Written in an accessible and readable style, it contains a number of serious factual errors. Most of these concern the Royal Navy. The Skua dive-bombers that sank the German cruiser *Königsberg* in April 1940 were RN aircraft of 800 and 803 NAS flying from the Orkneys, not RAF – a service that had consistently opposed dive-bombing. Kennedy's list of aircraft carriers sunk in action (page 296) includes *Furious*, which was paid off into reserve in 1944, worn out after a long and distinguished career. And on page 202 the author states that the battleship *Anson* was in Tokyo Bay for the Japanese surrender in September 1945, when she was in Hong Kong as part of the task force that liberated the colony.

In summary, this is a book that benefits from considerable research and which is beautifully illustrated, with coloured maps and graphs that help underpin Kennedy's thesis. However, the numerous factual errors mean that it cannot be recommended without reservation.

David Hobbs

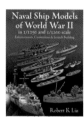

Robert K Liu
Naval Ship Models of World War II in 1/1250 and 1/1200 Scale: Enhancements, Conversions & Scratch Building
Seaforth Publishing, Barnsley 2021; hardback, 160 pages, illustrated with 300 colour photographs; price £25.00.
ISBN 978-1-5267-9391-1

Robert Liu is a former biomedical scientist who later became an accomplished jeweller and photographer. He emigrated to the USA after the Second World War and began making miniature model warships as well as writing about all aspects of scale modelling and, returning to his scientific background, on the behaviour of endangered fish. In his introduction Liu explains that time spent model-making, researching and photographing modelling subjects provides a very natural and rewarding way of working with his mind and hands. He also describes the worldwide community of individuals who collect models at these scales and the firms that have manufactured them. Further chapters, which amount to roughly a quarter of the book, describe the production methods used by these companies and his own tools and techniques, enhanced by an extensive array of colour photographs.

The remainder of the book comprises chapters on various types of warship, including British, US Navy, French, German and Japanese vessels, all shown as originally manufactured and at various stages of modification and painting. The mix is fascinating and ranges from the French battleship *Jean Bart* and aircraft carriers such as *Shokaku*, *Pretoria Castle* and *Manila Bay* to CAM ships, convoy rescue ships and many others. Categories such as cruisers and destroyers are represented by models from various nations photographed alongside each other so that they can be compared. Some chapters are specific to a single ship or small class, such as those describing models of the armed merchant cruiser *Jervis Bay* and the fighter catapult ship *Springbank*. The author's enthusiasm for his subject shines through and he makes the point that some models have a historical value of their own, making it wrong for them to be tampered with, even if their appearance were to be improved. Models are shown at varying stages of restoration or modification, and most of the finished results are impressive and highly detailed. It has to be said, however, that some are not quite up to this overall high standard. In some cases this is no doubt due to the quality of the original manufactured item; as Lieu points out this is variable.

In summary, this is a book aimed specifically at readers who collect, scratch build or modify model warships and is broadly successful in this. Those who are not model makers or collectors might find this examination of the subject ship models and their brief histories to be interesting but would probably find other reference material to be of more value. It is recommended to model makers and collectors at 1/1200 and 1/1250 scales, but those more interested in the ships themselves should look before buying.

David Hobbs

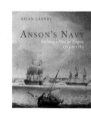

Brian Lavery
Anson's Navy: Building a fleet for Empire 1744–1763
Seaforth Publishing, Barnsley 2021; hardback, 208 pages, extensively illustrated in colour and B&W; price £40.00.
ISBN 978-1-3990-0288-2

In many ways a 'prequel' to the same author's classic *Nelson's Navy* (Conway, 1989), this handsomely produced, large-format title is centred on the period of the 'Seven Years War' (1756–1763) but actually covers much of the wider 18th century, both in terms of the background and consequences of the war itself, and George Anson's career and influence. Compared to the earlier title, the book has a far less obviously charismatic central character, and also a much less clear story arc. However at least Anson, the son of a minor Shropshire squire who became a slightly unlikely central figure in the Royal Navy's rise to global pre-eminence, got the chance to live on into retirement (if briefly), rather than meeting a premature and awful, if heroic, end.

The book's sub-title actually is slightly misleading, for

Lavery's text makes clear that this was more of an era of ongoing but often fairly piecemeal reforms, rather than any sort of consistent imperialist programme, with Anson frequently the presiding figure rather than the driving force. The fact that he kept few records himself does not help the historian here. The author is also sufficiently un-awed by his central character to note that in contrast to his notably successful active and administrative careers, he was also quite ruthless and prone to favouritism.

Lavery ranges widely and confidently over such diverse subjects as the technicalities of ship design, construction and fitting, uniforms (prior to 1748 officers designed their own), dockyards, naval diet (predictably pretty appalling), medicine (even worse, though genuine improvements were starting to happen during this period, thanks to James Lind, 'the father of nautical medicine'), discipline, logistics and much more. Of necessity each area gets no more than a relatively quick overview, but the reader nevertheless gains a comprehensive picture of the navy of the era, of its strengths and its weaknesses. Gunnery, for example, was getting seriously good; signalling, in contrast, was a shambles. This was bad enough in itself, with even mundane evolutions such as ensuring that ships were replenished with fresh water potentially fraught with difficulty, but in battle it could be catastrophic, and arguably cost the unfortunate Admiral Byng his life. Indeed the execution of the luckless admiral looms large over the whole story, an episode which Lavery clearly finds quite horrific but which he nevertheless succeeds in putting into context.

The book is generally well illustrated, with numerous contemporary paintings and engravings, often reproduced to pleasingly large size, and a jacket featuring a wonderful painting by Dominic Serres the Elder of men-of-war off a bucolic yet still recognisable Plymouth in 1766. Unfortunately many of the maps are terrible. That small caveat apart, this fine title provides an excellent introduction to a pivotal period in the development of the Royal Navy and its resulting influence on Britain and the world.

Stephen Dent

Jeremy Stoke
More lives than a Ship's Cat: The Most Highly Decorated Midshipman 1939–1945

Pen & Sword Maritime, Barnsley 2022; hardback, 288 pages, illustrated with 73 B&W photographs; price £25.00.
ISBN 978-1-39907-136-9

Gordon Alexander Stoke, MBE DSC RN was, at the age of 20, the most decorated paymaster midshipman in the Royal Navy. This book, written by his son, describes Stoke's extraordinary wartime service, from entering the Royal Navy at Dartmouth Royal Naval College as a special entry cadet in January 1940, through his wide-ranging wartime career, which resulted in him being one of the few to gain five campaign stars: Atlantic, Africa, Arctic, Italy, and the Pacific.

The author draws primarily on his father's letters home, initially to his parents and subsequently to his girlfriend (later wife) Doreen. These letters are remarkably balanced for one so young; as the war progresses so does the tone of the letters as the former schoolboy is matured by experience. However, they are also modest and softened as he plays down his own gallantry and often makes light of the terrible conditions experienced, both to appease the censor and so as not to worry his family. Where the letters leave gaps in the story, the author has done well to supplement them with a strong, well-researched narrative, further enhanced by the addition of other first-hand accounts.

Mick Stoke fitted more into his war service than most do over an entire lifetime. He was torpedoed twice in HMS *Glasgow*; continually bombed in Tobruk, suffering direct hits on his office and accommodation; survived torpedoes and mines on *Queen Elizabeth*; served in some of the most dangerous Malta convoys, including the Battle of Sirte; was bombed day and night in Bone, Algeria; was on the HQ ship at the Salerno landings, then torpedoed inside the Artic Circle, and finally served at D-Day and in the Pacific. Along the way he earned a DSC for his courage and an MBE for bravery, once confessing to Doreen that his greatest fear was to be found wanting when called upon. Stoke was a very brave young man who certainly had more lives than a ship's cat. An enthralling read.

Phil Russell

Erminio Bagnasco and Augusto de Toro
Italian Battleships: *Conte di Cavour* and *Duilio* Classes 1911–1956

Seaforth Publishing, Barnsley 2021; large format hardback, 280 pages, illustrated with nearly 300 photographs and drawings in B&W and colour; price £45.00.
ISBN 978-1-5267-9987-6

This book was originally published in Italian as two volumes. The material in it is not all new, but is essentially a compilation of everything we now know about these ships.

It begins with an account of Italian dreadnought development, which began with the influential *Dante Alighieri* and ended with the uncompleted fast battleships of the *Caracciolo* class which, despite their modest (and dated) protection scheme, would have been armed with eight 381mm (15in) guns and propelled by geared steam turbines capable of driving them at 28 knots. Sandwiched between these two types were the five dreadnoughts of the *Cavour* and *Duilio* classes, the construction of which was plagued by infrastructure problems, in particular the supply of good-quality armour plate.

The book then procedes with a detailed technical description of the ships as built and a comprehensive account of the radical modernisation of the two surviving

*Cavour*s that includes an analysis of their performance during work-up 1937–40, followed by a similarly detailed account of the modernisation of the two *Duilio*s. There is an interesting discussion of the rationale for reconstruction and of the decision to rebore the original 305mm main guns to 320mm, with consequent adverse effects on rigidity and (possibly) dispersion. The rejection of bulges (in order to keep the increase in displacement within the permitted limits and maximise speed) effectively meant that the ships sat deeper in the water, and immersion of the belt at deep load became an issue. The retention of the original bow in the *Cavour*s was likewise problematic. Although the *Duilio* conversion was more successful, in part due to lessons learned but also because the ships were given secondary and HA batteries modelled on the brand-new *Littorio*s, the authors are of the opinion that it was of doubtful value, as these ships were unable to stand against any of the new or newly-modernised battleships of their likely adversaries.

The second part of the book has a blow-by-blow history of the four modernised battleships during the Second World War and their subsequent fates, followed by four useful appendices detailing colour schemes and camouflage, gunnery performance, movements during the Second World War, and damage sustained.

Both parts of the book are heavily illustrated with photos, maps and tables, and the 'technical' section by the superb line drawings of Roberto Maggi. Reproduction is excellent: the drawings, which are often reproduced up the page in order to maximise scale, are given space to 'breathe'. The translation is adequate but not always idiomatic. Some sentences do not read well, and there are errors and confusions in terminology, particularly regarding the Italian *torre* (variously 'tower' or 'turret'). There are also some surprising errors concerning the rival French Navy: the battleships of the *Lyon* class were never 'on the building ways', and the dates given for the laying down of *Richelieu* and *Jean Bart* are well wide of the mark – in the case of *Jean Bart* by almost two years!

Despite these flaws this is an essential reference for these ships, with comprehensive data and superlative illustration. It is an excellent complement to the book on the battleships of the *Littorio* class (Seaforth 2011) by the same authors.

John Jordan

Andrew Cunningham
A Sailor's Odyssey: The Autobiography of Admiral Andrew Cunningham

Seaforth Publishing, Barnsley 2022; paperback, 720 pages, 20 B&W photographs; price £25.00.
ISBN 978-1-39909-295-2

Many readers will be familiar with this autobiography, first published in 1951. In it Cunningham explains how he dealt with the many challenges he faced, from deciding the fate of the French fleet at Alexandria after the fall of France to his frustrations with the lack of appreciation of his position by his superiors. The narrative is all the more cogent because of the author's honest self-reflection.

Understandably, Cunningham's primary focus is the Mediterranean theatre during the Second World War, with accounts of the crippling of the Italian fleet at Taranto, the victory at Matapan, and the Royal Navy's support for the army during the North Africa campaign and during the siege of Malta. He does so in an understated manner, accepting where things could have been better and acknowledging the efforts of his subordinates; along the way we see his relationships with Churchill and Eisenhower flourish. However, Cunningham's story embraces his own personal journey. Entering the Royal Navy in 1898 he learnt his art in destroyers, which were to remain his lifelong passion. He was there at the start of true joint operations, and he ended his career as First Sea Lord after serving almost 50 years, a period of profound technological change.

A Sailor's Odyssey is a strikingly lucid and absorbing memoir, rich in detail. This new edition remains faithful to the original save for a new preface by Cunningham's great nephew Admiral Jock Slater. It is an easy and very engaging read and remains a relevant and indispensable source, telling the human side of command. The author's thoughts about leadership, duty and discipline are still relevant and pertinent today. A true classic, highly recommended.

Phil Russell

Les Brown
ShipCraft 27: British Sloops and Frigates of the Second World War

Seaforth Publishing, Barnsley 2021; paperback, 64 pages, heavily illustrated in colour and B&W; price £16.99.
ISBN 978-1-5267-9387-4

Seaforth's well-established 'ShipCraft' series aims to provide modellers with an overview of a particular class or related group of warships, and to outline the various kits and accessories available from which to model the prototypes. Most of the volumes published to date have followed a largely standardised 64-page paperback format and the present book is no exception. This approach encompasses: design and operational histories; a review of current and past model products; a Modelmakers Showcase of completed examples; and extensive black and white and colour drawings to assist with the reproduction of detailed appearance and camouflage schemes. A concluding list of selected references provides valuable pointers to further research. As with earlier titles, the book benefits from a strong, consistent design theme and high-quality production values.

The book is broad in its scope. While the various interwar and war-built sloops are a major area of emphasis, the book also covers the frigates of the 'River', 'Loch' and 'Bay' classes, the 'Castle' class corvettes and a number of US-supplied escort vessels. This means that the coverage given to any particular design is necessarily brief. However, respected author and modelmaker Les Brown does a good job in providing the overall design context for this diverse group of warships while high-lighting of some of their more significant achievements. The relevant parts of the text are supported by an extensive range of high-quality black and white images. The five pages of colour and six pages of black and white drawings produced by experienced illustrator George Richardson are another area of strength.

The extensive scope of the book's subject matter is also reflected in the review of model products, which ranges from 1:2400 scale wargaming models from the American GHQ's 'Micronaught' range to 1:96 scale kits produced by Deans Marine that are suitable for radio control. The large number of products described is something of a double-edged sword, as there is often insufficient space to provide a meaningful assessment of a particular kit's strengths and weaknesses. The broad nature of the subject matter and a few errors of detail in the captions and elsewhere also suggest that the modelmaker would be wise to undertake additional research rather than relying exclusively on what is essentially an introductory text before attempting to represent a particular ship. These minor criticisms aside, *British Sloops and Frigates of the Second World War* represents another valuable addition to a series that is proving attractive to both the modelmaker and general enthusiast alike.

Conrad Waters

Douglas C Dildy and Ryan K Noppen
German and Italian Aircraft Carriers of World War II

Osprey Publishing, Oxford 2022; softback, 48 pages,
50 illustrations (20 in colour); price £11.99.
ISBN 978-1-4728-4676-1

This attractively-presented little volume provides a brisk account of the air-capable ships designed for Germany and Italy from the earliest days of naval aviation and of the aircraft intended for them. During the Great War the two countries fought on opposite sides; in the Second World War they were on the same side as part of the Axis. Neither completed a carrier between 1939 and 1945, sparing the Allies the daunting prospect of one or more battleship-carrier combinations threatening the Atlantic or Mediterranean supply lines.

More than half the pages, including a fascinating two-page cutaway labelled colour drawing, are devoted to the *Graf Zeppelin*, launched with pomp and circumstance in December 1939 only to be seized, desolate and neglected, by the Red Army in April 1945 and expended as a target. The proposed wartime conversions, namely the heavy cruiser *Seydlitz*, passenger liners *Europa*, *Potsdam* and *Gneisenau* and ex-French light cruiser *De Grasse* follow, described and illustrated by coloured profiles but without plan views.

For much of the interwar period Italy, together with its overseas territories of Libya, Italian East Africa and the Dodecanese, was considered a giant aircraft platform, with carriers unnecessary. War showed the limitations of this approach, and a belated carrier programme was put in hand. The only fully-fledged carrier, *Aquila*, converted from the liner *Roma*, was nearly ready for trials when the September 1943 Armistice intervened, ending any possibility of completion. After many vicissitudes, *Aquila*'s sunken remains were broken up postwar; the much simpler conversion of a second ship, *Sparviero* (ex-*Augustus*), was abandoned partway. Conversion of the badly damaged heavy cruiser *Bolzano* to an (unillustrated) auxiliary carrier/fast transport never began. The seaplane carrier *Giuseppe Miraglia*, the only Italian air-capable ship to operate during the Second World War, is given due prominence.

An overall assessment of the book is not easy. The title provides the brief, and the authors endeavour to stick to it. The 1914–18 material is irrelevant to the Second World War situation as, in contrast to the navies of Britain, the USA and Japan, there was no developmental continuity. The inclusion or exclusion of material often seems arbitrary; for example, although many of the 1930s proposals for newbuilt or converted Italian carriers are included, there is no trace of Wilhelm Hadeler's numerous wartime diesel projects for the *Kriegsmarine* (published comprehensively and at length in *Marine Rundschau* in 1972). Aircraft are illustrated in profile but not in plan.

Readers will find much more detailed material on German and Italian carriers and carrier projects in the annual *Warship* and the quarterly *Warship International*. Overall, this is a delightful primer, worth a B+ for effort and a B– for result; a book of twice the length would merit much higher grades.

Ian Sturton

John Fairley
The Royal Navy in Action: Art from *Dreadnought* to *Vengeance*

Pen & Sword Maritime, Barnsley 2022; hardback, 150 pages,
around 100 largely colour illustrations; price £30.00.
ISBN 978-1-39900-949-2

As suggested by its title, this book is essentially a compendium of paintings and other artworks illustrating the RN's wartime activities from the First World War to the present day. The book is split into three main parts dealing, respectively, with the First and Second World Wars and the postwar era. Each of these parts is further subdivided into a number of chapters that focus either on events or aspects of the period in question. For example, the section on the Second World War encompasses chapters entitled Early Years, Convoys and U-Boats, D-Day, and Famous Ships. There are also a number of appendices; these appear to have only passing relevance to the rest of the book, comprising an eclectic series of reprints of documents such as the Western Approaches Tactical Policy April 1943, and a press release announcing the

October 2020 assembly of the UK Carrier Strike Group for the first time.

The book adopts a layout in which the various paintings are dispersed amongst an extensive text that provides a general context to the events and themes depicted. The artwork encompasses the work of a wide range of artists dating from historic 'greats' such as WL Wyllie (erroneously given as 'W M Wyllie' throughout the captions) and Charles Pears through to more recent painters such as Terence Cuneo and the contemporary Ross Watton. Notable omissions, however, include Frank Watson Wood and the prolific Eric Tufnell. In general terms, the paintings are well-chosen and clearly reproduced. However, the reviewer felt that a more adventurous layout that presented some of the more complex paintings over two pages would have produced a more attractive result.

It is, however, the overall focus of the author's text that is most open to debate. This is aimed squarely at providing a broad background to the events depicted in the various paintings and their historical significance. The frequent use of contemporary quotations is a notable feature and serves the author's aim well. The approach is probably satisfactory for the casual reader but comes at the expense of a lack of a detailed explanation of the particular scenes, and could result in the naval enthusiast feeling short-changed. Biographical detail about the artists who produced the various works is also quite patchy.

The book also suffers from a lack of effective editing. A number of paintings are clearly misplaced – for example, that of the interior of the postwar nuclear-powered attack submarine *Spartan* in the Second World War section. When combined with more than a few textual errors, this lack of attention to detail further undermines the book's overall appeal.

Conrad Waters

Steve R Dunn (ed)
British Naval Trawlers and Drifters in Two World Wars: From the John Lambert Collection
Seaforth Publishing, Barnsley 2021; hardback, 208 pages, numerous B&W photographs and line drawings; price £35.00.
ISBN 978-1-5267-9486-4

This is the fourth in a series of books from Seaforth that traces its origins to the publisher's acquisition of the extensive collection of drawings by John Lambert (1937–2016), a renowned draughtsman. In contrast to the previous books, which focused on warship armament, this volume illustrates the naval trawlers and drifters that formed a major but often underappreciated part of the Royal Navy's materiel during the period in question. Another important difference is the extent of the introduction contributed by editor Steve R Dunn. This, encompassing almost two thirds of the entire book,

is arguably of equal importance to the plans themselves.

The structure of the book reflects the broad division between its written introduction and the drawings from the Lambert archive. The former is divided into two parts, each concentrating on one of the World Wars and comprising a number of chapters with a thematic approach, exploring subjects such as the ships themselves, the missions they were called upon to perform, and the realities of life on board. The text is accompanied by an extensive series of contemporary photographs, mostly of specific ships but also of their equipment and crews. These chapters provide important context to the drawings that follow.

The drawings section likewise follows the split between the two conflicts. It encompasses ten sets of illustrations from the First World War and a further twenty from the Second. Most are of trawlers and drifters, although some depict the key weaponry and equipment typically carried by these vessels. The vast majority are produced across two pages and typically contain a series of profile and/or plan views, frequently with significant annotation. Although necessarily reduced in scale from the originals, most are clearly reproduced with legible text. An exception to this general rule relates to a few original builders' drawings found in the Lambert collection, which have not reproduced as well as the draughtsman's own work.

British Naval Trawlers and Drifters is a high-quality book that benefits from a strong design ethos. The editor's introduction provides an invaluable complement to the drawings, being further reinforced by the selection of photographs. Potential criticisms include the lack of detailed information on the design of the more numerous, Admiralty-ordered ships, the absence of tabular data on the same and the lack of an index. These comments aside, the overall result suggests a publisher that has made a significant effort to honour the legacy of a recognised expert with whom it will have enjoyed a lengthy collaboration. Accordingly, this book represents a fitting epitaph to one of the most significant naval illustrators of his generation.

Conrad Waters

John D Grainger
The British Navy in Eastern Waters: The Indian and Pacific Oceans
The Boydell Press, Woodbridge 2022; hardback, 319 pages, 3 maps; price £85.00.
ISBN 978-1-78327-677-6

Charles Stephenson
The Eastern Fleet and the Indian Ocean 1942–1944: The Fleet that had to Hide
Pen and Sword Books, Barnsley 2021; hardback, 320 pages, 20 B&W photographs, 14 maps; price £25.00.
ISBN 978-1-526-783615

The British Government's bold post-Brexit 'Integrated Review' included what was described as a 'tilt' towards the Indo-Pacific region that, among other things, would manifest itself in the Royal Navy returning to a part of the world that it had – at least in theory – abandoned some 50 years earlier. Both of these books trace the history of Britain's navy across a vast area of the globe often referred to as 'east of Suez', but from very different perspectives. Grainger presents an overview which stretches from the earliest voyages of discovery to the present day, while Stephenson's book focuses on a specific two-year period during the Second World War.

Grainger's account starts with the explorers, among them Drake, Cavendish and Lancaster, whose circumnavigatory voyages revealed vast riches that were already being exploited by the Dutch and Portuguese. He then traces the rise of the East India Company, supported by its heavily armed Bombay Marine naval force and militia. Although this agent of the British nation constituted a triumph of private enterprise that brought fabulous wealth both to the Company and to the State, its semi-autonomy was understandably regarded by both Government and people with some suspicion.

The author uses a considerable range of secondary source material to trace the long and diverse history of the Company as a naval power across the littorals of several continental landmasses and many island groups. As the Royal Navy grew in stature it increasingly rendered support, and the author successfully explains the complex interweaving of naval power between the Company's own armed trading ships, the Bombay Marine, what became the Indian Navy and the Royal Navy itself. The eventual demise of the East India Company, the years of *Pax Britannica* and the establishment of the Australian, Indian and New Zealand Navies were all milestones towards the eventual eclipse of the Royal Navy's influence in the East of Suez area.

This is a huge canvas, and John Grainger draws on his considerable experience as a naval author to give the reader an overview and hopefully a stimulus for further research.

Charles Stephenson's book has a much narrower focus: the period 1942–44, when the Royal Navy's Eastern Fleet was compelled to adopt the highly unusual role of a 'Fleet in Being'.

Stephenson prefaces his study with an overview of Britain's defective prewar planning, which culminated in the sinking of HMS *Prince of Wales* and *Repulse* in late 1941 and the fall of Singapore. Thereafter, Admiral James Somerville had the unenviable task of keeping a foothold in the Indian Ocean, commanding at first a motley collection of mostly antiquated battleships and cruisers, a force that was being constantly eroded by the demands of more pressing campaigns elsewhere. His chances of survival in combat against the modern Japanese carrier-based task groups were slim indeed, which forced Somerville effectively to hide his ships in the vast wastes of the ocean until reinforcements materialised – a strategy that drew criticism in certain quarters. Gradually, the situation did improve, thanks to the arrival of modern American carrier aircraft which, by

1944, allowed Somerville to take the offensive with carrier-led attacks against the Japanese-held territories in the Dutch East Indies; these became the blueprint for the campaigns of the newly-formed British Pacific Fleet in the spring and summer of 1945.

Stephenson's meticulous account is supported by a wide range of both primary and secondary sources. This is a rarely discussed topic, but nevertheless relevant if one is to appreciate an important interlude in the long history of the Royal Navy in a region it was soon to abandon for the last time.

Jon Wise

Alexander Clarke
Tribals, Battles and Darings: The Genesis of the Modern Destroyer
Seaforth Publishing, Barnsley 2022; 176 pages, numerous B&W illustrations; price £30.00.
ISBN 978-1-39900-949-2

This book aims to assess the significance of the large British interwar 'Tribal' class destroyers and the subsequent even larger 'Battle' and *Daring* class designs in the context both of the Royal Navy's contemporary operational requirements and their place in the service's destroyer development. It is the first book written by author Alexander Clarke, one of a new generation of naval historians who have come to prominence by means of the internet and social media.

Tribals, Battles and Darings is divided into seven chapters that adopt a broadly chronological approach. The first looks at the cruiser and destroyer requirements of the Royal Navy in the 1930s and seeks to explain the process by which the 'Tribal' class was conceived and built. The following two chapters cover, respectively, the periods of 1939–1940 and 1941–1942, and are largely focused on the operational service of the class. Chapter 4 then turns to the origins and development of the 'Battle' and *Daring* classes before a return to the operational theme in Chapters 5 and 6. These take the story to the end of the Second World War and into the postwar era. The concluding chapter looks at the legacy of a series of ships the author describes as 'back pocket cruisers', including their relevance to the circumstances of the current Royal Navy.

The author's text is supported by a wide range of black and white photographs as well as a number of ship profiles and other illustrations originating from the builders' plans contained in the National Maritime Museum's collection. Disappointingly, the latter are not accorded the full-colour reproduction seen in many other Seaforth publications, while the book's relatively small (20cm x 26cm) format tends to obscure much of the finer detail. More positively, a long list of archival and secondary sources points to the extensive research that supports the author's work. Surprisingly, however, there is no reference to the Ships' Covers and other material held by the National Maritime Museum that form indispensable aids to understanding the design development process.

Dr Clarke has set himself an ambitious challenge in attempting to describe the design, operational achievements and legacy of three large and significant classes of warship whose entry into service extended for a period of more than two decades. This challenge is exacerbated by the fact that the selected ships do not form part of a continuous design process, being interrupted by the smaller 'J' to 'N' and various 'Emergency' destroyer classes.

A substantial part of the book is focused on recording the operational service of the 'Tribal' class and this is one of the author's relative strengths. These chapters benefit from the significant archival research that has supported the author's work, allowing many of the ships' actions to be recorded in considerable detail. However, coverage is somewhat inconsistent and understates the important role played by the Canadian and Australian units of the class. The loss of HMCS *Athabaskan* is dealt with in just two sentences, while there is nothing about HMAS *Arunta* and her role in the Battle of Leyte Gulf.

The quality of the book's analysis is variable. While the author seems to have a good general understanding of the period in question, his detailed knowledge is sometimes suspect. For example, when describing the conception of the 'Tribal' class there is no mention of the 50-strong cruiser target adopted in the early 1930s, while the influence of Stanley Goodall is referenced despite Goodall not yet having been appointed DNC. There is little information on the alternative design concepts considered before the 'Tribals' were ordered and no tabular data whatsoever on ship characteristics. The section on construction is largely taken up with a lengthy digression into the selection of some of the ships' names.

The author's tendency to digress on similar lengthy tangents, such as the influence of Third Sea Lord and Controller Reginald Henderson or the ideal structure of the current Royal Navy, is often at the expense of the book's core subject matter. When combined with a tendency to write lengthy sentences that resemble a stream of consciousness, these form a material hindrance to following the book's core arguments. While containing some material of merit, *Tribals, Battles and Darings* ultimately falls short of being a definitive work.

Conrad Waters

WARSHIP GALLERY

The Imperial German Navy 1890–1918

In the absence any submission for this year's Warship Gallery, we asked regular contributor **Dirk Nottelmann** whether he had any unusual/interesting photographs of warships of the Imperial German Navy in port during the period 1890 to 1914 in his collection. The following pages are the result. Dirk has expanded the period in question to 1890–1918, and supplied the detailed and informative captions.

In 1909 the piers of the Imperial Dockyard Danzig are crowded with a variety of laid-up and briefly reactivated vessels. Closest to the camera is the coast defence vessel *Heimdall*, having just returned from the annual autumn manoeuvres, for which she had been reactivated one last time before the war. To the extreme left of the photo her half-sister *Ägir* can be distinguished by her unique boat cranes. Astern of *Ägir* is a group of small cruisers. The innermost of these, *Gefion*, has begun to deteriorate after being laid up following her last refit in 1904; she would never recommission. Next is *Gazelle*, which shared a similar fate: after her return from the Caribbean in 1904, she was re-boilered in 1905–07, only to be laid up again until the outbreak of the First World War. In 1915 she struck a mine, with extensive damage which proved too costly to repair, and was decommissioned. The next vessel, the diminutive *Schwalbe*, is nearly invisible; like her two companions she had undergone a reconstruction between March 1903 and April 1905, but remained in reserve afterwards. Outermost is *Geier*, the final unit of the *Bussard* class, which had returned from the Far East in 1905 and was partially rebuilt between 1908 and July 1909; the photo therefore depicts her immediately after reconstruction. She would return to service abroad in the spring of 1911, and was interned in the USA during the First World War. Above the bows of *Heimdall* can be seen the masts and funnels of *Siegfried*, name-ship of a class of coast defence vessels. (Author's collection)

It has proved hard to date this image due to contradictory details in published captions. The presence of the ironclad – 'baby-of-war' – *Oldenburg*, just visible in the distance to the left, sets the earliest possible date as May 1889. However, at this time *Bayern*, prominently located in the centre and identifiable by her name on the stern, had been decommissioned and would remain so for the next twelve months. The solution to this puzzle lies in the presence of *Bayern*'s sister ship next to her. The black and buff paint-scheme would normally identify her as *Sachsen*, but the latter had been the replacement for the former – the ships were never in service together. However, in the campaign of 1890 *Württemberg* had replaced *Sachsen*, which subsequently underwent a reconstruction for two years. For this single commission *Württemberg* would receive *Sachsen*'s paint scheme, and *Bayern* had re-commissioned at the same time, so it can finally be concluded that the photo was taken in the summer of 1890. To the right can be seen the after part of the aviso and former torpedo trials ship *Zieten*. (Author's collection)

S.M.S. SEEADLER.

The small cruiser *Seeadler* at anchor with an unidentified Chinese waterfront beyond; note the small sampans alongside. *Seeadler* belonged to the six-ship *Bussard* class, arguably the most influential class of German ships in foreign waters despite their rather small size (see the author's article in *Warship 2020*). Between 1890 and 1914 at least one representative of this class of small cruisers could be seen on station around the world, showing the German flag in distant waters. This photo was taken during *Seeadler*'s second long overseas deployment; she served on the China Station between 1900 and 1905, in the wake of the Boxer rebellion, before being ordered to the Africa Station. Returning home in the spring of 1914, she had the distinction of having served outside European waters for the longest period of time of any German warship: more than thirteen years. She would be downgraded from 'small cruiser' to 'gun-boat' when her legal replacement, the small cruiser *Karlsruhe* (I), became operational. At the beginning of the First World War *Seeadler* was towed to Wilhelmshaven for conversion into a mine storage hulk in the Jade bight; she suffered an explosion, the cause of which has yet to be established, at her anchorage on 19 April 1917, fortunately with no loss of life. (Author's collection)

Left: The inner Kiel fjord in 1895. Moored to their respective buoys are the ships of the 1st Armoured Squadron, the four-ship *Brandenburg* class. It comprised, from left to right, *Wörth*, *Weissenburg*, *Brandenburg* and the flagship *Kurfürst Friedrich Wilhelm* (nearly obscured by *Brandenburg*). Behind the latter ship, the two funnels of the imperial yacht *Hohenzollern* can be seen; she is moored closest to the flagship as one might expect, while beyond *Weissenburg*'s bow the aviso *Jagd* is visible. The large building beyond her has survived to the present. It housed the Naval Academy in those days, while today it is the home of the local Schleswig-Holstein assembly. In the left foreground, the outer end of the Imperial Dockyard's southern wall is visible. (Author's collection)

Editor's Note: We welcome submissions from readers for Warship Gallery. The sole requirement is that photos (ideally 8–12) are unusual, have a common theme, are of high quality and are accompanied by detailed captions. Proposals should be addressed to the Editor using the Warship email address: warship.editorial@bloomsbury.com

Old versus new! In the spring of 1892 the freshly commissioned coast defence ironclad *Beowulf* and the cruiser-corvette *Arcona* (II) share the same pier at Wilhelmshaven. The former, under command of the Kaiser's brother, Prince Heinrich, was commencing her initial trials from that port before moving to Kiel at the beginning of May; the latter would depart on 4 May for a seven-year deployment to the Far East, during which she would take part in the occupation of Kiaochow bight. Beyond *Arcona* can be seen the two funnels and one remaining mast of the ironclad *Kronprinz* of 1866 vintage, in commission for one last time despite her total obsolescence. An interesting detail on *Beowulf* is the absence of torpedo defence booms, although all the necessary fittings and the box for the torpedo nets are in place. Despite these preparations, she would spend her career without the gear ever being shipped. The reason for this is unclear, as her predecessor *Siegfried* had been so equipped, as were all of her successors up to and including *Hagen*. Any reluctance to fitting them would prove to be well founded, the nets being heavy and difficult to deploy, but the decision to remove them from all vessels would be made only about five years later, when the nets were found to be subject to extensive oxidation, losing their strength and thus their protective value. (Author's collection)

One of the crispest images of any German warship known to the author, this is the coast defence ironclad *Odin* in 1901, shortly before she decommissioned for reconstruction. Despite the obvious changes from her predecessors such as the heavy military mast and the absence of sponsons for the secondary guns amidships, she and her sister *Ägir* concealed their very different protection scheme from the public eye. This originated in an early (1891) proposal to up-gun the final batch of ships, changing the main armament to four guns in twin mountings similar to those to be fitted in the *Brandenburg* class. The extra weight had to be compensated by omitting the complete belt in favour of a 'citadel' amidships, while the ends were protected by a submerged armoured deck. In the end they would retain the planned arrangement of guns, as it was accepted that the extra work and expenditure would be wasted on these comparatively dated small vessels. In addition to reducing the total number of units from ten to eight, it was decided that the final ship, *Ägir*, would become a test bed for a variety of electric installations and a set of early watertube boilers to justify her completion. The later reconstruction constituted a (successful) attempt by Tirpitz to deceive parliament: the capability of these vessels was to be improved to make them fit into the terms of the recent naval law, with the ultimate aim of having them replaced by battleships. *Odin* would end her days being rebuilt as a merchant ship. (Author's collection)

It is July 1914, and the High Seas Fleet takes a brief break during the annual summer manoeuvres – for the last time in peace. Heading the centre column is the fleet flagship *Friedrich der Grosse*, flying the flag of Admiral Friedrich von Ingenohl. She had just been equipped with an enclosed admiral's bridge atop her conning tower; later in the war it would be nicknamed *Scheers Ruh* ('Scheer's rest'), after the famous C-in-C who led the High Seas Fleet (HSF) for two and a half years. To the left, the I. Battle Squadron is headed by flagship *Ostfriesland*, flying the flag of Vice Admiral Wilhelm von Lans, followed by *Thüringen*, *Helgoland* and five more (obscured) units of that squadron. To the right, the flagship of II. Battle Squadron, *Preussen*, can be seen, flying the flag of Vice Admiral Reinhard Scheer. She is followed by *Pommern*, *Hessen* and *Lothringen*, while the remaining four ships of the squadron are obscured. In the distance, between *Preussen* and *Pommern*, the large cruiser (*Grosse Kreuzer*) *Von der Tann* is just about visible. (Author's collection)

Left: One of the lesser-known vessels of the Imperial German Navy was the river gunboat *Otter* (II), designed especially to navigate the Yangtse river above the rapids. She was based at the town of Chongquing in Sichuan province, while the photo was taken downriver at Shanghai. This remote station needed to be able to communicate, via relay vessels on the coast, with the German base at Tsingtau (Qingdao), hence the comparatively elaborate W/T aerials seen here. *Otter* was built in sections at Bremerhaven so that she could be dismantled and shipped by steamer after conclusion of her trials in late 1909. Note the Chinese-style boats suspended from the davits, the river handling capabilities of which had proven superior to the standard boats of German manufacture. The gunboat was laid up and repatriated at Nanjing after the outbreak of the First World War, receiving the new name *München*. However, China seized her despite her civilian status in 1917 after joining the war, and incorporated her into the Chinese Navy under the name *Li Chieh*. In 1920 she dared to sail across the Yellow Sea under her own steam into the Amur River. Her ultimate fate is still shrouded in mystery. While the most relevant German source, Hildebrand (*Die Deutschen Kriegsschiffe*, Vol 5, 38), claims that she was sunk on 16 October 1929 on the lower Sungari River by Soviet air attack, Branfill-Cook (*River Gunboats*, 68) states that she was sunk at the same location on 12 October 1929 by artillery fire from the Soviet monitor *Sverdlov*. On the other hand Wright (*The Chinese Steam Navy*, 156) states that she was captured by invading Japanese forces and incorporated into the navy of Manchukuo under the new name *Li Sui* in 1931. Anyone who has more definite information is invited to write to the author using the *Warship* email address. (Author's collection)

Just over one year later on from the image to the left, September 1915, the world had changed considerably and the war had been in progress for more than twelve months. This photo shows an interesting variety of modern naval vessels in Wilhelmshaven roads. Closest to the camera, the small cruiser *Graudenz* is leaving the port, heading north. She is flying the flag of Rear Admiral Friedrich Boedicker, leader of II. Scouting Group, as a tempory measure before decommissioning in October to be re-armed with 15cm guns. Note the discharge of ash which had built up in the boiler rooms during her stay in port. Above her stern *König*, flagship of III. Battle Squadron – then led by VA Scheer prior to his promotion to C-in-C of the HSF – is visible, while to the right the torpedo boat *B 110* can be seen heading into the port on an opposite course. Beyond her, *Grosser Kurfürst* is training her main guns, while over the bows of *Graudenz* the funnels and masts of the large cruiser *Derfflinger* are visible. In the distance to the right, the facilities of Wilhelmshaven port can be distinguished.

In the spring of 1915 the first destroyers, officially still designated as 'large torpedo boats', came into service, having been constructed around propulsion machinery being built by Blohm & Voss for Russian destroyers of the improved *Novik* type. *B 98*, having joined the re-formed II. Torpedo Flotilla on 6 April 1915 as flotilla leader, is seen here entering inner Kiel port following gunnery trials – evidenced by the target float secured to the guardrails abaft the bridge. In the distance are three elderly units of the V. Battle Squadron which had been laid up in February with skeleton crews to supply the personnel for an increasing number of minesweeping and picket vessels. From left to right these are *Brandenburg*, *Kaiser Wilhelm der Grosse* and *Wörth*. The first and last named would soon get a new assignment, serving as floating batteries to defend the newly-occupied port of Libau (today Liepaja), while *Kaiser Wilhelm* served the same purpose at Kiel until late 1915; in 1917 she became a stationary training vessel for the Sonderburg torpedo school. (Author's collection)

Shortly after the armistice of November 1918, the small cruiser *Königsberg* (II) is at her berth alongside the 'coal tongue' at Wilhelmshaven, where the dark soil indicates the stocks of coal having been stored there in previous years. The cruiser was one of the few modern ships that had not been initially designated for internment, to enable her to serve as a relay between Germany and Scapa Flow. After the scuttling of the German fleet at Scapa Flow in June 1919 she became a replacement for the sunken cruisers and was stricken from the Navy list on 31 May 1920, ending her days as the French *Metz*. In the photo, a clear indication of the war being over is the colour scheme of the minesweeper *M 97* beyond the cruiser. During wartime these boats had been painted grey, some of them with a black band along the first strake above the waterline. This was changed to all-over black after the armistice, with the pendant number painted in large white numbers on both sides of the bow. Alongside the minesweeper two of the Navy-owned oil tankers are awaiting better days. Astern of this group, two boats of the 'iron flotilla' (*Eiserne Flotille*) of torpedo boats can be seen; the large *B 97* and the stern of one unidentified Schichau-built 'Christmas tree' boat, nicknamed after the exceptionally tall foremast in combination with a diminutive after mast. Both were likewise initially exempted from internment before later being distributed among the victors (*B 97* was allocated to Italy). Protruding over the rooftops of the buildings beyond, the cranes of the *Reichswerft*, formerly the Imperial Dockyard, Wilhelmshaven, are visible. (Author's collection)